WHITE KNEES
BROWN KNEES

Cover illustration: Iain McIntosh

ALL UNAUTHORISED TAXIS OR VEHS. PASSING THIS POINT ARE WARNED THAT THEY ARE LIABLE TO BE FIRED UPON.

WHITE KNEES
BROWN KNEES

SUEZ CANAL ZONE 1951-1954
THE FORGOTTEN YEARS

DOUGLAS J FINDLAY

INTRODUCTIONS BY
SIR JOCK KENNEDY & ACKER BILK

Discover Press

This first edition published in Great Britain in 2003 by Discover Press

Discover Publications Ltd
103 Henderson Row
Edinburgh
EH3 5BB
Scotland

A CIP catalogue record for this book is available from the British Library.

ISBN 0-905389-01-8 hard covers

Publishing executive: Jill Murphy
Printed in Great Britain by the Bath Press

_____

For those who never returned.

_____

Acknowledgement

Much of the factual data found in this book is by kind permission of Mike Hardy of the 1951-1954 Egypt Award Memorial Alliance. A special thanks is due to The Canal Zoners and the Suez Veterans Associations, who are doing so much to bring old comrades together again in a common cause.

Sadly, the deaths of many Service men, women and dependants in the Canal Zone are still shrouded in mystery. The Army and RAF Records branches have proved as co-operative as possible within the limits of the regulations, and their unfailing desire to help is appreciated. The Roll of Honour published here sheds new light, but it is to some extent anecdotal and I would welcome any further information readers could provide.

My sincere thanks to the many veterans for permission to use a selection of the hundreds of photographs supplied. Special appreciation is due to Charles and Doris Golder, Phil May, John Torrington and Bryan Waller for their valuable contributions.

Sir Jock Kennedy, Air Chief Marshal (Rtd), and Acker Bilk, Squaddie (Rtd), are warmly thanked for their introductory words.

The perseverance and patience of the publishing staff is acknowledged. Finally I have to thank those who unwittingly appear in Part One. Without them there would be no story to tell.

Douglas James Findlay
Glenesk
Canonbie
Dumfriesshire
DG14 0SZ

June 2003

FOREWORD

by Air Chief Marshal Sir Jock Kennedy GCB,
AFC, DL, RAF (Rtd), Lord Lieutenant of Rutland

This book begins with a light-hearted series of anecdotes about the author's early days in the Royal Air Force but it soon illustrates his concerns, and indeed anger, at the off-hand reaction of the authorities in London to the many deaths and kidnappings that occurred daily in the Canal Zone where he served out his extended National Service. This curious mixture of fun and seriousness continues throughout the book, although overall his sense of humour is mostly to the fore.

He was not to know that there is a world of difference between the Ministry of Defence and the Civil Service/political side. I can well imagine the pressures applied to reduce the embarrassing number of deaths reported and even to push the whole matter under the carpet.

I enjoyed re-living many of the episodes described. No-one joins the services for a life of ease, and nowhere else does one find the camaraderie and the mutual loyalty that develops in a bunch of young men thrown together in a situation of considerable pressure and danger.

I think the author slightly overdoes the hardships he and his mates suffered in those early days. I joined up early in 1946 as a regular airman on a salary of three shillings a day, with a shilling deducted as a saving and sixpence per week taken off as a 'voluntary' subscription to the RAF Benevolent Fund. He didn't know how well off he was – seventy bob a week indeed!

I commend this book to all those who served in the Canal Zone facing significant dangers and haven't yet had even get a putty medal for their efforts. Rudyard Kipling said it all when he wrote: "It's Tommy this, an' Tommy that, an' 'Chuck him out, the brute!' But it's 'Saviour of 'is country' when the guns begin to shoot."

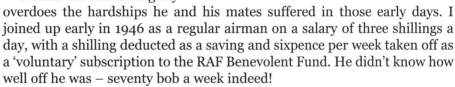

FOREWORD

by Bernard Stanley Bilk MBE, RE (Rtd),
also known as Acker

For me, this book is full of surprises. The author and I shared similar experiences in Egypt and more recently the unpleasantness of treatment for throat cancer. For some reason, I always thought that he had held a high rank in the Royal Air Force because when we meet, in typical RAF style, he never pays for the wine. It turns out that he is simply a Scotsman unable to break the habit of a lifetime. It was quite a shock to discover that he was only a lowly 'erk and one of us.

Although back home during the years 1951 to 1954, I was still interested in what was going on in Egypt but had no idea of how rough things were. Many incidents are uncovered for the first time and I found the book a good read.

My time in Egypt in 1948 and 1949 was spent mostly at the Engineer Plant Depot at Qassasin. There was, officially at least, no trouble at all if you discount the move down from Palestine and the first Israeli/Egyptian Six Day War in 1948. We were classified as on active service, for which we received a tanner (2.5p) a day and were subject to a very disciplinarian regime, even in the Engineers. This might have been due to the persistence of the 'klifty wallahs' who felt that our presence in Egypt was a sure sign of Allah's beneficence. Discipline was so strict that I was given a semblance of a Court Martial and awarded three months (eighty-four days) in the pokey for simply closing my eyes and mentally composing a tune while on guard duty. The sentence was prearranged and carried out in accordance with military procedures. Justice was severely blindfolded and given that day off duty.

At the time, No.1 Military Correction Establishment at Moascar was overcrowded and I was lucky enough to serve my first twenty-eight days in a cell at the regimental guardroom in a former British military hospital at Tahag. The glasshouse at Moascar was reputedly the model for the early Sean Connery film The Hill. The hill in the film was reminiscent of the one on the test park at the Engineer Plant Depot, and might actually have been it. Wherever it was, I have no doubt that it would have been built by Royal

Engineers' equipment. In the first twenty-eight days my clarinet playing improved tremendously, because the Regimental Police corporal was a real friend and he let me practise all day long in my cell – completely against King's Rules and Regulations. To add insult to injury, I was forced to serve an extra eighty-four days at the end of my two-year National Service to compensate the Army, although I received no pay during my incarceration. As a matter of interest, I keep in touch with that Regimental Policeman.

Reading this book has brought back memories of people and places I had long forgotten and I have to say that we were equally as hard up as the 'erks in blue. In the spares section of the Plant Depot at Qassasin were stored some four million Caterpillar diesel engine injectors, each with a recognised street value of £1E. The Royal Engineers would never resort to fiddling, but keeping an accurate count of four million items was difficult and presented opportunities. The cold Stella beers which were a necessity of life had to be paid for somehow. A Scottish sergeant from the pay section gave us a stark warning. "The Army is no daft, ye ken, and when the NAAFI takings are twice as much as the pay of the entire unit including the officers it's a sure sign somebody's on the fiddle." I was on the clarinet, so I was in the clear, but thereafter we cut down our Stella purchases from the NAAFI.

The most amazing theft by the klifty wallahs that I heard about was when they stole a Comet tank in full battle order. They hid it by building a ramshackle shed round it just fifty yards off the treaty road! In my time, the Egyptian workers were friends as well as employees and even in the periods when things became strained between Egypt and Britain, and fraternising was frowned, upon it was not unknown for us to sneak out to Qassasin, the nearest village, for a late night knees-up.

To accomplish this we had to detour round a Military Police post and cross part of the desert. On arriving at the village we were always made most welcome and enjoyed an evening of eating, drinking vast quantities of beer, and laughing a lot. The journey home in our inebriated state was always much more difficult than the outward leg, and had there been any animosity or hate from the locals we would have been prime targets.

The RAF boys clearly led a softer life, with pyjamas and bed linen, than we squaddies, but we were lucky and not only survived our tour but enjoyed most of it. It must have been the Brylcreem boys who upset the natives and caused all the problems.

CONTENTS

PART ONE: IF YOU CAN'T TAKE A JOKE...

Part two: The way we were

Part three: Sun, sand and sacrifice

PART ONE

IF YOU CAN'T TAKE A JOKE...

It's a well-known saying in all three
Services that you should not join up if you
can't take a joke. Part One of White Knees
Brown Knees relates the sometimes
hilarious, sometimes frightening,
experiences of a young Serviceman
pressed into extending his National
Service to three years by the lure of an
extra guinea a week. It was a hard-earned
sum. Serving in the Canal Zone of Egypt
made an indelible impression on the
author's mind and, no doubt, on the minds
of all the other men and women who
found themselves posted there.

ECHOES OF AN 'ERK IN EGYPT

*The telling of these stories has laid many of the
ghosts that haunted my mind for half a century*

Many books are written by those with worthwhile tales to tell of derring-do. For every one of that fortunate band there are thousands who were a little bit further away from the action, and as a result their contribution is often overlooked. They feel the same range of emotions as the hero but it has been said a hero dies but once, the rest of us a thousand times in our imaginations. My father earned a DSM on 'Q' Ships in the First World War and I was keen to match his effort. All I got was jankers on a regular basis. Strange that, when I tried so hard.

This book is partly for the legions of unsung heroes who simply did their bit in difficult conditions and went without thanks from our politicians. Mainly, it is for those who failed to return. Some died true heroes. Some suffered horrible deaths. Many died in accidents and some from natural causes. In every case, grieving relatives would wonder what might have been if their son or daughter, brother or sister had lived.

I hope this book will give an insight into the everyday life of an ordinary British Serviceman in Egypt. It is the story of an 'erk, RAF slang for an ordinary guy from the lowly 'other ranks', simply a number as far as the authorities were concerned, and is intended to evoke memories and make readers smile. As we used to say, if you can't take a joke you shouldn't have joined up!

The Army and Navy referred to airmen as 'crabfats', a reference to the blue unction that, before the RAF was formed, was used to treat the unfortunate condition that afflicts Servicemen who are less than selective in their choice of partners. In turn, we referred to Army personnel as 'craphats'. The Navy we mostly ignored, though we envied their mobility and reputation as happy-go-lucky characters – and the daily issue of rum that may have contributed to their philosophical attitude to life.

On a more serious note, I hope this book will bring to the notice of a wider public what it was like to serve King, Queen and Country, at home and abroad, during the turbulent years of the early Fifties. It would also be nice if this Government was to do something to right an obvious wrong instead of saying what people want to hear and then, once again, doing nothing. Justice demands, even at this late date, acknowledgement of the sacrifices made by so many.

Some of the blame for this book lies at the door of the then editor of The Shaky Do, house magazine of the Bognor Regis branch of the Royal Air Force Association. Having used a story of my wartime evacuation experiences, first published in the Scots Magazine, he asked for any other stories with an RAF theme. A dozen short stories later it seemed to make sense to join them up. Then, like Topsy, it just growed.

When we volunteered or were called up to the Colours, it was stressed that we were all subject to the Official Secrets Act and that for fifty years we would have to keep quiet about anything that we saw or did while in the service of the Crown. Well the time is up, and my freedom to pass judgement and express my opinions has been indulged to the full.

I firmly believe that many of us were psychologically damaged during our service. For years I would start awake in the middle of the night, bathed in sweat, convinced I was back in my billet in Egypt. The telling of these stories has laid many of the ghosts that haunted my mind for half a century.

The varying statements of eyewitnesses to any accident prove that no two people see things in exactly the same way, and I crave the indulgence of readers if they feel that I could have been more accurate in some respects. The stories are, however, fundamentally true. Every Canal Zone veteran I have had contact with has had a story to tell, and laugh about, and having served in the Suez at the same time creates an instant bond of friendship.

For years, the Foreign Office and Ministry of Defence have written off our service as of little consequence. The Foreign Office was anxious not to offend the Egyptian Government. They, and we, knew that the claimed death toll of only forty with another sixty-five wounded was nonsense. Hundreds were killed or died and thousands more were wounded and injured. Most did not die as a direct result of enemy action but it must be fair to conclude that had they not been required to serve in that theatre they would not have died there. We must honour and remember all of them.

I would like to acknowledge everyone who wrote to me, whether it was to submit photos, share stories or just to offer encouragement. All of your contributions have been very gratefully received, however it would have been impossible to include all the material I received in one book. Those whose pictures have been included are credited beside their photo. The list of helpers that follows is not comprehensive, but most will find themselves mentioned. Your encouragement and support has been invaluable.

I WISH TO THANK...

W Adams, Ellesmere Port

P Addison, Oxon

P Anderson, Aldershot

P Andrews, Southampton

D Atkinson, Halfmoon Bay, BC, Canada

A Bach, Salford

R Barrett, Redruth

R Barry, York

J Beach, Newton

H Beaton, Chislehurst

Mr Bernard, Middlesex

E Best, Sandal

J Bevan, Eccleshall

G Black, Portland

R Blake, Wilton

L Bradford, Rushden

D Bradley, Morley

R Brandon, Essex

K Brazier, Allestree

H Brockway, Gillingham

P Brummel, Godalming

G Burgess, Wigston Field

A Byrne, London

S Capon, Crawley

D Carter, Coverack

J Carter, Warrington

R Casson, Cumbria

J Catto, Pinner

J Chilton, Cirencester

M Chiverton, Niton

D Cleaton, Llandrindod Wells

I Cocks, Birmingham

D Cook, Nuneaton

R Cousins, Bromley

D Cope, Slaithwaite

T Credland, Winterton

R Curtis, Nottingham

R Davies, Llandudno

B Day, Madrid

P Denison, Luton

C Dixon, Cornwall

G Dixon, Cornwall

J Dunlop, Co Formanagh

D Dunstan, Redruth

J Edwards, Mowbray

F Egan, Bury

M Ellis, Stamford

R Entickap, Godalming

G Evans, Anglesey

R Evans, Plymouth

T Fahey, Manchester

L Faulkner, Liverpool

T Feeley, Manchester

H Fletcher, Sunderland

N Flint

E Fursdon

K Garrett, New Malden

N Good, Chard

T Gooch, Feltham

A Grover, Dunstable

M Hall, Syston

D Hardy, Nottingham

M Hardy, Devon

B Harrison, Pinner

S Harrison, Cannock

M Harte, Nottingham

P Hawxwell, Bexhill-on-Sea

H Heathe, Stafford

D Hewes, Normanton-le-Heath

R Hewlett, St Ives

J Heygate, Westgate-on-Sea

E Hudson, Abingdon

D Hurley, Somerset

J Ivatt, Horsham

P Jeffery, Newport Pagnell

M Jervis, Halkyn

P Jezzard, Hounslow

A Johnston, Liverpool

G Johnston, Liverpool

R Johnston, Newry

S Johnston, Molton

J Jones, Brynnoddfa

J Jones, Flintshire

D Kendall, Huddersfield

P King, Workingham

R Kirk, Allington

P Kirkland, Crewe

C Knowles, Clifton Upon Tyne

W Lane, Tavistock

R Latten, Pontyprida

C Lee, Cumbria

N Lee, Malta

Mr Len, Peterborough

N Lester, Willenhall

D Levett, Robertsbridge

A Lewis, Coven

D Lines, Hemel Hempstead

B Lone, St Ives

Mr Mason, Telford

C McEntree, Wetherby

B Menary, Dewsbury

H Menzies, South Wirral

S Merchant, Darlington

R Meredith, Newbury

J Nabb, Farnham

J Newton, Dudley

H Nightingale, Wakefield

I Paines, Oxon

M Palmer, Felixstowe

T Panter, Somerset

V Pender, Cornwall

D Polley, Rayleigh

Mr Pope, Wickham

R Potter, Manchester

H Powell, Harrow

D Powis, Dagenham

L Powis, Birmingham

E Price, Sutton Coldfield

G Purnell, Nuneaton

J Reading, Leicester

E Reeves, Lowestoft

S. Ricketts, Allington

W Rines, Wiveliscombe

S Robinson, Portrush

J Rutty, St Mary Magdalen

K Sankey, Ormskirk

B Saunderson, Hull

R Scurrah, Chesire

E Sear, Banstead

F Sephton, St Helens

J Sermon, Evesham

E Simmons, Darwen

S Smith, Carlisle

G Stacey, Doncaster

A Stanley, Leicester

H Stanley, Colwyn Bay

G Stoney, Winchester

A Stott, Cleveleys

N Stringer, Vejle, Denmark

A Sutton, Chateris

T Taylor, Newquay

J Thompson, Cranleigh

M Timms, Devon

R Trotman, Lydney

J Waldron, Hemel Hempstead

J Waller, Southend on Sea

L Warbuton, Taunton

N Watkins, Pontardawe

K Whitfield, York

T Wilkins, Waterlooville

R Wilson, Romford

R Woodfield, Alcester

R Woods, Hounslow

R Walters, Basingstoke

WHILE ON ACTIVE SERVICE

How much danger does it take, and how many lives must be lost, before Whitehall considers service to be 'active'?

The first victim of war is truth. The old maxim is as true today as it ever was, and is demonstrated by the collusion of successive British governments to conceal the true story of the 1951-54 emergency in the Suez Canal Zone. The burning question of whether the troops who served there were on active service has only recently been settled despite the existence of Cabinet papers dated 29 November 1951 that confirm the fact. Only when the papers had to be made public under the 50-years rule did the Government admit the truth it must have known all along.

Documents until now treated as privileged information are being read with interest by those who were in the Zone at the time of the conflict; but some are still kept from public view. The most widely publicised incidents – the attacks on the Egyptian Police barracks and the Bureau Sanitaire – were among the few fully reported. Thirty-three British Service personnel were murdered in the weeks before the action, but I believe the long-overdue decision to react to Egyptian provocation was in response to another, equally despicable, atrocity which occurred some weeks earlier and which is recorded later in this chapter.

Governments have always been prepared to accept the deaths of 'other ranks' as inevitable, since they are expendable – it's what they get paid for, after all. In this case, civilian deaths are also disregarded. Does the murder of a nun, a teacher of the children of the Moascar Garrison, gunned down in cold blood inside the convent of St Vincent de Paul, count for nothing? It helps to massage the figures if anyone not wearing a military uniform is excluded from the total of deaths.

It was stated recently in Parliament that the thousands of troops rushed to Egypt were merely to replace native labour and to guard and protect 'military installations' from theft. All news of action was dismissed as trivial, or suppressed, and those serving depended on news from home to bring them up to date on any reported events. Hundreds of incidents that caused death were never reported to the Press at home because the Forces were not on active service, or so Parliament was informed at the time.

Try telling that to the redcaps who, acting in their bounden duty, were lured into ambushes by the Egyptian Police and shot dead. Tell it to the parents of the eighteen and nineteen-year-old boys who were shot, or to the grieving relatives of the hundreds of other dead who lie buried in Egypt. Tell it to the families of the fallen who have yet to have explained to them how and why their loved ones died. It is beyond belief that a dispatch rider killed when slicing into a terrorists' wire stretched across a road at head height can be classified as a 'road accident casualty'. Yet that is how such deaths were officially recorded.

There is also the curious reporting of a Cameron Highlanders incident. It was said that a major and a private were blown up by mines that lay on railway lines, but a brother officer witnessed that they were in fact shot dead by terrorists. Nearly every British unit serving in the Canal Zone suffered casualties, and every disciplinary charge sheet was headed with the acronym WOAS (while on active service), with punishments more severe as a result. The first British troops to arrive from Palestine in 1948 had received sixpence (2.5p) active service pay there, and that sum continued to be paid in Egypt

The main difficulty faced by those serving in Egypt was knowing how to assess the mood of the natives at any given moment. In one spot they might be smiling and bartering with the troops, while only half a mile away a mob would be rampaging through the streets. There were several settings of alert. Red was when things were really rough, with everyone confined to camp unless on essential duty. Vehicles would carry escort guards and travel in convoy, led by redcaps driving a Land Rover with a wire-cutting piece of angle iron mounted in front. Red-and-amber indicated a slightly less dangerous state of affairs. At this level we would still travel in convoy but could cut down on the escort guards and dispense with the Land Rover. While we were out of camp we had to keep in groups, each man armed with a rifle and ten rounds of ammunition. This was an unpopular state of alert because, if an Egyptian grabbed the barrel of your rifle in an attempt to steal it, the obvious way to shake him off was to make a hole in his chest with a bullet. Despite the provocation and possibly life-threatening situation, to do this could – and did – lead to men being put away in the glasshouse. The rules of engagement were not clear on several points and we were under orders not to be nasty to the Egyptians.

The next stage was amber, when a pickaxe handle was substituted for the rifle. This was more or less the prevailing state if you were allowed out of camp at all, and whole regiments were issued with pickaxe staves. Egypt must have cornered the market in these handy 3ft-long implements of defence. I never saw a green alert in operation, but old sweats used to wax lyrical about the good times when the only condition was green.

The First Battalion Durham Light Infantry was based on the outskirts of Ismailia, and part of their duty was to supervise the few

D POLLEY

Land Rovers were fitted with girders to cut the wires stretched across roads by terrorists to decapitate motorcyclists and escorts standing in vehicles.

Egyptian labourers who still worked for the British. Because the labourers were inclined to be light-fingered, they had to be searched before being allowed home each night. A National Serviceman of the DLI was searching a worker when he located some contraband concealed in his djellabah. As he called to his sergeant for assistance, the next labourer in line stabbed the young soldier and seriously injured him. He was taken to hospital by ambulance and the DLI understood the soldier to have been killed.

Almost the entire regiment left camp armed with their wooden staves, as required when walking out. Formed up in line, they marched through Ismailia striking every Egyptian they met and, as there were no exceptions to this hastily introduced rule, the streets were cleared very quickly. A riot was narrowly averted and, like many others, this incident had to be hushed up.

Whitehall and Parliament seem to take the death of commissioned officers much more seriously than those of other ranks, perhaps because they consider such attacks as being on their own kind, so it was not until the following incident – involving an officer and kept secret at the time – that the VIPs were shaken out of their complacency and finally applied pressure to halt the carnage.

On 17 November 1951, after a series of carefully orchestrated riots that had lasted for days, loudspeaker vans toured Ismailia announcing that things were more or less back to normal, the town was in bounds, and families were free to enter the shopping area after being forced to stay indoors for nearly a fortnight due to non-stop trouble in the streets. A Major Wharton of the RASC, his wife and two young sons, decided to take the opportunity to buy some English newspapers. They were accompanied by their close neighbours, Flying Officer Henry Snelling, his wife and son, and Mrs Clegg, the wife of an RASC captain. Experienced in the unpredictability of the native population in times of conflict, Major Wharton was armed with a

G EVANS

The elegant Egyptian sailing boats on the Suez Canal were in sharp contrast to our military vessels.

Sten gun secured to his waist by a chain dog lead, and Flying Officer Snelling wore a belt with a fully-loaded automatic pistol and spare ammunition. The ladies wore bright summer frocks and the kids were in shorts and T-shirts. They were chatting and laughing when they heard the sound of rifle fire close by. The officers shepherded the women and children into a side street where they crouched beside a wall as bullets whistled and struck the brickwork over their heads.

Realising that the gunfire was coming from the police station, the men tried to attract the police's attention, with Snelling shouting to them to stop firing. They sent the kids scuttling for the cover of a heap of masonry at the other side of the road, and bullets threw up dust behind their heels as they ran. Moments later, the women followed the children across safely. Then, as the two officers made their dash, Mrs Wharton thought she heard a thud and a gasp; but both men seemed all right and this was not a time for asking questions. By now the gunfire had intensified. The police had brought shotguns into play. While the two plucky officers returned fire in the hope of making them keep their heads down, above the din the sound of maniacal laughter could be heard coming from the police station.

Across a wide pavement was the open doorway of a house owned by a French family of their acquaintance. As the fusillade returned from the Sten gun and automatic pistol caused the rate of fire from the police station to slacken, the women and children made a dash for the doorway and safety. At first they waited for the men to join them, but such was the intensity of firing that they had to retreat to the rear of the house. Later it went quiet, and the women, who could see the pile of stones but not the actual spot where they had hidden, called out in that direction. There was no reply. Some time later there was a knock on the shutters and an English voice told them it was now safe to return to their homes. Then incoming rifle shots struck the window frames, suggesting the reassurance was a little premature. The women and children spent the whole night lying on the floor to avoid stray shots through the window.

Throughout the night, Army and RAF patrols rumbled past outside, and in the morning a heavily armed patrol arrived to take them home, but there was no news of their husbands' fate. Later that day, Lt Col Ronald Menage, CO of the RASC, arrived to break the sad news that the two officers had been found riddled with bullets and badly battered some distance from the heap of stones. Their medal ribbons had been torn off and their weapons were missing. The officers' bodies had been dragged along the street to

be photographed for the Egyptian Press for use as propaganda. News of the murders was kept from the troops in the area, as the British were keen not to upset the Egyptians. Surely no one could consider an incident like this to be anything but an example of being on active service; but Whitehall did. Even Sir George Erskine, the General Officer

E SEAR

In the strictly non-politically correct style of the time, we referred to these boats, which plyed their trade on the grossly misnamed Sweet Water Canal, as the "WOG Navy".

Ismailia, 1952.

Commanding, was fired on while on duty in the Aden area. His ordeal was not too frightening since crack infantry units and highly trained redcaps surrounded him. He might have been horrified, however, had he known that I, a virtually untrained 'erk, was one of a hastily formed detachment of RAF men drafted in to protect him and his residence on the outskirts of Ismailia when his regular guard of paratroopers was called away at short notice.

When my white knees and I arrived at the accounts section at RAF Deversoir, a solitary Egyptian was still employed there. He wore European dress and was a perfect gentleman who resembled David Suchet's television

interpretation of Agatha Christie's Hercule Poirot. He had a light, mincing walk and a faint aroma of curry seemed to exude from his pores, although mercifully, unlike us, he did not sweat a lot. He had boundless patience in teaching us to speak Arabic and offended no one and kept his political opinions to himself. Each day he travelled from Ismailia and was punctuality itself, despite being threatened by terrorists because of his connection with the British. He was convinced that the terrorists would leave him alone if he minded his own business. He even brought in samples of the threatening notes that were slipped into the shopping bags of European women by the Daughters of the Nile, a notorious female terrorist-support group.

One day he failed to turn up for work and we surmised that the threats, or the terrorists, had got to him; but three or four days later he reappeared wearing a turban. Well, not exactly a turban, more a huge white bandage encasing his head. He had come to tender his resignation. The Durham Light Infantry had achieved in one night of anger, following the stabbing of one of their own, what the whole Ismailian terrorist movement had failed to do in months. He was a brave man, and did not deserve such treatment from his friends, the British.

Before landing in Egypt we were told that we were going on active service and our pre-

guard mounting instructions were couched in such terms. As more information comes to light and previously secret documents are released, many things unpalatable to the Government of the day will be revealed.

A Mr Tony Blair of 10 Downing Street, London, is now aware of the situation, so all should be well and he will make matters right. The very same Mr Blair stated that he was prepared to pay in blood for the removal of Saddam Hussein. One thing we could be sure of was that is that it would not be Mr Blair's blood that was spilled.

British troops seem likely to be sent on active service anywhere in the world. The RAF is short of fighter planes and soon, if a plane crashes on an airfield, the local fire service will have to be called out to deal with the situation since the specialist RAF fire service is being disbanded. The Navy has few ships and even fewer operational helicopters. The Army is mothballing tanks and merging regiments. All the Services are paying off middle-ranking NCOs, the backbone of any military service, before they qualify for full-term pensions. Recruitment is falling in all the Services. All this in an attempt to save money. Meanwhile, commitment of our troops constantly increases.

If the country cannot afford to maintain its Armed Forces, we should not contemplate waging war.

SIGNS OF THE TIMES

*Who could resist signing up to join Ginger,
the hoardings star, in the sun? Pity you
couldn't choose where the sun would shine...*

Why would anyone want to join up once the war was over and there was an abundance of work in Civvy Street? The answer was that National Service had been introduced and, with it, the certainty that every able-bodied youth would be obliged to serve a minimum of two years in one uniform or another. The certainty of being called up, even if the actual date was deferred through study or apprenticeship, engendered a spirit of 'you might as well get it over with'. In those days, to qualify as a tradesman you had to serve a poorly paid apprenticeship lasting several years. To serve all this time training and then to have to revert – just when wages would have real value for you as a qualified tradesman – to 28 shillings a week as a National Serviceman would be unbearable.

Being called up was something of a rite of passage, and those who missed it were often resentful. For ninety-nine out of a hundred, it was the first opportunity to leave home. Parents accepted it cheerfully because they believed a boy's sergeant major would be like a second mum – someone who made sure everyone was back to barracks and in bed on time, and who would never be talked back to.

By this time the demobilisation of all the 'hostilities only' Servicemen had been completed, and veterans were everywhere, filling the heads of gullible young men with tales of action in foreign parts. Policemen, tramcar conductors, rail staff and anyone who wore a uniform of any sort sported campaign ribbons. Even cinema doormen wore their medals with pride, and every conversation seemed to start with: "I remember one time in Cairo... (or Rome, Berlin, or anywhere that sounded mysterious or exotic)". Lines were shot and stories embellished and exaggerated with every retelling. To youthful ears it was all very exciting and we could hardly wait. We had missed the war and some older men, free at last from the tie of reserved occupations, grabbed the chance to finally wear a uniform. Some ex-Servicemen who missed the security and comradeship of the Forces rejoined.

Others did the same because they found it difficult to settle into a civilian routine. All was not as it should have been, or at least as they thought it would be, now that they were home. Johnny slept in his own little room again but it was smaller than he remembered. The rosy-cheeked girl next door who had written to him throughout his service had omitted to mention her addiction to nylons, chewing gum and the ubiquitous Yanks. She now spoke with a transatlantic drawl and, through ever-moving jaws, referred to 'the pictures' as 'the movies'.

At work, his former apprentice or the draft-dodging mate with flat feet, a dicky ticker or a punctured eardrum, was now his foreman. His paltry gratuity was soon spent, despite the scarcity of everything. A 'foreign' holiday was a week in the Isle of Man or Blackpool, and don't forget your ration book. Life was unexpectedly dull compared to the memories of Service life in sunnier climes.

My knowledge of life in the Royal Air Force, my preferred service, was limited to the annual Air Training Corps camp. I knew no one ate the crusts on RAF bread, and the clearing of tables was entrusted to orderlies who walked along them pushing a wide-headed railway platform style broom. I also knew you were expected to cheer like mad if anyone smashed a plate. It hardly seemed grounds for rushing out and joining up.

Everywhere, advertising hoardings exhorted men to rejoin. "Ginger's back," the legend advised. "Come on in and join him." Ginger was depicted as a sun-tanned, white-toothed youth lounging on the wing of an aircraft with his forage cap on the back of his carrot top. In this new, improved RAF, oil and grease were surprisingly foreign to engine maintenance, so the spanner in his hand was in pristine condition. In the background, a NAAFI van was staffed by a gorgeous Ginger Rogers lookalike with a dazzling smile and come-hither look. She was enough to make the average male consider signing on, but that was not my reason.

In the offices of the Electricity Board's stores, we sat on high stools at even taller desks that would have been instantly recognised by Messrs Marley and Scrooge. We used Bob Scratchit pens that sprayed ink in all directions. We should have worn protective cuffs but none was available, and the ink gave our fingers a racy blue tinge. The only concession to modernity was the use of the Kalamazoo system of record-keeping, which was the latest thing. Calculators and computers were light years away.

My arch enemy worked in the general office up the road from the stores building. As he had completed his National Service, he used to rile me with tales of what was in store for me once I was in uniform. We played tricks on each other all the time. The day of my nemesis dawned when, out of the corner of my eye, I saw him sidling round the loading bay in his sneaky approach to the office door. Through the frosted glass panel above the handle I saw his hand rest on the doorknob and could hear him engage in some lively badinage with the counter hands. His hand was removed from the handle for a moment. I seized my chance, picked up a waste paper basket and hid behind the door. The hand reappeared on the knob and it turned and opened inwards towards me. I pounced.

"Got you, you bastard!" I shouted in glee as I forced the wicker basket firmly over his head. The screwed-up bits of paper cascaded down over his shoulders on to his lovely dark suit and the pencil-sharpening shards and other bits of detritus stuck to his Brylcreemed hair – a complete triumph. Unfortunately, it was the wrong man. Who would have thought that the managing director would chose that particular moment to visit our office? He glared at me through the basket's wickerwork bars, showing surprise, shock, indignation and a hundred other emotions. Even though I removed the basket quickly and made a fair effort at brushing the worst of the debris off him, he was singularly unimpressed and deaf to my protestations that it was all a mistake.

"Come to my office at three o'clock this afternoon," he hissed, then left abruptly.

A breath of fresh air seemed a good idea, and I have to admit to being a mite depressed as I strolled along, looking at the ground. Just then I happened across a former chum from school, positively glowing with self-satisfaction and with no ear for my troubles.

"I've just signed on for the RAF," he crowed. "If you sign for an extra year on to your National Service you get an extra twenty-one shillings a week." A tramcar appeared and ten minutes later I was in the recruiting office in Princes Street signing my name and three years of my life away. An extra year did not seem long, and by making my mark I was certain of going into the Air Force as well as getting all that extra cash.

I had been in the RAF for only a few weeks when an advertising slogan, supported by a drawing of a cut-in-half car, appeared, aimed at serving airmen. "What would you do with half a car?" it enquired. Half a car translated into £250 as a signing-on inducement. Had I been serving as a National Serviceman or had it been available in Princes Street, I might well have been contracted for five years instead of only three. As it was, after the first few months, I realised that even three years was going to be a long time away from mother's cooking and the comforts of home. The RAF never released details of how many serving airmen were tempted by that half-car offer.

At three o'clock that afternoon I appeared on the carpet before a refreshed managing director. He was wearing a different suit, shirt and tie, so he must have kept a spare set in his office. It was a forgettable experience.

That I would be gone in a month weighed in my favour, and the RAF would not require a reference. Under the circumstances, I avoided the ignominy of being fired. As I was to be a regular, they would have no obligation to keep a job open for me on my return. I think he was glad about that, too.

I missed joining up in company with my pal by two days. He was in the first intake of three-year men and I was in the second. He enjoyed the life of Riley in the sun in Rhodesia. I got my share of the same sun all right, but it was shining down on the Canal Zone. He saw no action at all and quite resented the fact. So much so that he started to wear a Brigade of Guards tie and joined the police force. He just loved a uniform.

SAND IN THE CABBAGE

*As we came to realise, the Services have ways
of dealing with every possible eventuality*

Squarebashing is good for you and every young man today would benefit from a spell of it. If you doubt the veracity of this statement, just ask anyone who experienced it.

The huge boots that you thought were the ugliest objects you ever set eyes on were transformed, in time and with no little effort, into the most comfortable things you ever wore on your feet. They attained a mirror finish never since seen on any other item of your footwear.

The floor of the barrack room was treated with reverence and never trod upon once it had acquired its gleaming finish. This was achieved through endless effort with a buffer that weighed a ton and brought sweat to every brow. Having brought it to perfection from then on your every move was made by slipping about on pads of felt to preserve the quality. You became so possessive of it that you resented any contact between the barrack room floor and the tackets on the soles of the boots of any officer or NCO who might visit while on their lawful duty. Knowing the amount of elbow grease that would be required to restore it to its natural brilliance made you dislike the wearers and this was all part of the military master plan to bind you together as a unit by giving you someone or something in common to hate.

Your mug and eating irons, when not displayed on your immaculate bedding layout, were carried back and forth to the mess hall every mealtime. After use your knife, fork, spoon and pint mug were carefully washed in cauldrons of boiling water and then, before being restored to their designated spot on your bed, given a final inspection and polish. The family silver could not have been better respected.

You learned to darn a sock and press a uniform, and even to iron a shirt. You ate everything put before you and gained weight and muscle and, through exercise, achieved a level of fitness never before experienced. The system that never allowed you a moment of time to call your own between reveille and lights-out was designed to banish thoughts of homesickness and convert callow youths into men in the shortest possible time. It did a decent job of it.

We fired our trusty .303 Lee Enfield on the range and in my case, the target being so tatty, sawed the legs off it with machine gun fire from the deadly accurate Bren. If memory serves, we were allowed just ten rounds of practice with the rifle and half a magazine on the Bren. In the French Foreign Legion it is not unusual for a recruit to fire five or six hundred rounds during basic training. The Wehrmacht in Germany in 1942, a time when every spare round was needed on the eastern front, allowed even their young non-infantry recruits to fire off between two and three dozen rounds during basic training.

The next time I handled a rifle would be a year later on active service, and before being issued with this lethal weapon we were given no additional arms tuition. Little wonder we

From DA to conscript crop... National Service recruits learned that 'uniform' referred to haircuts as well as strange-feeling garments and footwear.

were in as much danger from our comrades as from the enemy. We also learned the rudiments of unarmed combat, which seemed a very rough pastime that we would never need in the future. You mixed happily with all sorts from any background and found something to like in everyone you met. A lot of time was spent instructing us in the 'panther' crawl and stressing to us that movement and reflection were the two things most likely to give away our position to the enemy, and vice versa. The Korean war had just kicked off and we wondered if we were being prepared for action there.

Having built up our courage we had to face our Tab One and Tab Two injections. They were not particularly painful when administered but within a day or two everyone spent their time ensuring that nothing bumped into a seriously swollen arm. Later a yellow-fever injection delivered fresh from the refrigerator stung a bit during the process but one suffered no after effects whatsoever.

We were volunteered en-mass to donate a pint of blood and in exchange we were promised a pint of beer – free. On the day the ale became tea and a biscuit. Although all of us were first-time donors we agreed that giving blood was easy peasy. When I stood up and moved towards the tea and biscuit table everything blacked out and I came to lying back on a bed with an instruction to stay there immobile for twenty minutes. I was fussed over so much that my tea was completely overlooked. It may be that the others got their pints of beer while I was lying there but if that had been the case I'm sure I would have heard about it. My blood was nothing special but I was given a little receipt for my donation and a written invitation to call again at anytime, anywhere. It seemed that blood, even mine, was in great demand.

The food was not as mother used to make, but after a fortnight's service the entire intake was hungry enough to eat a horse, and for all I know did. Good rations ruined would be a kind description but, being in starvation mode due to the unaccustomed exercise, we devoured all that was put before us and prayed for seconds. That was until the day that wet sand and cabbage was ladled onto our plates; it was the final straw, something had to be done. Someone would have to register a complaint in the strongest possible terms. There was enough civvy left in us to feel that we deserved better.

The scene in the huge dining hall was typical of the era – hundreds of starving teenagers, all muttering bitterly about the food. A self-important retinue headed by the duty officer strolled at a leisurely pace between the tables. A step behind the officer was a cook sergeant in crisp, freshly laundered whites. A corporal followed, and he was followed in turn by a hapless leading aircraftsman clerk clutching a clipboard.

"Complaints… any complaints?" the officer queried benignly, confident that he would never be answered.

He led his troupe with a measured tread. Never, in all his time in the service, had there been a single complaint about the quality of the food. Soon he would be off to the mess to enjoy a gin and tonic followed by a tasty steak washed down with a decent claret. Food rationing did not affect the officers mess.

"Any complaints?" he gently called in a bored voice. Silence, apart from the odd clatter of colliding knives and forks, reigned supreme.

At one table, resentment was simmering near boiling point.

"Go on, Jock," a chorus of cowardly regional voices urged.

"Tell him about the sand in the cabbage."

"It's not right…"

"We should do something about it."

"You tell 'im, Jock. We're right behind you."

Jock should have known better, but after only sixteen days of service he was sodden behind the ears. The siren voices continued their blandishments for action. His urge to speak out became irresistible. He rose to his feet and spoke the fateful words in his broad Scottish accent.

"Yes, sir. I have a complaint, sir. There's sand in the cabbage."

This time the silence was absolute, with eating irons suspended in mid-air.

"SAND IN THE CABBAGE!" roared a very surprised duty officer. "Did you hear that, sergeant? Airman here says there's SAND in the CABBAGE."

"In the CABBAGE, sir? SAND, sir? Do you mean there's SAND in the CABBAGE?" The sergeant was aghast.

"Corporal, what's all this about," he demanded. "This airman 'ere says there's SAND IN THE CABBAGE."

At the end of the line, the poor 'erk was standing, white-faced. The corporal turned on him and shouted: "What's all this about, YOU! Is there sand in the cabbage?"

The message had arrived at its terminus and instant action was required. The 'erk peered at the plate. His reluctance to confirm or deny the evidence was clear. "Well yes, it COULD be sand that's in the cabbage but, there again, it could be something else. It does look as if there's something in the cabbage," he advised the corporal.

The corporal shook his head mournfully and muttered unbelievingly: "Sand in the cabbage." Turning to the sergeant he repeated the 'erk's findings.

"Yes, sarge. It definitely looks like sand in the cabbage."

I skived off and spent the day walking around the camp looking as if I was on an official errand

The sergeant repeated the awful news to the duty officer. During these exchanges the hall was deathly silent. Not a plate moved. It was as if everyone had stopped breathing. The silence was absolute.

"Sorry about that, lad," sympathised the duty officer in a really kind and gentle voice to underline his concern. "Good of you to draw our attention to it. We'll see what can be done to improve matters. Take his name, sergeant."

Right down the line it went... take 'is name... take 'is name... take 'is name.

"3508595 FINDLAY, SIR." Although still only rookies, we had been taught how to address an officer, even if it was through three other people. My answer, as it were, went up through the ranks.

In the teeth of an icy snow-bearing north wind at six o'clock the following morning, 3508595 Findlay was introduced to a pail of ice-cold water and a pyramid of Southport sand-encrusted cabbages. An irate cookhouse sergeant, without a shred of humour in his being, barked a stern warning to his newly appointed cabbage-washer assistant.

"If we get a single complaint, you'll spend your entire service here."

The sergeant cook had been on duty all night and was due off at 6am. I spotted the change over and surmised that the new man would not have been informed of my existence. Anything was better than staying to complete the chore. I skived off and, armed with a piece of paper, I spent the day walking around the camp looking as if I was on an official errand. But word of my fate had spread.

That day a little after noon saw the familiar retinue, a different duty officer at its head, making the rounds of the dining hall. "Any complaints? Any complaints?" His query was in vain as hundreds of voices, all spitting sand, chorused in unison: "NO, SIR. NO COMPLAINTS."

As we all eventually came to realise, the Services have ways of dealing with every possible eventuality.

It was about now that the RAF decided that we were smart enough and had enough respect for the uniform to be allowed out of camp for an evening. We headed for Liverpool in a rush. Freedom is a heady brew and on that first evening I met my own Liverpool lovely. Young love, particularly the chaste variety of that era, was a powerful emotion. She must have thought that I was her kind of chap because we wrote to each other for years. Jimmy Young was top of the hit parade during those weeks with a song called They Tried To Tell Us We're Too Young, and he might have been singing it just for us. Jimmy also kept warning the listeners about the dangers of the Tennessee Waltz, but it was the Pier Head Polka that did for my romance. That was in the future, and luckily none of us had a crystal ball.

Christmas was approaching and snow fell heavily, rendering our new-found marching skills useless. We were instructed to dig our heels into the ice and this, much to our surprise, kept us upright. A little snow was not going to interrupt our squarebashing. How the people of the Wirral tolerated such weather conditions was beyond me but, as I was there only in November and December, my judgement was perhaps clouded.

To get us used to the possibility of guard duties we were rostered to do something called fire piquet. Our boots were just beginning to

W O RINES

A band from the Royal Scots playing on the fo'c'sle of HMS St Kitts, Suez,
11 August 1954. I think the double-bass player might have been teetotal.

take on the first glimmer of a shine when we were obliged to patrol in eight inches of snow, and two discoveries were made. Leather boots are not waterproof and soaked boots do not shine. The wind was whistling in off the sea at about forty miles an hour and our greatcoats did little to stop it. We froze. On our second tour of duty from 2am to 4am (we had not yet mastered the 'hundred hours' clock) when we left the cosy guardroom we found that the wind had died away. It was too cold to snow, or so we were told, and every step crunched as we plodded through the ice-topped snow. We spotted a glow shining under the door of a toilet block. Like the good fire piquets that we were, we decided to investigate what could have been a life-threatening fire, but the door was locked against us. We had received no instruction on what to do if we actually found

a fire and surprisingly little force was required to shove open the door where we found happiness in the form of an oil-burning stove. Its job was to keep the pipes from freezing and it thawed us out nicely. We discussed what we should do and since the discussion was wide ranging it took all of two hours. In fact, we were a few minutes late in clocking off.

The next day there was a bit of an inquest as to why the fire piquets had not discovered a break-in at a toilet block. Six of us had been on duty and since the other two pairs denied all knowledge we did the same. The camp covered a vast area and we couldn't be everywhere. With six weeks service behind us we could march like airmen, and our uniforms having been altered to fit, we looked like airmen. Christmas leave was granted and we dashed off home like little boys.

LEARNING TO BOX CLEVER

*The redhead who couldn't resist a uniform,
and the bully who tried to terrorise the billet*

My very first leave from the RAF passed in a flash. We Jocks would have preferred a Hogmanay break, but this would have upset the smooth running of the well-oiled RAF machine that turned callow youths into impressive fighting machines or, as in my case, fairly timid airmen. Wherever I went on that first leave I was chided for not turning up in Air Force blue. For me it was wonderful to be in anonymous civvies again after weeks of being inspected at every turn to ensure that my shoes were burnished or my buttons polished.

Surprisingly enough, I had been invited to the Electricity Board dance and party, being held in a posh venue on Princes Street during the festive season. There would be no high table at this bash and I was pretty sure I would be able to avoid my old adversary, the boss. He was no doubt still simmering over the indignity he had suffered at my hands, while I had more or less forgotten all about it because my seven weeks in the RAF had been filled with adventure and seemed to have taken forever. But to my former workmates, those seven weeks since they last saw me had probably seemed like only seven days, and my decision to turn up at the party in uniform proved to be a wise one.

As an ex-colleague, I was much more popular now than I ever had been as a fellow employee and, as people do, my former colleagues hatched a conspiracy with the aim of getting me so drunk that I would make a complete prat of myself. But they had overlooked the power of our drill instructors that could still control their charges at a range of over 200 miles. We had been warned of the dire consequences that would befall anyone who besmirched the good name and uniform of the RAF in general and West Kirby Training Establishment in particular. The plotters failed in their attempts because, when pressed to have a whisky - and a double instead of the ordered single was invariably delivered - a crafty swift spurt from a soda siphon shot the whisky on to the thick tablecloth on the temporary bar, and left only water in my glass.

That night I gained an undeserved reputation as not only a hard drinker but also one who could hold his liquor exceedingly well. At the end of the night I was bold enough to ask a vivacious redhead if I could escort her home, and the uniform had to take the credit for her agreement. It had a lot to answer for, because in civilian clothes she would certainly never even have noticed me.

My newly acquired marching skills made the long walk to her home an easy stroll and just how she managed after a night of dancing in her high heels never crossed my mind, and neither did the possibility of hiring a taxi. Arriving at her parents' house, she led me purposefully to a small potting shed at the bottom of the garden. Though my heart was really in Liverpool, this girl's hair was flame red instead of mousy brown, her eyes a lustrous green instead of hazel, and she was two or three inches taller than my love of two weeks. Her figure was what could only be described as statuesque, and her little red dress did much to accentuate her curves, all in the right places. She revealed that she was free from entanglements and, dewy-eyed, broke the news that her former boyfriend had managed to kill himself while riding a motorcycle. Her one major regret was that they had never consummated their relationship, and suggested that her next boyfriend would not be so denied. I got a distinct impression that if I made a sincere-sounding expression of honourable intent, her knickers would be off. She scared me stiff, no pun intended, and I knew I was out of my depth. This was heady stuff, and in the immortal words of the famous Sunday scandal sheet, I made my excuses and left.

We all have 20-20 vision with hindsight and I still kick myself for being so gauche. I could have had one girl at home and one away and received two letters a week instead of one; but at eighteen we all have an attractive innocence about us. It may seem hard to believe, but I was really looking forward to the second half of my squarebashing stint.

The list of things I had never done would fill a book, and to start with, I had never been south of the Border before I joined the RAF. I had never had a girlfriend, and I had never needed to stand on my own two feet. I liked it and returned to West Kirby determined to enjoy my second stint of squarebashing.

The mind definitely plays tricks on the unwary and I had forgotten just how basic the conditions were, the early rising and the enforced cold water shaves, it was not at all like home. We had all over-indulged at home on leave, and getting us back into shape was clearly a priority for the drill instructors. They had four short weeks left to turn us into airmen they could be proud of at the passing-out parade. The RAF is very keen on fitness and sport, and my contribution consisted of doubling round the assault course carrying a Bren gun in punishment for nodding off during a lecture on said armament. It got very

heavy after the first circuit and I ran – or rather staggered – round the course three times before reaching the desired state of total collapse. Stripping and cleaning a Bren gun and then reassembling it are not easy tasks when you slept through the initial instruction.

I also tried out for the wrestling team with unfortunate consequences. The large physical training instructor who was gently putting me through my paces took umbrage at being unexpectedly floored by my simple leg trip. His annoyance was clear when he whirled me round the boxing ring by my feet with only my elbows in contact with the surface. The skin came off and resin entered the wounds, entailing a trip to the sickbay where my elbows were strapped straight by plaster bandages. This, too, was to have unfortunate consequences, but it made me the smartest man on parade as I swung my rigid arms shoulder-high.

Back in the barracks our would-be bully (there's always one) was on the look-out for any weakness in the others that he could exploit. He claimed to be ex-merchant navy, boasted about a successful amateur boxing career, and took advantage of my absence at ablutions to mess up my freshly made bed. Due to the limited use of my arms, I had had difficulty trying to make it and been kindly assisted by the recruit in the next bed.

Knowing from the smirk on the bully's ugly face that he had done the dastardly deed, I invited him to make good the disorder, advising that a refusal would result in my taking steps. His smirk had by now become a sneer, so I bent my knees, grasped the rail of the nearest bed and stood up. The bed toppled over. I repeated the procedure and in a flash six or seven beds were strewn about. He charged down the hut in a most un-boxer like manner in an attempt to flatten me in front of everyone in the hut. It was now that my Air Training Corps time paid off, as the handy PTI of our unit had instructed us well in self-defence, telling us that if an opponent rushed you, he was playing into your hands, with his weight and strength being added to your own in defeating him. The theory worked a treat in the gym when both parties knew their respective roles; but this was my first chance to put the lesson into real practice. When the bully was close enough, I raised my straightened arms, gripped his shoulders and fell backwards to the floor, pulling him to me as I rolled. My feet found his stomach and, by pushing hard with my legs, I succeeded in making him airborne. He flew through the air like a daring young man who had missed his trapeze, and landed on the upright leg of one of the beds I had turned over. He was instantly rendered *hors de combat*. His mouth was still working, however, and after he stopped screaming from pain, he started yelling threats of dire retribution. They were quite bloodcurdling and if they had been put into practice, I would have been of no further use to the Air Force. But I detected a note of bluster in his outburst, and agreed to accommodate him when we were both recovered. I was amazed that it had gone so well. My billet mates now thought I was an expert in martial arts, and I thought it prudent to let them go on thinking it.

Boxing being the first love of the RAF, every new intake was expected to provide raw material for the entertainment of permanent staff. Our bully boy was extremely keen to make his mark, and every spare minute he was found shadow boxing, wearing a pair of scarlet gloves he had brought from home. He sniffed in time to his jabs and upper cuts, and he looked quite impressive as he jinked about. We wondered how he would fare when he boxed with a shadow that could hit back, and looked forward to the prospect of him getting his come-uppance in public.

As our camp facilities were first-rate, other military camps in the area made use of them. Thus an inter-service boxing competition was arranged. An Aberdonian in the next hut was reckoned to be a certain winner for the RAF team as he was a farm boy with big hands and broad shoulders. He said he fought southpaw, though he had never

In the immortal words of the Sunday scandal sheet, I made my excuses and left

actually been in a boxing ring. His declared tactic was to take whatever his opponent could throw at him and then nail him with a haymaker right hand that had never let him down. His adversary looked much smaller but was within the same weight limit, and we were very surprised when Jock, sound asleep, was carried out of the ring within the first quarter of the first round.

The opponent our 18-year-old would-be bully had drawn was a Royal Marine Commando, liberally tattooed and looking to be in his late twenties, so it was clearly a mismatch, man against boy. The Marine's hair was thinning and his face bore ample evidence of many previous encounters, and some scars which could only have been caused by blades. He had muscles on his kneecaps and wore regulation gym shoes, while our boy sported white calf-length boxing boots with long frilly tassels.

In the first round our man ran backwards round the ring, hotly pursued by the man with the pretty pictures on his arms and legs. The referee interrupted after two minutes by stopping the race and insisting that the pair start to box. Our man was having none of that and, although he sniffed a lot and his arms flailed about quite a bit, by the end of the round neither man had landed a blow. Applause is only permitted in amateur boxing during the intervals between rounds, and the deathly silence was only interrupted by the voices of fellow marines instructing their man to "Chin 'im, Bill." The referee took the opportunity of speaking to our man, clearly offering to cancel the bout on humanitarian grounds since there must be less messy ways of committing hara-kiri.

In round two, our man took three or four steps back and then launched an unexpected attack on the marine. The punching was crisp, clean and in clusters, and the hapless Marine's legs began to collapse. He sat on the middle rope for an eight count and bravely jumped up to continue, but the referee stopped the fight a few seconds later. To add insult to injury, our man was awarded a cup for being the best fighter of the night.

I resolved that there was no way in which the Marquess of Queensberry would be permitted to stick his nose into any confrontation between this whirling dervish and me; it would be in the dark where no one would see the half-brick in my hand. However, in the end, we never did square up to each other. His reputation having been made during the boxing match, some little doubt must have made him reluctant to risk losing it against a sneaky individual like me.

Scotsmen enjoy an unjustified reputation for being unruly and aggressive, though most of us would rather run than fight. But my own stock rose some days later when a drunken Irish recruit ran amok threatening all and sundry with a bayonet-fixed rifle. It was Kelly's odds that it was not loaded and I assumed he would not really stick a fellow Celt, so a sudden grab and a swift kick in a sensitive spot brought that particular excitement to an instant end.

Squarebashing was certainly educational but sooner or later you have to sit your exams and move on. Our exam was the much-dreaded passing-out parade and we spent a lot of time making sure we would get it right on the day. It is hard now to imagine the grinding work that must have gone into the preparations for that event. Failure meant being back-squadded and starting all over

again, so when it was discovered that a recruit genuinely did have two left feet, I suspect that on the day he would be made to report sick or something of that sort. Today's Army passes out in fairly small numbers, but in National Service times there were hundreds in every intake. My experience in the Air Training Corps not only gave me a different service number but also taught me how to march well, and I was therefore given the signal honour of being the parade's right-marker. This meant I was first on the square and, as it turned out, the last off it too. We had a band and a man with many rings on his wrists to take the salute and inspect the ranks of airmen who open ordered, and quick and slow marched, and generally showed off their new-found skills. When the parade was concluded and the brass hats had retired to the officers' mess, we remained to be informed of our future postings. It was done alphabetically, and I was to find out how it feels to have a name starting with Z.

A married man from our billet was a joiner in Civvy Street and therefore a bit older. Due to his call-up having been deferred, he was drafted to Gibraltar. We actually felt sorry for him, though in reality the jammy devil had landed a dream posting. Others went to the various trades training centres up and down the country. The authorities didn't jump from E to G, but all the other Fs received their instructions and I was ignored until, at long last, I was left standing quite alone on the square on my right-marker spot.

"Right, Jock, you lucky lad. We've wangled a home posting for you." My heart gladdened. Yes, Jock, it's Scotland for you – RAF Kinloss. As I marched smartly off the parade ground, I felt it had been worth the wait, since Kinross was in Fife and only about 30 miles north of Edinburgh, my home town. I would have been happy to stay at West Kirby within a 20-minute train ride of Liverpool, but this was the next best thing. For some reason, my life never seemed to turn out in accordance with my best-laid schemes.

ONE L OF A DIFFERENCE

*In which I receive a geography lesson from
British Rail and a treat from the CO's wife*

When I presented myself at Waverley Station's booking hall in Edinburgh, the oaf behind the British Rail counter sneered at my proposition that my travel warrant contained a typing error, and took great delight in informing me that Kinloss was in the frozen northern wastes near Inverness. So much for my promised 'home' posting! This would be hours, if not miles, further from home than Liverpool. I was not happy.

At Kinloss halt there was a surly porter, a crane, a wheelbarrow and a shed, but no sign of transport provided to take new arrivals to the RAF airfield. The porter nodded northwards and said the camp was "about a mile up the road". It turned out to be a Scottish mile. In the unseasonably warm weather I set off carrying every item of clothing issued by the Service, plus some of my own – a greatcoat, full webbing and packs, with a bulging kitbag stuffed with civilian clothing slung across the top. I strode off, confident in the knowledge that a car or van would come along and offer me a lift, but not a single vehicle passed me. There's a technical term for the condition I was in when I reached the guardroom – knackered. The snowdrop on the gate asked where I thought I was going, as he had no information on new arrivals.

"I've been posted to 45MU for trade training," I explained.

"Tough, that," he said. "They've all gone on leave." After a basic training camp like West Kirby, where everyone marched about

and either shouted or got shouted at, this laidback attitude was a bit of a culture shock.

"I'll tell you what," he added. "I'll put you up in the prefab and you can go on leave tomorrow." The prefab was a temporary building next to the guardroom where waifs and strays could be accommodated when visiting the camp. True to his word, the next morning I was off home again, my rail fare paid by a grateful nation. This was the kind of Air Force I would be happy serving.

Kinloss showed definite promise. A palatial new NAAFI was under construction and it would have every home comfort for the lads. Trade training was easy for me since the RAF had plagiarised the Kalamazoo system as used by the Electricity Board. All I had to do to qualify as a leading aircraftsman was memorise the numbers of the various forms unique to the mysterious RAF system of changing and losing items, and the promotion was worth 7 shillings a week. Had the base been sited in Kinross or, better still, at the bottom or our street in Edinburgh, I would have signed on for life.

Just to prove that it was a military base, something happened to me that I had thought was the stuff of fanciful legend. Six of us were hauled from a snug office to carry out a vital task. The important job that took us from our studies was to water the CO's garden while it was raining hard outside. We protested to the sergeant who proved that he had, in spades, what was required to make progress in the service. "Go and get your groundsheets," he ordered. "A spot of rain never hurt nobody."

The groundsheet has yet to be discovered and exploited by dress designers, and it's not even a military secret. It is a simple rectangle of waterproof material six feet by three feet wide which, when laid flat, provides a dry surface to lie down on. It works really well if you have overhead cover. The clever bit is that at a certain point on the edge is a collar device, which allows it to be worn as protection against the heaviest rainfall. Unfortunately, when donned for this purpose, it resembles a poncho with a low point front and rear, and high points at the sides, ensuring that the wearer always gets saturated. It is, however, a dual-purpose garment, and much more useful when providing a backdrop for kit, during inspections.

Once we had collected our groundsheets we, as AC1s, were entrusted to make our own way to the CO's mansion, while the sergeant, his duty done, sloped off to the sergeants' mess for a pint or a lie-down or whatever it is sergeants do in the afternoon. A knock at the door was rewarded with a quizzical look from the CO's glamorous wife, who agreed that it was ridiculous to water a garden while it was raining and directed us to the back door where we were admitted to the kitchen and served with coffee, cake and biscuits. A pleasant hour was spent discussing the shortcomings of the RAF in general and a thick sergeant in particular, and when the rain eased, we returned to our studies.

Wednesday afternoons were devoted to sport, and since there was no rugby team at Kinloss, I tried out for basketball and found myself picked to represent Coastal Command (North) against a team of infantrymen from Fort George. Rugby is a rough game, but when it comes to dirty play, basketball leaves it standing. As it is a non-contact sport, one could believe it would be all jolly hockey sticks and very polite, but this is not so. An elbow in the face in the first minute made my mouth bleed throughout the game, but the culprit was identified and a running battle ensued where shirt-pulling was *de rigueur* and the odd punch quite acceptable. In rugby, however rough the action is on the field, it is left there, and the losers applaud the winners off and join them for a pint afterwards. Emerging from the dressing-room, my basketball antagonist and I headed for each other to settle things when I noted that not only was his uniform a different colour from mine, and fashioned from much better material, but that he sported a single pip on each shoulder. I would like to report that we shook hands and all that, but we did not. Instead, we headed for our respective coach transports, muttering to ourselves and hoping to meet again when out of uniform.

Thereafter, I gave up rough games and instead swam in the Elgin baths on Wednesday afternoons. Behind the aircraft graveyard at Kinloss stand the tallest and whitest dunes of soft sand you could ever hope to discover, and as a hobby we used to hurl ourselves from the top and make a gentle landing 20 or 30 feet below, then scramble back up and do it again. We never swam there because the sea was icy cold even at the height of summer.

At the time we were training in accountancy, some medical staff were undergoing basic nursing instruction. When a plane crashed high on a mountain, the young medics were pressed into service to recover the bodies. The discovery that the corpses were frozen into weird shapes and that limbs had to be broken to make them fit into the body bags came as a shock to the trainee medics. After this incident, many of the embryo Dr Kildares remustered to other trades.

We lost count of the times we stood in the freezing gales in the pre-dawn light at Aviemore station where the snow lay twelve feet deep, never thinking that one day it would be a famous winter sports centre. We did notice the snow and were always surprised to find that Kinloss never saw a single flake due to the tail-end of the Gulf Stream, which flows into the Moray Firth.

To make life bearable and to beat the system, I teamed up with a stores handler, another lad from Edinburgh, and we often hitch-hiked home together at weekends. To finance this expensive exercise each week, he acquired a pair of the rather snazzy overalls as worn by RAF engineers, and I worked the oracle in the office to keep the records straight. We had a buyer for every pair, and the sum realised was just enough to pay for our return train tickets, and a cup of tea and a wad in the station buffet. We were lucky, and our appropriation of stock went unnoticed.

Some others were less fortunate. One ass, seeing two bicycles coming towards him on a dark and windy night, decided to scare the riders. His bike had no lights and as he zoomed between them it was his intention to cry out and give them a fright. He did create fear and he did indeed cry out – not "Yah-boo" as might have been expected, but "Oh ****!" as he struck the radiator of a three-ton truck fitted with high-mounted, but tiny, side-lights. Another cyclist riding in similar conditions failed to notice that the Shackleton aircraft parked on the hangar apron had its engines idling and lost his head, literally, as he rode along. Like a headless chicken, he kept going for some distance. After this incident, two more medics asked to transfer from hospital work.

Looking back on the living conditions we tolerated, it has to be acknowledged that they were quite primitive by today's standards. With thirty men to a hut, every other having sweaty feet, the pong must have been awful, but the RAF had a plan to offset this and improve hygiene. Showers after sport and swimming ensured that, apart from the dedicated soap-dodgers, everyone was rinsed at least once a week. Every billet was issued with a 'bath book' and, by signing it, each airman was required to confirm that he had bathed at least once that week. Those who

The groundsheet has yet to be discovered and exploited by dress designers

cheated were frog-marched to the ablutions and scrubbed down in an extremely painful manner. It was about this time that the phantom crapper put in an appearance. This despicable apology for a man left a calling card in the bath that he had presumably just used. We became so paranoid about being accused of being the guilty party that we bathed in groups to confirm the cleanliness of the bathhouse before we left it. The phantom would sometimes strike in the middle of the night, bringing snowdrops and fire piquet orderlies under suspicion, and it went on for months as he evaded every snare set to catch him. In his own way, he was as successful as Jack the Ripper had been in London's East End.

I had settled in nicely at Kinloss when my name appeared as one of twelve bound for an overseas posting. We all fervently hoped that the phantom would continue his disgusting work after we left or we might gain notoriety as the dirty dozen. The day we left, the new NAAFI opened.

Being in the transit camp at Wharton was very much like joining up all over again. This time the uniform being issued was KD or khaki drill, which meant we were heading for a hot country, so we asked: "Why all this woollen gear?" A wiseacre in the Electricity Board who had served abroad had solemnly warned me of the dangers of lying on my bed with my stomach unprotected while the overhead fans were sending cool air down on me. He advised that I must always wear a towel folded across my midriff otherwise I would get what he delicately referred to as a stomach upset. I never so much as saw a fan in two years but I certainly got my share of the runs, the trots and Delhi belly.

Knee-length stockings and thick vests, long trousers and shorts were all on the shopping list. The official order on shorts was that they were to be worn knee-length, and the old joke about long shorts or short longs was bandied about. When we got to Egypt we found that they were worn well above the knee, but whether this was through natural shrinkage or the work of the camp tailor we had yet to find out. New medical and dental inspections were carried out and we had to

brush up our knowledge of fieldcraft.

Our progress through transit had its lighter moments. On one occasion the draft was to be punished for some imagined wrong, not just a few other malcontents like me but more than 500 or 600 men. A route march was ordered and two other supposed ringleaders and myself were dragged from where we were hiding in the ranks and propelled towards the head of the column,

making me for the second time in my life the right-marker on a parade. We were 'shunned, 'ight-turned, and marched off in quick time by the centre and, as we passed out through the main gate, we were 'eft-wheeled and a huge crocodile-trudged off towards Preston.

Fortunately there was a bend in the road not far from the main gate and a very conveniently located bus stop. We could hear the shouting voices but their owners were concealed from view. If we could not see them, it followed that they could not see us. Saying a fond farewell to the second row that was now promoted to front row, the three of us skipped across on to the pavement, turned our backs to the marchers, and turned up our greatcoat collars. The whole parade passed us by and when a bus came along we jumped on board and had the joy of waving to our comrades when we overtook them. We alighted at a roadside café about a mile along the road and were eating fried egg on toast and drinking a refreshing cup of tea as the marchers trudged past. We thought it prudent to ignore them this time.

Everything had gone like clockwork and we were free; but it did not take long for the euphoria to wear off and the realisation to dawn that we were technically absent without leave. Getting back into camp might not be all that easy, but providence always smiles on the righteous, and today was our day. On our slow crawl back to camp we spotted some contractors' lorries driving in and out of a side gate which, in typical RAF fashion, was unsupervised. We dived in and made for our billet as casually as we could. Two hours later, our bedraggled and totally exhausted mates returned, and we were much relieved to find

Inniskilling Fusiliers wait to board HMS Triumph bound for Egypt in 1951. Did it always rain on embarkation days?

no one had grassed on us. It was a small victory, but a victory all the same.

We managed a visit to a variety theatre in Blackpool where we and the landladies of the town, who are admitted free, comprised the entire audience. Some of us were invited up on stage to make complete fools of ourselves. This we did joyfully, and performers and spectators alike had a good time. As always, the RAF kept us short of cash and we were promised a payday once we boarded our troopship. It seems that men due to sail overseas got ideas of staying at home if they had cash in their pockets, so the RAF were taking no chances.

A hitch somewhere down the line was experienced and additional leave awarded. We had used up our embarkation allowance so the few extra days were by way of a gift, though it was probably cheaper for the RAF to send us home than feed us at the camp. Buses were laid on, a pay advance of a few pounds issued, and we were off. On the way home, a fellow-Scot from Edinburgh quizzed me on whether I would be prepared to join him when he went AWOL. His actual words were: "Stuff this for a game of soldiers. I'm definitely not going back... how about you?" He then modified his statement with: "At least until the boat has sailed." Although I admired his spirit, my ancestry is littered with cowards so I found it easy to turn down his invitation, convinced it was all talk.

When the weekend was over, there was an empty seat next to mine on the bus journey back to camp. Jock MacLennan had kept his word and gone on the run. Back at Wharton the waiting continued till at last we were loaded into the carriages of a private train bound for Liverpool's Pier Head. We passed the time by playing cards. No one had much in the way of cash but, as they lost their few shillings and dropped out, the kitty kept getting bigger. 'Sharp' is too derogatory to describe my ability at pontoon and poker – 'skilled' is the expression I prefer. Having been promised a payday once we were on board, the men played carelessly... so I did very well.

We had just disembarked at the siding in Liverpool when we were ordered back on to the train. The Empress of Canada, all 45,000 tons of her, had been caught by a sudden gust of the rain-bearing wind and knocked her rudder against a stone buttress. A check for damage would have to be made by divers before she could be allowed to sail. Back at Wharton, we were just in time to see Jock MacLennan being ushered into the guardroom with his wrists in handcuffs.

As we entered the huts, the Tannoy announced that on the morrow, following an early morning pay parade, buses would again arrive to take us all home. Those who wished to leave earlier could do so. I was the only one in our group with any money and my gains at the tables had me home that same night, tucking into Mother's cooking. It was the last leave I would get for two years.

The pilot made no mistakes this time and as we filed aboard to find our mess deck our friend MacLennan, who had spent the extra holiday behind bars, was given a room of his own – in the brig. Once the boat was too far from shore for him to try swimming for it, he was released without charge.

The RAF could be kind.

WHERE FLYING FISHES PLAYED

*Children's Encyclopaedia pictures came to life as
we arrived at Port Said, but no one mentioned
the Canal Zone was far from being a playground*

It was not all that bad for us on the promenade deck since we were protected from the worst of the weather by the various decks above. It was the scarlet-jacketed band who were suffering as they stood on the dockside like bedraggled dogs, with water pouring from them, and their shiny brass instruments filling up regularly. These are, by the way, fitted with a little tap to allow the excess water to be drawn off and on a day like that they had probably jammed the drain hole open. They were playing a selection of lively marches and because you can tell from the music produced how happy or otherwise the players are, it was clear that they were ecstatic. We were going and they were staying. It was 1951 and our job was to save the Suez Canal for the world.

The Empress of Canada weighed in at an impressive 45,000 tons and she was leaning against the dock at an alarming angle. Every Serviceman and woman on board had rushed to the Pier Head side of the ship to see if any one had turned up to wave them goodbye. I had hoped that my Liverpool lovely would have used her lunch hour from Littlewood's Pools to come to see me depart but I was disappointed. In the absence of friends, we waved to anyone we thought might wave back. Many of the lady soldiers and airwomen were in tears while we men, made of sterner stuff, felt like crying but did not dare. This King and Country stuff is over-rated when you get right down to it.

Some Jeremiah said that the pouring rain

was nature crying for those who would not return but we banished that thought from our minds. Thousands of little square sheets of toilet paper were thrown overboard as a substitute for the streamers that are scattered from luxury cruise liners as they set sail. We had seen it hundreds of times in the movies and we roared with laughter and cried out in delight as the sodden squares of paper stuck to everything they landed on. The bandsmen, their instruments, the jetty and the crowd of supporters, all received their share. We were still laughing as we noticed rather than felt the ship glide away from the pier. So we were finally on our way, even if the ship was a bit lopsided. We stopped laughing then, and did not smile for the next five days.

King's Regulations decreed that toilet paper, troops for the use of, would be issued only every fifth day irrespective of any emergencies. For nearly a week every scrap of paper was carefully hoarded and guarded. Out-of-date magazines and newspapers commanded a premium and even treasured letters from loved ones were sacrificed to an urgent need. As if that was not bad enough, it was discovered that toilet doors do not exist for other ranks on troopships. Food must have been distributed and order restored, because lights out found us sleeping snugly in hammocks for the first time in our lives.

The crack of dawn coincided with the crack of portholes bursting open and green seawater flooding into our mess deck area. As the ship heaved and rolled on its eight-point

This huge green sea broke over us and we were soaked to the skin in an instant

perambulations the Irish Sea sloshed from side to side and end to end of our sleeping quarters. Those who had been foolish enough to leave their kit on the floor discovered it among dozens of other items in the unsanitary scum that was last night's supper floating on top of the seawater. Timing my dash with great precision I managed to make the companionway with my feet dry. Up top, the salt air swept away the stench of the mess deck but lining the rails were hundreds of wretched retching seasickness sufferers. I felt fine as long as I kept my face to the wind, and in the back of my mind was advice from seafaring cousins that seasickness is all in the imagination. Get a square meal inside you and in the unlikely event that you became ill you would be equipped with something to throw up. It was a theory that had yet to be put into practice. As I fought my way back down below and the stench hit my nostrils it triggered my downfall and I rushed back aloft to claim a space on the rail. In time I did go down to breakfast, a meal attempted by a select few and consumed by a mere handful, I managed to chew on a dry bread roll.

My attack of mal-de-mer was bad enough for me to discover that if you are really ill you don't hope to get well – you hope to die. No one had warned us that the Irish Sea can be a wilder stretch of water than the Bay of Biscay. Two of us were on an outside companionway

ladder fully a hundred feet above the waterline when we saw a wall of green water fast approaching. We shouted for any others to hang on for dear life and we clasped the steps in an unbreakable bear-hug. This huge green sea broke over us and we were soaked to the skin in an instant and later got queer looks as we wandered about in KD only two days out.

Sailing on an overloaded troopship is really quite boring once you get your sea legs, and the inevitable card schools and housey-housey sessions flourished. On deck it was freezing cold, and down in the bowels of the ship it was roasting hot, making shipboard life an ideal breeding ground for colds and influenza. After a few days, the green fields and whitewashed cottages of Portugal were seen on the port side. It looked appealing, but no one imagined holidays to Portugal by air would become commonplace within a few years. Later, when we saw the Rock of Gibraltar through the dawn mist, we felt that it was not much to look at but still something to write home about. The ship ploughed on into the Mediterranean and there was no doubt about it, even in November, the temperature was rising.

Excitement was mounting because we were stopping off in North Africa at the port of Tangiers. It took an age to get to the dockside and, as in Liverpool, everyone wanted to look out from the dockside of the vessel. The Tannoy and daily orders had repeatedly made it clear that everyone would be staying on board. Too late we discovered that anyone who was cute enough to ignore the Tannoy and change into dress uniform and present him or herself at the top of the gangway would be allowed ashore. With hindsight I believe that somewhere in King's Regulations there must have been a rule that troops had to be allowed to stretch their legs while on voyage if at all possible. Clearly they did not dare let us know this or the boat would have been delayed several days while the braver spirits were rounded up from the Casbah.

A BYRNE

The carrier HMS Triumph en route to Suez in December 1951, carrying troops of the Inniskilling Fusiliers, the Highland Light Infantry and a contingent of Military Police.

A BYRNE

Sleeping quarters on the Triumph made fifty to a billet seem like the Hilton Hotel.

The vengeful squaddies ranted and raved and swore and cursed but to no avail

Since there was nothing else to do everyone lined the rails with the hope of sighting women. We saw none but we did see the smartest man any of us had ever seen wearing a uniform. He was an officer of the French Foreign Legion striding out in boots that shone like glass, wearing a full cape that floated in his wake, and a dark blue kepi with the neck shade down. He looked as fit as the proverbial butcher's dog and in comparison we were a rather scruffy and flabby lot. We kept on looking at nothing in particular but entertainment was on its way.

The vendor of oranges slowly made his way along the quayside. He had to move slowly because his rickety barrow was laden with a pyramid of oranges. You had the impression that if one from the bottom row was dislodged the barrow would empty as the rest flooded in all directions. As he came nearer we could hear his cry.

"Oranges! Finest juicy sweet oranges. Lovely oranges Very refreshing" He stopped opposite where my group were lounging and rewarded our interest with the widest grin imaginable. He was in Arab dress but instead of having the swarthy skin of the North African he was black-skinned. From his position he could read the shoulder flashes of some of the regiments represented in the crowd. Taffies were greeted in broadest

Welsh, and had it been dark he could easily pass for someone from the valleys. His Geordie for the Coldstreamers was flawless and he asked if any Newcastle Brown was available and offered a swap for oranges. He could have made a living in Britain working for the BBC since he was not only fluent in all European languages but a master of regional accents as well. Entertaining as he was, no one fancied his oranges. He coaxed and pleaded, laughed and joked, but still no takers. Now I have always been a sucker for a good sales pitch and even today I buy things just because the salesman has a good line in patter. I decided to buy if I could do a deal, and he was becoming desperate.

"Two bob a dozen! Come on, who'll be first to get a bargain?" I couldn't resist.

"Here you are mate, but I've only got a half crown."

His voice mocked my pianos-and-kippers Edinburgh accent. "Your change will be right up, sir. By the way, when did you last walk down Princes Street?" His crack got a laugh from the lads.

My half crown was prudently wrapped in paper in the way my mother used to wrap up her donation to the Salvation Army when she threw it from our tenement window. In return for a donation, the band would meet a request for a favourite hymn or psalm, and although my mother donated regularly she never got him with the big drum.

I was going to get sustenance instead of soul food. "Here's your change, sir." Some coins were jammed into an orange and thrown up to me some thirty feet above. I caught it and examined the content. An aluminium coin about the size of a half crown but weighing only the same as a tanner was the biggest one. There were also two smaller, no doubt worthless items that I did not recognised.

"Have you got your change, sir?" he queried solicitously. "Now for your oranges." He threw up two in quick succession. One landed in the sea; a soldier caught the second and promptly disappeared into the crowd on

En route to the sheltered waters of Port Said, an experience shared by many thousands of troops.

H STANLEY

deck. "Never mind Jock, sir," he reassured. "You'll get your dozen oranges as ordered." True to his word he kept throwing them until I had a dozen succulent oranges stashed in my battledress blouse. Some had joined the first one and splashed into the sea. Others were stolen but I got my quota and I thanked him warmly.

"Right, who's next?" he cried. Coins showered down. He produced a piece of paper and a pencil and made elaborate notes.

"Right, Jock, twelve for you?"

"Only six for you, Paddy?"

"A dozen for you, Taffy?"

All orders were acknowledged in an appropriate dialect. It went on and on and the pennies kept coming from heaven.

"I've another barrow load round the corner so there's plenty for everyone. You'll all get served. Just ask Jock. Never fear..."

He was a superb salesman. Having collected every last penny from the cobbles he slowly eased up the shafts of his barrow and

wheeled it away. The defrauded squaddies went mad. They pleaded to be allowed down the gangplank to run after him but the redcaps caps were impassive and they had their orders and any that were going ashore had long gone. The vengeful squaddies ranted and raved and swore and cursed but to no avail. I was even accused of being in cahoots with him as part of the scam. I later worked out that he must have earned at least a pound an orange. Like the lady of easy virtue he sold it but still had it to sell.

We sailed that night. Porpoises accompanied us and flying fish crash-landed on deck, while at night the phosphorous on the wave crests glinted in the moonlight. We settled down into a routine, and now that everybody had his or her sea legs the cruise became enjoyable. Lifting ourselves up to our hammocks by arm movement alone and easing down into them became simplicity itself, and I found it so comfortable that I wished that I might always sleep in one. Had it been possible, I would

Our first glimpse of Egypt... The entrance to Port Said. February 1951.

gladly have signed on for the Navy and done my best to acclimatise myself to the rum ration.

One day followed another with nothing worth noting apart from a persistent rumour that one of the wives, going out to join her husband, had set up a business venture that depended upon a plentiful supply of eager males. Where better to set up such an enterprise than a troopship? However, despite diligent enquiries she was never identified. Everyone had heard of at least one person who had been accommodated, but it was always a bloke who knew a bloke who told his mate that...

About a week out of Tangiers it was noticed that the sea was no longer blue or even grey but had turned a dirty brown. Twelve hours later, still out of the sight of land, a peculiar smell assailed our nostrils. It was the stench of Egypt and would stay with me for more than two years. When we left Liverpool it was raining, and when we arrived in Port Said it was raining, but the rain was warmer.

When I was a child, my mother fell for the blandishments of a door-to-door hawker and bought a set of the Arthur Mee's Children's Encyclopaedia. It turned out to be a source of wonder and information throughout my childhood. If Sue Lawley ever invites me to take a luxury to a desert island it will be that set of books. I had read all about the building of the Suez Canal had studied the many pictures of its progress to completion. When we glided into harbour at Port Said, Arthur Mee's old photographs came to life. The fez and the djellabah, the bumboats, the statues and waterways – and it seemed as though nothing had changed in a hundred years.

It was well past noon by the time we disembarked and boarded buses for the journey to our various camps. In the time-honoured way of the military, no one told us where we were going, and the names would have meant nothing to us anyway. After a time the bus would stop and names from a clipboard were called out, buddies were separated forever, and the bus would move on. At last we arrived at RAF Deversoir, and my name was among those read out.

A TIN MAN IN HOT WATER

The invitation to play the role of Tin Man was quite appealing. But it wasn't a festive panto that the station warrant officer had in mind

Aerodynamically speaking, the Royal Air Force cheesecutter cap is badly designed. In a stiff breeze it will roll along quite happily, but even when it gains a respectable speed its take-off potential is poor. Once off the ground it has a tendency to dip and dive, jinking about in no particular direction, until it crash-lands. When it does fall to earth, if the wind is strong enough it rolls off again quite cheerfully. This condition of geniality was evidently not shared by the stout figure chasing it down the road. He had difficulty in bending down at all, never mind far enough or quickly enough to snatch up his cap in the few moments that it lay still. He would get close in the calm between gusts, but each time a fresh blast of wind would send it on its merry way again.

Newly arrived at Deversoir and on our way to our billets, we enjoyed a grandstand view from our vantage point on the back of the 3-ton truck. Enjoying the anonymity of a crowd, we felt it our duty to shout advice to the perspiring, red-faced, slightly balding figure in blue. My particular advice, had he heeded it, would have brought instant success.

"Move yourself, you dozy person. Get in front of it and try a flying tackle."

And, just in case he did not already know it: "You're out of condition. Move yourself!"

These remarks were a direct crib from my squarebashing days at West Kirby, but before I could see whether or not he had acted on it the lorry had taken us out of view so we never did see the end of the chase. It was a minor incident that was going to have far reaching effects.

We were only a few of the 50,000 reinforcements pouring into the Canal Zone in November 1951, and accommodation was scarce. My Nissen hut, No. E4, was one that had been hurriedly converted from a RAFA bar. The wooden bar was still in situ but the beer pumps had gone, and our beds were not regulation issue but the kind used by campers. They were fragile self-assembly devices made of canvas and what looked like wire coat hangers, but made up into a surprisingly comfortable bed. Once in the bed, though, complete stillness was essential as the slightest movement caused it to topple onto its side. As the beds were only inches off the ground this was not dangerous but they were crammed so close together that falling out caused a domino effect, and half the billet's 'erks ended up on the floor.

On being allocated a hut you cleared a space, made your bed, and then made the best of it by lying on it. Your kit was dumped on it at other times. I was immediately detailed for guard duty so I hoped my bed and other equipment would still be there in the morning, since I was leaving it with a crowd of strangers. There was quite a rigmarole to be observed on signing-in at a new station and it could be a fairly leisurely and lengthy business. To draw bedding and be put on the ration strength were obvious priorities but signing-in at the medical and dental centres much less

R BENJI

The main gate at RAF Deversoir. It was always busy, so stags passed quickly.

urgent. As a skive, and with careful planning, it could be made to last for days or even weeks.

One such signing-in point was to the SWO, the Station Warrant Officer. The Wing Co was a poor deluded soul who thought he ran the station but the seat of power was the SWO. At Deversoir, he was reputed to be an amiable individual, who had never been known to hurt a fly. He was also a man with an uncanny gift for remembering voices and I had barely opened my mouth to the clerk in the outer office when the SWO himself accosted me.

"You, laddie," he ordered. "Into my office!" The discussion that ensued, was a bit one-sided. It started quietly enough.

"A dozy person, am I?" It was not really a question, more an aide memoir for me. My reply was reasoned. It mostly consisted of short, sharp protests.

"But sir! Me, sir?" And even a forlorn attempt at: "But if only..." and "but how was I to know?"

It was all to no avail. His voice got louder the angrier he became, and his face got redder until I felt that a seizure might save the day. He really was completely out of condition but I felt it likely to prove unhelpful to mention it again, and in time he calmed down. It would have proved embarrassing to charge me since my observations on his size and condition, which would come out in evidence, were patently true.

You don't become a SWO without learning a few tricks, and he suggested that I was an ideal candidate to volunteer to become a member of the guard of honour for the station. He no doubt thought that this would be a subtle way of punishing me, but I loved it. Marching about and showing off had always been big with me and I found it easy thanks to my years in the Air Training Corps. He also insisted, after consultation with his corporal, that I was a suitable candidate for a special and secret duty at Christmas, then only a few weeks away. They could not explain the duty as it was very hush-hush and I had to tell no one. I was so intrigued that I signed my name and as I left his office I heard the tail end of a whispered conversation between them, but the words 'suitable outfit' and 'tin man' were all I could decipher. It was very mysterious but they had unwittingly given me a clue.

This would be my second Christmas in blue. My first fell during squarebashing at West Kirby when we were all allowed home on a short leave. We returned to camp to hear talk of a strange ritual that had taken place during our absence when officers and sergeants had served the men, not only early morning tea, but breakfast and dinner as well. A skeleton staff of cooks had naturally been on duty but the whole thing sounded like a jolly affair, especially as free beer and other goodies were handed out. We were later told that it was a tradition throughout the British Services going back hundreds of years.

When you are not given facts, conjecture comes into play. In my case the mention of 'tin man' made it rather obvious that some sort of jollity was being organised to entertain the boys on Christmas Day. Clearly a parody of the Wizard of Oz was being planned and a yellow brick road would be laid out round the tables in the dining hall. Dressed in a rusty suit of armour, the cowardly lion and straw man by my side, we would prance along it behind our very own Dorothy. Dorothy would be a senior officer or even the SWO himself done up in a gymslip, pigtails and red shoes and it would be a brilliant wheeze that would

Christmas celebrations in the 1952 RAF Deversoir Signals Section. The poor dears were excused guard duty as they sometimes had to man the telephones at night.

bring the house down. Later we would enjoy refreshments and a visit to the sergeants' mess at the very least. If they wanted a re-run for the married patch crowd, a visit to the officers' mess was not out of the question. This was a secret I had no difficulty in keeping from my billet mates, since to tell would spoil their fun.

My costume was not a good fit, as the Wellington boots were two sizes too large and the rubberised apron several sizes too small. They afforded little protection against the spray of hot soapy water as yet another scorched and food-encrusted tray crash landed in the cauldron of boiling water before me. I had unwittingly but, fair dues to the SWO, quite willingly volunteered to work in the tin room of the kitchens at Christmas so that the usual sufferer could enjoy his dinner in comfort. My Christmas dinner consisted of the odd snatched mouthful of roast potato and a tin of pears purloined from the larder when backs were turned. I think the SWO regarded that honours were even between us, since he never picked on me again.

While I was up to my elbows in soapsuds and everyone else was enjoying the festivities, a group of Egyptian terrorists murdered a nineteen-year-old Royal Artillery gunner. This piece of news was kept from us, as usual.

CHRISTMAS DAY MENU – 1953
RAF FAYID

BREAKFAST
Grapefruit, Tomato Juice, Cereals, Porridge
Grilled Ham, Fried Egg, Fried Tomato, Fried Bread
Tea, Coffee, Bread Rolls, Marmalade, Butter

DINNER
Cream of Tomato Soup
Roast Turkey, Cranberry Sauce, Roast Pork, Apple Sauce, Meat Stuffing
Roast and Creamed Potatoes, Cauliflower, Garden Peas, Rich Brown Gravy
Mince Pies, Cheese and Biscuits
Apples, Oranges, Mixed Nuts
Cigarettes, Bottles Beer, Minerals

BUFFET SUPPER
Cold Boiled Ham, Cold Roast Sirloin of Beef
Sliced Tomatoes, Potato Salad, Vegetable Salad
Scotch Trifle, Fruit Salad, Fruit Jelly, Assorted Gateaux
Christmas Cake, Chocolate Biscuits
Tea, Coffee, Bread, Butter, Jam

A typical Christmas Day menu... this one from RAF Fayid, 1953.

BANG! WHO WENT THERE?

*Who owned those eyes glinting in the darkness... just
some prowling animal, or a terrorist bent on murder?*

I had been in Egypt less than twenty-four
hours when I found myself detailed for
guard duty. We assembled at the guardroom for inspection followed by a reading
of the Rules of Engagement. Before opening
fire on the enemy (anyone prowling about
inside the perimeter fence could be more or
less guaranteed to be the enemy) a fairly
lengthy rigmarole would have to be observed.

"Halt! Who goes there?" was to be shouted
in a loud voice. The British Empire having
been what it was, it was assumed that the
world would be familiar with the words. If
this initial sally failed to engender a response,
the ante was raised.

"Halt or I'll fire!" delivered in an even
more strident voice. If the intruder was deaf,
or a non-English speaker, you would then be
required to repeat your order, but in a
stentorian scream. Unless you had detected
the potential intruder at some distance, he
would by now have passed you by, and you
would be following him into the camp. The
reality was somewhat different. The shouted
warnings, and the firing of your weapon,
were sometimes transposed to: Bang! "Who
went there?"

On arriving at your designated guardpost,
which could be anything from a perch on top
of a shaky tower, a thirty-foot high roof, or a
patrol on foot, you invariably put a round up
the spout of your trusty Lee Enfield .303, and
fixed your pencil bayonet. No military person
would be foolhardy enough to sneak up on
you. On the contrary, even your relief, whose

arrival was anticipated, would approach
whistling or singing loudly. The char and
wads, or the duty officer, would arrive by a
noisy three-ton truck or Land Rover. It was
therefore a safe bet, that if you came across
anyone unannounced during your lonely
vigil, he was going to be an enemy, and if you
didn't shoot him instantly he would shoot
you. Immediately after discharging your rifle
you would repeat the mantra: "Halt, or I'll do
something nasty."

On my first guard duty, after the lorry had
dropped me off and the rest of the detail had
cheerily waved me good-bye as they departed
for more favoured posts, I was left in complete
darkness in the middle of nowhere. When my
eyes became adjusted to the gloom I
discovered a structure about ten feet tall and
clambered on board. The platform was about
eight feet square, without a guardrail, and on
it I discovered a heavy-duty motor vehicle
battery and a lorry headlamp concealed in a
short cardboard tube. One crocodile clip was
connected to a battery and the other was lying
on the floor. Knowledge gleaned during
service with the Electricity Board served me
well and when the second clip was attached to
the power source I had light. Holding the light
at chest height I discovered that its beam
failed to reach the perimeter fence that I was
charged with guarding, so the action seemed a
bit futile.

In addition to my armaments I carried a
Very pistol with six cartridges – two white,
two red and two green, which meant that

selecting the correct shade in an emergency was likely to be tricky. While burdened with the mini-searchlight, which needed two hands to hold, I was virtually holding up a juicy target for a sniper. Even if he missed the light he could possibly hit me. I tried holding it to the left and the right but even if he was a rotten shot I was still at risk and my arms quickly tired. The best position was on the floor where I could hold it in place with my boot and still hold my rifle at the ready.

Suddenly I caught sight of a pair of eyes, reflected by the light beam, staring at me unblinkingly from the darkness. I zeroed in on him but as I did so I spotted, out of the corner of my eye, a second pair of eyes concentrating on me. Whipping round suddenly to check behind me I couldn't miss two pairs of eyes side by side about thirty yards away. I was surrounded. My bowels have always been fairly regular but suddenly messages were being sent from there to my brain suggesting urgent action. I had a round up the spout, so that was all right, but had to try to remember the correct sequence in which the various coloured shells of the Very pistol were to be fired. Was it red or white for a first alert signal?

In trying to extricate the pistol from the carrying bag I moved my foot and thus the searchlight. A pair of eyes darted sideways

This birdseye view of RAF Deversoir shows how difficult it was to guard. In the dark, you were as likely to bump into an Egyptian trying to rob it as a mate trying to guard it.
In daylight, it was not unknown for airmen working on the satellite dispersals to be shot at from the other side of the wire.

R BENJI

along the ground. Such a movement was beyond the capability of man. It was a pi-dog, and I deduced that all the eyes belonged to pi-dogs, the ubiquitous scavengers of Egypt and the Middle East. I was instantly braver than I had been moments before. When my relief arrived, singing loudly and out of tune, I mentioned my fright.

"You must be new," he divined. "We always shoot first and ask questions later."

This policy had little effect on those intrepid Egyptians who looked on an airfield as a place of plenty, provided by Allah to meet their needs. They managed to steal things that were securely nailed down and were of no obvious value or use to them. On one occasion I arrived at the top of a thirty-foot high revetment (part of a protective three sides of a square erected to protect aircraft from bomb blast), to discover that the searchlight which should have been there – an essential part of my defensive equipment – was missing.

Two hours later I asked my relief if he had heard an explanation as to why we were on stag in the dark. Naturally he knew nothing. That whole long night the guards sat thirty feet up in the air seeing nothing at all. Back at the satellite guardroom telephone enquiries were made. No, the searchlight was not being serviced; it had just disappeared over the fence. Naturally, the RAF was much too busy to mount guards during daylight hours and as this site was in a far corner of the airfield the theft must have been fairly straightforward. What the thieves used it for is a mystery.

By one of the strange coincidences destined to put the wind up new arrivals, I was woken during my first session of heads down by the duty corporal. He asked, very politely, if I would be prepared to volunteer to respond to an urgent cry from help from the bomb dump guard. Ensuring that others would be going as well, and that I was not being mistaken for hero material, I agreed.

"I see no ships, not even ships of the desert." Me, on the look-out at the water filtration plant. The tower later fell down, injuring the guard on duty.

The searchlight, operated from the roof of the nearby furniture repository, had picked out the thieves who were right inside the bomb dump among the packing cases. The sentry could not fire at them for fear of setting off some of the ordinance. As November the fifth had been and gone such an act would not have been appreciated. By the time we arrived they had managed to get outside the wire of the bomb dump but were thought still to be in the grounds between it and the perimeter fence. This particular piece of wasteland was covered in elephant grass fully ten-feet tall and we fearfully plunged in with bayonets fixed and one up

J THOMPSON

The control tower at RAF Deversoir, one of the station's best guardposts. 1953.

the spout. The guard commander told us to take no chances since the terrorists were likely to fire first if in danger of being discovered. "Halt or I fire!" was officially suspended. This drastic step meant that whoever found any of them was definitely at risk. Only twenty-four hours before, I had been safe and sound on the good ship Empress of Canada and here I was risking

my neck. We tried to keep in a line, judging by sound how near our comrades were. We poked at the long grass with our bayonets ahead of every step but the enemy was long gone. Back in the satellite guardroom, rolled in a blanket and drifting off to sleep, I thought to myself: good heavens, this is real soldiering, and I thought I had joined the RAF for a quiet life. On one celebrated occasion an intruder was captured inside the perimeter wire and handed over to the snowdrops who did not know what to do with him, so they put him in a cell and fed him chocolate and other goodies. At last the Egyptian police arrived to interrogate the prisoner and from the reports we received they beat him almost to death in our cell. When the Egyptian plod carried him out to their ramshackle van to spirit him away everyone was sorry that they had been sent for and vowed we'd never to do so again. Naturally the wog police – as we referred to them in those days – would report to their superiors that he was in that condition when handed over to their custody and we lost another round in the propaganda war.

The perimeter fence at Deversoir was fully seven miles long and therefore well nigh impossible to secure. An armoured car drove along it late each afternoon to check for any obvious holes or missing sections and we guarded strategic points. The furniture repository was next to the bomb dump so a nest of sandbags was built on the roof. Its searchlight could constantly sweep along the boxes of bombs and if one went off it would provide some protection from the blast. The water filtration plant was an essential element of survival, so a tower had been erected there. The armoury naturally needed a guard, as did the generating station. Each group of Nissen huts and the tented lines required supervision, as did the Beach Club, married quarters, control tower and various other places considered vulnerable to attack. Little wonder we did so much guard duty.

Some posts were considered better than others. The Beach Club, cut off from the camp and where three of you were dropped off together, was much desired. You had company, of a sort, sleeping away on comfortable chairs. The Great Bitter Lake ebbed and flowed, noisily for a tideless inland waterway, and if an attack came from seawards the enemy would have the

advantage. A dark night would be required for such an enterprise and Egypt is justifiably famous for the darkness of its nights. On the other hand, on a balmy night when there was a decent moon it was idyllic. On a rough night in winter it could be creepy and the guard was often in an extremely nervous state. One night someone within the camp fired a shot at something that in all probability was the product of a fevered mind. The bullet whistled over the head of the Beach Club guard. He could see nothing but decided to fire back. His bullet startled the guard on the water filtration plant tower so he fired at nothing as well. The battle raged fiercely but was of fairly short duration as the ammunition issue was only ten rounds a man. No one was hurt and everyone was commended for being so alert.

One of the best posts without question was the air traffic control tower where brewing facilities were available throughout the night. The guard sat at ease, protected from the chill wind by acres of glass, surveying the swinging searchlights. If any of them stopped moving he would have to get off his bottom and telephone for help. On some patrols there was no searchlight and a Very pistol was carried in lieu, so the lucky control tower guard was required to keep a sharp look out for flares. If a light stopped moving it was a sign that one of three things had happened. One, the guard had been shot and the post was under attack. Two, the guard had fallen asleep. The third and most likely option was that the light had been kept mobile by a length of string while the guard crouched beneath the protective sandbags and the string had broken. If a light beam stopped moving for any length of time either the entire guard would be turned out or a Land Rover containing one snowdrop sent to investigate.

On the main gate guard the time passed quickly since you had lots to do and tea was passed to you at regular intervals. The armoury was a lonely site and your duty was to patrol round the lighted veranda non-stop. As it was a normal rectangular building one always felt that on turning a corner a terrorist might be waiting in ambush. An armoury packed with light weapons was an obvious target. I recall once at the start of a stag having a flying beetle of considerable size strike me in the face as it shot out of the darkness into the attractive light. It was stunned and so was I, but my reflex action was to whack it to the ground where my highly polished size-nine crushed it flat. I carried on patrolling and by the time my two hours were up not a trace of the beetle was to be found. The ants in Egypt work round the clock.

The power generating station was, for me, a creepy place. A duty engineer used to sleep in a tent close by so you had company of a sort, but the noise of the generators was at a level that ruled out conversation. If he was on the prowl with his oilcan in his hand the first you knew about it was when a hand tapped you on the shoulder with the offer of a mug of char. A toilet roll would have been a more appropriate offering.

The tower at the water filtration plant had clearly been built in a rush and in due time it fell down, injuring the guard on duty quite seriously. Two sheets of corrugated iron, about two inches apart and filled with sand, formed a protective layer on two sides. If a sniper fired at you from the other two sides it would be jolly unsporting. The weight of the sand made the thing sway alarmingly as you climbed aboard but once up there the view was fine until darkness fell. You had no torch but there was a fixed light over the shed containing the filters. The bulb, although bright enough, was awkwardly sited and ruled out reading on duty.

An Arab house was nearby and ground nuts or melons could be bought in season at ridiculously low prices. Rumour had it that in the village about half a mile away an ATS deserter had set up house with a desert prince. I made numerous enquiries in my limited Arabic and it was confirmed that a fair-skinned bint lived in the locality and I was even invited to pay a visit to see for myself. I lacked that kind of courage. Rumour also had it that a young Arab girl who sometimes walked past the post on the other side of the wire was a bit of an exhibitionist. Ten ackers would be rewarded with a flash of young beaver as she lifted her djellabah. I never met anyone who would admit to having had this exciting experience but I feel sure that she got her share of coins and the donors, separated by a ten-foot barbed wire fence, their share of frustration.

Perhaps the best guard duty of all was on the sleeping quarters. You wandered about between the Nissen huts and tented lines, armed with a rifle and a torch, keeping an eye open for intruders. Despite the vigilance of the guard our hut radio suddenly stopped playing one night. By the time the shouting had died down we realised that someone had opened the billet door, snipped through the power cable, and made off with our much-prized radio set. We found the guard and his torch and followed the footprints directly to the perimeter fence. Footprints and wheel tracks in the sand showed that the same thieves had acquired a motorcycle. How they lifted a motorbike over a ten-foot high barbed wire fence was a puzzle, but everyone knew that a determined Arab thief could steal anything. We were told that a favourite trick was to oil their naked bodies so that grabbing them was nearly impossible. Alternatively they would roll in the sand, making them hard to spot, but this could be an old sweat's tale.

Once when I was shuffling to the toilet block in the middle of the night I was alerted by   a little dog barking at something in the darkness. The billet guard was soon on the scene and we discovered that the dog was trying to attack a snake. It was not big, as snakes go, but it had reared up and was swaying back and forth. Its head, some eighteen inches off the ground, seemed surprisingly high for a body that looked to be only half an inch in diameter. I instructed the guard to kill it and he looked at me as if I had taken leave of my senses.

"Kill it yourself if you fancy your chances," he retorted, handing me his rifle with bayonet attached. I toyed with the idea of shooting it but if I missed or the bullet ricocheted I could be very unpopular. Now that reinforcements had arrived, the terrier took a back seat and became an interested observer. The snake turned its beady eyes on me and there was hatred in them. All the books that I have read insist that if you ignore a snake it will take the hint and slide off about its business. This one was obviously not a great reader.

It was High Noon: the snake or a terrified airman, poison-laden fangs against cold steel. It could, of course, have been a harmless grass snake but I was no expert and was taking no chances. A sudden lunge with the bayonet and I don't know who was more surprised. The point of the bayonet had pierced its body dead centre about four inches below its head, and it demonstrated its dislike for me. Its head could not get far up the bayonet but the rest of its body did its best as it coiled round the barrel of the rifle. It was clearly still very much alive but I had the upper hand and I folded it over and over stabbing each time until its whole body was skewered like meat for a barbecue. Still it fought on.

Its eyes seemed to blaze with hatred and it kept trying to get up the rifle at me spitting and snapping. I hate cruelty in any form and it was clear that I was being cruel to this poor snake. The truth is that I was driven by fear and fear alone and the kindest thing I could do was to crush its head flat quickly, and this I did. As I pushed his body off the bayonet, prudently using a long piece of wood, it seemed to come to life again and wriggled about for quite some time. Returning the rifle to the guard, who was looking at me with

High Noon... beady-eyed snake against terror-stricken airman, its poison-laden fangs against my bayonet's cold steel

what I took to be admiration, I made for the toilet and then went back to bed.

In the morning no one in the billet believed me when I related my adventure. My proof lay outside in the sand, or at least it had done but the ants had been busy. All that was left was what looked like a smear of grease in a shape that could have been that of a snake. It was measured and found to be 2ft 5in long. The type was never identified.

The fates conspired against me when, for some incomprehensible reason, I was appointed duty storeman in charge of the satellite stores for a night. These stores were an isolated group of buildings situated in the centre of the airfield and miles from human contact. Even on a good night it was a cheerless and desolate place, so I was very cheesed off with the appointment. Every other night we had guard duty to suffer and this was one of the precious nights off. I would have a night on guard immediately followed by a night as duty store man, and then another night on guard. Three nights of broken sleep was not fair in my opinion, but naturally it is the squadron leader's opinion that counts.

Within the cluster of Nissen huts there was supposed to be a small cache of everything that was stocked in the main stores. In the unlikely event of fire damage to the main stores or a bomb being dropped on them we could carry on functioning by using the goods in the satellite stores. I know for a fact that there were even half-hundred weight bags of horseshoe nails on the shelves so we were ready for anything.

In an emergency, which occurred out of normal business hours, the duty storeman could issue any bits and pieces that might be required because the RAF never sleeps as far as the supply of equipment is concerned. The snag in this well thought out scheme was that my speciality was accounting procedures and I could not differentiate between a C and a B flange sprocket to save my life. If I had to open up the stores I did not know where the light switch was, never mind where things were located. The technical term for putting someone with my level of knowledge and skill in such a position of responsibility is known in the trade as a 'cock-up'.

My duty period was from 18.00 hours to 06.00 hours, which for any reader who has forgotten, is 6pm to 6am the following morning. No NAAFI for me, and not being on the approved list of guard posts, no char and wads in the middle of the night either. My place of duty was a tatty, weather-beaten tent outside this highly important outpost. The tent contained a tiny camp bed with a telephone on an extension cable, a bunch of keys that I was to guard with my life, and a dim torch. I toyed with the idea of opening up the stores to see if I could find a fresh torch battery but thought better of it.

The Ivy Benson all-girl band, who brought enjoyment to everyone and more than that for some. 1953.

Defending the keys with my life would be all that I could do because no rifle had been issued to me. It was going to be a very lonely vigil. Near the tent was a fire alarm device consisting of a metal triangle suspended from the arm of a pole and a length of steel rod – metal triangle for the striking of – to summon assistance.

Darkness fell minutes after I arrived on site. This was going to be a very long night made longer by the fact that I was missing a special event – the much appreciated treat of

D CARTER

a visit to the beleaguered troops by the Ivy Benson All Girl Orchestra. We had not set eyes on a woman for months and I was missing the sight of at least a dozen scantily clad delights.

I had been fortunate enough to see Frankie Howerd when he paid us a visit and he went down a storm with only the support of "her" at the piano. The roof would come down when actual girls were on display. Guard duty made me miss out on a visit by Miss Joyce Grenfell but I knew that in the future I would be able to catch up on her show. I could not make the same promise to myself in respect of Ivy Benson's remarkable musical feast because immediately following her tour she was obliged to reform the orchestra as a trio or a duo. The former members of her famous all-girl orchestra were busy signing on at various ante-natal clinics up and down the UK. Their visit was obviously enjoyed even more by a fortunate few than by the majority of the troops.

Since it was dark I had no option but to go

to bed and try to sleep as the torch would not last long if I tried to read. I was lying there trying to rid my mind of the injustice of it all and settling down to endure my lonely watch in the utter blackness of the night, when a police Land Rover roared past and someone took the liberty of throwing a piece of four by two timber at my tent. I thought little of it at the time, as the poor old snowdrops have a weird sense of humour due to being mother-less and fatherless and universally unloved. I kept the piece of wood intending to call at the guardroom in the morning claiming to have been injured by the unknown, but easily traceable, assailant. With a bit of lead swinging and some sincere acting it could be worth a couple of days off. In the cool of dawn's early light a closer look at my trophy brought the realisation that the day could herald misfortune. It bore the legend "INCENDIARY" scrawled in white chalk.

A golden rule in the RAF is always to read daily orders, which are to be found posted at several convenient locations throughout every station. There is therefore no excuse whatsoever for any airman to be unfamiliar with the latest news concerning the camp. You could find yourself promoted, drafted, or being sent off on a course of instruction to improve your prospects. Glory be, it could even announce your release date. In Egypt, where daily newspapers were non-existent, orders should have been read avidly. They were a source of authorised information but since nothing exciting ever seemed to happen they were largely ignored. Failure to read daily orders could lead to jankers and on this occasion it did so for me.

"Did you read daily orders yesterday?" our elderly warrant officer inquired within minutes of my arrival at the accounts office. He was forty years old if he was a day and his only desire was for a quiet life.

"Certainly did, sir. I read them every day," I lied.

My dear friend the Wing Commander tried the case for reasons best known to himself, so I was going up in the world. To give him his due he heard me out, and having had a couple of days to mull things over, my story was watertight and would lead to the instant dismissal of all charges.

"It was like this, sir. When the incendiary landed on my tent it set it on fire, sir, and I only just got out myself." I had taken the opportunity to belatedly read the said orders. "I rang the alarm bell for a good ten minutes but no one must have heard it because no one came to my assistance." The Wingco must have been a Sherlock Holmes fan. "Why did you not use the telephone to raise the alarm?" he queried in a gentle voice. An encouraging, or so it appeared to me, smile on his lips.

"The tent was on fire, sir. It destroyed the telephone. I did all I could to raise the alarm. The daily orders were quite specific, we were to treat the exercise as the real thing."

"Ingenious" was the word he used to describe my defence in his summing up of the case. Sleeping in a burned out tent on a burned out cot seemed to weigh heavily against me. His tariff was the usual of fourteen days jankers, which entailed reporting to the guardroom every hour on the hour from 13.00 hours to 22.00 hours and at 06.00 hours. Worst of all, horror of horrors, banned from the NAAFI for the whole fortnight.

Almost everyone who served in the Canal Zone did guard duty at some time or another. Common to all was the fright experienced at the first sight in the darkness of the reflected light from eyes. Were they human or those of the night prowling pi-dogs? The sudden change from daylight to total darkness in the space of a few minutes. The surprising cold at night. The fear of the unexpected. The loneliness. The joy of a char and wad in the middle of the night. The deep instant sleeps on a concrete floor while others bustled about trying not to make too much noise.

The bed bugs. The trauma. The welcome first streaks of dawn. The smells, the sights and the sounds of the changing season. The timelessness of Egypt.

Privy but no privacy

*Even life down on the farm had not prepared
me for the privations of the Egyptian loos or the
creepy crawlies we had to share our beds with*

I have never understood lavatorial humour. I was nearly seven on the day the Second World War broke out, and within the hour, I was evacuated from the modernity of a city flat to the Nineteenth Century living conditions of a farm in Lanarkshire, in rural Scotland. It was more of a smallholding than a proper farm but it had a byre, a hayloft, and other sundry outbuildings. The smallest of all was a tiny wooden shed about thirty yards from the back door of the farmhouse. The vegetation was lush and each yard of the journey was a leg wetting one for a seven-year-old, but it was fitted with a highly efficient ventilation system that kept offensive odours at bay. This device was cheap to run, being wind-powered, and cold air breezed through the gaps between each plank used in the construction. Toilet rolls were replaced by tiny squares of newspaper suspended from a nail at a convenient height.

As you would expect in such rural surroundings there was no mains lighting, so the farmhouse depended for lighting on oil lamps. There was no running water either so night-time emergencies depended on the use of china chamber pots from the Victorian era. The use of these delightfully decorated items necessitated a rather unpleasant ritual each morning that has since been banned in Her Majesty's prisons.

Drinking water was drawn from a well fifty yards down the lane and kept in buckets until required. Water for the animals came from butts which collected the abundant rain that fell with such monotonous regularity, and to heat water for washing purposes a kettle permanently dangled from a hook over an open coal fire. School, a two-mile walk from the farm, was a bit backwards in an academic sense and when I arrived I was a year ahead of my age group. Three years later when I returned to city life I was a year behind my peers and I never managed to catch up. However, each day at school afforded a real treat since the building had proper flush lavatories.

You might think that living under these conditions would have prepared me for the rigours and deprivation of life in the Canal Zone, but you would be wrong. Bad as life on the farm was, nothing could be worse than the toilet facilities we endured in Egypt.

Having said all that, we did our best to keep things as hygienic as possible with flies and bluebottles forming the number one enemy. However long an airman was resident in the place he was attacked from time to time by stomach bugs and forced to spend long periods stuck within the portals of our multi-seated ablution blocks. Others had it worse.

In many regimental depots, set up in empty desert areas, the loo was simply a hole dug in the sand. A telegraph pole laid across the gaping hole provided a precarious seating arrangement but gave no privacy to groups of users. Hessian sheets protected the crouching figures from public view but left a lot to be desired by way of design. Economy of scale was achieved by flushing only once a day. Flushing is perhaps the wrong word to use to describe a defaulter pouring diesel oil down a trench and setting fire to it. The RSPCFBCC* would not be pleased to be appraised of this method of dispensing with human excrement and inadvertently killing off the creepy crawlies.

At Deversoir the most important job on the camp, bar none, was carried out by a special flying squad of cheerful and uncomplaining souls. To a man they were dysfunctional in the olfactory department and received only sixpence a day extra for 'special' duties. I think that they deserved a gold watch. The sight of the honey wagon tearing through the camp, the irrepressible crew sitting on top of the bins

chatting and unconcernedly munching sandwiches, and the whole followed by a thick black cloud of assorted and presumably hungry insects is one that will stick in my mind always. Well done, lads!

When old soldiers meet and lamps are swung it is surprising how often the topic of 'bogs' crops up. The Royal Navy has its 'heads' in the bow of each ship. A visit to HMS Victory in Portsmouth Dockyard shows just how primitive the toilets were in the Nelson's day. In the modern Navy it seems that water flows constantly beneath the rows of seats in the heads. A regular source of fun is to wait until every stall is occupied and then send a lighted newspaper floating down the line like the fire ships of old, and the sequence of shouts and

Inside billet H3 at RAF Deversoir. I rarely saw a billet as tidy as this in Egypt, so it must have been ready for an AOC inspection.

H STANLEY

screams is compared critically with previous efforts. As always, new boys come off worst. Old hands who trained on HMS Ganges, the boy entrants' stone frigate, tell of the embarrassment of discovering that the partitions between toilets were only waist high.

At RAF Deversoir, an artist of wartime vintage had decorated the inside of certain stall doors with exceptionally good drawings of the famous Jane. It was not unknown for men to queue up to use that particular stall leaving undecorated ones unclaimed and empty. Some no doubt had a date with Mrs Hand and her five lovely daughters. The en suite facilities enjoyed today are this 'erk's idea of heaven on earth.

The reference to Mrs Hand brings up the vexed question of sleeping partners. Some might challenge the very idea that without exception everyone who served in the Canal Zone shared his bed with a partner or partners at some time or another. The subject under discussion is, of course, bed bugs. They emerged quite spontaneously at certain times of year – probably during their mating season, which was practically all the time. Some swore that if each leg of a bed rested in a can of diesel oil you would not be troubled. In my experience nothing could stop them and infestation was unavoidable however extreme the precautions. We were issued with biscuit-type mattresses and from time to time everyone in the billet would be engaged in the fight against the little horrors. Leaving your mattress out in the mid-day sun was supposed to help, but I think that the little beggars enjoyed it.

The sovereign remedy was to pass the flame from a cigarette lighter along the stitched edges of your mattress. As you slowly eased it along, the satisfying sound of snap, crackle and pop could be heard as the bed bugs sizzled. The eggs seemed simply to melt in the heat but the proud parent came to the boil before bursting open and splashing OUR blood about.

Flies were everywhere and much more of an irritant than bed bugs. Sometimes we would hold a fly hunt in the billet and everyone would join in. The door would be wedged shut and the window screens inspected for holes, which were then sealed. Insect killing aerosol sprays were a thing of the future, and as none of us had a proper fly swatter, armed with rolled up newspapers we would attack. Swatting away, however long it took, until every fly was a corpse. We would then lie on our beds to recover, completely exhausted after such unaccustomed exercise. Instantly someone would discover that at least one fly had eluded our keen pursuit and we would jump up and continue our mission convinced that if one was left alive he could summon reinforcements through the ether. As we slumped for a second time on our charps, or as some would have it our pits, we would spend a blissful time pest free. Inevitably, sooner or later someone would burst open the door and enter, bringing with him the makings of another hunt. We eventually reduced the nuisance of flying insects to a minimum by acquiring a chameleon.

One pest that never troubled us was mice. This was strange because scraps of food were often left lying about and stored in lockers. Quite near to my bed head was a mouse hole in the wooden skirting board of the billet and I often used to wonder what had become of the former occupants. This was not brought about by a Mickey or Minnie Mouse fixation, prompted by the Walt Disney cartoon shown in the camp cinema, but just idle curiosity.

The one thing that we had plenty of in Egypt was time. My modest bookcase boasted a copy of Topham's Company Law and an educational treatise on how to write modern business letters. I bought it at a bookshop in Ismailia from a gorgeous Greek girl, who could have sold sand to Eskimos, so selling books to airmen was a breeze. It was only when I got back to camp that I discovered that it was a pre-typewriter Victorian publication that instructed that to end a letter 'Your obedient and very humble servant' was being a bit pushy. There was also a chapter on the care and maintenance of quills. In any event their presence prompted approving remarks when any commissioned officer carried out a kit inspection. They may have looked interesting but in truth they were rarely opened. Thinking about how to put the world to right would be more my scene as this could be done from a prone position. If during a lengthy thinking session I dozed off to sleep I could be anywhere at all. Often it would be home to my own bed where I could actually smell my mother's cooking, and then I would wake up to reality. Curiously enough this same phenomenon exists to this day. It happens less frequently now but it still occurs. I start awake, bathed in sweat, convinced that I am back in bed in the billet at Deversoir.

One day I spotted the rear end of a mouse framed in the mouse hole. Its tail must have been wrapped round its body because it was not sticking out as might have been expected. This would have made him easy to capture. Quietly I leaned over and gripped its rear between finger and thumb and started to pull. It came out all right but kept on coming. It was a snake! I stopped pulling and yelled for someone to witness my discovery. Women are said to make a fuss and jump on chairs when they see a mouse but they are like SAS troopers compared to airmen when there is a snake in the vicinity. In a flash my billet mates were standing on beds and lockers and, in one case, the windowsill. My recent encounter with a viper had found me christened the Snake Man of Deversoir. A bit like the Birdman of Alcatraz but without the knowledge and expertise. The idiots thought that, devoid of fear, I had pulled it out on purpose. No wonder we were mouse-free. To a snake a mouse is like steak and onions or a good vindaloo and strangely enough we never saw

H BROCKWAY

'Home sweet home' to many who served in Egypt. Such luxury and space mean that this must have been officers' quarters.

The perfect billet... Stella on tap. By the time that I moved in it was a pub with no beer.

the snake again. Perhaps it disliked having its tail pulled in public.

Although the Arabs were said to hate our guts there was one group of airmen who claimed that they could not only move freely among them unharmed but were invited into their homes and feted. They were offered tea, melon and groundnuts in season and the warmth of their reception seemed quite genuine. They were a self-contained unit with a fairly grand title. Among the crew was a leading aircraftsman with a decent BSc degree from a redbrick university. The task of this unit was to rid the area of mosquitoes to the benefit of all. We, as a precaution against attack, were obliged to wear long trousers and our tunic sleeves rolled down as evening approached. This team was a law unto themselves and went into the breeding grounds of the beasts wearing shorts and stripped bare to the waist. Wherever they

found stagnant water they covered it and the surrounding area with kerosene.

I wangled an educational trip out with this team and it led to my being able to visit an Arab's house. It was actually a mud hut and even the internal furniture was mostly constructed of clay. As our host chased the hens off a sort of recess in an inner wall, swept along it with a witch's broom and invited us to sit, his wife and daughter fluttered about apologising because the house was not tidy – just like women at home. We were offered tea and melon. I refused the tea but accepted the melon. My BSc acquaintance, to my surprise, accepted the tea. He explained later that he had seen the kettle come through the boil and that would have killed any germs. In his scientific opinion, my melon was much more likely to give me a good dose of the trots. You can't beat education.

In exchange for this lavish hospitality the

house and its environs were liberally doused with finest Vampire fuel. I hoped that no one would strike a match until we were well clear.

It was getting dark before we set off back to the camp and I was becoming anxious because we did not have a single rifle between us for defensive purposes. The team was completely unfazed.

"The tom-toms will have warned of our position and where we are heading, so we are quite safe," announced our intrepid leader. He had much more faith than I had, but we returned to base without incident.

It was kept quiet at the time, but had they known the fate of a major who was operating a similar mosquito-spraying unit on behalf of the United Nations, also unarmed, they would not have been so confident. He was captured and tortured. When his body was found he was buried up to his neck in sand with his testicles sewn into his mouth.

I had a long walk back to the billet and parts of the ground enclosed by our perimeter fence were quite barren. By now it was very dark and the wind was rising so that I could neither hear nor see anything at all. Without the slightest warning I was struck full in the face and body by something huge but soft that nearly knocked me over. It was the surprise rather than the force that unsettled me.

I had discovered yet another pest, tumblin' tumbleweed. My nerves were not in good order at all.

* Royal Society for the Prevention of Cruelty to Flies, Bugs and Creepy Crawlies (if there's not one in being there should be).

R BLAKE

Fanara Wharf on the Great Bitter Lake, 1952, showing the tent lines with the cookhouse and NAAFI buildings to the rear. Today it's a 'des res'.

OF FIDDLES AND CLARINETS

Beating the system was seen by many as a bounden duty. Fiddles played all around. One squaddie chose another instrument, and the world hummed along

Most airmen of my acquaintance were permanently broke during their Service careers. A National Serviceman told me that the week he was called up he borrowed a pound from a fellow recruit and he repaid it after the first pay parade. He borrowed and repaid it throughout his two years, and by the end of their time neither man could be sure who owed the pound to whom. This was not as unusual as it sounds.

At home as a seventeen-year-old I seemed to manage quite well on pocket money of ten shillings a week, and the remainder of my £3-something pay was handed over to my widowed mother. My starting pay in the RAF was forty-nine shillings, but after allowances to home and to the bank I was left with fourteen shillings as spends. My naivety was my downfall. What I had overlooked was that at home there was a bread bin, always full, and the makings of a sandwich close at hand. The biscuit barrel was never without a selection, and Mother acted like a benevolent banker who made loans but never called them in. Now toothpaste, boot polish and a dozen other requirements found in cupboards at home had to be bought. Blanco... what was that? You had to have some.

Realising within days that I had underrated my financial needs, I went to see the folks in administration. I discovered, to my dismay, that allotments being processed could not be altered until basic training had been completed, and that was fully twelve weeks

away. By the time basic training was over I had developed some expensive habits. I bought tea in the NAAFI! I wrote letters that needed stamps and envelopes and a writing pad. How National Servicemen on twenty-eight bob a week managed is beyond me. By the time I was trade-trained – a rehash of what I already knew – I was upgraded to leading aircraftsman. My pay leapt to seventy shillings a week, but I was living proof of the adage that expenditure invariably rises to meet any increase in income. I was still permanently broke.

Our aim was to find someone with money, someone who had a need that we could meet, and relieve him of his money in return for satisfying his desires. The word money is used to identify any negotiable commodity. I was saddened, but others were cheered, by the discovery of a group in our camp in Egypt with peculiar needs. Today they might be considered happily balanced people but in our day they were classified as perverts. Meeting the demand for their particular fetish was the perk of the stores wallahs who issued rags.

Bales of shoddy were sent out from the UK in huge numbers because the demand for rags was never ending. The bundles were completely sterile having been treated before dispatch so handling them was quite safe. The issue was not weighed or measured in any way and it was mostly a matter of help-yourself. An astute store man noted that instead of simply grabbing a handful at

J B WALDRON

Standard Vanguards as sold for £120 by the British Government when they withdrew from Egypt. Photographed in 1953.

random, some airmen were extremely choosy and valuable time was spent sorting through the heaps of shoddy. In among the woollens and the cotton goods would be old brassieres, or even better and more valuable, pairs of well-used knickers. This action was not lost on the stores 'erks.

From the moment of this discovery no one had access to newly arrived bundles before the stores crew had removed any articles of value. A flourishing market developed and expanding waistlines indicated that the cookhouse was the likely centre of corruption. One pair of knickers hung up in a billet for all

to see, and perhaps drool over, were valued at steak and chips plus peaches and custard.

They had clearly started life as a pair of bloomers, airwomen for the use of, but the WAAF in question had an arty background. The long legs had been cut off with the edges neatly hemmed. Red silk ribbons had been woven round the leg openings and round the waist and some embroidery had been added, all clearly for the purpose of stimulating the male eye. I bet the lady who wore them is now the life and soul of the old folks' home.

Beating the system was a game played by most airmen at some time or another during their service. As we were always short of funds, other currencies had to be created to make life a little more pleasant. Every trade had something to barter and we at RAF Deversoir had it off to a fine art. The Royal Navy had its currency in the form of the rum issue. According to naval tradition, on his birthday a member of the mess deck would be offered 'sippers' by his mates and 'gulpers' perhaps from his winger or best friend. If you agreed to stand in for a duty, the quantity offered and received was negotiable. For 'sandy bottoms' you had to save a life, but it was an excellent system understood by everyone. In the RAF, it was much more hit or miss.

A few of us owned motorcycles and at that time trials and scrambling were immensely popular. To be effective, a trial course requires mud, and this in Egypt is as scarce as hens' teeth. However, we needed mud, so mud we would have! We had the entire assets of the huge stores buildings at our disposal, so price was not a problem. Three large holes would be dug in a quiet part of the airfield and a refuelling bowser summoned. Then a thousand gallons of diesel would be shared between the holes in double quick time. We had our instant mud and normally it would remain fluid for about twenty minutes. Our riding skills improved and everyone was happy. Taxpayers back home would know nothing about it and the discreet movement of paper would cover the loss.

Socks were among our most valuable commodities since the constant sweating, particularly of the feet, caused them to disintegrate in a surprisingly short time. The Air Ministry laid down the approved rate of sock consumption, without thought to where the airmen were serving. What might be reasonable for Whitehall was completely inappropriate for the tropics, but as a sergeant might well say: "Rules are rules!" We store-wallahs had a source of great wealth right under our noses and the demand for socks, under or over the counter, always outstripped supply. We could no more resist

providing these creature comforts than a drowning man resists a passing straw. With many hands dipping into the same sweetie jar the losses mounted rapidly and it was not easy to account for a shortfall of such magnitude. But we were prepared for this. We had the Woolly Bug Farm.

All other items of equipment were straightforward in accounting terms. Spanners broke and the evidence was there for all to see, and 99.5 per cent of our stock was quite valueless for barter. A jet engine is a wonderful thing, being an example of the latest technology and all that, but demand on the black market was limited. To offer one to a cook in exchange for an extra sausage was to invite ridicule. Only socks had a universally recognised value but their losses had to be accounted for somehow.

We had inherited the Woolly Bug Farm under conditions of great secrecy from some old sweats long demobbed who had served in in the halcyon days when trading prospects included Abdulahs and other fez-wearing entrepreneurs. Their envious lifestyle had been financed by freely trading with all-comers, some of whom were visited in the privacy of their homes and offices.

When the British eventually withdrew from Egypt, the Government tried to sell off virtually new Standard Vanguards for a paltry £120 each. Demand was low if not non-existent. Some said this was because buyers would be identified as pro-British, which would result in revenge attacks mounted on them or their new cars, but we knew that it was due to the price being charged. If they had come to our outlets we could have halved the asking price.

The deal that the old sweats were most proud of was selling a huge £6,000 diesel-powered generator for big money to some Egyptians. It was rumoured by our time that it was used to streetlight a suburb of Ismailia.

Readers might consider this a tall tale, but the RAF used some weird and wonderful accounting procedures dreamt up during the war years when ingenuity was at its most valuable as it kept units going when bombs were falling. It was generally known as the exchange principle. For example, a length of string could easily serve as a shoelace. Why indent for a supply of scarce shoelaces when you had stocks of string? A stirrup pump (fire) could be adapted and converted to a motor vehicle pump (tyre inflation) without too much trouble. An exchange form could be raised and stock records altered, all in accordance with approved procedures. It would happen like this.

The £6,000 electric generator, having been spirited from the airfield by a feat of legerdemain worthy of David Copperfield, was converted by a complex series of ingenious alterations into something smaller and smaller until at the end of its labyrinthine journey it had metamorphosed into a pump (bicycle) of Bakelite construction. This easily broken item was recorded as received in the stores in a condition of "damaged beyond economic repair" and scrapped. The trail was not only complex but the brains behind it had introduced blind alleys, deliberate mistakes, conversions back to an original device and then gone off at a tangent to another loop in the trail. It was all clever stuff.

The old sweats concerned in the scam were surprised to be woken in their civilian pre-dawn hours by the Special Investigation Branch of the RAF. Several PC Plods supported them, and our heroes were marched into Her Majesty's secure custody by that fine body of men. I know all this because I was the one of the chosen few who followed the yellow brick accounts trail on the instructions of the white-kneed SIB specially flown out from the UK. We became so engrossed in the challenge that instead of helping out our old allies we got caught up in the excitement of the chase. Sorry lads, if you happen to read this. We eventually tracked down every last piece of paper and unravelled the mystery. The one piece of the jigsaw left missing would have revealed the identity of the buyer and how much he paid for it. It was from these

same old sweats who sold the generator that we inherited the Woolly Bug Farm, which was located in the rafters of the stores building.

You can't be too careful with woolly bugs, for you can hardly advertise for replacements. Their presence could be acknowledged only twice a year (an acceptable incidence ratio), or when the sock cupboard was particularly low. Every repository of material has to hold a stock check at some time to ensure the contents tally with the ledgers. Using the Woolly Bug Farm in our cover-up operation meant a portion of carefully tended livestock would be required to make the supreme sacrifice for the greater good. On one occasion we were driven to act because we were completely out of socks despite the ledger showing the warehouse contained 500 pairs.

"We've discovered woolly bugs in the stock, sir!" The announcement would be relayed to the squadron leader with due solemnity.

"Destroy all the infected stock by burning without delay," would be the inevitable rejoinder.

Sometimes, if it would not interfere with tiffin, he might decide to inspect the damage. In this case, he would be informed that the correct procedures to combat a woolly bug attack were in hand and the remainder of the stock was already a smouldering pyre. Naturally, a solitary example of a woolly bug, rustled from the farm, would be produced as irrefutable evidence of the outbreak. The unfortunate bug would then be publicly sacrificed in the flames. King Solomon himself would have been hard put to accurately divine not only the quantity of socks consumed by the conflagration, but also what had actually been burned in the first place. Our bacon and eggs had been saved, and the priority requisition signed by the squadron leader, when filed, would nicely balance the books for the forthcoming check. Once again we could all sleep easily in our beds, and it was business as usual until the next time.

This chapter is probably written to justify my participation in the many fiddles that

Old pals from the Engineer Plant Depot (Egypt) at Qassasin meet up again. From the left: Ron Pickering, Acker Bilk, John Britten and Harry Gardner. It was John Britten, sadly no longer with us, who gave Acker his first clarinet. Unlike some who hit the big time, Acker Bilk still holds dear his old friendships, and appeared on TV in support of the Egyptian Medal Campaign.

were available during my Service. It has
always been thus. Acker Bilk, also a Suez
veteran, is a shining example of how the
system works to the benefit of all. After being
caught asleep at his post when on guard he
was sent to the glasshouse for three months,
which extended his service by that length of
time. Fortunately for him, there was no room
at the inn: the Crystal Palace was full. He was
obliged therefore to serve the first six weeks
of his time in the camp guardroom.

John Britten, a friendly lance jack who had,
'acquired' a military (short two-piece)
clarinet gave it to Acker to help him pass the
time of day in his lonely room. Naturally it is
against King's and Queen's regulations that
anyone in custody should pass their time
profitably or enjoyably. Though many heard
his practising, raids on his cell always drew a
blank and freak radio waves were blamed for
the unusual sounds. The clarinet, when not in
use, was concealed in the leg of his Army-
issue bed and a friendly early warning system
kept him safe from discovery. The rest, as
they say, is history.

The world enjoyed Acker's Stranger On The
Shore so much it bought several million
copies. I like to think that the shore he had in
mind was that of Lake Timsah, the Great
Bitter Lake, or even the Canal itself.

In the manner typical of bureaucrats everywhere, the British Government continued to
pour money into the Canal Zone even though
they knew it was only a matter of time before
they threw in the towel in the battle against
the Egyptians. At Deversoir, the airfield
construction crews sweated in the midday

sun to extend runways and aprons for
aircraft. This was work priced in millions
rather than thousands of pounds.

The only people to benefit, apart from the
Egyptians, were the Third Battalion Grenadier
Guards, who shared part of Deversoir camp.
Their drill sergeants went potty at having a
real barrack square to march their men up
and down on. Naturally this could not be
done during normal business hours as
practised by the RAF – 6am to 1pm. During
these hours the odd Vampire fighter was
liable to taxi about. Noel Coward's song about
mad dogs and Englishmen should have
included a line or two about guardsmen.
When the sun was doing its worst, out
marched the Guards. Being sensible types,
the RAF, after tiffin, would lie down in the
shade. You have no idea how annoying it is to
have your slumbers broken by loud voices
shouting instructions to 'eft wheel and by the
clomp of hundreds of heavy boots as they 'eft
wheel to order.

Acker Bilk was with the Royal Engineers,
and, when not dozing on guard duty, they
spent further millions on maintenance of
the infrastructure of the entire area. The
troops were kept short of cash and if they
were paid at the active service rate it must
have been only coppers.

When we finally left Egypt, the graders,
bulldozers, tractors and other earth-moving
equipment dug a huge hole in the sand. They
then buried themselves deep underground,
with the last machine putting the lights out.
So far as I know, they lie there to this day.

PLANET OF THE ROCK APES

*As darkness fell, one of the officers fired a nervous
shot at something that 'resembled a rock ape'.
It turned out to be his unfortunate colleague*

Members of the RAF Regiment have been called Rock Apes not (as you might think) for as long as there has been such a regiment, but only since 1952. As they once guarded the Rock of Gibraltar it is tempting to assume that similarities were drawn between them and the Rock's other hairy residents. The story that there were cases of intermarriage is also not proven. The truth is more mundane, but interesting nonetheless.

RAF Regiment officers are a strange breed. Obviously all that foot stamping has effected the cranial department over time. A normal RAF officer is a slothful individual with a desire to serve his years and retire on a substantial pension. Commissioned aircrew are a bit different, with an in-built desire to emulate birds. In time they discover that every move they make is pre-arranged, and as soon as their bodies and reflexes pass the peak of perfection they are pushed aside by younger entrants to the profession. Thereafter they are employed only as glorified bus drivers.

RAF Regiment Ruperts long to become fighting soldiers, and spend their spare time in manly pursuits. Hunting and fishing are much favoured, as a consoling hip flask can be carried in the field without attracting criticism. It might be untrue that it was a combination of hip flask and rifle that had them dubbed Rock Apes, but here's how the story goes.

Two intrepid RAF Regiment officers serving in the Aden Protectorate Levies at Dhala, in the western area of the country, decided to amuse themselves by shooting at the baboons – locally called rock apes – that came down from the hills in the cool of the evening to forage for food, throw stones at the Levy camp and generally make a nuisance of themselves. The locals treated them as vermin.

As darkness fell the two officers became separated. On hearing a rustling sound from some bushes on a rocky outcrop one of them fired a nervous shot. Unforunately, he had not waited until his target was clearly defined before firing. Running forward to inspect his trophy, he was horrified to find his colleague, a Flight Lieutenant Mason, lying there with a hole in his chest. The bullet had just missed his heart. His life was saved by swift medical attention following an overnight journey by a medical team from Aden and a 'casevac' by air the next day. Months of hospitalisation followed, but he made a full recovery and was eventually able to return to duty.

Death and injury to Servicemen in far-flung outposts of the Empire were common enough and seldom rated a line in the newspapers at home, and the incident escaped attention till the subsequent board of enquiry. In a plea of mitigation, the accused party stated that in the half-light his intended target "resembled a rock ape". This comment became an oft-quoted part of the Regiment's folklore.

At the I joined RAF Deversoir, so did the RAF Regiment. No 5 Wing consisted of 26 and

28 Squadrons, both in light ack-ack roles, and the poor souls had to rough it until they had cleared the ground and erected their tents. These would be home-sweet-home for the next two and a half years.

They then moved to RAF Habbaniya in Iraq, which seemed like a Butlin's holiday after Deversoir. There were three swimming pools, 28 miles of tarmac road, and US-style taxi cabs to drive Servicemen anywhere on the camp for one shilling. They had RAF and Army ladies to look at and speak to – if not to touch – in stark contrast to Egypt, where the only glimpse of a white woman was through the wire around the married patch.

In addition to providing ack-ack fire in the event of an air attack on the camp, the Rock Apes did guard duties elsewhere. The warriors in blue kept the Abu Sultan bomb dump and the Air Officer in Command's houseboats on Lake Timsah safe. They also spent some time at Bir O'Dieb on the Red Sea, where shooting sharks was a popular hobby. It is hard to believe that the men had actually wanted to stay at Deversoir rather than move to Iraq.

Among their duties were guarding the Vampires of 32 Squadron, an illustrious outfit formed in the Royal Flying Corps days. It still exists at Northolt in the guise of the Queen's Flight. The other two Squadrons were 213 and 249, both now disbanded. This country will surely live to regret the slashing of its defence ability, as we never seem to learn the lessons of history. How odd to hear the Secretary for Defence say that he had the wholehearted backing of the Prime Minister in retaining the right to first strike with nuclear weapons. I wonder if they have thrown away their Campaign for Nuclear Disarmament medals.

In 1942, in the very early days of the RAF Regiment, soldiers from many regiments became airmen overnight and wore either a blue battledress blouse with khaki trousers or vice versa. The Brylcreem boys have never fully accepted them as real airmen. Their officers were drawn from almost every line regiment, and standards of drill and discipline varied depending on who was in charge. This mixed bag of RAF Regiment officers was an odd lot, as the following will illustrate.

Jankers were so frequently awarded to our billet members that instead of fixing up our own webbing for these occasions we assembled a spare set – we ran the stores, remember – for general use. On one unforgettable evening, when half a dozen of us presented ourselves for inspection we discovered that the duty officer had newly arrived in Egypt and was from the Regiment. He was a young man, anxious to make a name for himself and to qualify as a flying officer. He actually lined up the defaulters and INSPECTED us. This was not playing by the long-established rules of the game. He referred to us as a 'shower', which was fair enough, then decided to check that we were carrying the prescribed equipment.

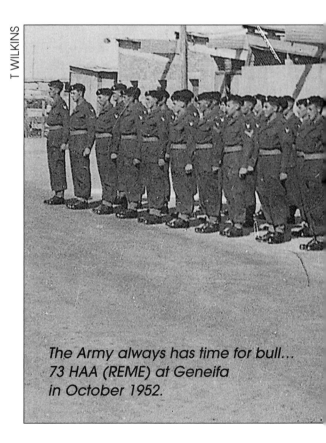

The Army always has time for bull... 73 HAA (REME) at Geneifa in October 1952.

Dirty brown liquid was found in water bottles, and then my unopened small kit was pounced upon.

"What's in it?" he shouted in American Marine Corps style.

I quietly told him that it contained a change of underwear and my physical training kit. A proper RAF officer would have taken my word for it, but he had ideas of his own and insisted that I unpack it.

I had as much idea of what it contained as a child has when opening a Christmas parcel. First a wad of cleaning cloth emerged like a rabbit out of a hat. I thought he would be really pleased that cleaning my rifle took such a priority in my life, but it was not to be. When I produced the next item, the oldest and mangiest pair of PT drawers you ever set eyes on, he actually changed colour. He was a very unhappy RAF Regiment-type person and, vowing that we had not heard the end of the affair and that it would be extra jankers all round, he stormed off.

We never heard any more about it and I can visualise some senior non-Regiment officer calming him down with words like: "There, there. Don't you worry about it. You can still order your own men about as much as you like." He would get used to our little ways.

Elsewhere I have said some unkind things about RAF Regiment recruitment but I am happy to report that recently, only fifty years on, I received a letter from a former regular who served with 26 Squadron. He has studied hard since leaving the Regiment and I have to admit his printing is not at all bad now.

The RAF Regiment has come on a lot since those days, and the drill shown by the Queen's Flight is second to none. In Egypt the Regiment was used in many difficult situations, and deservedly gained the admiration of the many Army regiments with which it served.

NOT-SO-PRIVATE PARTS

Trouser-dropping is not embarrassing in itself. It's doing it in front of two or three thousand other men that has particularly embarrassing potential

As in the other Services, a condition caught due to indiscreet liaisons was considered to be a self-inflicted wound and punishable accordingly. If an American was unlucky enough to become infected, his stay in hospital qualified him for a Purple Heart medal in recognition of his injuries. In the RAF, the reward was jankers. All recruits were shown horror films featuring unlucky ladies and gentlemen who had been less than careful in their choice of sexual partners. They were suffering the extreme results of untreated contagion and it was a frightening sight. Fortunately the bulk of recruits were virgins. Although a few did boast of successful conquests they were mostly, and rightly, classified as liars.

Behind the guardroom at each camp was a small office known as the early treatment room. When leaving camp one could call in for a free issue of condoms, but few did this unless they were going swimming. A condom is an ideal waterproof container for the small denomination notes issued in Egypt. When returning to camp after a drunken night out, an 'erk's visit to the early treatment room was a way of wordlessly boasting to his mates that his evening had been crowned with sexual success. Whether or not he used the wonderful selection of creams and lotions, it proved evidence of his virility and attractiveness to women. We had little need for the room, though, because we were mainly confined to camp for months on end.

For the truly desperate there was a very famous one-legged purveyor of pleasure who plied her trade close to the Moascar Garrison outside Ismailia. I had the dubious pleasure of seeing her in action on one occasion while acting as an escort for a stores truck. Fifty or sixty squaddies, who according to the variety of hats and caps represented most units of the Army, were waiting patiently in a line that stretched round several corners. At the front of the queue a paratrooper was beavering away quite unperturbed by the fact that he was operating in full view of the passing throng. Dusk was falling and Peg-Leg was leaning against a wall supported by a crutch on one side and the shoulder of her next customer on the other. They were conversing animatedly. Perhaps a discussion about the prevailing price was in progress, but we shall never know.

From the back of the lorry I had a grandstand view of the scene but was not near enough to establish details of her possible age, or to judge her chances in a Miss World contest. One man who swore that he had a close look at her stressed that she was, or had been, a real beauty. Quality information from many sources proved that she had plied her trade for at least ten years. She may have lost her leg by being run over by a British vehicle and have been receiving a pension, but whatever her reason for setting up in business she was completely faithful to the British Forces. For long service to the Crown she certainly should have qualified for an award of some sort or another. I have no idea of her scale of charges, but her industry must have made her a fairly wealthy woman. A persistent rumour states that the Egyptians eventually killed her for fraternising with the British, but this has never been confirmed.

Although we were only fifty miles from Cairo, none of the thousands of Servicemen who were rushed out to reinforce the Canal Zone ever saw the city, the Sphinx or even a pyramid. When the conditions were considered quiet enough for us to leave camp and visit Fayid or Ismailia, we carried a rifle and ten rounds of ammunition, or a pick handle. Ismailia was a pleasant enough place but the Blue Kettle Service Club was on the point of closing down when I visited, and a mere shadow of its glorious past. There were no European women at all to be seen. A few plump elderly ladies swathed in black djellabahs crouched by the roadsides offering swift 'couch shufties' for a few piastres. Some touts offered the jig-a-jig services of young Greek or French girls if one cared to visit the out-of-bounds areas. It was surprising how many could be tempted after consuming enough Stella. Anyone daft enough to fall for such an invitation could easily finish up with a knife between his ribs.

The ubiquitous shoeshine boys were a more persistent menace. The offer of a shoeshine for only ten ackers quickly became a threat to douse the buyer's best KDs in liquid black polish if a revised demand of fifty or 100 piastres was not met. A swift and vicious kick from the polished or unpolished boot was the only effective remedy, and as a defensive strategy it worked best before the initial offer was made. It did little for Anglo-Egyptian relations, but was most satisfying for the Serviceman concerned.

Being lusty young males our dreams concerned female company, but few of these dreams came true. The military, having hundreds of years of experience controlling men and keeping infection to a minimum, had long ago decided that an annual check-up on the venereal health or otherwise of the troops should be written into the Regulations.

For everyone concerned it was embarrassing. The examination would establish the facts. Called the FFI parade, it would discover whether we were indeed free from infection.

This annual rite of passage in the Royal Air Force of my generation was known unofficially as a short-arm inspection. Those suffering the indignity and those whose duty it was to see it carried out shared the embarrassment equally. Everyone, regardless of rank, was required to drop his trousers in an official manner to be checked. When I say official manner, I should point out that no actual drill exists for the manoeuvre. No "Undo braces, two three," followed by "Drop 'em, two three." King's – and subsequently Queen's – Regs were silent on the subject, probably due to the difficulty of framing a suitable drill and series of commands that could apply to every branch of the services. Highland Regiments would require suitable instructions to lift kilts, and introducing a system for female Service personnel would be a veritable nightmare. It would need to be a combination of both the trouser and kilt orders. Something like "Skirts up, two three," quickly followed by "Bloomers down, two three." The mind boggles.

Trouser dropping is not embarrassing in itself since we all do it every day. It's dropping them in the presence of others that causes the problem. To do so in front of two or three thousand other men has particular embarrass-ment potential as the size and style of the parts exhibited could cause derisory laughter, envy or – in extreme cases – astonishment. Just imagine the consternation and loss of dignity to any poor sod whose examination led to the discovery of anything worthy of scrutiny by higher authority.

The actual mechanics of the drill should perhaps be explained. The Medical Officer and sundry others from the scab-lifting branch of the Service would be seated in a row of chairs, each separated from the other by about ten feet. The venue could be a drill hall, an aircraft hangar or even in the open air if the weather was clement. Each examiner was armed with a short stick or a pencil. This instrument was known in medical circles as a prodder. The men were herded into queues before each station and they would move forward slowly, dropping their trousers on command when their turn came. The examiner would first peer at the objects suspended before him, looking for parts that might be missing, interesting holes or deep craters. Then he would use his prodder to shove the dangly bits to the left and then to the right in a search of livestock. Crabs were occasionally located but, despite rumours, lobsters were not. The final act was to deliver a sharp blow with the prodder to the membrane virile to see if any multi-coloured matter flew or dripped forth. If something amiss was suspected the Medical Officer himself would take a gander and deliver an expert opinion. To find anything was extremely rare, and happily 999 times out of 1,000 nothing would be found. That said, in a camp of 2,000 men the law of averages meant two poor souls were likely to be exposed. For me the most worrying aspect of the event was that the prodders were not sterilised between customers.

Though FFIs were rare, one would imagine that they could be organised without a hitch, but this was not always the case. Young airmen were shy and tended to require the close proximity of friends in deciding which queue to join. If rumour had it that a certain medical orderly suffered from bent-wrist syndrome his line of potential customers might be short or long depending on the proclivities of those queuing, or simple curiosity.

An inspection was duly arranged for us at Deversoir, and to understand the shambles that followed, one must first bear in mind that few of us airmen had even glimpsed a female for over a year. In addition, the gauche young men who had been sent out from the UK had been toughened and roughened up into troops whose knees were extremely brown. The FFI was an alfresco affair, and faced with the prospect of examining well over 2,000 men the MO pressed anyone who was suitably qualified into service to complement his tiny staff. One such conscript was his attractive and nubile young wife, a former nursing sister. No doubt it had seemed to be a bit of a laugh in the mess when first mooted, or perhaps it was by way of a cheap birthday treat for her.

In any event, when she was spotted sitting demurely in the middle of the row of medics every man jack became determined that she would have the joy of testing his tackle and that no one else would get a look in. The other examiners had about a dozen men each in their queues whilst the adorable Mrs. MO had the rest. The Station Warrant Officer yelled and shouted in vain at the men, who had no intention of moving. The object of lust changed her seating position and the herd moved with her in a solid phalanx. When the lucky man at the front of the line dropped his trousers he would show a marked reluctance to pull them up again. Trousers were dropped in anticipation before the instruction was given, and men in adjoining lines flashed in her direction, leaving their rightful inspectors to talk to the side of their heads. They hoped to interest her into changing her seating position again. It had to end, though, and she was retired from active participation. Dozens had fallen instantly in love with her and elated proddees told and retold the story of their experiences to the less fortunate who had been at the back of the queue.

"She gasped in surprise when she saw mine," one lied without a blush. "She spent longer looking at mine than at anyone else's," claimed a second. "She winked at me. Honest, she did." This from a front-runner in the liar-of-the-year competition. Needless to report, not a single case of infection was uncovered.

Meet the neighbours

The infrequent periods of truce were the ideal time to stock up on food and to get to know the locals better

When King Farouk was forced into exile the crowds who had approved his every excess and cheered his appearance in the streets instantly switched their support to General Naguib. The General, a man no one had seen or heard of, became Egypt's hero overnight. Suddenly his picture was everywhere. The General could be identified in most of the Press photographs by the fact that his head was circled in pencil or dark ink.

A new spirit was in the air and our authorities decided that it was now safe enough to visit Ismailia without a rifle and ammunition – or even a pickaxe shaft – as long as we stayed in groups of two or three. Arriving in the town, three of us from the equipment section agreed to stick together come what may. There was safety in numbers and we would do our best to enjoy what delights were on offer in case the shaky truce disappeared again.

Our first surprise was finding a fruit-drinks stall – the first we had ever seen – and, we felt, a great idea for Blackpool or Margate, or even a national chain. The idea was so simple and inexpensive: a row of blenders was lined up along the counter and the shelves behind were laden with individually priced fruits of every description. Bottles of milk and a bucket of ice cubes completed the set-up.

We knew better than to ask for ice in our drinks since it had probably come direct from the Sweet Water Canal, and we were unhappy about drinking from a glass that had been washed in water from the same source. My Granny used to say: "You'll eat a peck o' dirt afore ye die," but I was not keen to eat it all at once. I didn't know how much a peck is, but I had already had my share, as a cursory inspection of our cookhouse would confirm. There must be an element of truth in the old Army saying: "He saved the entire regiment when he shot the cook!" And the more familiar: "Who called the cook a b*****d? Who called the b*****d a cook!"

Anyway, having chosen a banana, a peach, a small bunch of grapes and an orange, I watched them dissolve in seconds into a lovely mushy mess as the blades of the glass-fronted liquidiser whirled. I had never seen such a machine before and was fascinated by it. When ice-cold milk was added it was food fit for the gods, and the fruit was at its peak of ripeness. At home you might have to add syrup but here it was perfect. It was so delicious we all had seconds.

The inner man was satisfied and the fruits must have released something into our bloodstreams that intoxicated us like alcohol, because the next thing we knew we were sitting on horses. None of us had ever ridden before and the driving seat was a considerable height off the ground. We didn't have a driving licence between us, so the lack of a brake or steering wheel seemed not to matter much as we paid a deposit against late return of the nags. I now know that the correct procedure is to instruct your mount to "walk on", and if this is successfully accomplished you can later try "trot on". Having never been faster than that, I can't advise on the order for gallop, a lack of knowledge shared by Pat Eddery, Frankie Dettori, Keiron Fallon and a host of other jockeys who have since reduced my fortune by a considerable amount. We had no time for those namby-pamby commands, and I doubt if the horses understood English anyway. A cry of "Imshi!" and a dig from our heels in best John Wayne style made our mounts shoot off into the rush-hour stampede. The car horns did nothing for the horses' composure as we dodged in and out of the traffic.

We were not all that worried about the animals, as they were expendable. It was our own lives and limbs that really mattered to us. About then I realised that my nag was fitted with a combined homing sensor and anti-theft device, in the form of an Arab urchin clinging to its tail and charging along behind. I had been too afraid to use the riding crop provided, as the animal was moving quickly enough, but found it helpful in ridding me of my unwelcome strap-hanger.

The reins were quite useless as a steering device since the horse had obviously been programmed to stick to a set route on every outing. I wanted to turn right, and hauled on that rein. The steed, which appeared to have a mouth of steel, turned left, and I very nearly went over the handlebars. The animal slowed down and trotted back to its owner, who was not best pleased with the loss of his Arab assistant. Doubtless he thought we had clocked up some additional miles during the hire. Having had enough excitement for one day, we decided on a sightseeing stroll.

We wandered along the beautifully kept streets of the French and Greek quarter, a

Terrorist attacks were easy to arrange against off-duty troops. You always had to watch your back in Ismailia. 1952

stark contrast to the Arab part, with Out of Bounds signs at every street opening. As we wandered along, an Arab riding a brand new bicycle, the frame still wrapped in brown paper, came alongside and spoke to us in Arabic. When he realised how limited our knowledge of the language was, he switched effortlessly to excellent English.

"Fancy some entertainment boys?" he

E SEAR

queried. It had been a great day out so far, so we thought we'd take a chance.

"What kind of entertainment?"

He gave us a very old-fashioned look, glanced conspiratorially up and down the street, and breathed: "Girls."

This was more like it. We had heard the old sweats talk about the houses with the little red lights above the door, which were definitely not an indication that Bass beer was sold within.

"What kind of girls?" we asked, with the films showing the result of untreated infection still fresh in our minds.

"Young girls: Greek, French, Cypriot and Egyptian. You can take your pick. None of them older than fifteen."

The offer was irresistible even to me, the

voice of caution in our trio. We were lusty nineteen-year-olds, virgins to a man, but keen to widen our experiences. Was it legal to have it off with a fifteen-year-old? In Britain it was out of the question, but women aged much more quickly in the East, and we had heard some got married as young as twelve. There would be no harm in looking, but how much would it cost? We put it to the linguist.

"It's a pound whichever girl you choose but you mustn't waste my time. You look all right though, so I'll take a chance. It's only a few yards down the street."

This would mean going into the out-of-bounds area, but it was only a few yards and, there were three of us. He slowly pedalled ahead and then, as if struck with a sudden thought, stopped.

"Are you sure you've got the money if you do decide to have a girl?"

"Of course we've got the money."

"Let me see it then."

I was becoming a bit suspicious of this guy.

When he found out that we couldn't get by in Arabic he must have known that we were new and inexperienced; suckers for old tricks. All of us were by now deeply wary but the thought of the young girls allayed our fears. I decided that I would let him see the colour of our money and I produced a pound note, but held it firmly in both hands showing only the middle part.

"There are a lot of forgeries about," he cautioned. "Make sure that it has the same number on the back as on the front."

I fell for his trick. Still gripping the note firmly, I turned it over, but I turned my hands over too, and more of the note was exposed. In a flash he grabbed it and, standing up on the pedals to gain extra purchase, he was off. I ran after him.

Elsewhere I have stressed my aversion to physical exertion, but my feet had wings that day, and hard as he pushed his bike I was still gaining on him. We must by now have been fifty yards into the Arab quarter, but nothing was going to part me from my pound. He

Vendors on the outskirts of Ismailia, near the French Quarter – the only area the Forces were allowed in on weekend recreational visits. 1952

R WOODS

Char up! Welcome tea and wads from the ubiquitous NAAFI truck. By February 1954, volunteers had returned to the Canal Zone to provide this essential service.

shouted out to an accomplice, who darted off the pavement to meet him. As their hands touched he cycled off while his mate darted up an alley. I didn't know who now had my cash but the guy on the bike was my target.

I had broken the world record for the hundred-yard dash in Service boots, but he was still twenty yards ahead and now I was making no impression on the gap. It was then that I realised that I was quite alone. I had only turned one corner during the chase, and was able to work out the beeline back to safety. On the way I passed an Egyptian bank, with its ancient and badly-uniformed guard leaning against a wall. I told him that I had been robbed and that the culprit was riding a bike that would be easy to identify. My difficulty was in finding words to explain the paper wrappings on the machine. An elderly Egyptian couple wearing European dress, happened by and stopped to help. They translated and explained details of the bicycle

to the guard. He shrugged his shoulders, indicating that his sole responsibility was the bank, so I asked the couple to convey a message to him that caused them to blanche and protest that such a thing was impossible and they would not dare translate it. Giving him a guarantee in English that I would shoot one of his fellow countrymen at the first opportunity, I departed in a huff.

During those few days of calm, two squaddies driving a NAAFI truck at the tail end of an Army convoy became detached from the vehicles in front and the lorry was never seen again. Their bodies were recovered from the Sweet Water Canal. Worse still, there was a determined rumour circulating that a WAAF had been kidnapped, raped, mutilated and killed. Following that incident, rioting by incensed Air Force and Army personnel was only narrowly averted. At that time a terrorist was being rewarded with a bounty of £100 Egyptian when he killed a British officer; other ranks were valued at less. That sum represented eighteen months' wages for an ordinary soldier in Naguib's army. and the situation was so serious that one troopship bringing out families was turned round at Port Said and sent home.

My reunion with my two buddies was frosty in the extreme and I would never again trust either one of them.

I was on guard the following night, and although my experience was limited I was put on stag with a newly arrived Aberdonian to show him the ropes. We were detailed to wander the far reaches of the camp and see if we could detect intruders. The armoured car crew had spotted a freshly opened hole in the fence on their teatime patrol, but they had pretended not to notice. The bluebottle in the unction was that no one told us where the hole was located. My companion, Jock Barclay, who was later to become something of a star in the Mouth Organ Band – although he actually played an accordion – was an ideal companion on patrol. Unlike my mates in Ismailia, he could be depended on.

As we crept silently along the internal railway line, I saw a flash of white up ahead. We already had one up the spout and I signalled for confirmation of my sighting, but Jock had seen nothing. Then I saw it again and this time I got a nod of agreement, but the object was gone again by the time I raised my sights and drew a bead on the target area. There could be no doubt that the white flashes were djellabahs, which meant that there must be a gang of intruders and no question of being able to send up either a white flare to help with vision or a red one to summons help. I had told the idle policeman in Ismailia that I was going to get one of his pals and this looked likely to be my chance. A third white flash crossed my sights and, being ready for it, I fired. Firing a .303 Lee Enfield at night causes a huge muzzle flash, in addition to the report which deafens the operator. It is not recommended that you stay

in the same position for too long after firing, since the enemy now knows your whereabouts and may well fire back. To thwart this possibility, the instant I fired I rolled forward and resighted my rifle from a new position about a yard to the left of my previous one. Jock had his rifle to his shoulder, ready to give covering fire and take up the fight if incoming shots arrived.

Nothing. Utter silence. Had I shot him dead? Had it been the same man flitting about, or had he been part of a gang? We waited for a suitable time then crept forward, but could find nothing of interest. We reported the incident to the satellite guardroom, so our relief had something to think about when we bedded down.

Determined to find the body, or at least signs of a successful ambush, I made my way to the site the next afternoon. It was a wild and lonely place, as Private Frazier of Dad's Army would have said; an area virtually neglected, and not patrolled for weeks on end. There was no sign of blood, but by working back from the fence to where I had discharged my rifle I could reassess the position in daylight. The djellabahs I saw had been the sails of boats on the Sweet Water Canal passing between two clumps of tall elephant grass. I kept this knowledge to myself.

Negotiations were taking place between the Egyptian Government, now led by Colonel Nasser, and our Government. The Egyptians were running rings round our chaps who, being the old-school-tie brigade, believed everything that they were told. The Egyptian propaganda machine let it be known that Britain was on the run, so suddenly the Egyptians became genuinely friendly towards us. We even went so far as to appoint a local as billet batman and hoped that it was going to be like the old days we had heard so much about. The business acumen of the average Egyptian is keen, but our Mohammed's was razor sharp and he agreed to look after two billets if we would pay him 25 ackers each per week. He would act as billet orderly, making the beds and sweeping the floor, washing the windows and carrying out other chores as required. He would wake us with char in the mornings and keep our boots immaculate. When we returned to our huts after tiffin he would be waiting to welcome us with a huge toothy grin, happily pointing out the work he had done, with a gleaming billet to prove it. Our pay was £3.50 a week in today's money and Mohammed was pocketing at least £12, so little wonder he smiled a lot.

He was also one of the strongest people I ever met. In the streets of Fayid I saw a circus strong man effortlessly bending six-inch nails with his bare hands, and Mohammed was in his league. I was the only one in our hut who bested him at arm wrestling, and I only managed this by ensuring that he had pitted his strength successfully against a dozen others before I had a try.

All good things come to an end, and after only two weeks the talks between the governments broke down. Mohammed was gone and rioting returned to the streets. It was controlled from Cairo and could be turned on and off like a tap. During the lull in hostilities I managed to fit in a visit to Fayid on my own, and found it a pleasant enough little place and quite different to the impression I had gained from the back of a three-tonner. The larger Ismailia was the

Egyptian boats on the Sweet Water Canal. Can you believe the sails could be mistaken at night for djellabahs?

G EVANS

town we preferred to visit on the few occasions an out-of-camp journey was possible.

It is difficult to believe the deprivations suffered by troops during this campaign. An accumulation of little things made life so unbearable, starting with flies, bugs, sweats, and then more flies. One of my skives was serving on the catering committee of the camp, and it was then that I discovered just how little was allowed by the Government to feed a man. It was in the region of one shilling and tenpence – less than 9p – a day. With hindsight, the catering staff did a magnificent job, but all Servicemen reserve the right to grumble about the quality and quantity of food provided. To turn a diet from edible to rancid took a matter of hours, and how the pre-war troops survived in India on five-year tours is difficult to imagine. The death rate from disease and food poisoning must have been high, although many changed regiments so they could stay out there. Some did a full twenty-year tour and only came home to be demobbed on pension. They must have lived on curries to disguise the taste of rotten meat. It might have been a case of *cherchez la femme,* since a few undoubtedly had native concubines and children. A return to home life in the UK would have seemed a return to chilly squalor.

A few years ago I had the honour to attend the disbandment of the Second Battalion Scots Guards at Glencorse Barracks, outside Edinburgh. What a difference forty-odd years has made. Access to the sergeants' mess was barred not by a sentry but by an electronic push-button device, and despite valiant and desperate efforts we could not attract the attention of the serious drinkers within. Fortunately, one thing in the Army has remained constant: there will always be defaulters. One such individual was engaged in sweeping up leaves outside the building. Whether he was a busted sergeant or not we never discovered, but he rattled off the eight-digit open-sesame as quickly as he could his

regimental number.

An immaculately turned out pipe band marched into the mess at two-thirty in the morning and entertained us with a spirited display of piping, drumming and Highland dancing. As if this was not enough, 'supper' was announced and we were fed a delicious range of curries with all the trimmings by a team of immaculately turned out cooks who wore crisply starched whites and were happy to smile at their squiffy guests in the wee small hours. Having spent the night in the old officers' mess we discovered that breakfast in the Guards is served at some ungodly hour before dawn. As a result we were obliged to visit a Little Chef to calm our shaking hands.

The best Service food I have eaten was the nosh produced on one of HM's nuclear submarines, where a tiny galley feeds almost 150 matelots four meals a day. The quality is consistently high, and even on a three-month undersea deployment it never becomes repetitive or unappetising. We know that submariners are well paid, but they deserve every penny. Even so, their living conditions of hot bunking, crammed together like sardines wherever there is space to lay one's head, are much better than we experienced in the Canal Zone.

Fayid was where we bought melons and other fruits to complement our bangers and mash. Not long before I was due to come home there was a window of peace, which lasted a fortnight. Pete Davy, a Londoner from Islington who played a mean double bass, risked his cash to buy a suit fit for the bright lights of the Smoke, where he hoped to launch a professional career in music. He provided the tailor with a photograph from a newspaper showing his requirements, and the only additional intelligence the poor man had to go on was Pete's waist, chest and inside leg measurements. The suit, collected in seven days, would have been a credit to Saville Row. While waiting for some last-minute alterations, we wandered about and found a museum in the town. It had two principal exhibits, one of which was a boat riddled with bullet holes that had been used by someone at some time to cross the Canal on the way to a triumphant victory. It probably commemorated the only time that the Egyptians won anything.

The other exhibit was much more interesting: a genuine mummy. Being in Fayid it was not behind glass. The mummy was within touching range and visitors were actively encouraged to satisfy their curiosity and prod away. The face and hands were waxy, and parts were still swathed in ancient bandages. A notice informed readers that only separate groups of males and females should be within the viewing room at any one time, and the reason soon became apparent. Above the genitals was a little trap door, which when lifted revealed that the cadaver was male and not all that well endowed. It may have disappointed some of the ladies, but it swelled the chest of some of our lads. However, I'm not sure how well they might measure up 4,000 years from now.

It was in Fayid that I discovered I had a yellow streak about a foot wide running down my back. This is not something that one likes to admit to, although some might refer to my cowardly action as one of prudence or even self-preservation. I am still unhappy about it fifty years on. How I came to be in Fayid on my own, unarmed, is lost in the mists of memory. I was walking along a pathway crowded with native pedestrians. There was a Land Rover with a couple of redcaps overseeing the throng, and there may well have been another group of security people at the other end of the pavement. As I strolled past I spotted a very large Egyptian lolling back on a dwarf wall. His European suit sagged open in a provocative display, and tucked into the waistband of his trousers was a Colt .45 automatic pistol. He was obviously set on demonstrating his disregard for the authority of British troops. I did a double-take but walked on as if though had noticed nothing. He might have been an Egyptian plainclothes policeman, but I doubt it.

Hindsight makes me realise that this must have taken place during one of the few peaceful periods of the emergency. He could have been the cheese in a mousetrap

Ancient and modern forms of transport in Egypt. In 1952, a bus like this, with its driver, disappeared completely.

H STANLEY

*Egyptian Military Police were allowed a presence in the Suez Canal Zone
under the terms of the treaty with Britain. We were never quite sure what
they actually did. This pair are on duty outside RAF Fayid.*

designed to lure an unarmed Serviceman
into an ambush, since there were lots of
Egyptians about. Having walked on for a
few yards I retraced my steps and
confirmed, at least to my own satisfaction,
that he was definitely armed. I drew the
attention of the redcaps to the situation.

"What do you expect us to do?" was the
discouraging reply. "There are only two of
us." In vain I pointed out that if they gave
me a weapon there would be three of us.
The MPs were much more interested in

directing foot traffic than engaging in anti-
terrorist activity. The outcome was an
angry altercation between the RAF and the
Army. I was getting nowhere and stormed
off back down the walkway. Fortunately
the Egyptian had gone, because in that
mood I would have challenged him with or
without a rifle, hoping that the two MPs
would be watching my back.

It was very much an anticlimax when I
caught my bus and returned to camp to
bore everyone stiff with the story.

HEAVY HANDS ON TRIAL

The most excited man in camp was our squadron leader, who ran the boxing team and thought he had discovered a new white heavyweight hope

In the good old days when National Service was still part of Service life, skiving was a way of making it all bearable, and it even permeated the consciousness of regulars. You could walk around all day displaying a piece of paper or, even better, a coloured file, and your time was your own.

Daily orders usually contained something or other which had prospects for a good skive. A court-martial was one such opportunity, and even had the blessing of our superiors who probably thought it was a good way of striking fear into our hearts. They could not have been more wrong, and we recognised it for what it was – the ideal way of having an official loaf.

Not that a court-martial was a regular event, even in a big camp like RAF Deversoir with about 2,000 inhabitants. I doubt if we had more than three during my time there. The one that sticks in my mind was to do with assault and battery committed by a rather large airman on a much smaller one. Although at first sight this would seem to be a case of a bully taking advantage, it was nothing of the sort. The victim was, by common consent, a pain in the posterior and long overdue for a good punch in the mouth.

He received this one night in the NAAFI, delivered by the larger man – who did not even rise from his seat – as a warning against annoying him further. Such was the force of the blow that several of the victim's teeth flew in all directions and he had to be taken to the sickbay for urgent dental treatment.

Thus, inevitably, enquiries had to be made. Eventually the larger man appeared on a charge and was duly awarded fourteen days' jankers that barred the miscreant from enjoying the limited delights of the NAAFI. The smaller airman, whose mouth had by now healed, took a delight in riling his former aggressor during this period. Time passed.

On a pay-day evening some weeks later, the pair found themselves seated opposite each other in the NAAFI at a late hour, after a fairly heavy session on the Stella beer. The smaller man, doubtless emboldened by the beer and confident that he had a licence to bait the larger man, became extremely objectionable. His surprise was obvious when he received yet another, much harder, smack in the mouth from the larger man, who again simply leaned over the table.

This time the punchee was unconscious, lost the rest of his teeth, and had a broken jaw into the bargain. The most excited man on the camp was our squadron leader who ran the boxing team and thought he had found a new white hope. If this man could knock other men out from a sedentary position, what could he achieve from an upright one after some elementary instruction in the pugilistic arts? The squadron leader talked of little else but "heavy hands", and fought valiantly if vainly to have the whole incident hushed up so that his prodigy's career would be unsullied by a violent past.

The prosecution did not have free rein at the overcrowded court-martial. The NAAFI had been packed with airman getting rid of their meagre earnings, but strangely no one had actually seen anything. Some thought that someone had fallen down drunk and injured himself, while others attested that the smaller man had unaccountably head-butted the big chap's hand. In any event, the incident was seen as nothing but a pals' tiff. Inevitably, since courts-martial are not overconcerned with facts or indeed justice, a spell in the glasshouse was handed down. Rumour had it that had the accused was presented with a provisional contract – quickly drawn up by our squadron leader – to become a professional boxer when back in Civvy Street, but he was not interested. The story of the reluctant boxer had a sting in its tail however.

The snowdrops were quite unused to having a violent prisoner in the cells and gave him an extremely hard time during his stay. Protected by their stripes, and in a position to throw their weight about, they did just that by ordering him to do menial tasks, and they laid on other unnecessary indignities. On the night before he was due to be taken to the military prison to be punished, something very strange happened. The line of tented police accommodation positioned directly behind the guardroom was flattened by a human hurricane. Mayhem ruled as every head that poked itself up received a blow from the iron fist of an upright, sober and unknown person. Only one copper escaped injury, but the rest of the snowdrops were in a sorry state when seen the next morning after sick parade. The obvious suspect was safely locked up in his cell and regretfully ruled out in subsequent enquiries.

The rumour mill buzzed to the effect that a decent, about-to-retire snowdrop, disgusted by his colleagues' antics, had 'accidentally' left a cell door ajar while nipping off on an errand – and returned in time to relock the door and give his prisoner a cast-iron alibi.

The truth will never be known, but many are convinced that a potential world heavyweight boxing champion slipped through the podgy fingers of our portly but ambitious squadron leader. Lots of us simply enjoyed a good two-day legal skive.

Nurse! Nurse!

When you face misfortune, such as being admitted to hospital, you can tell your real friends by the way they rally round. No one came to see me

The very sand in the Canal Zone was hostile to British Servicemen. Any cut or graze sustained by playing football or simply tripping over would turn septic before you could blink. If the Egyptians had cribbed the secrets of flushing toilets and hot and cold running water from the Romans, theirs would have been a better country today.

As far as the RAF is concerned, airmen are not entitled to go sick without giving due notice to the medical branch. To be classified as ill, you must report to the medical hut carrying a small pack containing a toothbrush and other items needed for a night in a strange bed. Only if you are at death's door will you be transferred to hospital by ambulance. An ex-RAF ambulance is an excellent second-hand purchase as it is likely to have virtually no mileage on the clock.

Normal treatment for every condition is a No 9 tablet. It is a treatment of legendary effectiveness that has kept the British Army on its feet for hundreds of years. "If your bowels move regularly, there can't be much wrong with you," is the answer universally espoused by all military medical men. The reader will notice that I do not use the term doctors, but a vague one of 'military medical men'. They will do almost anything rather than admit a man to the wards, since it ties them down a bit and keeps them off the golf course. I managed to get into hospital two and a half times during my service.

The half-visit hardly counts because it lasted only about an hour. It was suspected that I might be handling food during my time at the Beach Club, so I had to produce a sample stool for testing and present it in the smallest box you ever clapped eyes on. The difficulty of achieving this feat is not suitable reading for a book like this. The result of the visit was the granting of a certificate proving that I was not suffering from the dreaded lurgy, or anything else for that matter.

My second visit was much more serious. I have always been a martyr to influenza and when I get it I am pole-axed. On this occasion it was late at night when the 'flu struck with classic symptoms – dry throat, headache, pouring with sweat but shivering with cold all at the same time. Merely rising, getting dressed and assembling my small pack were chores, and I had no interest in breakfast. If you manage breakfast before sick parade you are malingering. I made it to the queue at the sickbay and waited in misery to see the MO. His assistant was an LAC like myself, and so well qualified to take my temperature. Seconds later, I was tucked up in bed in hospital. I had attained the aim of every airman. Sadly, I hardly remember it, as I slept my stay in hospital away. The MO was clear in his diagnosis. It was definitely a case of malaria.

Four days later my temperature was normal and they chucked me out. The MO was adamant that all I had suffered was a severe dose of influenza. Whatever it was, I had it twice a year for ages afterwards.

It was during my visit that a serious case of flat feet was admitted, though I suppose 'flat feet' is an exaggeration; it was flat foot, singular.

Some airmen are not too bright and one such discovered by accident that if a lorry runs over your foot in desert conditions, it simply pushes it down into the sand and does no actual damage. A cretin who had seen this demonstrated used it as his party piece and had a habit of performing it to new arrivals from home. One day he demonstrated his technique on sand-covered tarmac, and the result was not a pretty sight. The quality of an RAF boot saved him from amputation, but he limped for a long time afterwards.

My next hospital visit was much more newsworthy, as I came out in a head-to-toe rash. Well, not really a rash, more small pustules that made me want to scratch until I bled, and then some. It was going to be good for two weeks of luxury five-star-hotel-style living. I was to be rushed into isolation, but our hospital did not have such a place so I was put in the corner bed of a ward, three bedspaces away from the nearest inmate. No one, especially the medical persons, would come near me. The MO shouted to me across the ward an enquiry as to whether or not I knew what my trouble was. I guessed it was associated with my heavy woollen vest. The Wee Oriental Gentleman who 'did' for the camp was none too fussy where cleanliness was concerned and probably used the Sweet Water Canal for rinsing purposes.

My stay became routine and even boring. Once a day the MO would enter the ward and, staying at a safe distance, would ask how I felt. Twice a day an orderly – masked, gowned and gloved – would approach the bed treating me as if I was radioactive. Using tongs, he would tear off a piece of cotton wool from a large roll of the stuff and then wet it in calamine lotion dispensed from a carboy. Having dabbed a part of my anatomy, he would then discard the cotton wool into a bin for burning. We got through a considerable amount of wool and lotion this way and

although it did bring instant relief, it was shortlived. Three times a day I was served with a meal, but my plate, knife, fork and spoon were treated as special and kept well apart from those used by the others. After a few days, I was able to play cards using my own individual pack. Someone would deal, and my card hand would be held up to me so that I could select the same cards from my own pack. This interaction with my fellow-sufferers kept me sane, a statement that might be disputed by my billet and workmates at Deversoir equipment section.

When you face a misfortune like being taken to hospital you can tell who your real friends are by the way they rally round to visit you and bring you gifts. No one came to see me.

Once the pustules had subsided to ordinary spots and then to angry red marks I felt fine and was enjoying the luxury of the place. On his next visit the MO carried in my offending vest in tongs. "Wear this tonight in bed and we'll see if it flares up again," he said. "I have to admit, it's got me beat."

That night, just before lights out, an orderly passed me the vest and supervised me putting in on under my pyjamas. He used a set of tongs to do this and stayed at a safe distance. Immediately after lights-out, I took it off. I was not going through that torture again for anyone if I could help it. When the orderly on the next shift watched me remove my hastily donned vest first thing in the morning, I was clear of spots. It ended my holiday, but in any case I was becoming bored and a little lonely being in my exclusive corner.

I had to see the doc before being discharged, and he wondered aloud if he had discovered something worth a letter to The Lancet. He told me to return at once if I felt anything peculiar happening to me. His knowledge impressed me no end when he supposed it was "probably just one of those things".

Delivered from a safe distance, his parting remark proved that he was still on the ball.

"Bowels okay, old man?"

S SMITH

*I was never lucky enough to be taken to a proper hospital like this one,
to be treated by Princes Marina's wonderful lady nurses. My illnesses
were dealt with on our camp by amateur, but enthusiastic, orderlies.*

EGYPT CALLING

*No guard duty, no parades, no sign of an officer
in command. This sounded like a job for me, even
if it meant sharing a tent with Simon and Nigel*

I was bored rigid, cheesed off, fed up to the back teeth with the never-ending routine of office work. Active service brought few rewards, and the punishments awarded for what might be seen as mere misdemeanours in the UK were severe. Fall asleep on guard duty and you were straight into the glass-house without passing Go. And rightly so, as lives were at stake. People were being shot dead, often by their own colleagues. Somehow, the RAF never quite got the hang of clearing their weapons when coming off stag. It was a regular offence for a loaded rifle, with one 'up the spout', to be left leaning against the wall of the guardroom while we slept. If it fell or was kicked over by someone deep in slumber, the result was a very loud bang. If you heard it, you were probably okay. If you didn't, you were probably dead.

The troubles were serious enough for us to be permanently confined to camp. Although I have never been in a jail, I imagine that conditions in an open prison in the UK would have been preferable to our state. The food would have been better for a start, and the flush toilets that we dreamed about a reality.

Even rain would have been welcome. As people do, we vowed that when it eventually fell we would luxuriate in it and enjoy the freshness of it. But in the event of even the slightest shower, we always ran like chickens for shelter. We worked in the morning, slept in the afternoon, and if not rostered for guard duty, bored each other silly in the evening. We repeated incidents from our lives that we

had told and retold ad infinitum. The NAAFI was gloomy and virtually out of bounds to those of us who spent our fortnightly wage in one afternoon of riotous living. The following thirteen days were spent looking forward to the next blow-out.

Things were so bad that when I started to attend evening art classes I produced dark and sombre paintings. I had discovered it was possible to qualify for a correspondence course with a college in the UK and that all costs would be borne by a grateful RAF Education corps. I believe I was the only person ever to achieve this distinction. To qualify and prove I could study under desert conditions, I was obliged to pass university entrance examinations in English and Modern History. This took so long to arrange that by the time my correspondence course came through I had only a couple of months left to serve. This stands as another classic example of forward planning by the best brains in the Royal Air Force.

One glorious morning I read this small ad in station orders: "Scriptwriters/announcers required for local duty with the Overseas Forces Broadcasting Service."

It gave details on how to apply, so in my first off-duty moment that very afternoon I sat down at the typewriter in a deserted office and waited for the muse to strike. Eventually I dashed off a short script for a limited number of voices which, I convinced myself, had great promise. I enclosed a letter of application and waited. If nothing else, I knew that I had a face suited to radio broadcasting. God be praised, a letter arrived inviting me to attend an interview at their studios near Ismailia. My imagination clicked into overdrive. A studio! No doubt there would be a comfortable green room furnished with ice and a cocktail cabinet and possibly air conditioning? I would give Cliff Michelmore a run for his money. Transport was arranged, somewhat reluctantly, and I set off full of excitement.

The studios were a cluster of small tents miles from anywhere in the outer reaches of the Moascar Garrison. Two characters who could have been the inspiration for Julian and Sandy in the radio show Round The Horne welcomed me. They wore identical cravats, long-sleeved jackets turned up at the cuffs, matching suede desert boots and no military symbols. Hanging on a hook was a jacket sporting corporal's stripes, so I assumed that in the real world they were mere mortals. They invited me to address them by their first names, Nigel and Simon. From time to time they addressed a pair of legs glimpsed in an adjoining tent the lower section of which had been rolled up to allow verbal exchanges. Their owner's name sounded like Tarquin, so they were obviously three of a kind.

My opened correspondence was lying on a desk, and Simon pulled out my attempt at a script, glanced at it, and announced: "It's not the sort of thing we use, is it, Nigel?"

Nigel, who seemed to have no idea of what it was all about, enthusiastically agreed: "No, no. Not the sort of thing we use at all."

"Anyway," Simon said, "we'll give you a test."

I was invited to sit at a radio console fitted with a microphone, and was handed a sheet of paper while Nigel and Simon retreated to the far side of the tent and donned earphones to listen to my effort. I started to protest that I had a desire only to be a scriptwriter and not an announcer, but Nigel cut me short.

"We have to do everything for ourselves here. Isn't that correct, Simon?" I was not sure whether he had said "here" or "dear" and felt a little bit uncomfortable.

Simon agreed, of course, and went on to say how arduous the work was – "Sometimes it's after midnight before we finish!"

No guard duty, no parades, no sign of even a junior officer in command. Imagine having to work only from 8pm to midnight providing links to radio programmes from the UK. This sounded like a job made in heaven – a job I now decided I really wanted, even if it meant sharing a tent with Simon and Nigel.

But of course there was the test. I looked at the paper to discover that it was simply a long list of tricky names. I found Kirkcudbright, Kirkcaldy, Llangollen, Dun Laoghaire and a few other obvious tongue-twisters easy. Some were trickier. Cholmondly, Mainwairing, and the Scottish pronunciation of Menzies caused a difference of opinion. I was trying to show I was very butch and interested in arranging programmes for any Jocks out there. Jimmy Shand, Harry Lauder and other 'och aye the noo' performers were under-represented on the airwaves, I argued. To my surprise, they seemed impressed – even by my test efforts.

"How long have you got left to serve out here?" one of them asked.

"Eleven months," I said, and they gasped.

"It'll take a year to get rid of your Scottish accent!"

My face must have betrayed my thoughts. Surely there was an opening for a Scots voice? But I was ahead of my time; it would be 1972 before Auntie began to tolerate regional accents.

"Out of the question," said Nigel and Simon.

At the end of my interview they said they would let me know when they had talked about my ideas with 'higher-ups'. If by 'higher-ups' they meant Tarquin, his legs were giving nothing away. And naturally, I heard nothing more from them.

Of the next fifty years, I spent thirty-nine living in England and being understood everywhere. If Simon and Nigel read this – I still have my Scottish accent.

These photographs were taken at the Forces Broadcasting Station in Fayid, which was mainly a music station but also held inter-Service quizzes.
Above: Presenters and production team at work in the studio.
Below: the REME Workshops quiz team with two of the station's presenters.

BATTLE OF THE BUREAU SANITAIRE

It was a big flap. We were expecting an attack. But the weapons we drew were never fired. Not far away the Lancashire Fusiliers were fighting and dying

To be wakened from sound slumber in the middle of the night is bad enough, but to find that all 2,000-plus personnel on the camp have been similarly treated is disturbing to say the least. I woke to find lights on everywhere, the Tannoy blaring out confusing messages, Land Rovers and lorries buzzing about, and even our Vampire fighters warming up. The airfield was under attack!

No sergeants brought us a nice cup of tea that morning, and we dressed hurriedly before being formed up and then doubled to the armoury to draw our trusty .303s. Unfortunately, hundreds of others had got the same instructions and, in scenes reminiscent of Dunkirk's beaches, lines of men stretched out in long queues in every direction. The issue of ammunition confirmed that the balloon had gone up. We were issued with fifty rounds each instead of the usual ten.

An officer then appeared, clutching some secret plans of the airfield, and we stores personnel were directed to some imaginary trenches sited near the perimeter wire. The trenches were marked on the plan but no one had actually got round to digging them. As equipment bods, the answer was simple for us: open up the stores and issue shovels, sand for the digging of, but no one in authority thought of it so nothing was done.

The heroic RAF Regiment were specially trained in airfield defence and they were clustered in a tight circle manning their ack-ack guns in the dead centre of the camp. They would defend the skies, and if the Egyptians should manage to break through into the camp they would have plenty of warning.

Digging by hand in the soft sand seemed to be a simple matter and the first few inches of depth easily achieved. Thereafter, the sand took the side of the Arabs and fell back in as fast as we threw it out, so we eventually abandoned the futile effort although not before we had built a pile big enough to hide behind. After that, we sat around smoking and yarning until dawn broke.

The rumour mill had been working overtime all night long and it was reported as fact that an Egyptian army, led by tanks, was fast approaching the airfield. Once we were out of commission our air superiority would be lost and Egypt would have a field day, so the airfield had to be held at all costs. As far as we knew, no proper preparation had been made for this eventuality, but the drawings looked great and a defensive strategy had obviously been discussed very late at night in the officers' mess.

Our fighters took off and returned, but no reports of them opening fire filtered through to us, and any excitement we had felt soon evaporated. At long last we were ordered back to the armoury to hand in our weapons, following a battle in which we had not fired a shot. It was time for breakfast, and then straight to work – quite unaware that not far away, at the Bureau Sanitaire and nearby police station in Ismailia, the night had been much more eventful. We knew nothing of other conflicts until letters from home, enclosing newspaper cutttings and photographs, arrived from worried families. The Lancashire Fusiliers in particular had had a very rough time of it, fighting and dying while we were enjoying our late breakfasts.

Propaganda stated that only regular troops were engaged, but National Servicemen were in fact among the ranks too, and they were killed alongside their regular comrades. The same source stated that the British lost four dead with thirteen injured, while the Egyptians lost forty-one dead, with seventy-three wounded and 886 taken prisoner. The British death toll included – in today's terminology – 'blue on blue' deaths.

It seems certain that the Egyptian police had been infiltrated and reinforced by scores of crack Egyptian troops – if that is not a contradiction in terms – and clearly these were very brave men. Perhaps 'fanatical' might be a more accurate description of them, because when they found themselves outgunned, they fought on. It must have come as quite a shock to them to discover that tackling British soldiers who could fire back was a whole new ball game compared to the killing of unarmed civilians and off-duty troops.

In the weeks leading up to this incident sniper fire and other guerilla tactics had killed thirty-three British soldiers. In a typical incident, two redcaps had called at the police station on police business aboard their Land Rover. They were cordially invited to drive into the premises then ruthlessly shot dead.

Only a week or so before this stunning

The metal-muscle behind the British presence in the Canal Zone. Cromwell tank and Sexton SP gun at Waterloo Camp, Fayid, 1951.

N GOOD

RAF Regiment gun drill at Deversoir, with the station cinema in the background. They practised regularly and assiduously but never fired a single round in anger.

event, another horrific incident had at long last sent shock waves through the high command. General Sir George Erskine, who was in overall charge of the Canal Zone, finally lost his temper and forced the politicians at home to agree that he should act. In a mealy-mouthed way they agreed, but being anxious to avoid offending the Egyptian Government they laid down the condition that British troops should try at all

costs to avoid conflict while attempting to disarm Egyptian forces. The battle lines were drawn: 600 so-called auxiliaries of the Egyptian Army were defending the Bureau Sanitaire, with a further 340 manning the police headquarters, backed up by sixty regular policemen-fanatics.

At dawn on 25 January 1952, our troops moved in. In typical British fashion, loudspeaker appeals were directed at the Egyptians asking them to surrender and give up their arsenal of weapons. As each broadcast was made the reply in gunfire became fiercer, and at 09.00 the British were forced to launch their attack. Two companies of the Lancashire Fusiliers aided by three 50-ton Centurion tanks and fifteen armoured cars, plus a company of parachutists, attacked the Bureau Sanitaire. A company of Lancashire Fusiliers, supported by three tanks and three armoured cars, made a dash for the police headquarters.

It is hardly surprising that, faced with 600 well-dug-in troops, the first assault on the western wall of the Bureau was forced back under heavy rifle fire. Most of the accurate fire was coming from the roof where blue-coated Egyptian policemen – probably the crack troops of legend – were positioned. The Lancashire Fusiliers secured the roof of an adjacent and taller building, where Bren guns soon eliminated the opposition. This basic military tactic accounted for most of the Egyptian dead. Meanwhile, Centurion tank fire punched holes in the north wall to admit the armoured cars and infantry, and by 10.30am the auxiliaries who formed the defence began to weaken.

At the police headquarters the captain in charge defiantly shouted that he and his men would rather die than surrender. But when he got news of what was happening at the Bureau Sanitaire, and realised that he would undoubtedly be granted his wish if he persisted in his defiance, he changed his mind.

This incident was not big enough to be described as an act of war, but it was much more serious than a policing action. It caused riots in Cairo and great consternation in the British Parliament. The wireless operator's log giving details of the various actions that took place can be examined in the chapter EYE IN THE SKY later in this book.

J I JONES

Valettas of 204 Squadron from RAF Fayid flying over the Suez Canal on 5 September 1951. This was the only time all eight aircraft were airborne together (the eighth contains the CO photographing the others).

RESTING IN A FOREIGN FIELD

Although it was an arduous and often unpleasant duty,
and mostly we hadn't known the deceased, we understood
that being part of a Guard of Honour was a privilege

I am told that the military cemetery in Fayid is a credit to those who look after it. I hope this may bring some solace to those whose sons, husbands or loved ones lie there. As a press-ganged member of the Guard of Honour for MEAF Deversoir I became all too familiar with the cemetery. At that time the graveyard where we buried our dead was quite undeveloped, at the far side of the present cemetery. We would slow-march, with arms linked and coffin on shoulders, from the main gate to the last resting place of the unfortunate bloke in the box.

Most deaths were the result of enemy actions ranging from cowardly assassinations of unarmed women and their families to the random killing of solitary Service personnel – a regular target. Mines, booby-traps and wires strung across roads to decapitate dispatch riders or Land Rover crews were old favourites. Opportunist actions like firing on convoys from the safe haven of occupied flats, while British troops were forbidden to fire back, were frequent. On the few occasions the Egyptians tried open military confrontation, they inevitably seemed to come off second best. When young and inexperienced British Army drivers were killed by being run off the roads by Egyptian lorries and buses their deaths were recorded as resulting from traffic accidents.

A great number of genuinely accidental deaths occurred too, and many could have been avoided if rules had been enforced. I had been at Deversoir for just over a week when I saw my first dead men – ten of them. They were killed when a 15-cwt truck overturned a few hundred yards from the guardroom on the main road outside the camp. I was on guard duty but off stag when we were turned out at the double to give what help we could. It was too late. When dim torches were flashed over the faces of the casualties trapped under the truck it was noticed that all their faces were black. Someone with medical knowledge suggested this might be because when a heavy weight is placed on a person's chest the face turns purple. We tried in vain to lift the lorry manually but the task was completely beyond our frenzied efforts. There were no survivors, and even those who had been thrown clear and landed on the relatively soft sand of the roadside were dead.

We learned later that the victims were eight privates from the East African Pioneer Corps, a British private and a major on their way back to barracks from a work detail. We were surprised that although it had taken us just ten minutes to rise from slumber and run to the scene not a single man had survived. No other vehicle was involved and we surmised that the driver must have fallen asleep, letting the vehicle run off the road so that it flipped when a wheel hit the sand.

For fifty years I believed this was a road accident, but the MoD has now officially admitted that the incident was the result of an ambush. In the time it took us to get to the site the terrorists must have murdered any survivors. Our torches were dim and there

S J I SMITH

Fayid Military Cemetery as it was in 1952. Sadly, most of the graves contain the bodies of Servicemen who never reached their twenty-first birthday.

was a lot of blood about. It was only when the bodies were examined later that the evidence came to light. More than eighty members of the African Pioneer Corps died serving in Egypt, which strikes me as disproportionate. Their death rate was twice as high as that suffered by the most vulnerable British unit, the Royal Army Service Corps.

Most deaths in our camp were caused by accidental discharge of a weapon but we did have a couple of cases of deliberate shooting and our share of suicides to add to those that came from natural causes. One natural death was a new posting, whose reputation for prowess as a soccer player preceded his arrival, and of whom great things were expected. Playing at centre-half, he was over six feet tall and broad with it. After a couple

of weeks to acclimatise to the heat he turned out for a game against the Grenadier Guards. He was the only member of our team who measured up to them, and the rest of our players looked like David to their Goliath.

There was an unusually large crowd there to witness his debut, as we were out to 'stuff' the Grenadiers, who were unpopular because they had a tendency to shove their way to the front of the NAAFI queues. They acted as a mob, while we were a group of individuals. To see the Grenadiers get a public humiliation on the soccer pitch would have been sweet, but our potential star proved to be a washout. Two yards slower than anyone on the pitch, he was brushed aside in every challenge. It surprised no one when he was substituted early in the second

CANAL ZONERS

Fayid Cemetery today. A place of pilgrimage for many Servicemen.

half. I happened to be near enough hear his excuses: "I couldn't get going and felt really drained. It must be the heat, or maybe I've got a bug. I'll need to see the MO." None of us believed him, thinking that he was just a duff player who had chatted up his prospects. Two weeks later, he was dead.

The MO had carried out a blood test and discovered that he was at an advanced stage of leukaemia, so it was little wonder really that he couldn't get going. We ate our words, and realised that he had been a bit of a hero. He must have driven himself beyond reasonable limits to turn out on the football field at all. It also raised doubts about the thoroughness of pre-embarcation medical examinations.

For the guard of honour, a murder or

sudden death from an unknown cause was bad news. A post-mortem examination had to be held, and a lead-lined coffin provided in case the body had to be re-examined at a future date. If the deceased was big and heavy it added to our problems, and the final straw for us was if he happened to be of the Roman Catholic faith because the local priest was known to be fond of his own voice and long services.

The pattern was always much the same. The lead lined coffins were badly made, with the lid never an exact fit – which left gaps between the screw fittings. Our Land Rover or 1500-weight truck hauled the coffin to the cemetery on a flatbed trailer at high speed to reduce the risk of attack. The Union flag, which should have reverentially draped the casket, flapped like a freshly laundered sheet on a clothes-line as we hurtled along the pot-holed roads. This rough treatment may have contributed to the state of the boxes when we unloaded them. Refrigeration was an unheard-of luxury and storage facilities for bodies were so poor that they deteriorated quickly in the heat.

Arriving at the cemetery gate we would dismount from our transport, buff up our shoes on the backs of our socks, and fall in line to pick up the coffin. It was usually mid-morning and very hot, and once we had been kept standing for a considerable time holding the body aloft we would become aware of unpleasant odours emanating from within. Bluebottles and flies have a keener sense of smell than us, and they arrived in squadrons. They would shuffle through the gaps, then re-emerge without wiping their feet. Their first port of call was our faces. Our hands were fully occupied and there was nothing we could do to shake them off, apart from blowing at them through the sides of our mouths.

The priest afforded some light relief as he bore a striking resemblance to Old Mother Riley and wore his biretta at a very jaunty angle. His cassock and other finery looked like an old-fashioned dress and did nothing for

B B DAY

The grave of Sister Anthony in Ismailia Cemetery, 20 January 1952. She was murdered by Egyptian terrorists because she taught British children. There are further details of this incident in the Roll of Honour in Part Three.

splashing the stuff everywhere and leaving our faces dripping wet. Just as we were drying off nicely, a second spray would arrive over the top of the coffin from the other side. All this would take a full ten minutes while the coffin seemed to became heavier and heavier, and our weakening knees shakier and shakier.

These formalities completed, he would set off at a very slow meander, swinging his smoking handbag again and chanting in slow time as we followed. The usual burial party consisted of six men, and every ounce of strength was needed. The walk to the graveside could be 300 yards or more, with us slow-marching to attention, our knees now and then buckling, and our shoulders screaming out for relief from the sharp edges of the coffin which cut into them. Carrying a burden of nearly 3cwt in a smooth and level manner is no easy task.

Sometimes we knew the deceased; mostly we did not, but we always understood that it was a great privilege for us to provide this last duty for a fellow serviceman. Each year on 11 November, I remember those I had the honour to carry.

Finding something to smile about was our way of lightening the gloom, and did not reflect our lack of concern for the deceased. The Services have a system designed to keep even the dead in their allotted place, so we only buried other ranks. Men of equivalent rank carried NCOs, and a sergeant major was entitled to the whole bit – an entire company would turn out for him. I presume

him since they were much too short. His skinny legs, and toes that pointed inwards, gave him a comical air as he walked. His sincerity was unquestioned. He was thorough, and even with a sparse congregation like us he would milk the occasion for all it was worth. The only bit he missed out, thankfully, was the collection.

His incense burner – which poured out acrid smoke – mercifully helped to combat the flies, although the smoke also enveloped us and he would wander around muttering incantations and waving the burner until it literally began to hurt. With our eyes stinging and our noses twitching, we must have appeared to any onlookers to be genuine mourners instead of pressed men.

The priest was a dab hand with the holy water, and used plenty of it. No doubt the water was meant to benefit the deceased, but he would walk down one side of the coffin the ceremony is the same for officers. At the end of the service we would stand to attention in front of the open grave as a volley of three shots was fired in close proximity to our ears. This would render us completely deaf, and our hearing would only return as we neared our base half an hour later. However, the War Pensions Department takes a dim view of an application for a pension claimed for deafness on these grounds, as I can personally verify.

Depending on the period you choose, the casualty figures can vary; but hundreds lie in Egypt. Graves of service personnel, families and support staff can all be found in the Canal Zone; and every story is a sad one.

At the infamous Battle of the Police Station in Ismailia in 1952, a National Serviceman earning less than £2 a week crouched behind a wall to recover his breath, and a 50-ton British tank reversed through the wall and killed him. Two commissioned officers and two redcaps were killed in separate incidents in the lead-up to the actual fighting that day.

It is now galling to think that any British Government would tamely hand over the Suez Canal to the Egyptians on orders from the USA. Perhaps it was this political humiliation that has made successive governments want to forget about the thousands of Servicemen who suffered hardship and deprivation simply doing their job. I believe that, had the politicians shown just a fraction of the grit and determination required of those they sent to do their dirty work, the outcome could have been very different.

It is food for thought to remember that more than twice as many people died in Egypt as in the Falklands conflict. Whatever the cause of death, every victim deserves to be honoured and remembered.

P ANDREWS

*The 32 Squadron Vampires based at RAF Deversoir
which took part in a Coronation Day fly-past in 1952.*

W L S LANE

*16 Parachute Brigade beating retreat at Jenefa Camp on Coronation Day.
Bill Lane, of Tavistock, Devon, who served with 33 Parachute Light Regiment
Royal Artillery in Jenefa and then in El Balah Camp, provided the picture.*

ONE OF OUR AIRCRAFT IS MISSING

*It was a plane mistake when the 'R' in the fly-past
to greet the new Queen became a 'P'. Surely it was
a bit much to blame a certain 'erk in the stores*

One of our aircraft is missing." A portly and extremely irate desk-flying Squadron Leader in the Equipment Accounts Office at MEAF Deversoir delivered the sombre words, not in the measured tones of John Arlott or John Snagg in a wartime BBC broadcast to the nation, but loudly in 1952 in sunny Egypt. His face was reddening to a deep, life-threatening purple as he screamed his announcement. Finishing on a note well above high C, he concluded in an ominous hiss: "And I want to know the reason why."

Everyone in the office was suddenly very busy. The Warrant Officer, eighteen months from pension, gave a gentle cough before discreetly disappearing into his office-cum-retirement-waiting room. Simultaneously, the Halton-trained boy-entrant corporal, who knew the answer to everything, shot out of the door to lurk beside the clay water jar on the veranda. Everyone else bent their heads low over their ledgers. Old Ebeneezer Scrooge would have warmed to their apparent industry. Our fat controller, usually such a benign man, was now a raging doolally cross between captains Bligh and Queeg. He swept the room with blazing eyes until they focused on me. The buck was going to be passed in no uncertain manner. Perhaps a few words of explanation at this point would help the reader grasp the situation.

The new Queen was about to be crowned, and for some there was great excitement in the air. Due to the impending coronation our workload had increased. There was much to do. A Serviceman from every base in the world had to be sent to London to line the proposed route of the procession. We all envied the lucky lad chosen from our camp – until he returned and booked himself straight into the sick bay. There, several penicillin injections were administered to his backside through a huge syringe with a long needle. That would teach him where and when to find romance.

Displays of a military kind were arranged everywhere in the mistaken belief that Her Majesty's loyal troops enjoyed extra bull. Someone somewhere thought it would be a bright idea to arrange a fly-past by the Vampire fighters from Deversoir. A casual enquiry as to the number of operational aircraft available was answered by a glance at the ledger in our office. You might ask: why didn't someone simply count them?

Anyway, twenty-two intrepid birdmen would form the letters 'E II R' and everyone would think it a wonderful wheeze, followed by "Jolly good show. Pink gins all round."

I, for one, thought the Queen had a cheek to style herself as Elizabeth the Second since we in Scotland had never had an Elizabeth the First. As usual, no one asked for my thoughts, although perhaps my occasionally-expressed opinion explains the delay in the receipt of my knighthood.

We never found out where the fly-past took

The cover of a Coronation Day programme.

The Coronation Day menu from RAF Fayid.

Coronation Menu

Breakfast
0800 - 0900 hrs

Porridge — Milk
Cornflakes — Milk
Grapefruit
Fried Ham
Fried Eggs
Grilled Tomatoes

Dinner
1230 - 1330 hrs

Cream of Tomato Soup
Roast Turkey — Cranberry Sauce
Roast Pork — Apple Sauce
Force Meat Stuffing
Sage — Onion Stuffing
Macedoine Vegetables
Cauliflower — Mornay Sauce
Dauphine Potatoes
Anglais Potatoes
Giblet Gravy
Tinned Fruit Salad — Custard Cream
Cheese — Biscuits
Tea — Coffee — Lemonade — Bread — Butter

High Tea
1730 - 1930 hrs

Creme St. Germain
Cold Boiled Ham
Cold Roast Silloin Beef
Shredded Lettuce
Marinate Beetrots
Sliced Tomatoes
Chipped Potatoes — Bottled Sauce
Tinned Fruit Salad — Custard Cream
Fresh Fruit
Tea — Jam — Butter — Bread Rolls
Assorted Gateaux

R JOHNSTON

place, but a question was asked in the House as to why the RAF thought 'E II P' was a suitable tribute to the new Queen. At a push they could have changed it to 'E + P', as Eddie and Pauline might decorate their Fiesta's windscreen, and all would have been well.

Anyway, a buck had started moving. The spokesman for the Air Ministry failed to provide a satisfactory answer in Parliament and the parcel was passed, inexorably and inevitably, downward. In due time it landed in my lap.

In vain I pointed out that if it had been a missing screwdriver there would have been no such furore, although the stocks of both items are kept in identical ledgers. In fact, the system's designers obviously had so little faith in its operators that they included a cross-reference check at the bottom of each page to make it leading aircraftsman-proof.

I thought that everyone, especially the apoplectic Squadron Leader, was being unreasonable. Surely the fault lay with the pilots who did not have the wit to realise that

a 'P' is not an 'R'. Just what all the fuss was about was all beyond me.

"YOU," shouted the two-and-a-half-ringer, "ARE A LEADING AIRCRAFTSMAN AND SHOULD NOT MAKE MISTAKES!"

This was his final word before going off for a good lie-down to recover from his exertions. I feel it was at that moment that any chance of my ever gaining corporal's stripes went right out the window. My goose was well and truly cooked. The nature of the crime was so heinous that I would be required to appear before the station commander to answer the charges.

The Group Captain had no sense of humour or proportion, but he did sympathise to some extent. It was out of the question for him to fail to support his drinking companion. "You are unique, Findlay," he assured me. "In all my years of service I've never seen a 252 issued by a Squadron Leader before. I think I'll have it framed."

I was the one who was framed, but fourteen days' jankers soon passes. As they say, if you can't take a joke, you shouldn't join.

In the centre of this picture is my nemesis, Squadron Leader Farley. We never saw eye-to-eye on how the Air Force should be run. Here he is seen applauding as the CO's wife, Mrs Philpott, presents the station cup to Terry Taylor, captain of the equipment section's football team.

T TAYLOR

THE HANGMAN FLIES IN

*A Royal Signals truck was parked close by the
execution shed. But no message arrived from
the Home Secretary to stay Pierrepoint's hand*

On 17 April 1950, Gunners John Goldby and Robert Smith, together with Driver Edward Hensmann, RASC, who were all from Fayid, decided that life was dull and that they would see what delights Cairo had to offer. They armed themselves with Service revolvers and ammunition, borrowed a Land Rover for transportation, but they wore civilian clothing as posted orders decreed for visits outside the Canal Zone. Before they set out they sold various items of Army equipment to finance the expedition.

By nightfall they were broke and their Jeep had disappeared. It was agreed that they in turn would pinch a car to take them back to their unit, where they would face the music. They located a garage but a night watchman-cum-taxi-driver guarded it. They agreed that Hensmann would knock him out and restrain, him while the other two selected a car with sufficient petrol in its tank to get them back to the Canal Zone. The watchman saw them coming and went outside to greet them. Hensmann then tried to force him into the garage office but he, either a resolute fellow or scared rigid, would not or could not move. A gun was pushed into his back to encourage him, and unfortunately it went off. As the taxi driver staggered into the street, Hensmann shot him through the head. Goldby and Smith later claimed they did not witness the shooting, as they were inside the garage attempting to start a vehicle.

They fled the scene on foot, and sold two of the revolvers to finance the purchase of a car to be used for the return to camp. They made a getaway, and although there was some suggestion of the involvement of the Egyptian police, they were eventually arrested in a cinema in Ismailia, no doubt due to the tracing of their car purchase.

Although Hensmann had pulled the trigger, the prosecution claimed that they were all equally culpable for the offences of attempted robbery with violence and murder. The prosecutor, Lt-Col R S Gulliver, made the case that since Goldby and Smith knew that Hensmann was intent on using force to achieve their ends they were equally guilty in law. He regretted that the Egyptian authorities would not co-operate with the British Military Police and that his case was therefore incomplete. This today would be enough to have the murder charge dismissed, but not at that time. After a three-day trial all three were found guilty of murder and sentenced to death.

Albert Pierrepoint, in the garb of a full colonel, was flown out from England to carry out the sentence. He changed into civilian clothing on arrival and was introduced throughout his stay as Mr Clough, although it was common knowledge as to who he really was. The night before the hangings, he spent a convivial evening in a sergeants' mess where he signed autographs.

The gallows were erected in an old disused railway repair shop warehouse close to Fayid village. A gallows was constructed to hang all

The locomotive inspection shed, which housed the hanging pit at Fanara.

W WARREN

three prisoners at once and the executions were carried out at 7am on 31 August 1950.

Just before Pierrepoint, the hangman, pinioned their arms behind their backs, he said to the three that he was breaking with tradition and offered to shake hands with all three because they were soldiers and there were no hard feelings on his part – he was just doing his job. The first two accepted his hand, but Hensmann push it away and said: "I'll come back and haunt you, you bastard."

Pierrepoint's replied: "To do that, son, you'll have to get in the f*****g queue."

Four members of the Egyptian Ministry of Justice witnessed the ceremony and some high-ranking officers of the British Army. Rumour had it that the Egyptians attended to ensure that the executions were actually carried out. This was yet another example of the Foreign Office bending over backwards to appease the Egyptian Government, who had demanded that the death penalty be awarded. Three British deaths for one Egyptian death seemed quite acceptable to them. Within an hour of conducting his gruesome task, hangman Pierrepoint was flying home from Fayid. Some suggested that his actions had been unlawful as he was not authorised by the Egyptian authorities to act as a hangman in Egypt. If this was true, he could have been charged with murder.

It has been widely reported by those who attended the court martial that no one thought that Goldby and Smith would be sentenced to death due to the circumstances of the crime. Hensmann's body is buried at a different angle to all the others in the graveyard. Goldby and Smith lie buried in the usual manner, which presumably indicates something of the thoughts of those in authority.

Another grave that lies at an odd angle is that of Corporal Tom Houghton in Moascar cemetery. He was convicted and judicially hanged for the murder of two regimental comrades, Captain Herbert Walter Mason and Corporal F J Carter, during the evening of a supply depot dance in March 1952.

Captain Mason had been dancing with Iro Hadjifoti, a twenty-year-old considered by Corporal Houghton to be his girlfriend, and Houghton created a scene and was required to leave the dance. he stormed through the camp recklessly firing a Sten gun. Hearing the gunfire, Captain Mason accompanied by the duty corporal, W. Carter, went to investigate and Houghton shot them both down. Seven bullets were found in the body of Captain Mason. Houghton later claimed that Captain Mason had ordered him not to keep company with the girl.

Rose Heilbron QC was flown out to prosecute the case. Percy Grieve, the defence counsel, told the court that Houghton was a "decent man" who had suddenly lost all control and that it was clearly a crime of passion. He had suffered delusions about his supposed relationship with Miss Hadjifoti. The Army psychiatrist gave evidence that Houghton was either mad or in a jealous rage when he committed the murders. He was found guilty and sentenced to death.

Curiously enough, Corporal Houghton seems to have been reduced to the ranks as an additional punishment before being hanged, because his grave is marked as that of a private. He was the last British Serviceman to be hanged in Egypt. Albert Pierrepoint, the public hangman, again officiated.

An eye-witness reports that when Houghton, who had been held in solitary confinement within the prison, boarded the vehicle for the 200-yard journey to his date with Mr Pierrepoint, he did so without assistance and with a firm step as if he was simply boarding a bus for a routine run to town. The RAMC were in attendance, and it is thought that something may have been administered to him to help him through his

W WARREN

The hanging pit used in the executions of Hensmann, Smith and Goldby.

ordeal. A Royal Signals radio truck was parked close to the shed in case a last minute reprieve was received from the Home Secretary in London. No such merciful message arrived.

Following each of the hangings, the bodies were handed over to Royal Military Police for burial in Moascar cemetery.

The tariff for murder clearly varied in line with the attitude of the Foreign Office at that time. At a later date, a soldier and an aircraftsman murdered an unarmed Egyptian police officer in Fayid, following a drinking binge. They were promptly removed to Britain where a court martial awarded them a mere six years' imprisonment.

Dear John

With no telephone and letters taking a fortnight,
the RAf had an enlightened system to cope with
bad news. We all need to use it at some point

In Beau Geste, P C Wren describes the high incidence of 'sand and sun madness' among French Foreign Legionnaires after they had spent extended periods in the scorching African interior. The same thing seemed to happen to us. There was a general acceptance of unreasonable behaviour which, if not actually classifiable as madness, must have come close.

Take the case of the airman determined to get sent home to Blighty. Having washed one foot in a strong antiseptic solution and dressed it in a single new sock, he placed his foot in a brand new unlaced boot; then shot himself in the foot. But he did this metaphorically as well as physically, because once his foot (minus a toe) had healed, there was no question of being sent home. The story of his meticulous preparations had become common knowledge throughout the camp, and the powers-that-be decided such courage and resourcefulness should be rewarded. He was duly promoted to corporal. They were clearly as daft as he was. He was henceforth known as Hopalong, but limped out the rest of his tour quite happily.

Another airman, a former jockey, stated forcefully and loudly in the course of a heated debate with a much larger colleague that the only way to settle the issue was for him to shoot his bigger, more eloquent adversary. So he picked up his rifle and did just that. The man died as a result of the shot. The tariff was seven years, if memory serves me right, and no doubt it would be served in a civilian

nick in the UK. Not exactly a recommended route home. Less drastic, but equally bizarre, were the actions of the group who thought it would be a hoot to put some chairs and tables – complete with parasols – on the apex of the NAAFI roof. Each of the three men guarding the NAAFI that night was given a spell on jankers for failing to detect the incident or capture the culprits who, needless to say, were never found.

In the opinion of many, the maddest of all was a strange chap who lived a solitary life in a one-man tent alongside a piece of essential equipment only he could operate. Once his two-and-a-half-year sojourn was over he was sent home. Six weeks later he was back living in his little tent for another tour of duty. He was definitely strange, but looking back I believe we were all a little abnormal in the way we behaved. Stress plays tricks on the mind, although those suffering from it may be genuinely unaware of this.

When anyone had a domestic crisis – most frequent among married men – the problem was magnified by distance. We had taken two weeks to get to Egypt and it took letters ten days to a fortnight to make the journey in either direction. This meant that the first inkling of domestic trouble was two weeks old before the unfortunate airman found out, and it would be nearer a month before his reaction would get back to complete the exchange. Fifty years ago international telephone calls were out of the question for people like us. Jet travel today means that you can breakfast in London, lunch in Cairo and be home in the UK again for high tea. In those days we felt isolated, and depended on letters from home to bring good news.

Over the years, the RAF had worked out an enlightened policy to deal with the recipient of a 'Dear John' letter. He only needed to pin it up in the barracks or billet for all to see and he was free to do his own thing for a reasonable period. Mates would cover his duties. He could get drunk, run and hide, weep or curse until the pain had passed. It was an excellent system that kept many out of the guardroom.

My own 'Dear John' was not unexpected. The romance started during squarebashing, and she was the most beautiful girl in Liverpool. Her home was in the suburb of Knotty Ash, where Ken Dodd was later to discover jam butty mines. In those far-off days a chaste relationship was normal, and it took several dates before a parting peck on the cheek was considered acceptable behaviour. From this little acorn grew a strong friendship. Letters flowed between us. On my way to the transit camp en route to the Middle East I managed to meet her for an hour in a railway station in the middle of an afternoon and, though our physical contact went no further than usual, we made promises.

In Egypt her letters arrived weekly and I religiously wrote in return. I did not exactly keep them tied together with a pink ribbon, but I did keep a bundle in my locker. One of the topics she eventually raised was the fact that many of her friends were getting engaged. Some had even married. Later her thesis was that most of her friends went dancing on Sunday nights at the Pier Head

R JOHNSTON

Lucky lads! Ladysmith Camp, Fayid, 1954.

R CURTIS

Pin-ups on a billet wall. This would not have been permitted at Deversoir, where they were confined to the insides of locker doors.

Ballroom and she stayed at home, even though she was "not even engaged". She asked if it would it be all right if she went out dancing occasionally. The situation was well beyond my experience and I needed to discuss it and seek advice from a wiser person.

Our hut corporal had joined up during the last days of the war and had been given the rank of sergeant air gunner. Opting to stay in the Service, he had remustered to clerical duties and was now corporal in charge of the camp post office. He seemed pretty old, being twenty-seven or twenty-eight and married. He was an astute man and had planted some fast-growing shrubbery along the side of the Nissen hut most affected by the sun, and installed an irrigation system to feed the

puny plants. A few months later the hut was much cooler, protected by a profusion of foliage. He was the man to ask for advice so I presented my problem.

"Do you want to marry this girl?" was his first question.

"Yes, but not yet," was my non-committal but truthful reply, and eloquently expressing my doubts I added: "She hasn't met my mother yet and I've not met hers." I thought it was normal to have parental approval, a decent job, money in the bank, and good prospects before putting a ring on a girl's finger. He seemed encouraged by my reply but dropped a bombshell.

"You do realise that she is already going out dancing and, if I'm any judge, she's met a guy she quite fancies."

I was stunned. How could she? It was unfair competition, with me being thousands of miles away and he being close enough to put his arms round her to quickstep. I was sick with frustration and helplessness, but what could I do? My father-confessor corporal had the answer.

"Tell her that just because you're stuck in the desert away from women, that's no reason for her not to enjoy herself. Tell her that you love her and that you trust her and that you'll be home in a mere seven months and then you can discuss getting engaged."

He was impressively shrewd. I carried out his instructions to the word and, after a few more letters that were chatty but cool, I got the old, old story. She had gone dancing as 'I' had suggested and met a jolly Jack Tar who, being a fast worker, was keen to get engaged. I wrote back a nice letter congratulating her, though by checking dates and other clues it was clear that the corporal had been spot-on.

To punish her I removed her photograph from my locker and stowed it away with her letters. I would never again trust a woman, but since I had fully expected to receive my 'Dear John,' I did nothing outrageous over it.

Deep down, I felt a bit of a berk.

POMP AND POLISH

*The tidiest you'll see an RAF base is at an AOC's inspection.
But when I visited an Army friend's camp I discovered that
guardsmen even have to sleep to attention*

Christmas comes but once a year, and so does the inspection by the Air Officer Commanding. Active service in the Canal Zone of Egypt did not excuse us from that dreaded date in the calendar. He would find everything in apple-pie order, as such inspections are not done randomly or unexpectedly but with a reasonable period of notice. Everything stopped when the announcement appeared in daily orders. Gallons of white and RAF-blue paint, brushes, cleaning cloths, sandpaper, sugar soap and the like were issued to everyone who could move. The entire encampment had to be clean, cleaner and cleanest. Even the ever-changing sands had to be controlled and fleets of Land Rovers and lorries dragged hessian carpet up and down to obliterate any trace of footprints or tyre tracks.

The lunacy continued unabated and, since no one could predict which areas of the airfield our bigwig would choose to visit, every part had to be brought up to scratch. If he could be delayed in the officers' mess it would reduce the number of sites he might visit. In the unlikely event that he turned out to be teetotal, however, there was no knowing what he might unearth.

In the equipment accounts office we polished ledges under desks and placed painted stones in pretty lines. In the stores an excessive application of elbow grease ensured that bins and their contents shone brightly. For a week before the air officer's visit not a single case of food poisoning was traced back to the kitchens, and hospital patients were emptied out of their cots and reduced to medicine and duty to tidy the place up. On duty we painted and cleaned and polished, and off duty we painted and cleaned and polished. Flies were eliminated, as the little blighters could leave footprints on gleaming glass. Not even recruits on the night before passing-out parade were as highly strung as we were before the critical inspection by the man with the all-seeing eye. We grumbled to each other that if we had wanted this amount of 'bull' we would have joined the Brigade of Guards, but I knew better than most the extent to which the Guards go to maintain their deserved reputation for smartness.

A friend from home was serving as a National Serviceman with the 1st Battalion Scots Guards at the golf course camp near Port Said, and I was granted weekend leave to visit him. I had no difficulty in hitching lifts to this centre of culture shocks.

Every guardsman had his head shaved at the sides and back, and they marched about with a crick in the neck to see where they were going under the peaks of their caps. They ate out of mess tins and clomped about in large shiny boots at all times, even when dressed in denim fatigues. Every bed in every tent had kit laid out on it unless it was actually occupied. Guardsmen were required even to sleep to attention.

During the day there was a slight change in direction of the prevailing winds; while during the morning a soft, dry breeze blew in from the desert, by afternoon it would be damp from passing over the sea. This minute change in temperature brought a faint bloom to the khaki coloured webbing as it lay on the beds, and meant that all of it had to be re-blancoed twice daily. In the RAF we blancoed our belts and sundry equipment at the first sighting of a blue moon, but then only if we saw pigs in flight.

My appearance no doubt shocked the guardsmen, and probably induced apoplexy in the Regimental Sergeant Major, but everyone was too polite to say anything. The Guards are said to be comprised entirely of gentlemen, and on the Queen's birthday you can hear the proof when the parade ends. The order is given: "Gentlemen, to your duties, dismiss."

My friend Harry Bremner, who had become a blue-eyed boy in the Guards following successful exploits on the rugby field, took me for drives in his Bren gun carrier and generally kept me out of view as much as possible. Soon after my weekend with them he was promoted to lance sergeant as a reward for this thoughtfulness.

They are a bright lot, the Scots Guards, and it was from them that I was instructed in the art of smoking undetected during the night, while on stag. A spent .303 cartridge is a smidgeon larger in diameter than your average fag, so a lit cigarette inserted into it receives just enough oxygen to keep it alive. It can then be very discreetly puffed upon, without any giveaway red glow, in perfect safety. At the approach of the guard commander it can be thrown aside, pocketed or laid somewhere safe. The favourite method of disposal was to seal the open end of the cartridge case with the thumb, cutting off the oxygen supply, and concealing the whole in the closed fist. In the subsequent standing to attention the thumb is to the front, in the approved Guards fashion, and the illicit substance safe and sound and hidden by the fingers. If a salute is called for, as the arm sweeps up

the object can be thrown away; the further the better.

The 1st Battalion Scots Guards had taken over responsibility for an area of the docks formerly secured by the less enthusiastic troops of a normal line regiment. Guardsmen, however, do guard well. On the night they took over they shot and killed three Arab thieves. On the second night their tally dropped to two, and after that they shot no one at all because word had got out to leave that particular area well alone. Not that this dimmed the enthusiasm of the officers and NCOs.

My pal was due to go on stag the day I arrived and nothing, not even an important though unscheduled visit by the RAF, could alter the roster once your name was on it. So, with nothing better to do, I tagged along as an interested observer. Ten men were detailed for duty so, in Guards-fashion, twelve paraded and ten duty men dusted and polished each other as though they were preparing to guard the Queen at Buckingham Palace. When further improvement was impossible the two spare men CARRIED

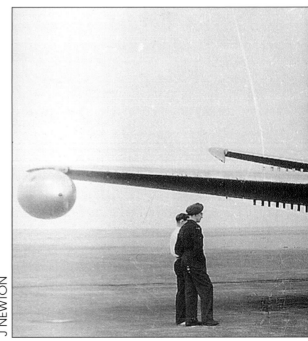

J NEWTON

Right: Me and my lifelong friend from home, Harry Bremner, who was serving with the 1st Battalion Scots Guards at Golf Course Camp, Port Said.

H BREMNER

Below: A Canberra being refuelled at RAF Shallufa in March 1954, during it's record-breaking flight to Austrailia.

P BRUMMEL

Above Vampires of 32 (F) Squadron at RAF Shallufa in 1951.

Above: A Meteor of 32 Squadron geared for target towing.

D LINES

their comrades on to a barrack square fashioned from rolled and flattened sand, and placed them carefully in line. This line was confirmed as accurate with a length of string and within a few minutes an officer, a sergeant and a corporal appeared. At sight of them the detail visibly tightened up though still technically in the at ease stance. Then came the stentorian order in trooping the colours style:

"AT-TEN-SHUN!"

Ten feet crashed down and the view was completely obliterated by a cloud of fine sand, which gradually settled on the previously pristine guardsmen, kept so clean by their thoughtful comrades.

The RAF has its share of mad people, but this condition is not a prerequisite for service as it is in the Guards. In the RAF people go crazy over time, while in the Guards they are mad from day one. I was delighted to get back to the comparative sanity of RAF Deversoir. The rumour that when an applicant to join the Army attempts to complete his questionnaire using the wrong end of the pencil he is immediately drafted into the Guards is not true; he is directed to the RAF.

On the day of the AOC's visit two men were detailed to each Nissen hut to provide a warm welcome, should serendipity attract our man to this or that particular door. The whole station sparkled and every man on it was smartly dressed in freshly laundered and starched uniforms. No real RAF work had been done on the base for over a week, but that was considered a small price to pay. If our wing commander did not get the anticipated pat on the back at the end of the inspection we would be in for it.

A tale is told about an AOC who just happened to visit our Nissen hut during an inspection tour. Having found the billet immaculate, he called the billet orderlies to the centre of the hut to congratulate them on the high standard achieved. It was then that he spotted some pencil marks on the table and he demanded an explanation as to why the surface had not been sandpapered clean prior to his visit. An orderly explained that for a number of years only stores personnel had used that particular hut. They had invented a game and the pencil marks and initials recorded their results. When asked to explain the rules the orderly pointed out that it was simply a recording of the member-lengths of the residents over the years. Most of the marks and the sets of initials were between three and five inches from the edge of the table. The AOC laughed and stated that he had risen through the ranks and that he would create some goodwill by joining in the fun. He boasted that he could beat them all and asked for a pencil to be handy before assuming the position – 'prepare to throw'. It was at that moment that the orderly pointed out that we all threw from the far side of the table!

This AOC's visit was all a bit of an anti-climax, since he failed to visit any part of the camp in which I had friends and acquaintances. He did visit the officers' mess, and reports were that he was no stranger to the gin bottle. Perhaps he became tired and emotional, but he left satisfied. We could again leave footprints in the sand, get admitted to hospital if we became unwell, and lay down our paintbrushes for another year.

Having spruced up the camp for the flying visit of the air officer, someone thought that rather than let all that 'bull' go to waste it could be utilised to improve the RAF's image as the scruffiest of the three services. The spit and polish had a curious effect on the CO and he wanted to show his station off to the world. An air display would be the answer, and the idea proved to be so popular with Army units looking for a skive that entry was restricted to one lorry or bus from each unit. On the base we went to ground because a cry went up for volunteers to control parking, act as guides, do some guarding and bar access to parts of the camp best left unseen.

The object of the exercise was to impress the craphats. It would raise the morale of the not concur with those of the Air Ministry. Despite all that, and some grumbles from the 'erks, the show would go on. The day arrived, and only the main gate was to be used. This would ensure that the carefully drawn up parking arrangements for the hundreds of troops expected to attend would work according to a meticulously prepared plan. I was posted as guard on one of the closed gates, and warned that no relief could be

Dragonfly Helicopter with me on board after the air display. None of my photographs taken from the air came out.

squaddies camped up and down the Suez Canal by showing off the state of readiness the boys in blue maintained. Our Vampires were the eyes of the entire command, and their constant patrolling was a visible sign of our superiority in air power. Early warning of any moves by the Egyptian army was guaranteed, and we would bomb and strafe them out of existence before our comrades in khaki had rolled out of bed. When our visitors saw how meticulously we cared for our kit, buildings and aircraft they would be overawed. Not everyone appreciates that for each member of an aircrew it takes fifteen ground crew to keep him operational. It therefore follows that at a ratio of fifteen to one, Air Force personnel dislike aeroplanes, as without them life would be much easier. If this is taken to its logical conclusion – if we could do without the kites – we could all go home. Of course, the views of the author may

H STANLEY

guaranteed since every spare bod was being grabbed and allocated duties on an ad hoc basis. That said, to leave my post would guarantee a court martial and probably a hanging.

My KD was starched to perfection, although my shoulder flashes and leading aircraftsman badges had all but faded away due to the excessive exposure to ultraviolet rays. Though I say it myself, I was very smart.

My shoes had been bulled till they sparkled in the sunlight. As a perk of being in the equipment section I was wearing a prototype of the new cheesecutter caps. The whole ensemble was very fetching and rather spoiled by the need to carry a .303. Directing traffic and carrying a rifle at the same time is quite tricky, and I solved the problem by upending the gun so that the butt was at my shoulder and the foresight near my knee,

213 or 248 Squadron flying upside down over the Canal. Vampires were hard enough to fly the right way up.

leaving both arms free. Many drivers had previously visited Deversoir using the gate I was guarding and predictably tried to turn into it. I solved this problem by crossing the road and waving them towards to the main gate from there. It was fairly quiet when I took up my duty, but it was enlivened by a contretemps with some of the native labour still employed on the base. The powers-that-be did not want them in the camp, as it was felt that they made the place look untidy. Their usual route home was via this gate; but it was barred and locked, and I told them in Arabic to take themselves off to the main gate where they would be allowed out. They were very unhappy because it entailed a walk of about half a mile, which would have to be retraced once they were outside.

The people at the main gate wanted nothing to do with them as they were expecting visitors at any minute, so the workers were shooed back to me. For a time it was like a game of ping-pong, and the argument became more and more heated. At the start I was *Sahib* but later I was something that I could not translate, but understood anyway. They showed a keen grasp of the phonetic alphabet, as they were 'foxtrot oscared' up and down, before at last I used my initiative and allowed them to climb over the gate. They managed this with such alacrity and ease that I suspected they did it regularly at night.

The traffic began to build up and I re-crossed the road and took up a position opposite the gate. Once I got them rolling, the three-tonners behaved like sheep and were content to follow one another down the road. My gate was on the Ismailia side of the camp and the majority of the traffic was coming from that direction, so I was kept fairly busy and was high profile when an extraordinary thing happened.

I was looking very smart and acting very officiously when I heard a shout from a lorry laden with troops, all sitting upright on seats in the back. The sergeant in charge was standing on the passenger seat, his upper body protruding through the circular hole in the cabin roof designed to mount a defensive machine gun, and he was calling his men to attention. With the strident cry of "eyes left," he threw up his arm in a cracker of a salute while his men's heads swept to the left. His hand quivered by his right eye, and his back was ramrod straight. I did the decent thing and threw him a casual RAF officer-style salute in return. The vehicle immediately behind copied his actions and from then on I took the salute from all and sundry, even from a RAF 15-cwt truck. It made me wish that I had a suitable dais to stand on. Eventually the flow of traffic slackened and a solitary Bedford was approaching. I could tell that the NCO in charge had no intention of paying me his respects. I haughtily pointed a finger at him, then at my shoulder, and was rewarded with a belated, if rather hurried, acknowledgement of my newly invented rank.

I was delighted when my relief turned up, as I felt that I had pushed my luck far enough. Back in camp, as a lowly LAC once more, I managed to cadge a flight in a Dragonfly helicopter and took some photographs of the camp in all its AOC inspection-type, highly polished glory. Unfortunately, none of my pictures came out, and the photo I have of the flying machine during my time in the air was taken by someone else.

NOT-SO-EASY RIDER

While I was daft enough to spend my pay and time on a motorbike, young ladies were earning the gratitude of other Servicemen on holiday in Cyprus

Buying a motorcycle was one of the more stupid things I did during my stay in the Canal Zone. Control was very lax: a crash helmet was thought effeminate, and bare legs and arms were the order of the day. On one of my few excursions outside the camp, as I rode along carefully keeping to the well-used main road to avoid losing my head to a hidden wire, a large American car drew alongside me and the nice Egyptian family within waved to me. They pointed at the bike while suggesting that I pull over and stop. Now, however nice people appear, this is no guarantee as to their intentions. I gave them the internationally recognised 'V' for victory sign, wound up the throttle, and roared ahead.

We British have always believed our motor industry products to be superior to Detroit's steel and chrome monsters, but on a long straight road there is no substitute for horsepower. The driver easily overtook me and again the finger-pointing and hand-waving was repeated. This time I paid more attention to the occupants and discovered that they were mostly children. I took a calculated risk and stopped, but left the engine running just in case. The bike had been converted for trial use and, at a push, I could go off-road where the big car could not follow.

The reason for the semaphoring quickly became apparent. The seam of the petrol tank was leaking and my legs were now glistening with the highly volatile fuel. A spark would have seen me in a bad way. I thanked the Egyptian family and quickly checked the fuel level, which proved sufficient, in spite of the leak, to get me back to camp, and I was off. At speed the dribble of petrol was dragged clear of my legs by the wind, and it is probable that, being in complete ignorance of the danger, I could have run out of fuel miles from anywhere. Had that happened, I could have lost not only the motorcycle but also my life. My future riding was confined to camp.

Even in camp the bike brought problems. It was a daft purchase, brought about by my 'Dear John' letter. The money I had saved could have bought an engagement ring for my faithless girlfriend or I could have left it in the bank. It could even have bought me a holiday. I had not had the bike for long but was already fed up with it. Securing petrol was a bind and trying to stop others using it when I was on guard duty was impossible. It made even less sense when I considered that I had only a few months to serve. Holidays in Cyprus had been authorised, and from the information gleaned from the first few lucky ones to qualify, it seemed perfect. Airmen were not obliged to stay resident in the tents at Golden Sands, Famagusta, but were free to make alternative arrangements. This was before partition and the whole island was there to be investigated and enjoyed.

The best of the nightclubs was the Spitfire, where nubile young ladies down from the central mountains were keen to save enough for a dowry as quickly as possible. This they did by touching up the holidaymakers, their hand movements concealed by low hanging tablecloths, while encouraging clients to buy drinks. The value of the gratuities earned in this manner reflected the gratitude of those being caressed. Extra sums could be earned against convenient walls in the vicinity of the establishment, and the highest rate was earned from any airman found sufficiently attractive to share their quarters with for the duration of his holiday period. There was a surprisingly reasonable weekly rate for this.

To the young ladies, saving hard to secure their futures, attractiveness seemed to be entirely governed by wallet thickness. Most of them took part in all three enterprises each night. The overnight person had to realise his entitlement to the goods was from the early hours when she came home, until she left for work late the following afternoon.

I would have liked a bit more exclusivity had I been in a position to make a purchase, but the rules were the rules. I learned all this from one of the first to visit. The drill was to go to a bar, engage the girl of your choice in light-hearted conversation and arrange a midnight tryst, leaving your cigarette lighter with her as security against her being stood up. No show, no return of cigarette lighter. It

Me on my very expensive pride and joy.

A postcard showing the Golden Sands holiday camp in Cyprus. The back of the card says the camp shop gave "every consideration to H.M. forces on leave." They weren't the only ones.

H BROCKWAY

sounded an admirable arrangement. I knew that if I went to Cyprus, every penny I had would be lavished on women despite the risk to my health. In truth, as the girls dealt exclusively with Servicemen with no previous opportunity for illicit sex, the risk was minimal. But there was still a risk and although I had no girl at home waiting for me, I felt sure a nice one could be found.

To work out the best value for my money, I took a sheet of paper and wrote the positives on one side and the drawbacks on the other, illustrating the attractions and price of each choice. I was always a bit mean and the thought of a few months' use of the bike and the return of the purchase price when I sold it was the clincher. If I bought the bike I would go home with cash in the bank. Going to Cyprus, I would be soon broke and probably return to the UK in debt. All for a few golden memories.

Yes, I'm the idiot who bought the motorbike and I've regretted it all my life. I could go to Cyprus now at any time, but I'll never be able to go there as a young man or recapture the eagerness of youth. Perhaps if I drove round some of the mountain villages I might see some black-dressed old crones, the girls of yesteryear who generated such excitement. Anyway, I had some good times with the bike.

Having scrounged a big new packing case from the stores, I used it as a garage, digging it into the sand at the side of the Nissen hut. I attached a makeshift alarm to the construction because Egyptian thieves pinched such items from inside the camp. Terrorists did raid us, but they left my machine alone. Instead, they fire-bombed the nearby photographic building, making a spectacular blaze. Anxious not to alarm us, the authorities claimed a dryer had been left switched on overnight, but we knew better.

One morning, when I returned from yet another guard duty just after 6am to inspect the bike as usual, inside the 'garage' I found four large, silver paper-bound boxes. Thinking they might be an early gift of oil or something from Santa, I took a closer look. Each box contained two thousand cigarettes – eight thousand in all – and me a non-smoker! I mentioned to the lads in the billet that I was going for breakfast and that whoever had been leaving 'rubbish' in my shed had better move it before I got back. I very much enjoyed my square egg (a product of convenient mass production) and headed

J THOMPSON

The JAPIC (Joint Aeronautical Photographic Intelligence Centre) Section building, which caught fire after terrorists bombed it. 12 & 13 April 1953

back to recheck my garage. The parcels were still there. It felt strange to be heading for the guardroom of my own volition, since every other time I had been in jankers uniform. I addressed the snowdrop on duty:

"I've found some cigarettes in my bike shed."

"What's that to do with us?"

"There are quite a lot of them."

He looked at me quizzically. "How many?"

"Eight-thousand."

Now he was interested. The questions came thick and fast. "Where? When?"

And then: "Let's have a look."

With my luck, they would have disappeared and I would have a lot of explaining to do. The Land Rover, cigarettes and myself returned to the guardroom.

"Where were you last night?"

"On guard duty."

"A likely story, ideal alibi, dead easy for you to nick 'em." I did not like the way things were shaping up. So I thought I had better ask a rather obvious question.

"Where are they from?" His eyes clouded with the effort of concentrating his mind.

"How would I know?"

In a case like this there is clearly only one thing to do – lock up anyone connected with the case. That is how I came to be banged up in a cell, with my pleas ignored that my squadron leader should be informed. I suppose it was resolved relatively quickly in police investigation terms, but eight hours is a long time in a cell when you are blameless. I was freed and two villains from the equipment section took over my cell. They were brought to trial and, since the cigarettes had been recovered, given a relatively light sentence of fifty-six days in the cooler. No sooner had they been dispatched than we began to find bottles of beer hidden everywhere, especially below the surface of the water in the 50-gallon drum which we used to irrigate our hedge. We dared not take them to the guardroom for fear of being locked up again, so in the late evenings, we sat under the sinking sun, glass in hand, drinking a toast to the two miscreants who made it possible.

My boat was approaching and I felt it time I realised some cash from the sale of my trusty 350cc Matchless. Alas, the bottom had fallen out of the bike market, particularly for those of only 350cc. When I did get a buyer, he was poorer than a church mouse and could only offer to pay by instalments on fortnightly paydays. I got something like £4 before I had to leave for home, but he promised faithfully to send it on. I knew he was lying, but I thought: what the hell, I'm going home. I still wish I had spent my £60 on the bints in Cyprus, or even on that damned engagement ring.

STEN GUN ALLEY

Lives were at risk when the Egyptians attacked us on the road. But when we launched a raid on a small village the stakes were not quite so high

The mention of a raid to some RAF types can evoke memories of dangerous night sorties and loss of life on a massive scale, or long hours of hard work on the ground. Our memories are more mundane. The Air Force in which we served still involved hard work and long hours, coupled with the dire inconvenience of living in the heat and smells of Egypt. The Egyptians were unfriendly and regularly fired at our motor transports, necessitating the provision of armed personnel to travel with the lorries. Above the passenger seat was a removable section of the roof, and by standing on the seat the escort could command a good field of fire. It also made him a prime target in the event of a sneak attack. The second escort rode among the goods. His first act before leaving the base would be to construct a sort of nest in the middle of the load, thereby providing a wall between him and incoming bullets.

Our particular Sten Gun Alley was found when approaching Ismailia. Blocks of flats provided an ideal site from which to shoot at the passing military traffic. The flats were well protected by a branch of the Sweet Water Canal between the buildings and the road, and we were under orders – which seemed cretinous to us – not to fire back if attacked, as local residents occupied the flats.

When we were shot at, our chances of locating the cowardly attackers were nil so we travelled at top speed on that stretch of road and the escort in the back kept his head well down.

Apart from the annoyance of a hostile population, which kept us confined to camp for months on end, life was tolerable. Until the cookhouse became Americanised. Instead of plates our food was served in plastic trays with indentations for various courses. Despite the 100-degree heat our diet was prescribed by the Air Ministry in England and was to be served throughout the world. Jam roly-poly and spotted dick were regularly featured on the menu, as were Irish stew, shepherd's pie and sausage and mash. If the temperature moved much over the 100-degree mark, lemonade made from a powder mixture was served up from the tea urns. It was invariably warm and had tea-leaves floating on its surface; but it was a gesture.

The introduction of the plastic trays was a major disappointment. Gravy or soup ran in rivulets into the custard, and tinned fruit would slide into the stew. Mixed-up food was not popular and complaints poured in to request a return to normal crockery. As usual, however, the wants of the airmen seemed to be ignored by those on high. The experiment with the plastic trays was not extended to the officers' mess.

I had completed a night on guard duty at the main gate on first stag – from six until eight in the evening – and the time flew by. I had to open and close the barrier, and check vehicles in and out. It was a well-lit post, with help a mere twenty yards away in the guardroom and a cheering cup of char surreptitiously delivered by a thoughtful mate. Being on first stag – which brought the sentry back on duty at midnight – cut down on sleeping time as no one slept before the second shift. Rolled in a blanket on the concrete floor, I fell asleep instantly at a few minutes past two in the morning; only to be rudely awakened at five and told to stand by to carry out a raid. In typical RAF fashion,

pre-planning had been overlooked and no instructions were issued to the bleary-eyed troops.

"When you get there," we were instructed, "put a round up the spout and don't put up with any nonsense from anyone."

"What are we looking for, Sarge?" enquired a plaintive voice.

"You'll know when you see it," came the rather unsatisfactory reply. We jumped into

H STANLEY

where murder can be legal!

One of the propaganda leaflets distributed mainly by female terrorists, who slipped them into the shopping bags of Army wives. They were also thrown into the various camps.

WARNING

To the British troops in the Canal Zone

This is a warning. Before we start to kill each other on a large scale would you be advised?

I guess you can't disobey orders...

But I suppose you can think... can't you?

Look here, Tom, Dick or Harry!

What are you fighting for?

Have you, or any of your relations, got shares in the blinking Suez Canal Company? Or the blasted oil corporations?

I doubt it.

So you are fighting for the fat capitalists of the City, who sit in their luxurious rooms, smoking their cigars, who exploit you and order you to fight the Egyptians, who want to be free in their own country, as you did in 1941 when Hitler wanted to interfere with your freedom. What are you fighting for? Your situation at home is precarious because of the shortage of food, manpower and the threat of bankruptcy.

Can't you see that Britain is bearing a far too heavy burden? It is the fault of your Government. Her forces are fighting in Korea and Malaya and are garrisoning innumerable stations all over the globe. Your Government refuses to be relieved of her burden in the Suez Canal.

And here you are, fighting in a barren, waterless tract 3,000 miles away from home, surrounded by a hostile population determined to carry on for ever an irregular warfare, like the Ismailian's battles of 18th November, 1951, with endurance and stubborn... without any leniency... till you get out...

The Suez Canal is ours. We cut it and we defended it in two world wars. We are determined to have it and keep it... whether you like it or not.

You will have no rest, no sleep... we will get you one by one, slowly but surely. We are at home and time is on our side.

WE WILL HANG YOU BY THE NECK FROM THE ACACIA TREES.
WE WILL FINISH YOU OFF.

The text of a leaflet delivered to the Royal Dragoons by the Egyptian post.

three Land Rovers and two three-ton trucks and roared out of the gates. Were we going to sort out the flat dwellers in Sten Gun Alley? We hoped not, because there were thousands of better-qualified infantry soldiers between Ismailia and Deversoir. We did not have far to travel though. We swept off the road and drove across country for about a mile, then screeched to a halt in the middle of a small native village that none of us knew existed.

"Right, lads," screamed a voice. "Get in about them!"

We wondered what exactly "getting in about them" was. Were we to shoot them dead on the spot? Even I thought that a bit extreme, and looking to see what the others were doing I leapt into action. With one up the spout and bayonet fixed I dashed for the nearest hovel. Knocking at the door was clearly out of the question, but a couple of hefty kicks swung it open and I charged inside, ready for anything. It was a bit of an anticlimax really. A couple of hens squawked, a dog barked and a terrified couple appeared with their hands raised aloft in the inter-national sign of surrender. So far so good. But what was I looking for?

After a cursory examination of a few obscure places where I thought a gun might be hidden I gave up and moved next door to repeat the process. Obviously the element of surprise had gone and if a terrorist was lurking behind the door he was likely to be armed and dangerous. This time the door flew off its hinges under a shoulder charge and I was in possession. Alas, the cupboard was bare or the residents had constructed the ultimate secret shelter, since I could not find it despite trying as hard as I could. I prodded here and there with my bayonet, and each time it met solid resistance; so there were no false walls or sliding panels. What the absent tenants would think on their return was not my business.

Before I could start on a third dwelling, whistles blew and the dogs of war were

called off. Someone else had made a discovery. 2,741 dinner plates, airmen for the use of, were recovered. The question was: who had stolen them?

The only native Egyptian workers who were allowed on the base were the 'gash wallahs'. They collected the swill and were rewarded with a supply of petrol in addition to a small stipend from a grateful RAF. How and when they had stolen the plates remained a mystery, but conjecture was rife that they had taken a few plates at a time over a period of months. The swill bins made an ideal hiding place because no one was going to rake through them on the off-chance of finding stolen goods.

Soon after that the hated plastic trays disappeared to be replaced by good old-fashioned crockery. I like to think that, in my own small way, I contributed to the restoration of civilised eating for the other ranks. I often wonder what happened to the trays. Perhaps they are hidden away somewhere in a small village in Egypt.

Other village raids were more successful. A few days before the battle of the Bureau Sanitaire and the Caracol, on 19 January, A Troop of B Squadron of the Royal Dragoons accounted for three terrorists who had exploded a bomb on the YMCA Bridge, killing two British Servicemen. A short time later one of the dragoons' armoured cars was damaged by a bomb thrown from the convent in which Sister Anthony had been murdered. This resulted in a large-scale search and clearance of the nearby Allied Quarter of Ismailia. The Para Brigade, aided by B Squadron of the Royals, recovered 80,000 rounds of 14mm ammunition which had been stolen from the BAD. Twelve Egyptians were killed or captured during this action.

Shortly after the events related above, the Royals received a letter by the Egyptian post, the text of which is displayed on the previous page. The leaflet was printed in Cairo by the Socialist Party and sent by the Ottoman Bank, Ismailia.

CHRISTMAS SPIRIT

We were miles from home, holly and snow, but our Egyptian Christmas at Deversoir was as memorable as they come

My third Christmas in blue, and I had yet to experience a real Royal Air Force one. My first had been spent at home and my second as a 'volunteer' in the kitchens, so I was quite determined to enjoy 25 December 1952. I still had eleven months to serve, but third time could be lucky and anyone in the service who did not make an effort deserved a rotten Yuletide. Few of us were terribly miserable, and spirits rose as the days passed and an air of goodwill permeated our souls. Even in a camp *sans* females, where the spirit of Christmas was mostly appreciated in bottle form, there was laughter and gaiety all around. At heart we were kids again as we wrapped and hid little gifts in our lockers, decorated our billets and created a tree. The RAF also did its bit, and 252s were issued less often.

A programme of festivities to suit all tastes was announced. On 23 December a kiddies' party and film show was to be held in the officers' mess, but obviously I was not invited. In the station cinema, Ronnie Ronalde would whistle his way through a programme that included his chart-topping success A Monastery Garden; a reminder of home and the tranquillity of civilian life.

After all that excitement, Christmas Eve would be a quieter day. The station Christmas draw would take place, followed by a free film show in the cinema, and night flying would not disturb the entertainment. Christmas Day would start with a church service in the early morning. (So we had a church in the station? It was news to many of us.) The billet judging competition would start at 10am and be completed by 10.10am, as not many billets were keen to receive visitors that early on a day off. There would be two sittings of Christmas dinner in the NAAFI and the airmen's mess, and at 1900 hours we would enjoy yet another film show.

Christmas dinner wasn't bad at all when you consider that the cookhouse had to prepare more than 2,000 meals. The officers and sergeants helped them out by serving and generally getting in the way. The generous issue of free cigarettes might encourage some elderly coves suffering from persistent coughs to consider suing the RAF for recompense, but such a claim would be unlikely to succeed. Cigarettes at that time cost five pence for fifty, and Stella around five ackers a bottle.

December 26 was a fun day, and a comedy football match was held between the officers and the sergeants. Naturally the officers were allowed a diplomatic win. We were keen to have an officers-versus-airmen game followed by sergeants-versus-airmen, but the sickbay could not have dealt with the casualties. The officers-versus-sergeants match was followed by an international. I can't remember which countries took part, but it was a spirited affair and the referee called it off when both teams were reduced to seven men.

The highlight of the day was a donkey derby and our glorious leader, Wing

CHRISTMAS DAY MENU – 1952
RAF DEVERSOIR

BREAKFAST
Grapefruit, Cereals, Porridge, Kippers
Grilled Bacon, Fried Egg, Grilled Pork Sausage, Tomatoes
Tea, Toast, Butter, Marmalade

DINNER
Cream of Tomato Soup
Roast Turkey, Roast Pork, Forcemeat Stuffing, Apple Sauce, Gravy, Onions, Roast
and Creamed Potatoes, Cauliflower, Peas
Plum Pudding, Brandy Sauce
Beer, Lemonade, Cigarettes, Mixed Nuts
Coffee

SUPPER
Cold Meats, Salad Varies
Fruit Salad and Cream
Cakes, Mince Pies, Christmas Cake
Tea, Bread, Butter, Jam

This was the only Christmas dinner that I was able to sit down and enjoy during my three years of service.

Commander Philpott, assisted by his delightful wife, started the race. He entered into the spirit of the occasion by arriving dressed as a costermonger, although it may simply have been his gardening jacket – who could tell? Squadron Leader Farley, our stores chief, was keen that I should run a book on the event. It was just as well that my lack of knowledge led to his request being turned down since I would have finished up minus my shirt, and even the extensive stores at Deversoir could not sustain a loss like that.

On no racecourse in the world has nobbling and cheating been so prevalent. Likely winners were dragged back by their tails, and one animal – a clear also-ran – was carried to the winning post and well clear of the field by supporters holding a leg each. The owner of the donkeys, renowned for his cruelty to animals, was reduced to tears. It was a memorable event.

Security in the festive season had to be maintained and, with our guard duty roster insisting that we parade every other night, I know I missed some of the entertainment: the Ronnie Ronalde concert I think. Perhaps I should have agreed to act as a bookie after all, because the squadron leader was all-powerful and likely to reward those who complied with his whims.

Yet another Christmas Day death occurred

as we were enjoying the festivities, and this victim was even younger than the previous year's. He was an 18-year-old private in the RASC. The news blackout worked again. We had no idea of the high death toll and only knew of those related to our own camp. Had we known that four or five men were being killed each week we would have been much more trigger-happy on guard detail, and the effect on the Egyptians would have been a political nightmare for the ~~faceless bureaucrats~~ authorities at home.

D L BRADLEY

Right: Deversoir station commander Group Captain Philpott and his wife after their donkey derby exploits.

Below: The magnificent Astra Cinema at RAF Ismailia, 1952. The explosions of terrorist hand grenades thrown over the wall often spoiled the enjoyment of filmgoers.

E SEAR

THE BEACH CLUB

Take an entrepreneurial Libyan, a PoW-built beach hut, drinks, food and games. Shake well and enjoy

Political tension was still high, and having more than 2,000 men confined to camp for months on end was not good for morale. We did have some entertainment when the open-air cinema showed a film, but this happened only when night-flying exercises were scheduled. Some said that the giant floodlit screen was the only way the flyers could find their way home at night. Although the pilots denied it, they never strayed far from the airfield, and circuits and bumps round the cinema often drowned out the soundtrack of the film. Complaining was regarded as a waste of time, but men did, and eventually the powers-that-be realised that something should be done to make life more tolerable for them.

The answer was to re-open the Beach Club. It had been built by German POWs and was a ready-made recreational facility just outside the camp proper, on the shore of the Great Bitter Lake. We guarded it at night because it was still furnished, and if an attack came from the sea our heroic guards would stop the enemy from over-running the married patch. A Libyan contractor called one day at the camp to enquire if he could bid for the camp laundry contract when we moved to Libya, as rumour had it we might. Instead he was talked into taking over the Beach Club for a peppercorn rent, to provide a mess for the other ranks. The officers, sergeants and even corporals had a mess where they could experience a change of scene and some civilised living. The other

ranks had the NAAFI, which was only open when it had beer. A NAAFI in the UK was a refuge where char and wads would be available, and egg on toast or even chips and Spam. It also stocked essential items like boot polish, notepaper and pens, and other mundane items we did not see at all in Egypt.

I cannot remember how I met this foreign gentleman, but we struck up a friendship. He didn't know what the men needed, and had no idea of how to run a mess. I had even less idea, though I kept that fact a secret. What I did know was what I would like.

After work each afternoon I would be picked up by car at the guardroom, and driven in state to the Beach Club. When I applied to the CO to allow the driver to collect me from my office in the camp, permission was refused. In my innocence I was quite oblivious to the fact that the special treatment I received caused some envy in others.

We opened the club with a bang on a Sunday morning, with a full English breakfast served at a reasonable hour for a reasonable price. It started with grapefruit segments, followed by cornflakes with ice-cold milk; then bacon, eggs, sausage, beans, fried bread, tomatoes, fried potatoes, Heinz Tomato Ketchup or HP Sauce – unheard-of luxuries in Egypt – tea or coffee, and lashings of toast; and all this for five bob. Business boomed.

Equipment was limited but we managed to organise table tennis and darts tournaments, and all in all it became a successful

E SEAR

An escort vehicle and the AOC's Humber Super Snipe, RAF Ismailia, 1952. His staff car was a little larger than the one that used to take me to and from the Beach Club.

operation. While the table tennis tournament was being organised a very large King Farouk lookalike appeared at the club, and announced that he had played the game for Egypt in the 1936 Olympics. I quite fancied my chances at table tennis, having once played a pat-a-cake game with a Helen Elliot, a Scottish lady champion, so I took him on. He controlled the table from three yards out and smashed my best shots all over the place. I failed to score a single point. As Egypt were also-rans in the Olympics it made me wonder how good the medal-winners must have been. I suspected my friend was a mysterious 'Mr Big' behind the Libyan, and had called to

check his investment. Perhaps it had been wise of me to lose.

I drew no wage for helping out at the club but my food and drinks were free. Since I rarely drank beer and never touched spirits, everyone was happy. My duty ended each evening at closing time, when I ushered the few remaining drunks off the premises before being dropped off at the guardroom after lights-out. Having to walk from the guardroom to my billet was an inconvenience, but it had to be tolerated.

A cabaret seemed a good idea for the Beach Club, but just how my Libyan friend got the artists smuggled out of Ismailia or

High-speed RAF rescue launch. The rest of the crew are below deck, sleeping off their mid-day tot of rum. Fanara, 1951.

M A HARTE

Fayid and into the club was shrouded in mystery. On the night the place was packed to overflowing and the Gilli-Gilli man, a close-up magician and conjurer, was world class. The skimpily- clad belly dancers brought the house down, and the rest of the acts were acclaimed as fantastic.

As I made my closing-time rounds I could hear someone singing lustily out in the darkness, but couldn't find him. His rendering of Rock of Ages finally gave him away, lying flat on his back behind a low wall and singing hymns and psalms in full Tom Jones voice. He was from the Welsh valleys and said he had signed the pledge before joining up, to please his religiously strict mother. Unfortunately he had enjoyed himself so much in the club that he had broken his vows and got smashed. He was overjoyed by it all and wanted to sing but, knowing none of the popular songs, sang the only ones he knew. In the morning he would be a sadder but wiser man, with a lot of explaining to do when he wrote home to Mother.

The party had been such a success that a few corporals, and even some sergeants gatecrashed it. When closing time came, two of them took exception to being ordered off the premises and a bit of pushing and shoving ensued; but I thought no more about it.

I began to notice my name appearing more often on the guard and duty storeman roster, and the Squadron Leader seemed to be finding extra jobs for me in the afternoons; I was clearly a marked man. It came to a head when I was informally called before the Group Captain to explain why I had been less than respectful to some drunken NCOs. As usual, my side of the story was not really wanted.

"You see," he explained gravely, "it's not really on, to have an airman running the Beach Club. And this thing about you having your own car and driver..." He shook his head negatively. "Not really on at all."

I fought my corner, but not well enough, as he concluded: "We really need someone with a rank doing that job." My suggestion –

that he issue me with as many stripes as he liked, on an elastic band: airman for the use of, only in the Beach Club, acting and unpaid – went down like the proverbial lead balloon, and I was told to pack it in.

I had served long enough to know when I was on a hiding to nothing. A tame corporal was foisted onto the Beach Club and its Libyan host, and within a few weeks the place closed down. My replacement did not have the facility of a courtesy car, but that was not the reason the club failed. It was simply that without impetus – and my daft ideas – nothing happened. The combined brainpower of the RAF leadership lost the other ranks an enjoyable facility that had raised morale no end.

D CARTER

RAF sailors in action. Not everyone knows that they received naval rum rations. 1952.

Use other exits

There are more ways to leave the Army than seeing out your term of service. You could go for medical discharge. Or get kidnapped

I will call him Dick to spare his blushes, even fifty years on. He squarebashed at the same time and place as me but we did not meet there. Both of us, having been allocated to equipment accounts training, were drafted to the same trade-training centre at RAF Kinloss. Dick, it has to be said, was his own worst enemy. I don't think that he meant to be a permanent pain in the backside, but his single-minded devotion to Number One completely ruled him out as a team player. When I arrived at Kinloss, dead on time as per my orders, I was immediately sent home for another seven days leave. Dick, who had to travel from Croydon, clocked in two days late. As a result he was kept hanging around while the rest of us enjoyed a buckshee holiday. We met when the maintenance unit reassembled and trade training began.

I was quite unique in the RAF as I was a round peg in a round hole despite not wanting to be one. My job at home had been clerking in the stores accounts office of the Electricity Board. I really wanted a change, but training to be a driver was oversubscribed. My time in the Air Training Corps had turned me against the Morse code, and doubtless because of this I showed great aptitude for dots and dashes when tested. No one asked me if I could type, which I could, at twenty-five words a minute. This would have proved ideal for teleprinter operating but I missed out simply because I did not think it was my place to volunteer the information. When I expressed a view to the personnel selection crowd that I thought I

would be well suited to working with them as it seemed dead easy, I lost Brownie points and was directed into stores accounting.

Dick was vague about his background. We became quite friendly, despite him being permanently homesick. In a matter of weeks he had used up his annual quota of leave. In the maintenance unit we had a means of earning additional leave, but it had to be worked for and Dick did not pull his weight.

In 45 MU we were stuck miles from anywhere as far as most of us were concerned. For me, what had seemed a local posting had put me further from home in travel time than I had been in Liverpool. With most of the personnel complaining that they were not getting the time off to which they were entitled, someone in authority had a sensible idea. Our main task was to upgrade aircraft by carrying out conversions. We had to add radar, guns, an extra wheel or whatever. The time to do the job was worked out at one day for one conversion. If 120 aircraft needed the modification we were allowed 120 working days to complete the task. By working evenings, Saturdays and Sundays we might finish the job twelve days sooner than the allotted schedule. Hey presto! That number of days leave for everyone on the team. It was a perfect plan to instil team spirit but Dick was not interested.

It was about then that he decided to seriously consider 'working his ticket,' as the action was colloquially known. This is not as easy as it seems. We regularly read of men

Working your ticket is much more difficult than might be thought

who, after thirty, forty or even fifty years on the run come forward to clear their names. They get arrested, spend a night in the guardroom, and are discharged in the morning with a pat on the head. Invariably their life has been ruined, and despite having changed their names and locations they have lived in permanent dread of that knock on the door.

At the other extreme you have the example of the Kray twins. When called up they were posted to a barracks only half a mile from their home. Any time they saw an open door they were off to Mother's house for tea. The Army kept dragging them back. When the twins were locked up, they beat up the redcaps and escaped to run home again. Eventually they spent as long in detention as they would have served with honour.

The Army eventually swept the issue under the carpet and decided not to bother re-arresting them. Just see where it got them: thirty years each, supping porridge – and no time off for good behaviour. If they had completed their service they would have realised that the military is a machine that cannot easily be beaten. It has all the answers, gleaned over hundreds of years of dealing with difficult men. In exchange for submission and obedience, it feeds and clothes you, looks after your health and even pays you. You may have to die, but so does

everyone. The Krays must often have regretted their excesses and wished that they had soldiered on.

Richard was not the type to fight the system. He would muck it about as much and as often as he could, but he did have a degree of intelligence. We discussed the 'train set' ploy, said to be infallible. This is the trick where the elbow is crooked on parade When the Serviceman is asked why, he explains that his toy train set has to be carried everywhere. The 'ticket worker' then assembles an imaginary set of rails, winds up an imaginary train and… you get the picture. Evidence that this ever worked in practice has never been found. Richard considered striking a NCO, or better still a commissioned officer, though violence was not his forte. This idea was disregarded on the grounds that if he struck an NCO it was likely that the NCO would strike him back, and give him a good hiding. Hitting an officer was ruled out when we calculated he would spend longer in the glasshouse than he had left to serve in the RAF, and conditions were better where he was. He was prepared to put up with some discomfort in exchange for his liberty, but not too much, and it was not easy to think up something original. Working your ticket is much more difficult than might be thought.

Dick confided in me that he was thinking of going AWOL because he was having trouble with his girlfriend. I suggested that he have a word with the padre, and in a matter of days he was off home on compassionate leave.

Extra leave in the RAF is difficult to come by, and some of the London lads actually took the drastic step of insisting that they needed to be circumcised. Following illness, a period of convalescent leave was normally given, but in this case it was not granted. The MO decided, despite the pain and discomfort of the operation, to treat the sufferers in the same way as those infected after being tattooed with an unclean needle. Thus circumcision was treated as a self-inflicted wound. If he had thought the operation essential, leave would have been granted. However these skivers enjoyed bed rest for days. Airman Solomon from the East End of London was incensed that he was not even considered for the operation.

When Dick returned from Croydon, crediting me with his good fortune, he sought me out for more advice. I could not convince him that, although geographically nearer, my home was just as emotionally far from Hut 29 as his was. I naturally asked how he had enjoyed his leave and he told a very strange story. His trip home had been arranged so quickly he did not have time to alert anyone with the news that he was on his way. He arrived in the late evening and took the opportunity to visit his girlfriend. Although her parents were at home, she was out at the pictures. He asked her parents to be sure to let her know that he would call round the following evening, made his excuses and went. But he did not go far; he hid in the bushes in the garden and waited. His girlfriend was very late back from the movies and – surprise surprise – she had a fellow in tow. Dick remained hidden as the couple kissed goodnight. At this point in the tale I suggested that I would have jumped out of hiding, giving them both the fright of their lives, kicked lover-boy up the backside and demanded an explanation from her.

"No, no," he protested. "I wanted to see how far she would go. She's supposed to be my girlfriend after all." He really was a dick. "I watched them, and they had it off on the doorstep."

Now I felt sure he would tell of the confrontation, and how he kicked her into touch instantly.

"What did you do?" I wanted to know.

"Nothing," he said. "I just went home."

There was method in this apparent madness from his point of view. It seems that their sex life had been intermittent. It should be remembered that these events occurred in the early Fifties, when attitudes were very different even if passions were the same. In my limited experience, a chap had to meet the folks and have his feet firmly under the table before a hand would be allowed to press on the breast area of a coat and several layers of clothing. That was sex life, Fifties-style. Dick's idea was to somehow blackmail his girlfriend into letting him have sex whenever he wanted it. Would it still work once she knew what he knew? He seemed not to have thought that through. I wondered how he could live with the thought that once he was off the scene someone else was enjoying the goodies. No wonder he was permanently homesick. It was not for his home, or his mum and dad; it was for a plentiful supply of nookie.

He came back to Kinloss a few hours late, squeezing the last minutes of freedom out of his furlough. Then he announced his master plan. His girlfriend was now his fiancée and his intention was to marry without delay, entitling him to more time at home. The padre again worked the oracle and we had a whipround in the hut to buy him a present. As some thirty men slept there, we raised a fair sum.

At about this time the camp tailor's premises were broken into. The only thing missing, as we were found out later, was the CO's suit. Mid-morning the whole camp was sent from work to our huts to stand by our beds. The quantity of debris and suddenly unwanted kit that was thrown out of windows and into the long grass was astonishing. We knew that the culprit had to be Dick, as he needed a wedding suit. Because we were the equipment hut, our lockers were particularly well stuffed with contraband. If Dick was responsible for us getting caught he would be a dead man. In Hut 27, only yards away, the suit was discovered and the hue and cry called off, but it had been a narrow squeak.

Dick was due to leave us again, and each time he went we had to do his work in the office, his fire piquet or other duties. A few days after he arrived back – two days late as usual – the administrative office sent for him.

Forms had to be completed so that his spouse could collect her marriage allowance. Three weeks later, Dick made a formal complaint about the delay in his wife getting her dues and an investigation was set in motion. It was reported back, after exhaustive enquiries in the Croydon area, that Dick was not married at all. The 'Ohs' and 'Ahs' had hardly died down before Dick, on the grounds that his prospective bride was pregnant, made yet another application for leave. The shame associated with such an occurrence had to be avoided at all costs, since the good name of the RAF might be besmirched. Only Dick and I knew that the responsibility might lie with the late-night opportunist who had made free with his girlfriend on his prospective in-laws' doorstep. Personally, I doubted if Dick's girlfriend was pregnant at all.

Despite everything that had gone before, Dick headed home again. It was about now that the i/c stores, the padre, the CO and the

RAF got their collective revenge. Bodies were needed in the Canal Zone of Egypt and Dick's name was at the head of the list. With the prospect of embarkation leave, we thought he would be happy enough. My name was further down the list, so Dick and I would set off for further adventures side by side.

At Deversoir, Dick took up where he left off, but this time leave was out of the question. He was determined to work his ticket, and he bought hashish through the perimeter wire from the natives. It resembled small cubes of compressed horse droppings, but Dick declared it top-rate stuff and good for hours of pleasant dreams. When posted as the billet area guard he would slope off back to bed in full kit, and we were daft enough to cover up for him.

Discovering that homosexuality was taboo in the Services, Dick determined to pose as one and to his, and our, everlasting shame participated with an equally bizarre tattooed Geordie in a sexual act which would have

Suez Square, the centre of Ismailia. Mid-1951. It looks peaceful, but it was the scene of many a conflict.

P BRUMMEL

horrified a vegetarian. The invited audience consisted of every resident of the billet. Only the Halton-trained corporal had the wit, decency and commonsense to quit the scene. What he did not see could not affect his stripes or his future prospects. Had word got out, both individuals would have spent a considerable time in the glasshouse before being granted a dishonourable discharge; but the secret stayed in the hut, dashing Dick's hopes. As a typically cynical punishment the audience, having enjoyed the spectacle and even encouraged the activity, sent them both to Coventry for the remainder of their time in Egypt.

Then on one bright and sunny morning, daily orders announced that leave could be granted in Cyprus. Golden Sands at Famagusta to be precise. Dick was up for it instantly since, like the rest of us, he had received no leave allocation for well over a year. Memory becomes a bit clouded here. Whether he went home directly from Egypt or via Cyprus I don't know. He was one of only two people who got back into the UK during their tour. Dick told us that he would not be returning, whatever the RAF said. He was short of cash and borrowed from everyone in the section. He did get home, and indeed he did not come back. Every penny he borrowed, though, was received by post within a fortnight. Well done Richard, but don't call us; we'll call you.

Another unforgettable character is Tony Rigden who has never filled in a football coupon, bought a lottery ticket or backed a horse in his life. He used up a lifetime's luck in Egypt in 1953. In the July of that year, while relations between Egypt and Britain had eased slightly, 3508672 LAC Rigden A. was enjoying a few beers with a couple of pals on a night out in Ismailia. The last bus back to RAF Abyad was due to leave at 9.30pm and, as the trio waited at the terminus in French Square, thirst overcame caution. Tony drew the short straw and his pals agreed to hold the bus until he returned with some Stella. The hotel was just a short distance away, and it

was common knowledge that if you went through a side gate, service would be provided via the kitchens. Tony got as far as the back door when two politically motivated local thugs threw a sack over his head and bundled him further into the out-of-bounds area and into a hovel somewhere in the backstreets of the town.

His mates kept the bus waiting and eventually sent for reinforcements, but no trace of Tony could be found. The hotel staff denied that any British Serviceman had been there. How could he have been? It was out of bounds. Usually such a story would end with the mutilated body being found floating in the Sweet Water Canal. Sometimes death was mercifully quick, but more often than not it involved sadistic torture.

At Deversoir, just up the road, we heard nothing of Tony's disappearance; but the news broke at home. Someone in authority in Egypt must have added his name as a bargaining counter to a list of demands given to the British Government.

Tony was smuggled to a military prison in Cairo. Conditions were terrible, with a permanently blocked hole in the floor for a toilet. A bucket was provided so that water could be used to flush. Tony tried this only once, for the result was a smelly, messy flood. He was issued with Egyptian cotton shirts and underwear, and his hair was cut to resemble the style worn by the locals. From there he was taken to a house and guarded by plain-clothed army men. His daily guard was a minimum of two men, and at night they slept across the locked doorway both inside and out. One of his guards, an officer, knew the words of the popular English song Moonlight Becomes You and sang it regularly to Tony, who always remained seated when in his presence, as he had heard tales of men like that.

The food was poor and Tony complained to an English-speaking officer. The result was the introduction to his diet of bully beef, which the officer insisted was a staple of the British Army and thus likely to be enjoyed by

Tony. He was fed it non-stop for the rest of his time in captivity. His captors kept quizzing Tony for information, although what value intelligence from an 'erk would be to a foreign power is hard to imagine. They played tough cop and good cop with him, but were clearly disappointed with the results.

In due time he was smuggled out of Egypt through Alexandria, then from Naples to Marseille, and on to Paris under constant close guard. His ordeal lasted for almost ten weeks as getting rid of him seemed to present a problem to his captors. Rumour has it that the Intelligence Service monitored his progress, and a message had got through that, if anything happened to Tony, the capture of the conspirators was certain. At this time capital punishment was still in vogue and the gang was certain to face Madame Guillotine. This warning of the dire consequences undoubtedly saved his life.

One day he was bundled into a car and driven to the centre of Paris where he was told to get out and go. Certain that he would be executed Tony threw himself to the ground as the car roared off. No shots were fired, and he got to his feet with a red face, suddenly aware of the curious stares of the promenading

A fine body of men, with a splendid collection of brown knee

Parisians. He made his way to the British Embassy, and in response to his knocking a concierge told him that his visit was inconvenient and could he call again tomorrow.

When he protested and gave his name he was hauled inside quite unceremoniously. It turned out that the Embassy knew that he was being held in Paris, but not his exact location. He was shipped back to England, given a new uniform and, surprisingly, ten weeks' pay. He was feted like a hero but was not sent back to Egypt as his time was nearly up. He feels that the whole incident was an embarrassment to everyone concerned, not least to the AOC who finally interviewed him, absolved him of all possible charges, and more or less very politely told him to p**s off.

Tony is a modest man and claims that he had very little to do with his adventure apart from being dragged along. He has visited Ismailia five times since his ordeal, and although the building where he was captured is no longer a hotel he cannot bring himself to enter the grounds in case it all happens again. His is a clear case of untreated post-traumatic stress disorder.

He still enjoys a drink, but Stella is not his favourite tipple.

8 AA Fire Command Battery, Royal Artilllery, at Tyne Camp, Ismailia, in 1954.

GAME FOR A LAUGH

*In a camp allergic to exercise, a sports day
looks like a bad idea. But with cash prizes,
it's not the taking part that's important*

It was decided to hold a sports day to boost morale and improve the health of everyone in the camp. We were all encouraged to enter at least one event and only genuine volunteers would be participating. The old Army idea of 'volunteering' where a sergeant pointed a finger at certain individuals and commanded: "You, you, and you!" had long gone. However, it was clear that the alternative to taking part would be unpleasant. A list of events was drawn up and an issue of little chits invited entries. To compete you simply had to sign your name against your chosen event, and there was something to suit everyone: jumping far or high, running short or long distances and throwing things. Cash incentives of undisclosed sums were promised to the successful competitors.

The results were disappointing, and something of a shambles. No one had volunteered to take part in the 'marathon', although it was considerably shorter than the normal twenty-six miles. Even a third of the normal distance would be liable to induce cardiac arrest in our fittest people and many of them had opted for the high or long jump. The shorter distances attracted their fair share of entrants but the realisation that a single throw would qualify you as a competitor, thereby avoiding a spell of guard duty or time in the kitchens, made field events the top attraction.

Officialdom restored a balance in entries by the simple expedient of adding a second and even a third event above the signatures on the slips of paper. Surprised faces discovered this when the selections were posted for us to read. Our portly squadron leader in the equipment section was a sports fanatic, with boxing his particular passion. Although it was clear that he never indulged in any form of exercise, he ran the boxing team and therefore considered himself an expert on fitness and training methods. He was determined that his section would triumph in the forthcoming Olympics and each of us was quizzed on our athletic history.

Being determined to do as little as possible, and having a phobia of running, I insisted that I had been schools champion in javelin, discus and shot. When questioned about my obvious physical frailty I managed to convince him that it was really a matter of technique and not one of strength. Once I had polished up my skills I would take on all comers. Since his knowledge of the matter was even more vague than mine he fell for it, but threatened dire consequences if I failed him. I could never understand why he took things so personally.

Whilst others faced the prospect of discovering what it feels like to run a quarter of a mile, I rested content that I would have an easy afternoon come sports day. Having volunteered for all three field events I decided to visit the physical training staff's hideaway in the hope of picking up a few tips. Upon my arrival the PTI nodded his head to indicate a shot, and then again to direct me to where some others had been practising. The circle was well marked, and various dimples in the sand indicated the extent of the competition's efforts so far.

It was about this time I discovered that, although not a natural athlete, I am a natural show-off and my loosening-ups and stretches were something worth watching. At school I had in fact putted the shot not too badly but had never merited a mention in dispatches, never mind been champion. The ball tucked into my neck under my chin felt right and my jiggling, shuffling hop across the circle created momentum. Using more than a little effort I threw it aggressively. It flew upwards as if fired from a cannon, and arced its way gracefully to land with a dull thud. I could tell it was a decent throw and trotted after it to see just how good it was in relation to those previously tossed. It was more than two yards further out than the best so far recorded, so I felt the event was in the bag. I carefully erased the evidence of my successful throw and strolled back to the sports hut.

No one had booked out a javelin or a discus so I thought I might as well have a try, but even through my rose-tinted spectacles the results were disappointing. The discus had a mind of its own and flew off at the wrong angle, bringing a curse from a sportsman speeding up for a try at the long jump. The javelin was heavier than I remembered and there was no hard standing to provide a decent run-up. However my enthusiasm for those events had waned now that I knew I had a win in the shot put more or less guaranteed, and I felt I had done enough training for our camp Olympics.

I sometimes wondered if the selection procedure for the Royal Air Force was lacking in some degree, because at MEAF Deversoir we had our share of halfwits. Some villages in England must have sorely missed their idiots when they joined up, and one such was Davy. Where Davy worked, or even if he worked, was never discovered but he appeared that day at the sports hut just as I was leaving.

Assuming that I had something to do with the place he asked my advice about running in the marathon. Now, his legs left a lot to be desired being better suited to a sparrow, but he had enthusiasm in abundance. That was how a few of us from our hut came to be accepted as his official trainers: after all, we'd do anything for a laugh.

The race distance was to be 10,000 yards so we instructed Davy (who reminded me of the Great Wilson, a boyhood hero of mine who featured in the Wizard) to eat as much as possible to give him the energy to last the distance. There would be no such thing as drinking stations en route so he would have to drink lots of water before setting off on the day. We also suggested that his practice should be over shorter distances and only every second day, since even his dedicated trainers found it irksome to hang about while he pounded away. For some reason connected with kinetic energy, which someone had read about, it was suggested that if he held a bunch of grass in each hand he could squeeze it at times of stress and it would keep him going. To give Davy his due, he carried out our instructions to the letter and confirmed that the grass-holding trick was most beneficial.

The great day came and groups of reluctant athletes gathered in clumps to await their moment in the sun. The officers were having a real field day, with many of them dressed in cricket whites. They carried flags, starting pistols, and deck chairs and mostly tried to look as if they knew what they were doing and were, thus, important. Sensing the confusion, dozens of unwilling contestants deserted.

My day was not wholly successful. My half-hearted attempt at the discus was awarded third place since it was the worst of only three valid throws by the entire field of competitors. My three attempts at the javelin resulted in two foot-faults and an unusual effort when the missile, having reached its optimum height, paused, then seemed to reverse and streak back towards its launch point. No

The programme cover for the Inter-Unit and Individual Swimming,
Diving and Water-Polo Championships held at Moascar.

The El Firdan band, which you can see on the following pages,
supplied the music at this tournament.

PRIZES

Mrs H.W. Heslop

has kindly consented to present the R.A.F. Canal North Inter-Unit Swimming and Diving Trophy. the Inter-Unit Water Polo Trophy and Prizes to individual winners and runners up

MUSIC BY

Royal Air Force, El Firdan Band

By kind permission of

WING COMMANDER R. E. CAESAR

Officer Commanding,

ROYAL AIR FORCE, EL FIRDAN

GOD SAVE THE QUEEN

R JOHNSTON

The RAF Volunteer Brass Band, El Firdan, in 1951. Some airmen would do anything for a good skive – even to wearing longs.

marks were awarded for interpretation or novelty, but I was not downhearted as there was still my speciality to come. The Tannoy made a call for the entrants.

I hoped my stroll to the mark was not too cocky, but since the majority of the contestants were only there for the skive, some very poor throwing was the norm. Many injuries from pulled muscles were claimed after, and even before, a single attempt, so the competition was whittled down to a precious few. I bent to pick up the shot and discovered that something was wrong. This was twice the size and weight of the one I had practised with, but when I complained to the PTI he was unimpressed.

"You must have picked up the ladies shot by mistake," he observed scathingly.

This monster shot was too big for my hand and seemed to obscure my vision when I brought it up to my face. Technique would have to triumph, so I threw myself across the circle and got rid of the thing. I avoided running out of the circle by a hair's-breadth and the throw was not only good but also the leading one. My strength had gone and my next two throws were abysmal but I did not care since my winning lob would bring me justified acclaim. However, one competitor, who worked in the blacksmiths, turned up late. He picked up the ball, took a step forward, and tossed it onwards and upwards. He did not need to throw another as he won by a mile. I was still secretly proud of my second place that netted five bob, and my discus effort that was worth a half-crown. Now it was time to have some fun with Davy.

The marathon was scheduled late in the afternoon when it would be cooler. The course consisted of laps round a quarter-mile oval. Davy set off, a bunch of grass in each hand, filled to the brim with water and his skinny little legs going like pistons. As instructed, he bided his time, but by the halfway mark he had lapped the competition so many times that everyone else had dropped out. The authorities decided that rather than hang about waiting

Me on the billet bicycle. The bushes in the background, planted to cool the Nissen hut, took only weeks to grow. They were planted by the post office corporal, a would-be author who lived with us in N3.

for him to complete the course they would call a halt to the proceedings and announce Davy the winner. We felt sure that our hero would want to share the celebration of his good fortune – and the ten-shilling prize – in the NAAFI with his trainers; but when we went to congratulate him he was nowhere to be seen.

There was no doubt that Davy was daft, but he was not daft enough to let us find him while he had ten bob to spend. Strangely, not one of his dedicated team of coaches set eyes on him again. A fine example of gratitude!

DEVERSOIR-SUR-CANAL

What a life! Sun, sand and swimming. Beer cans raining down from passing ships. A pity we were being shot at

Of all the RAF bases in the Zone, Deversoir was one of the best postings due to its position on the Canal. At the north end of the Bitter Lake, it was close to the water and benefited from cooling sea breezes. On a peninsula beside the camp was to be found the navigational control building which regulated the shipping traffic plying up and down the waterway. Near to the building, by a breakwater, was a swimming hole where the water was crystal clear and at least 30ft deep and therefore safe for diving into. It was there that I was able to study the sea horse – a tiny creature I had believed to be much bigger – in its natural environment as well as the small octopi found in fairly large numbers.

To swim in the Canal proper was put forward as just for the big boys, but I never heard of anyone drowning there. Swimming across the Canal was a permanent challenge surprisingly few airmen accepted. The heat haze created an optical illusion and at just over a hundred yards it was a lot further than it seemed. I swam to the other side several times, once or twice alone, but usually with company. There was not a lot to see, just stones and sand. I always felt that there might be some patient but hostile Arabs hiding there waiting for a soft target so I was not inclined to hang about. The day two of us were shot at marked our final visit to the far side.

My companion of that day slept in the bed next to mine and he was the leader of and inspiration behind the remarkable musical phenomenon Smokin' Pete Denison's Mouth Organ Band. Had the shooting been more accurate, Tin Pan Alley's loss would have been heaven's gain.

The other risk in swimming across the Canal was cramp, since we mostly swam after tiffin. It was easy for an unpractised swimmer to run out of puff, and a boat that had been a distant speck on the horizon could suddenly loom large and bear down upon you. With eyes just inches above the water it was difficult to judge distance and speed, and you had to decide to carry on or turn about. The danger of being dragged into the propellers was probably overestimated, but it gave the swimmer something to think about.

When coming from the north, the Ismailia end, the pilots seemed to speed up at the sight of the wide-open spaces of the Bitter Lakes. The boat crews were good to us, and more often than not cans of beer, tied to bits of wood, would rain down and splash into the water. The trick was to be close enough to grab the booty when wood and gift inevitably parted company on crash landing, but far enough away to avoid being struck by a missile. Lots of times we got the wood but not the beer, and it was extremely frustrating to see cans and bottles plummeting down just out of reach. When the sand dredgers came round, the operators must have thought it was their Christmas, Ramadan or whatever.

The only other items to come hurtling over the sides of the ships were French Foreign Legion troops anxious to avoid

This is the Bitter Lake area where we used to go swimming. The jetty and sunken barges are gone: now it's the playground of guests at the Helnan Morgan Hotel.

service in Indo-China. Not many succeeded, and those who did were quickly captured and handed back. This was unfortunate, as reports indicate that many of them were shot without trial when back on board their troopships. Later, when French ships passed through the Suez Canal, the legionnaires were battened down below deck under armed guard until out of temptation's way.

I'm no Rolf Harris but I harboured a yen to make a permanent record of the blue skies, yellow sand, green-topped palm trees and the different liveries of the shipping lines. I joined an art class in camp and discovered that a latent depression inside me jumped onto the canvas. I seemed unable to dip a brush into bright colours and instead chose black, purple, and deep orange and dark red. My brushes seemed to operate without input from me and I seemed to have no control over them. It was quite creepy. Moonscapes, and Mars and Venus with attendant satellites, appeared out of a matt black background, and painting after painting was on the same theme. When I became ambitious and tried to mix colours the result invariably was a muddy tint. When eventually my boat ticket came, I

tore up all my paintings. This enraged my instructor.

"There's no such thing as bad work," he claimed. "It's all part of the learning process and you'll regret it later. It's sheer vandalism."

He was right, and I do.

It was about this time someone decided that since there was a dearth of professional entertainment from home we should do it ourselves, just like Judy Garland and Mickey Rooney in the movies. I remember two items from the show. One was a thought-reading act that proved to be a hundred per cent accurate. It was uncanny. The maestro, an amateur newly arrived on camp, who would surely turn professional as soon as he left the Service, announced things known only to a few of us – the initials of the man in the third bed from the left in the hut, the Christian name of our warrant officer, the last three digits of the Service number of the tallest man in the stores section. It was quite inexplicable.

The other act that I remember gave us a spontaneous chance to be cruel. As in all Service concerts, the front rows were reserved for the brass hats, so we were in the darkness behind, giving us instant and unrestricted communication with each other. The last act was a popular officer who appeared on stage with an eight or twelve-stringed banjo, which I understand is fiendishly difficult to play. He was note-perfect and, like every other act, was cheered loudly. The audience demanded an encore, and it became clear he had practised only one tune and thus we had heard his entire repertoire. The eager audience seized on this. When he had played the same tune a second time there was foot stamping and non-stop cheering until it was played a third time. It was only when the demands for a fourth encore were at their height that everyone realised it had become a send-up. His popularity was, in part, due to his good nature and he waved and smiled as he was eventually allowed to exit stage left.

It was on the day I was leaving for home that a lad who had been in our billet for a couple of years confessed to me in strictest confidence that he had been the mindreader's accomplice, and the whole act was rigged. It had been put to him that giving the bored lads something to puzzle over could only be beneficial. I agreed to say nothing. Fifty years later, I am breaking my vow of silence.

RAF Deversoir had been in operation since the Second World War, if not longer, and German and Italian prisoners had been kept there. Some of the billets we had to reclaim due to the rapid expansion in personnel had previously contained WAAFs. It was easy to identify which the internees had occupied. They had made some effort to make the place more comfortable by laying walkways and enclosing areas in dwarf walls. They had left quality artwork on walls and had carved various objects d'art. Those billets previously occupied by the women of the Air Force were equally easy to identify. The crude graffiti and genital representations would have made the inhabitants of Pompeii blush.

Veterans who revisited the Canal Zone have told me that the Deversoir camp is out of bounds to visitors, though Fayid is open, and a much larger Ismailia, now housing a

Remember her? This painting on the mess hall wall at Deversoir was left by German prisoners in 1943. I do not remember her at all.

university, can be visited. The immaculate lawns of the Greek and French quarter have gone however, and it's a typical Egyptian town..

I would love to see a pyramid, and the Upper Nile is said to be quite lovely, but the only thing that would take me back would be the chance to sit by Deversoir Point and wander round a few of the haunts of my youth. It is possibly not at all as I remember it , but I confess that I would like to see it one more time.

In the years before 1950, the Suez Canal Zone, though never a posting of choice, was at least a tolerable place. The following poem may jog memories in those who enjoyed the amenities of the Blue Kettle in happier times.

What a delight on a Saturday night,
To stroll around Ish wearing mufti.
When after some Stellas, some of the fellas
Would ask a young girl for a shufti.

RED FOR DANGER

*The much-maligned Military Police rose several
points in the esteem of their brothers-in-arms
by being first on the scene in times of danger*

For a corps to be universally loathed is unusual. Presumably, before joining the Royal Corps of Military Police, the recruits are quite normal, so the training must bear the responsibility for the change in them and their attitude to their fellow-soldiers. If you examine the ninety-plus years of the corps' existence it's not difficult to understand the hostility towards its members universally adopted by the rest of the Army. In First World War their duty was to round up deserters, including the shell-shocked and mentally deranged, give them a hard time in the glasshouse, and return them to their units in time for them to go 'over the top' to certain massacre. RCMP men – or redcaps – stayed well behind the lines, the better to locate other deserters, and the only danger they faced was that of being late for lunch, dinner or having a few beers in the local *estminet*.

In the Second World War they were still employed well away from the battle zone. Their main duty seemed to be to awaken sleeping soldiers in rail stations, check that their leave passes were in order, and point out the fact that the soldier had the odd button undone. A charge sheet would follow the unfortunate squaddie to his new posting.

But things changed after D-day. Many of those snoopers found themselves, arms encased in snow-white armlets, directing the traffic right up there in the front line. Line regiment infantry fighting close by could keep their heads down, but red-capped traffic policemen, performing their vital roles, were sitting ducks and hundreds of them were killed. In the ebb and flow of warfare, enemy vehicles were often requisitioned and the man on duty at the crossroads had no way of knowing who was coming, or from where. Some were shot by snipers at long range, many died from close-up gunfire and doubtless some died from bullets made in the Midlands of England. Bombs and shellfire also took their toll. As a result, by the end of the war the redcaps' reputation had risen several points in the esteem of their brothers-in-arms.

The same can't be said for the 'crushers' in the Navy or the 'snowdrops' in the RAF. I hope their mothers loved them because no one else did. At the time of their serving in Egypt in the early Fifties, the RCMP were working hard at becoming unpopular again. Their tasks were dangerous in the extreme and they were invariably first on the scene in times of danger. Leading convoys in open Land Rovers, and being obliged to work closely with the treacherous Egyptian police cost them more than their share of men in the conflict. And yet they managed to get our backs up. Some of the following incidents involving redcaps are no doubt apocryphal, some could be exaggerated, and one or two might just be true.

While most of the pressed passengers enjoyed a relaxing trip on board troopships, the redcaps had to work. They were first on board the *Empress of Canada* and some dimwit on high decided that it would be nice if they shared their quarters with the Royal Marines. Being first on board, the redcaps selected the best bed spaces, dumped their kit thereon, and reported for duty. When the marines arrived they threw that kit into a far corner and took over the beds. The RCMP were not best pleased.

The duty of the military police on board was to patrol in endless circles to ensure that the rest of us behaved in a suitable manner. The marines were a tough bunch, many sporting 1939-45 war ribbons and therefore much older than the rest of the passengers, and they decided to control a conveniently sunny part of the deck. When a pair of redcaps approached, they were instructed to 'foxtrot oscar' whence they came. Indeed, whatever area of the deck the marines decided to claim as their own became a no-go area for the redcaps.

A distinct memory for me is of a marine showing off his badges, like those worn by Boy Scouts, each indicating a special skill acquired by the wearer. Their value to the nation was no doubt great, but to the marine himself the monetary value was what mattered. Long-service and good-conduct badges were the basis of a substantial pay structure. All were mentioned in direct relation to the daily rate paid. A parachutist's pay was perhaps a shilling a day, a marksman's crossed rifles garnered another four pence, canoe handling and diving were each worth about sixpence, as were motor-cycling and vehicle driving skills. The list seemed endless and, if memory serves me right, ski-ing and mountaineering were included. A nice twist was the way he related the values in beer volumes. "This 'ere is worth a pint. And that one is a whisky chaser." His round-eyed audience could only marvel and wish.

Another true story is told of an RMPC detachment which – having missed the plane home – was posted to a homeward-bound troopship. The cruise would be over the Christmas period and so, instead of the quick flight home and enjoying the festivities with their families, they found themselves keeping the peace between the Royal Scots at one end of the ship and the Highland Light Infantry at the other. The HLI were a strange lot. The previous year they had been obliged to celebrate Christmas and not the New Year, as they would have preferred, and they marked their disappointment by burning down the guardroom of their barracks. It seems that the trouble started when some HLI entered a bar and were greeted by a party of paras with the remark: "Oh, there's going to be dancing. Here come the girls." Not the most tactful of greetings. The HLI seemed content to fight with everyone.

The HLI and Royal Scots made a formidably muscular unit when they agreed to join forces and this was done when Lt Moorhouse of the West Yorks went missing. Informers were concealed in the rear of a covered Land Rover and an intelligence officer had them point out suspects. The Scottish troops conducted house-to-house searches and frightened the residents out of their wits. Lt Moorhouse eventually turned up and he does not appear in the Roll of Honour, so this story must have a happy ending.

The Blue Kettle in Ismailia was the focal point of much RCMP activity in days before the troubles started in earnest. Protection rackets and loan-sharking were rife in some regiments and members of the force, in mufti, infiltrated the place to discover and point out the gang ringleaders who always had plenty of spending money. Sometimes they were identified as the enemy and legendary and vicious battles resulted.

Once the duty men were called from the Blue Kettle to the scene where a just-married Serviceman had hanged himself. Though their response was fast, word of the incident had been slow to reach them and they found a fly-blown, maggot-riddled corpse. Where the wife thought her husband had been for the missing days is not recorded.

There was even a vice-squad detachment working in Ismailia then, and from all reports

C C KNOWLES

The Blue Kettle in Ismailia, focal point of RCMP activity before the troubles started in earnest (1950). I managed to visit it once before it closed.

they were kept pretty busy. I have yet to meet anyone who will admit to having contracted venereal disease during his service in Egypt, so the custom in such places must have been entirely restricted to those wearing uniform.

While the battle was raging over the Bureau Sanitaire and the Caracol a 'no looting' order was issued. The redcaps had to enforce it and this was more easily said than done. A foot patrol of two RCMP happened across a para officer with cohorts jemmying open a desk. The upholders of the law were ordered to get out, so they wandered off. The incident could have been entirely innocent and connected with the battle. Perhaps they were seeking blueprints or plans of the buildings, then again perhaps not. In any event, notebooks stayed firmly in pockets.

Another Corps member, hardly an untidy type, remembers seeing a detachment of French Foreign Legion troops and describes them as the smartest body of men he had ever seen. This confirms my remarks in regard to the officer that I saw from the deck of the troopship in Algiers. They are a credit to France and an object of admiration to every military unit, worldwide.

Homosexuality was a problem that needed delicate handling by the redcap SIB and, as some of them were still in their teens, it was amazing how successful they were in rooting out culprits. The homosexuals usually operated in secretive groups and preyed on young soldiers. In one complicated enquiry, the main culprit was the garrison sergeant major – who was convicted and imprisoned before to being given a dishonourable discharge from the Army. After sentence, it was revealed that his record included being found guilty by a court martial in Germany and reduced to the ranks for a similar offence. The decision not to sling him out of the Army had allowed him to continue to corrupt young soldiers.

It was not all doom and gloom being a policeman in Egypt. Having enjoyed a night of revelry with fellow officers, a Major Kenneth Syndall decided that an old field gun adorning a Royal Artillery barracks occupied by Mauritian Pioneers was just what he wanted. He issued a Form 118 to the guard commander and he and his inebriated friends wheeled it to the Provost Company Lines. Being in a merry mood he woke his men, showed them the spoils and then hid the gun in one of their tents. Inevitably, the RSM found out about the affair and the CO of the division was informed. Major Syndall was removed and a court-martial reduced him to the rank of second lieutenant before sending him back to the UK.

Things are never as they seem in the RCMP and they were warned, as were all the other drivers in the Canal Zone, of the dangers to be expected on the roads. A puncture or a breakdown on an empty stretch of road could attract, as if by magic, hordes of angry Arabs out of the desert. Should the incident involve injury to a native, a strange wailing would be heard and it would not be the siren of an approaching ambulance but the lamentations of extremely hostile natives bent on revenge. The odd Arab had been known to deliberately injure himself by coming into violent contact with a Service vehicle. A small pension from the British Government was enough to keep him at comparative ease, without the need to work, for the rest of his life. Although everyone who served in the Zone had heard rumours about such claims and tried to avoid them, it is only now that limited evidence has emerged to show such a policy did exist.

A former RCMP corporal describes his introduction to Egypt by his CO, a major, thus: "We stopped outside the RMP Duty Room and were 'fell in'. The CO was a frightening figure, mainly because we were fascinated by his cap-badge, a skull and crossed bones of the 17/21 Lancers. He did not greet with us in nice words like 'Welcome to Egypt, lads.' Oh no, all he said was: 'The first thing is that you must learn to shoot and to SHOOT TO KILL!' He then glared at us before carrying on: 'Those of you who are drivers must learn that if you collide with an Egyptian pedestrian or cyclist, you do not stop if other people are about. If none is about and the man is still alive, you reverse over him until he his dead, then drive away fast.' With that, he turned on his heel and left the squad pole-axed. It will be noted that there was no written confirmation of this instruction.

Despite their reputation, the Royal Corps of Military Police are a welcome sight when the chips are down. I offer this anonymous piece of doggerel in their defence.

WE CALLED THEM BASTARDS

The Service canteen was well crowded
with troops of every kind,
when a soldier came in feeling lonely,
a friend he was hoping to find.

In his hand he carried a letter
from his home that was so far away;
he wanted to study the message
from his dearest, and what she might say.

He then caught sight of the Redcap
sitting so quietly there.
"Excuse me, Corp," he queried,
"but have you a minute to spare?

I've just received this letter
but I'm afraid that I cannot read."
The copper took hold of the missive
and to read it aloud did proceed.

"Shall I write a reply to it, for you?"
The soldier then answered "Yes please."
And with that the husky young copper
brought a lonely soldier some ease.

And I thought to myself, they're all bastards.
It's a well known fact that they're mad
with power from a stripe and lanyard.
But that one... he must have a Dad.

COUNTING DOWN TO FREEDOM

Happy souls due for release were wheeled into the Squadron Leader's office to hear his recruiting homily, but in my case he decided not to waste his time

At some time anyone who survives military service has to face the prospect of returning to civilian life. For a regular who has served his twenty-two years this could be depressing; although nowadays, with the prospect of a golden handshake running to thousands of pounds, things are not so bad. Returning home was uppermost in the minds of National Servicemen and short-term regulars for months before their escape. We were sure we would return to a rosy-hued Civvy Street where anxious employers would welcome us into well-paid jobs and the girl next door would fall into our open arms. Life would be a dream...

But it wasn't, of course. It would prove to be a nightmare for all but the fortunate few.

Each morning another little cross would appear on the calendar; another day served, another step nearer to the boat. Each day seemed to become longer and longer. We were like kids waiting for Santa Claus. But open excitement had to be curtailed, and to less fortunate billet mates with longer to wait you had to appear blasé.

During the early weeks after newcomers' arrivals it was expected that you would teach them at every opportunity to get their knees brown, and it happened to everyone in turn. It was not the done thing to gloat about the approach of your ticket to Blighty. Cooks and others with suitable currency substitutes would purchase advance notice of names appearing on teleprinter reports of new troop movements. The less-well-funded had to wait until their names appeared on daily orders. The recipient of the glad tidings would completely unconcerned about the whole thing, while inside he was jumping with glee.

My release date was 13 November 1953, and I hoped to wave goodbye to Egypt at least a month earlier; but it was not to be. It was late in October before I was wheeled before the Squadron Leader for his little homily, delivered to anyone about to depart for pastures new. Happy souls due for release were paraded in his office to be told the same uplifting story. He was particularly sorry to see them go, as they had been so helpful and productive in their work. In fact, so diligent had this particular airman been – this applied to anyone the line was being shot at – that he had been considered for promotion since he was clearly NCO material. If he cared to sign certain forms which our determined recruiter just happened to have by him, in the fullness of time – subject to a few formalities – stripes could be virtually guaranteed. Barrack room lawyers picked up on the word 'virtually'. According to the Oxford English Dictionary it means 'in effect, but not in fact'.

Very few of the airmen so addressed were lawyers, but they could spot a phoney offer at 500 yards, and the Squadron Leader's re-signing success rate had been nil to date.

He tried another strategy which was equally unsuccessful. An airman could go home and take his demobilisation leave before signing on again. When he did this, he was entitled to the posting of his choice, and once back at Deversoir he would soon be visiting the corporals' mess. Naturally our intrepid leader failed to mention that such action would involve starting a new thirty-month tour of duty. When heads shook even at this splendid offer, his final bid was tinged with desperation. He would suggest that the airman leave the Air Force and give civilian life a try then, having found it was not all it was cracked up to be, rejoin. If he returned to Deversoir and the squadron, promotion was on the cards. Naturally, it could only be guaranteed if the Squadron Leader was still in command, and again the offer would be hedged about with such phrases as 'subject to establishment quotas,' and 'as and when vacancies arise'. It was so vague that there were no takers. Only the certifiably mad would have signed. We were not mad, only close to it with a condition known as being demob-happy.

When I appeared before him, the drill was suddenly altered. He looked up from his papers, feigning surprise.

"Oh, it's you Findlay."

"Yes sir," I responded, just in case he really was unsure.

He then said: "I suppose I'm wasting my time..."

I thought it worth a quip: "Your supposer is in perfect working order, sir." He sighed audibly. He could only have been reflecting on the past differences of opinion between us. Sometimes I was right but he, as Squadron Leader, always had the last word.

I greatly respected the man. Although he had never served as aircrew, he sported the ribbon of the Croix de Guerre on his chest. These are not handed out like sweeties at a tea party, and his was for bomb and mine disposal in the war. It must have been irritating for him to be reduced to the task of running an equipment section, however vital the work. The respect may have been mutual, because he described me in my discharge papers as having an 'alert brain' and a 'persuasive personality'. Even at this late stage the ball was still in play. I was standing to attention in respectful mode.

"March him out, warrant officer," he ordered, and I was duly removed. And so I gained the distinction of being the only man in the squadron's history not to have been given the flannel about extending his service.

By one of those strange quirks of fate, I recently met the Serviceman who took my place in equipment accounts at Deversoir, and he had no recollection of my Squadron Leader. Had I been daft enough to take up his offer – if he had made it – I would have returned to Deversoir to find both him and his promises long gone. Perhaps he could not face life there without me.

The clock ticked on until I was quite certain I had been overlooked and would be serving additional time. No doubt, if one knew where to look, Queen's Regulations must be riddled with loopholes to cover such contingencies. I dismissed thoughts of suing the Air Ministry as futile.

In early November I was moved to the transit camp near Fayid. I am not too bolshie myself, but I seemed to be surrounded by those who were, and we were not slow in advocating our point of view on the type of duty appropriate to men on their way home. We felt we should be allowed to loaf about in the NAAFI, but the RAF disagreed.

To keep us busy, we were put to shovelling the sand out of concrete bases with 12-inch retaining walls to prepare them for the erection of airmen's tents. The units were natural sand traps and the slightest breeze quickly refilled them. Strictly speaking we should have been enjoying our demobilisation leave of fourteen days, but it was clear we were going to be diddled out of that perk. Few of us had received a leave allocation during our service, so most of us reckoned the RAF owed us three or four months' pay. Applications for cash in lieu were instantly rejected, and suffering from this injustice we were viewed with deep suspicion by the camp staff. Having deserted

French Park with the Sweet Water Canal in the foreground. 1952. In peacetime the Canal Zone could have been a quality posting, but there's nothing the Egyptian Tourist Board could possible dream up to make me return to the Suez Canal Zone on a pleasure trip.

our posts at the sandpits we were tracked down and put in the charge of the guardroom sergeant. He was an odd individual and was permanently armed with a pace stick. It was clear that he did not know what to do with it, but he carried it everywhere as a badge of authority. He had probably seen a sergeant major in the Brigade of Guards doing his stuff, and assumed that this talisman was the source of the swank.

He had either been instructed or had decided off his own bat to teach us a lesson and had chosen picking up litter as a suitably demeaning task. The area to be cleared covered a good half-acre, from the front of the guardroom to the boundary fence along the main road. We were strung out along the length of the fenced area and equipped with litterbins. The jumped up snowdrop – who was probably acting unpaid – strode up and down behind us, pace stick under his arm,

peering out from under the slashed peak of his cheesecutter hat.

The traffic was heavy and the drivers and guards, noticing our lethargic approach to our duties, clearly jumped to the conclusion that we were prisoners under punishment. Today we could go to the Court of Human Rights and be awarded untold sums by the Government for cruel and degrading punishment. As it was, we were rewarded by the passers-by. Packets of cigarettes, bottles of beer, toffees, chocolate bars, and even money were chucked at us as we laboured away. Drivers who had missed giving us a treat the first time turned their lorries round and passed us again, throwing out largess that was gratefully received and applied as a balm to our hurt pride.

The poor stick man was beside himself with rage. Having little to lose, we completely ignored him and shared our communal loot equitably. After a time he realised that he was beaten and withdrew his working party from the field. We then sloped off and he, having had enough, pretended he couldn't see us go. He stormed into his guardroom where presumably he repolished his pace stick.

In the early afternoon of 10 November a Corporal Donnelly, who said he lived in Bray near Dublin, where he would soon be joining the family's very successful transport firm, borrowed ten shillings (a day's wages) from me until his pay parade that afternoon. By teatime he had left on an earlier flight and I never saw him again. Compound interest is a wonderful way to multiply one's savings, and I have worked out that he now owes me over fifty quid. Does anyone out there know a rich Irish family called Donnelly? Or even a family of that name that owns a horse and cart?

At last, on 11 November, with only two days of my contract left, I was due to board a York aircraft for the flight home. It looked as if the RAF might still make it on time.

On the night of the 10th I visited the NAAFI and, though virtually a non-drinker, drowned my sorrows by downing more bottles Blue-Star beer than was good for me. When the time came to stumble back to the billet I found that my pride and joy, my newly issued cheesecutter, was missing. Had the culprit been found, murder would have been done. All the anger, frustration and rage I had stored up over two years was ready for release. The red mist had descended and consequences would not have mattered. My last days of service were to be seen out wearing a borrowed, outdated, attention-seeking piece of headgear – a forage cap several sizes too small. And I knew my hangover would be as fierce as I felt.

But the day that dawned was one never to be forgotten. I was on my way.

An Airman's Farewe

Land of sweat and shirt that stinks,
Land of Pyramids and Sphinx,
Sweat rash, foot rot, and prickly heat,
Aching hearts and blistered feet.
Swarms of flies that buzz and bite,
Mosquitoes pinging through the night.

Land of scorpions, camels, bugs,
Henna, hashish, other drugs.
Streets of sorrow and of shame
Streets that never had a name.
Clouds of sand and dust that send
The sanest 'bod' clear round the bend.

Donkeys, goats, piard dogs,
Cut-throats, thieves and bleedin' 'wogs'.
Land where children in their teens
Sell souvenirs outside canteens.
'Baksheesh, baksheesh' is their cry,
By this alone they live or die.

Where typhoid thrives and gypo gripes,
Where 'wogs' smoke hubble-bubble pipes.
And every native, brown or black,
Just waits to knife you in the back.
Obnoxious smells, eternal strife
Oh! For my homeland and the wife.

⊃ the Canal Zone

Where men with 'prep chits' sit and gloat
While other dream about the boat,
Their only aim to dodge and skive
Until their 'clearance docs' arrive.
Their chief delight – to laugh and shout
At some poor 'erk whose just come out.

Land of Taabush, djellabah
'quoise tamaam, quoise kateer'.
Land of chi and mungareia
Moiré, chappatis, Stella beer.
Where one can often hear men say
'Thank God for the YMCA.'

Oh! For Britain's happy life
Where people never see such strife.
My tickets here - I'm going home,
Away from there no more I'll roam.
I'm on my way, it will be grand
To see green fields instead of sand.

Land of sorrow, filth and shame,
I've seen you once, no more again.
I leave you now with no regret,
The things I've seen I'll ne'er forget.
Native's heaven, white man's hell
This land, this Egypt, *fare thee well.*

Anon

FLIGHT FROM EGYPT

*Farewell to hot desert and Egyptian terrorists. And
back to cold Blighty and (hopefully) warm girls*

I am ashamed to admit that the Armistice
Day memorial parades and observance did
not even cross my mind in November 1953,
because I was going home – at last. The
York aircraft which the RAF used at that time
was an unusual model, with an entry door
that was so close to the ground a single step
could assist passengers aboard. It was a slow
steady machine. Passengers sat with their
backs to the engines, facing the tail of the
aircraft.

Every seat was occupied since someone
had failed to realise that a few planes would
be unable to transport home the huge
numbers delivered to Egypt by overcrowded
troop- ships. The passengers were a mixed
bunch, reflecting in microcosm the variety of
personnel serving in the Canal Zone at that
time. In addition to a wide range of uniforms
there were families with demented children
who seemed to think that the York was a
playground.

The excitement on board was infectious as
everyone was elated by the prospect of going
home, with the possible exception of the
aircrew. As the aircraft rumbled along the
tarmac, gaining speed to take off, I finally
accepted that I was escaping. I would soon be
rid of the stink of Egypt. My thoughts were
with the lads who still had time to serve, and
particularly with those I had helped to bury,
who would never be going home.

Our first stop was Malta. I had been
brought up on stories of the George Cross
island. Tales of the Gut and riding in gharries

were in my mind, and I hoped that we would
find time for a run to town.

After what seemed like an age of droning
away the plane slowly began to lose height in
her approach to Luca airport. We dropped
lower and skimmed over the rooftops of
Valetta, so low that we could clearly see the
streetlights and people milling about. Once
or twice we looked into houses where
curtains had not been drawn.

We sailed past the chequered caravan at
the approach end of the runway expecting to
land, but we flew on. The troops and families
were coming to life at the prospect of
stretching their legs, and the conversation
grew louder. Only the RAF personnel were
quiet, knowing that it was time we felt the
bump of the wheels hitting the ground.
Perhaps the pilot was more used to
Shackletons or Lancasters because he
showed a marked reluctance to touch down.

Fully convinced that he would stick on the
power and go round again, we waited
expectantly. He came lower still but failed to
make contact with the runway. Then, far too
late, he put the plane down and we rolled
along the ground at breakneck speed.
Reverse thrust is not possible on a propeller
driven plane, and the brakes must have
smoked a bit before they burst into flames.
We passed the caravan at the far end of the
runway and kept on going. We were slowing
down, but not quickly enough, and we
ploughed right through the perimeter fence
where the wheels dug into loose sand. We

finally stopped with the aircraft completely outside the airfield. Had we come to an abrupt halt, having the seats facing the tail would have shown its value. Most of the passengers – civilians and craphats – were quite happy with the landing, and had noticed nothing amiss until asked to clear out at the double. They would not have been so sanguine had they known that fourteen months later a York was to explode and crash at the same spot killing the crew of five, an Army private and forty-three RAF and RAF Regiment men who had just completed their tour of duty in the Canal Zone. When a plane has been involved in an accident the RAF naturally become concerned, and in this case they would not allow it to fly again until a qualified inspector had examined the undercarriage; but he was in the UK and it would take some time to fly him out.

We were stuck in Malta as dawn was breaking on 12 November. I had one day to serve. It seemed a good idea to utilise the time by arranging a quick visit to Valetta, but the authorities disagreed and permission was refused. We went to find the gaping hole in the perimeter fence, but it was already being repaired and an armed policeman was in attendance so we were unable to sneak out.

It would be many years before I visited Malta again, to discover that the bread is as delicious as any in the world. I recommend it. Try it with a squirt of olive oil and a splash of tomato puree. Good, but even better when washed down with a glass or two of the MacStagger.

Once the plane was ready for action we took off again. We saw Corsica, or was it Sardinia? We were tired by then and didn't much care.

The flight to Stanstead Airport was uneventful apart from a heart-stopping moment over Paris. The captain announced that if we looked out of the port windows we would be able to see the Eiffel Tower sticking up through the cloud cover. The inexperienced passengers moved to that side

of the plane for a better look, greatly unbalancing the aircraft. But the pilot's recent narrow squeak must have sharpened his reactions because the recovery manoeuvre he performed was quite brilliant. Stanstead looked green and lush from the air, and we landed without further incident. Many who had sworn to kiss the ground of old England chickened out when given the chance, since traditional British reserve returned to everyone the minute their feet touched the soil. Customs had to have their say, although what they thought we could smuggle beats me. Once the formalities had been observed we boarded buses for central London. None of us had a clue where Stanstead was, and every mile brought excited observations.

The weather was mild for November, but to us it was distinctly chilly. We noticed little apart from girls walking on the pavements, female shop assistants serving clients, women in general. On the plane we had seen the Service wives laden down with offspring, and therefore quite unapproachable. The women we were now looking at, and who waved in return to our catcalls and whistles, were real living and approachable dolls. None of us talked except to draw attention to a particular beauty that the others might have failed to notice. Our thoughts were concentrated on the forbidden fruits ahead; Carnation-topped salad that would surely be available in the city centre to ravenous young men. We agreed that the number one priority was to satisfy the lust that had built up over two years in the desert; indeed in some cases all our lives. This was long before the Street Offences Act, and we had been told hair-raising stories of how easy it was to have an instant romance in London.

It was approaching lunchtime on 13 November, the date that my release was due. To give credit where it is due, somehow a pay parade was organised and travel warrants issued. We were given a severe talking to, unheard by most of us, to the effect that we were still subject to military law. It was meant to remind us that we were still technically tied to the RAF, and subject to its discipline, for our reserve period.

Being issued with civilian clothes was a hoot. A cap or a trilby was the first choice, as at that time the advertising hoardings advised that if you wanted to get ahead you had to wear a hat. Sports coat and flannels or a two or three-piece suit was next, but no shirt or tie was on offer. We would have to make do with what we had – our fetching RAF-blue shirts and black ties. A coat was

G EVANS

The three ways down the Suez Canal: the Treaty Road, the Canal and the railway. We didn't care which method of transport we used so long as it took us nearer home.

also issued and I selected a rubberised riding coat with concealed leg straps. Equitation was not on my mind, following my first experience in Ismailia, but I thought it would be just dandy when riding my bike in the rain. There was a definite run on brown

shoes, since we had been forced to wear black ones for the last three years. A line of spivs outside the clothing centre offered to purchase the boxes of new clothes for a fiver, then a tenner. If this offer failed to get a positive response a last desperate attempt would be made – £15! They were doing lively trade but not with me. It had taken a long time to earn those togs and if I did not like them I would give them away or even burn them, but they were not for sale.

A small group of us arranged to hold a party that night. We would meet at Piccadilly Circus to enjoy a night on the town featuring a mix of wine, women and song. For once we would have plenty of money in our pockets. We separated and I dumped my kit at the left luggage office at King's Cross station before deciding how to pass the time before the reunion. I did what every red-blooded male does in such circumstances and took a taxi straight to Soho. I had it on good authority that the salt beef sandwiches on sale there were not to be missed, and I set off to find the famous shop.

To my huge surprise and delight I was accosted by ladies of every size shape and colour offering services to tired businessmen. At five-yard intervals this kaleidoscope of delight kept changing and one or two even opened their coats as an added inducement. The stockings, suspender belts and bras were flashed as a sort of foretaste of the possibilities to follow. It was all too much for me and I dived into a public house, as much to gather my thoughts as to refresh the inner man. I was almost a non-drinker and I suppose I overdid the refreshing bit because when I emerged I was ready for anything. The instant excitement of the free peep shows inflamed my senses and reduced the dread inculcated by the RAF's 'don't do it' films. The few beers, instead of cooling me down, had heated me up and as I still had plenty of time in hand before I was due to meet the lads. I decided to take a stroll.

A very attractive lady – with perhaps a

York aircraft similar to this were used to ferry military personnel back from the Canal Zone and were often the target of terrorist organisations. One crashed, probably due to sabotage by Cypriot terrorists, as it left Malta in 1956 (see of Roll Honour for further details). The York was a development of the Lancaster bomber with a larger fuselage and an additional tail fin. Those operated by Scottish Airlines had a poor maintenance record and constantly broke down.

M HARDY

little too much make-up on – whom in my fuddled state I took to be a vision of pure delight, asked me if I was interested in spending time with a naughty girl. Not half, I wasn't. But still I was held back by the residual fears of the possible consequences. My early religious instruction had made its mark, and I knew that anything exciting and forbidden was sinful and should therefore be avoided like the plague. There was no 'little room' at the back of the guardroom in the West End of London, but she really was gorgeous and I felt that I did not care about any possible consequence. She was Vicki Michelle from 'Allo, 'Allo come to life. She

was French and her business card nameplate described her as Madame Lulu, so it all seemed quite perfect. I always thought that the madame simply oversaw operations, but Lulu must have been a one-woman band because she seemed to be extremely enthusiastic and very keen to do business.

Although it was years before safe sex was Government approved policy it did run through my mind, and remembering the incident in the billet at Deversoir I asked rather tentatively if that particular option was available from her extensive repertoire. My former resistance evaporated when she

The Senior Service clear up after the Malta crash on 18 February 1956. (See Roll of Honour for more details)

replied in the affirmative with as much outrage as if I had requested an extra cube of sugar with my tea (sugar was still rationed). As I followed her upstairs to her apartment in Brewer Street I became hypnotised by the sway of her buttocks. They had a sensuousness that had to be seen to be believed, and were inches in front of me. Gosh! Excitement overcame me and, emboldened by her laissez-faire attitude, I reached out to caress those beautiful orbs; and instantly found myself back on the street, with a distinctly French flea in my ear. It seems that unspeakable antics were permissible once a client had crossed the portals of the boudoir, and presumably paid over his subscription, but correct behaviour was expected until that moment. She obviously had little experience of desert-weary, sex-starved, brown-kneed veterans. I decided that I would look her up again later when the boys hit town. By then, if business had been brisk, she would have forgotten all about my unprovoked attack on her delicious derrière. Perhaps if I had paid in advance I would not have been thrown down the stairs.

I still had a bit of time in hand, and in my tipsy state thought it prudent to check the times of train departures to Edinburgh. When I arrived at the station a train was due to leave in ten minutes and although it was a stopping train I decided that it would suit me. My reasoning was that the others might not show up anyway and if I went back to Soho I would definitely end up with my Madame Lulu, and who knows where that might lead.

Pure and unsullied I struggled across the concourse from the left luggage office laden down with my kit bag, a cardboard box of clothes, and other sundry items. I found the platform and in minutes the train drew out and I was on my way home. The RAF had got me demobbed on time after all, *sans* the leave due to me but with four hours to spare. All the little 'xxx's on the calendar had paid off and now, at last, I was a free man kissing goodbye to Service life. Then sleep must have claimed me because I can remember nothing of the journey.

I was to receive one last perk from my service in the RAF: on the number six tramcar to Marchmont the conductor, in acknowledgement of my deep tan, refused to accept my fare. Apart from that nothing had changed and the world had not even noticed that I had been away. However the nicest bit was still to come. The friendly conductor posed the question that Servicemen have been asked since time began.

"When are you due back son?"

I could smile and quite truthfully answer: "Never".

PART TWO

THE WAY WE WERE

They may be a bit fuzzy and faded, but in drawers and attic boxes across the nation lie photographs which tell of another time in a foreign land.

Many show comrades who may be out of touch but will never be forgotten.

The names of the Canal Zone veterans who kindly supplied the pictures and details on the following pages are included in the captions.

Even those pictures with scant information will hopefully stir some memories.

Norman Lester (sender) and his
two short pals, Jack and Dick.

Gene Booker in disguise.
(Sender: Terry Taylor)

Always a welcome sight: the NAAFI van serving up char and wads outside
the Accounts Section of RAF Shallufa in 1952. (Sender: Peter Brummell)

RAF Deversoir Rugby team at El Firdan. From the left: Back row - SGT Winter, PO Brian Middleditch, FO 'Chalky' White, FO 'Big Jim' Butler, FO 'Keen Type' Dicker, S/Ldr 'Max the Doc' Johnson, F/LT Diack, LAC 'Lofty' Trumper, S/Ldr Urquhart (ref). Front row - LAC 'Sandy' Sandoz, PTE 'Taff' Mackin, Cpl 'Taff' Thomas', Cpl 'Taff' Taylor, Cpl 'Joe Jewkes, FO, PTE Heard. (Sender: Terry Taylor)

AFS Abyad. From left: Back row - Les, Roy Kirk (sender), Dave, Robinson, Jock Watts, Chas Pervett. Front row includes- 'Jinj' Bedward, Paddy Donavan, Cpl Butler, Sgt Henry, Cpl Baker, Pat O'Mahony, Spud Taylor.

Family transport.
(Sender: Michael Harte)

Above: From left: Doug Findlay, Terry Taylor (sender), Herbie Sutcliffe, 1952.

Right: The phoney Xmas bar at RAF Deversoir. (Sender: George Evans)

The desert near El Firdan Base with Suez in the background. El Firdan means 'Land of the Lions.' (Sender: E J Simmons)

Tony Gooch and other members of C Company 1st Battalion Buffs on road block duties at Tel el Kebir.

The Railway Workshops football team 1952/53. (Sender: Peter Jeffrey)

Boxing Day 1954 at El Hamra. From the left: Ron, Jim, Michael Hall (sender) and Mal.

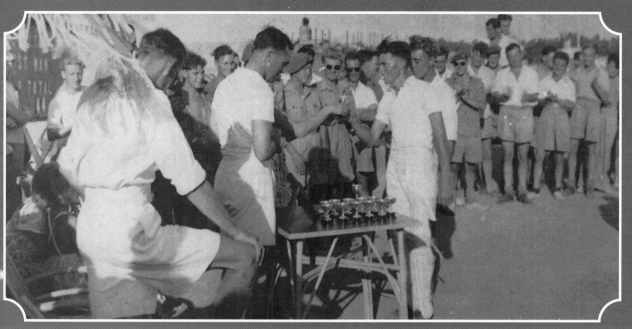

LAC Good receives his trophy after the 26 Squadron team won the Deversoir Cup in 1952.

Admin A, Cup and League winners 1950/51. From the left:
Back row - J Gorman, Hammon, Slater, Sloan, Todd, Cooper, Church;
Front row - Rounge, Clarke, Davis, Clarke, Carter (sender).

Terry Taylor and friends enjoy Christmas 1953, Egyptian style.

Above: A piper with the band of the Royal Scots playing on the foc'sle of St Kitts, 11th August 1954. (Sender: W O Rines)

Left: 1st Battalion The Royal Sussex Regiment. The char wallah in camp, 1950. (Sender: D S Levett)

Bomb Disposal Unit, RAF 128 MU, Abu-Sultan, 1953. (Sender: D Kendall)

51 MT Squadron on a visit to the Pyramids in 1955. Third from the left in the front row is Michael Hall who supplied the photo.

National Servicemen from REME LAD El Kirsh, attached to 38 Company RASC MELF 10, 1951. (Sender: I Cocks)

Brigadier Rendall CRA inspecting RHQ Troop 41st Field Regiment RA at North Camp, Moascar, 7 June 1952.(Sender: K L Garrett)

A toast to teatime in the El Firdan cookhouse, after a day's sailing on Lake Timsah. (Sender: E J Simmons)

Room 9, HQ BTE, Moascar Garrison, Ismailia, 1947. From the left: Back row - Geordie, Jack, Taffy, Willky, Dave. Front row - Duke, Walter Adams (sender), Ray, Brum, Clarky.

Ray Walters (middle) with his friend Charlie (right) enjoy their three-day leave at Port Fuad, which was just across the Canal from Port Said.

Motor bike scrambling was a popular pastime in the Canal Zone. (Sender: E J Simmons)

Terry Taylor (sender), John Smith, Herbie Sutcliffe, Dennis Edwards and friend enjoy a swim.

Norman Lester and friends, Dan, Nevill, Den, Phil, and Jeff standing on the peak of Mount Shubra.

Abyad Pipe Band in 1954. Ken Brazier (sender) stands second from the right in the centre row.

The Scrubbers. A Stanley and fellow Servicemen doing a bit of cleaning.

RAF Deversoir 32 Squadron basketball team. Sender Derek Lines is at the left of the back row.

AFS RAF Abyad. From left to right: back row - Cpl McGill, Chas, Cpl Driscoll, Paddy, Ken, Cpl Melia, Dereck Charge. Front row - Cpl Haskell, Tom Eden, Pop, Jock Carey. (Sender: S Ricketts)

Equipment Section, RAF Fayid, 1954 (Sender: R Johnston)

If I was an RSM! (Sender: R J Curtis)

Kit layout for inspection.
Jankers? (Sender: R J Curtis)

Some of the natives
were friendly!
(L R Powis)

1st Battalion Royal Sussex Regiment
complete a spell of guard duty and head
back to camp. (Sender: D S Levett)

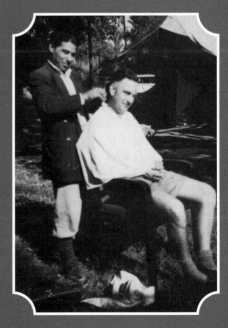

Lt John Chilton has his
hair cut by a
Palestinian 'lufti'. 1953.
Marina Camp Ismailia,

The Basketball League final. Deversoir v Abu Sultan, 1954. (Sender: H Stanley)

Christmas morning 1952 in the BBS at RAF Ismailia. (Sender: Eric Sear)

National Servicemen and Regulars, Suez 1953. (Sender: Mr. Byrne)

Kabrit Stores football team, 1954.
Back row - Moody, Warr, Jack, Burridge, Best (sender), Ainsclough, Cook.
Front row - Manchip, Hodson, Lever, Johns, Turk.

The good old lads. Reg Barret (second from left, back row) and fellow Servicemen in the desert, 1954.
Below: Derek Lines (second from right) and the 32 Squadron badminton team. League winners 1951/52.

An Egyptian lady from the village near RAF Deversoir, in her Sunday best.
(Sender: G Evans)

PART THREE

SUN, SAND
AND SACRIFICE

The forgotten deployment of 30 Line regiments, 10 regiments Royal Artillery, 2 squadrons Royal Engineers, 4 squadrons Royal Signals, 14 companies RASC, 2 depots RAOC, 3 REME detachments, ACC detachments throughout the Canal Zone, 1 Field Ambulance RAMC, 3 companies RCMP, RAPC base, 11 Royal Navy ships, 3 Commando brigades, 6 RAF airfields, 3 RAF support units, 3 RAF regiments, QARANC, WRAF, WRAC, RAFNS.

A LAND IN TURMOIL

A brief history of the British military
presence in Egypt from 1882 to 1956

A very hot sandbox, ten miles wide and 100 miles long with a ditch in the middle, is how the thousands of troops who were stationed there remember the Canal Zone of Egypt. The mid-day Summer temperature averages 38°C (100°F), with spells as high as 48°C (118°F) in the shade. At night the temperature drops almost to freezing. One climatic effect the British Forces never got used to was exposure to the regular sandstorms, from which there was no escape. Even under cover, sand and dust penetrated noses, ears and eyes, and if you were caught out in a storm it severely stung the exposed skin. A freshly painted vehicle could be scoured down to bare metal in minutes.

These were minor irritants next to the plague of flies which infested the area. A constant battle was waged to keep them off the face, arms, legs and, more importantly, food. The inevitable outcome was delicately referred to as 'gyppy tummy,' but more commonly known as 'the runs' or 'the trots.' The constant sweating, coupled with unfortunate practices of the dhobi wallahs, who sprayed water from the Sweet Water Canal through their teeth onto the garments they ironed, ensured that sooner or later everyone suffered from prickly heat. The rash started round the waist, the genitals and under the arms. Gentian violet, the sovereign remedy, liberally applied, was almost as embarrassing as the torture of itching and irritation brought on by the condition. At

night the flies thankfully disappeared, only to be replaced by their mosquito cousins.

Sleeves were rolled down, and long trousers replaced shorts at dusk to dissuade the gnats from making a meal of the wearer; but this was only partially successful. Mosquito nets over beds at night might have been effective but were not, to my knowledge, on the stores inventory during the years 1951 to 1954. Many troops suffered from malaria, and an outbreak of typhoid occurred at RAF Abyad in 1951. Egypt was not a healthy place.

The Suez Canal took ten years to construct, and was bound to succeed when it opened in 1869, since it cut 6,000 miles off the sailing distance from Europe to India. As with all major civil engineering projects the financial strains were great and the Prime Minister, Benjamin Disraeli, pulled off a spectacular coup in 1875 when Britain bought a controlling interest in the Canal for £4million. The Egyptian Government assumed that, since they had all but bankrupted their country building it and as it was on their soil after all, they would share the spoils. Britain and France drove a hard bargain, though, and excluded the unhappy Egyptians from the profit sharing.

Egypt traditionally claimed sovereignty over Sudan, but in meetings of European heads of state in the 1880s a new map of Africa was drawn, and Egypt and Sudan appeared on it as Anglo-Egyptian Sudan. An Arab uprising against Egyptian leader Khedive Tewfik, during which fifty European nationals were massacred in Alexandria, caused great concern in Europe in case it affected the Canal. As a result, British forces led by General Sir Garnet Wolseley joined with Egyptian troops and defeated the rebels in the battle of Tel el Kibir on 13 September 1882. This established a permanent British military presence in Egypt.

On 26 August 1936, Foreign Secretary Anthony Eden signed an Anglo-Egyptian Treaty freeing Egypt as a British protectorate and giving Britain control of the defence of the Suez Canal for the next 20 years. Britain was to maintain a force of 10,000 troops, confined to the Suez Canal Zone. The RAF, although based in the Zone, retained the right to fly over all Egyptian territory. When the Second World War broke out, British Forces were no longer confined and were free to move throughout Egypt to counter the threat posed by the Axis powers to the western borders of the country. British HQ moved to Cairo, and British Army camps and airfields were quickly established in many parts of western Egypt. Troops were sent out from the UK to reinforce the pre-war defence lines.

At the end of the war, Egypt was anxious to gain genuine independence. A gradual deterioration in Anglo-Egyptian relations resulted in Britain agreeing to withdraw her troops to the Canal Zone in 1946, in accordance with the Treaty. A further demand by the Egyptians that all British troops quit the Canal Zone by the end of 1949 was rejected.

King Farouk, ineffectual and generally despised by his people, allowed the Muslim Brotherhood (*Ikhwan el Muslimeen*) free rein to stir up trouble against the British presence. A religious movement, Ikhwan had been formed in 1928 with the express aim of getting rid of the British by political means. Many of its members deserted the movement in frustration at its lack of progress and resorted to guerrilla tactics, attacking British troops at every opportunity.

As always in the Middle East, oil had a bearing on attitudes. The loss of control over the Canal was seen as a threat to European oil supplies, and the Canal Zone was an ideal base from which to re-supply troops in Palestine, Iraq and Jordan. In a Cold War context, any threat to the Middle Eastern countries bordering the Soviet Union must be met. In 1947, Palestine was partitioned by United Nations agreement. The United States ordered Britain to leave Palestine and gave a deadline of May 1948. By 14 May, when the state of Israel was established, we were gone. On 2 November, the American Jewish vote swung the US election and delivered the desired result: a further term for the Democratic Party.

In his book Wings In The Sun, Air Chief Marshal Sir David Lee wrote: "The Middle East was in turmoil and when politics go sour, military action is not far distant."

The training given to the various Zionist gangs by British officers, including Orde Wingate of Chindit fame – skills that had been used against our own Servicemen – could cease. British troops in Palestine were offered £1 for a single round of ammunition, £300 for a rifle; for a machine gun you could name your own price. 45 Commando were the last British troops to quit Palestine, and when they left the transports were overloaded with valuable munitions and guns. Once at sea, this cargo was dumped overboard. Assets left behind included hospitals, schools, roads, aircraft runway installations and a host of other useful infrastructure.

Some troops were posted to Malta and Cyprus, but the bulk were sent to an overcrowded Canal Zone, so 156-transit camp at Port Said was bursting at the seams. It is little wonder the Egyptians became nervous. The huge concentration of our troops in a relatively small area made them vulnerable to a nuclear attack. In addition, Britain had an obligation to aid Egypt or Jordan in their defence, which made Israel unfriendly and later led to British-Israeli combat skirmishes. The RAF were forced to re-activate their 205 Group's Joint Fighter and Anti-aircraft

T PANTER

What all the trouble was about... the Suez Canal seen from the deck of an aircraft carrier. Under the Anglo-Egyptian Treaty of 1936, Britain was given control over the defence of the vital waterway until 1956. This splendid photograph by Tony Panter gives a dramatic impression of what it was like to sail along the Canal.

Operations centre, and at the same time the Army prepared and improved the Canal Zone ground defences.

While the the tension in Anglo-Egyptian relations eased slightly as our troops withdrew to the Canal Zone, the Israeli-Egyptian tension that had existed since 1945 became open hostility. The small but ambitious Israeli Air Force was a real threat to the Zone, and in 1948 they fired shots at patrolling RAF aircraft on several occasions, perhaps mistaking them for Egyptian planes. In none of those incidents did the RAF return fire. In January 1949, reports were received that the Israeli Army had crossed Egypt's eastern border and were making their way towards the Canal Zone.

Six unarmed photo-reconnaissance Spitfires of 208 Squadron took off from RAF Fayid on a Saturday afternoon to establish the Israeli position in the Sinai. When the had completed their sortie and turned for home a Spitfire was shot down by anti-aircraft fire. The pilot successfully baled out of the stricken aircraft. The three other Spitfires were circling the spot where he landed to establish an accurate fix on his position when they were attacked by a flight of Israeli Spitfires and all three RAF planes were shot down. Two of the pilots managed to bale out safely but a third was killed, along with the pilot of an armed Tempest sent to investigate the incident.

Many changes took place in Egypt during the period of Canal Zone occupation. Following the Israeli-Egyptian conflict in 1948 the Prime Minister of Egypt, Mahmud Fahmi Nokrashi, was assassinated by the Muslim Brotherhood, prompting the Deputy Prime Minister to crack down on them and arrest several of their members. In February 1949, the leader of the Ikhwan faction was murdered, almost certainly by the Egyptian Government's secret agents. Following a general election in June 1950, the anti-British Wafd Party were swept into power and gave the terrorists their unofficial blessing to attack British troops. They also pursued an openly hostile anti-British diplomatic stance. King Farouk was forced into exile in 1952.

'When politics go sour, military action is not far distant'

Air Chief Marshal Sir David Lee

General Naguib declared Egypt a Republic on 18 June 1953. He was, however, simply a stooge for Colonel Nasser, who waited a year before taking over in the spring of 1954.

During the years 1950 to 1954, tension was built up, and eased, on direct orders from Cairo, and it became clear that Britain and France were going to be forced to hand over the running of the Suez Canal to Egypt ahead of the time agreed by their Treaty. A major international crisis began on 26 July 1956 when President Nasser nationalised the Suez Canal, previously run by the Anglo-French Suez Canal Company. He did this in retaliation against Britain and the US for reneging on promises of financial assistance for his pet project, the remarkable Aswan Dam.

The problem for Europe, and in particular Great Britain, was the possibility of an interruption of oil supplies. Britain, France and Israel agreed to unite to prevent the seizure of the Suez Canal by Egypt, and in 1956 successful landings were carried out and the Canal retaken and secured. However, world opinion was against such imperialistic send-a-gunboat diplomacy, and Britain and her allies were forced to make an ignominious withdrawal at America's behest.

In fairness, all the prophets of doom were wrong, and Egyptian Governments continued the policy of making passage through the Canal freely available to all nations, with the exception of Israel.

Timeline of events in the Suez Canal Zone

1869
The Suez Canal opens.

1875
Britain buys a £4million controlling interest in the Anglo-French Suez Canal Company.

1880s
A new map of Africa, drawn at a meeting of the European heads of state, shows Egypt and the Sudan as Anglo-Egyptian Sudan, which contradicts Egypt's claim of sole sovereignty over the Sudan.

1882
An Arab uprising in Alexandria against Egyptian leader Khedive Tewfik sees fifty European nationals massacred and causes concern in Europe for the security of the Canal.

1899
An Anglo-Egyptian agreement restores Egyptian rule in Sudan; but as part of a condominium, or joint authority, exercised by Britain and Egypt.

1882
13 September British Forces and Egyptian troops defeat nationalist rebels after uprising at Tel el Kibir, thus establishing a permanent British military presence in Egypt.

1936
26 August British Foreign Secretary Anthony Eden signs an Anglo-Egyptian Treaty freeing Egypt from being a British Protectorate, but giving Britain control of the defence of the Suez Canal for the next twenty years.

1939 – 1945
British troops, previously confined to the Canal Zone, are free to move around Egypt to combat the threat of Axis powers.

1946
British troops are withdrawn to the Canal Zone at Egypt's request. A further request that British troops quit the Canal Zone by 1949 is rejected by the British Government, as the 1936 treaty states that they have the right to remain there until 1956.

1947
Palestine partitioned by United Nations agreement.

1948
14 May British troops leave Palestine. The bulk of them are sent to the Canal Zone, making the Egyptians nervous about nuclear attack from the Soviet Union.

1950
January Wafd Party voted into power in Egypt by a general election. They adopt an openly hostile anti-British stance, giving terrorists their unofficial blessing to attack British troops.

1952
King Farouk forced into exile.

1953
18 June Egypt declared a republic by General Naguib.

1954
17 November Colonel Gamal Abdul Nasser seizes power and becomes head of state.

1956
24 June Nasser elected as President.
26 July President Nasser nationalises the Suez Canal, previously controlled by the Anglo-French Suez Canal Company, after the British and French refuse to assist financially with the Aswan Dam.

1956
Britain, France and Israel unite against Egypt to prevent seizure of the Suez Canal.

1956
Canal retaken and secured by Britain and her allies; but they are forced to withdraw as world opinion frowns upon their actions.

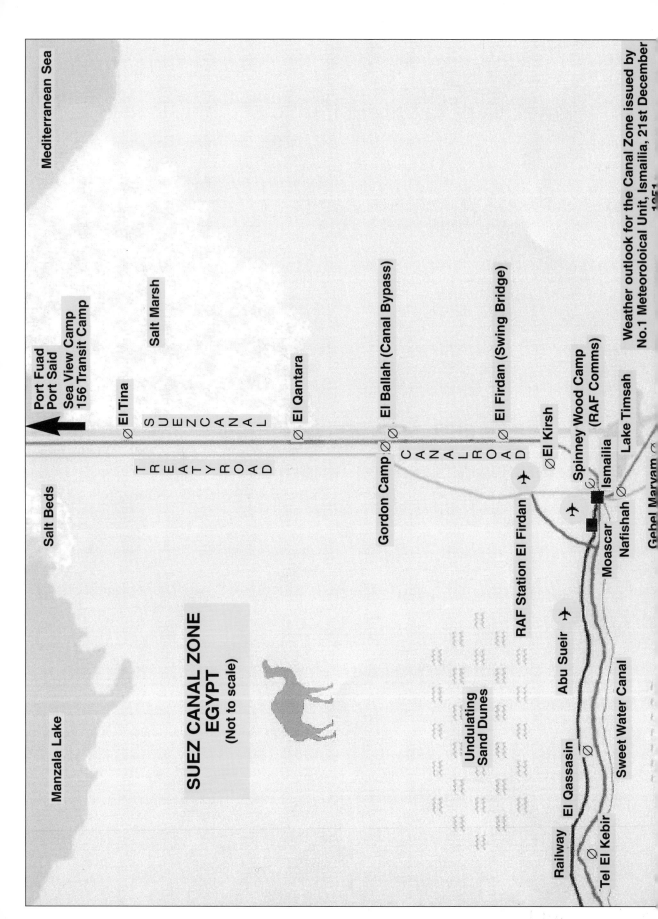

SUEZ CANAL ZONE
EGYPT
(Not to scale)

Mediterranean Sea

Manzala Lake

Salt Beds

Salt Marsh

Port Fuad
Port Said
Sea View Camp
156 Transit Camp

El Tina

S U E Z   C A N A L

T R E A T Y   R O A D

El Qantara

Gordon Camp

El Ballah (Canal Bypass)

C A N A L   R O A D

RAF Station El Firdan

El Kirsh

El Firdan (Swing Bridge)

Spinney Wood Camp
(RAF Comms)

Ismailia

Lake Timsah

Moascar

Nafishah

Gebel Maryam

Abu Sueir

Railway   El Qassasin

Tel El Kebir

Sweet Water Canal

Undulating
Sand Dunes

Weather outlook for the Canal Zone issued by
No.1 Meteoroloical Unit, Ismailia, 21st December
1951

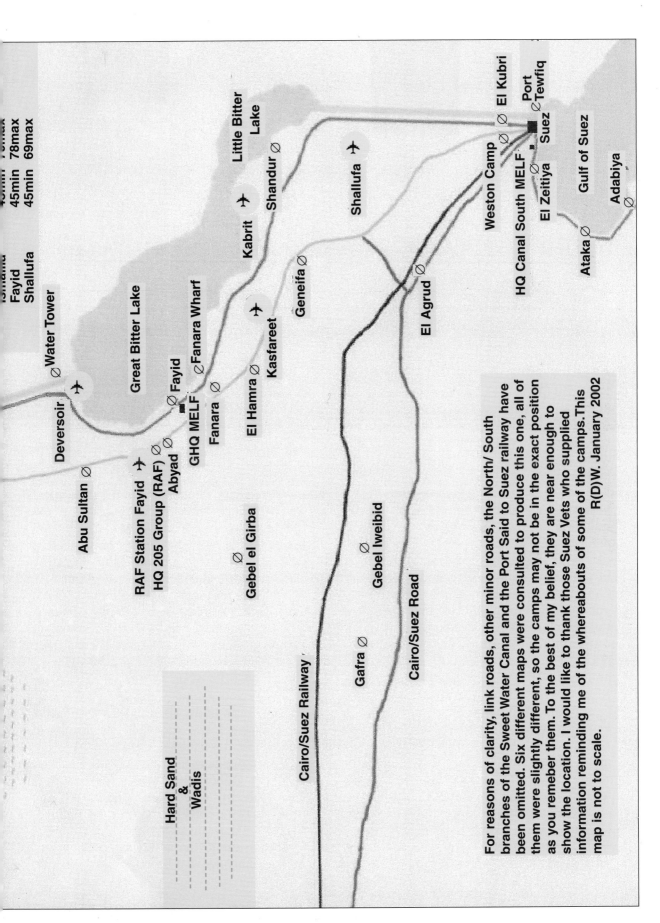

Ismailia Fayid 78max
Fayid
Shallufa 45min 69max

Water Tower ⊘

Abu Sultan ⊘

Deversoir ✈

Great Bitter Lake

RAF Station Fayid ✈
HQ 205 Group (RAF) ⊘
Abyad ⊘
Fayid ⊘
GHQ MELF ■
Fanara ⊘
⊘ Fanara Wharf

Gebel el Girba ⊘

El Hamra ⊘
Kasfareet ✈

Little Bitter Lake

Kabrit ✈
Shandur ⊘

Geneifa ⊘

Gafra ⊘

Gebel Iweibid

Cairo/Suez Railway

Cairo/Suez Road

El Agrud ⊘

Shallufa ✈

Weston Camp
HQ Canal South MELF
El Zeitiya ⊘
Ataka ⊘

El Kubri ⊘
Port ✈ Tewfiq
Suez ■
Gulf of Suez
Adabiya ⊘

Hard Sand
&
Wadis

For reasons of clarity, link roads, other minor roads, the North/ South branches of the Sweet Water Canal and the Port Said to Suez railway have been omitted. Six different maps were consulted to produce this one, all of them were slightly different, so the camps may not be in the exact position as you remeber them. To the best of my belief, they are near enough to show the location. I would like to thank those Suez Vets who supplied information reminding me of the whereabouts of some of the camps.This map is not to scale.

R(D)W. January 2002

NOW IT STILL CAN'T BE TOLD

Twenty-four killed in one month, yet the only death rating a mention in the Canal Zone News was that of King George VI. Today, the MoD is bravely getting round to revealing the secrets of the First World War

Servicemen with experience in printing and publishing were recruited from their units to produce the Canal Zone News that ran for some six months from 1951 to 1952. It was published three times a week, so the boys were kept busy. From the Union Jack on the masthead to the tailpiece of Home and World News it was essential reading for anyone who wanted to be on the ball. You could discover what film was being shown where and what radio programmes were due to be broadcast. The dangers of serving in the Canal Zone got a mention – a petrol bomb was thrown at the last lorry in an RASC convoy, but no real damage was done; Egyptian police claimed they had rounded up 500 suspected terrorists in the Canal Zone. A line under the Canal Zone News masthead stated: "Printed and published under the authority of the Commanders in Chief Middle East".

Among the editions that survive is No.42, Thursday, 7 February 1952, which is mainly devoted to the death of our beloved King George VI, and another on Queen Elizabeth, published on Saturday, 9 February 1952. However, during January 1952, twenty-eight servicemen, two merchant seamen and two British civilians were killed or died, but not a word appears in the Canal Zone News about their deaths.

The Christmas edition of Monday, 24 December 1951, is quite a cheery affair. The staff, all of them serving Service personnel, send greeting to the readers. To mark the

occasion the masthead was changed to the lion and unicorn, crown and shield. The Secretary of State for War and Army Council observes that our troops are serving under particularly onerous conditions in the maintenance of our rights in the Canal Zone.

In a short section on the Canal Zone, the News advises that the all-night curfew imposed in parts of Ismailia on the night of Friday, 21 December, was effectively observed. It reports that there were a few small incidents in the Zone. Searchlights were put out, explosives thrown at a water filtration plant and a train delayed south of Ismailia by an iron bar across the track. The Canal Zone News goes on to state that the amount of terrorist activity being claimed by the Egyptian authorities has been greatly exaggerated.

In December 1951, twenty Servicemen and four British civilians were killed or died. A few small incidents and twenty-four dead do not tally. As far as the News was concerned, there were no deaths in the Canal Zone during the six months of its production. In a two-month period, a total of fifty-six deaths were simply swept under the carpet. Perhaps the Canal Zone News was the sole source of information for Whitehall.

The happy news in the 1951 festive edition was that Father Christmas arrived at RAF Deversoir in a 600mph Meteor jet, his reindeer being unable to cope with the heat, which that day ranged between 42°f and 64°f.

In fairness to the authorities, freedom of information never has been a military priority, though I have been told that on some sites a sit-rep (situation report) was posted each day for the benefit of all ranks. This was not true of RAF Deversoir. Perhaps they thought it best not to inform us in case we started taking our guard duties seriously.

Astonishingly, half a century later, the Ministry of Defence still refuses to provide full and accurate information about the causes of Service deaths in Egypt in the years between 1948 and 1954. Can it be that the political sensitivities of those troubled times so long ago are justification today for this denial of the freedom of information that New Labour promised us? Or is it simply the obduracy of bureaucracy and insensitivity to the feelings of the families and comrades of the dead exemplified by the letter reproduced here. Certainly there is a political dimension to this determination to play down the emergency, which was highlighted by the failure to award a General Service Medal to those who served their country in this particular foreign field.

The warriors of the Honours and Awards Committee used a short lull in the troubles in Egypt in 1952 as an excuse to stop keeping accurate records, which perhaps partly explains the obvious confusion in Whitehall over what actually happened.

In March 2000, Dr Lewis Moonie, Minister for Veteran Affairs, stated that in Egypt only forty Servicemen were killed and seventy-five wounded. In November 2000, Geoff Hoon, the Defence Secretary, declared that a total of fifty-four Servicemen were killed in Egypt. In January 2001, two months later, Defence Services Secretary R.T. Coney reverted to the figure of forty dead and seventy-five wounded. Then in July 2001, Mr Coney produced revised figures of 613 dead, including civilians and Commonwealth personnel.

The facts slowly emerging show the true figures to be much higher. The Army accepts that six men disappeared and have no known graves, but the number is at least ten. Casualties who were evacuated to other areas and subsequently died of their wounds are excluded from any list, as the authorities did not keep records of this kind of information.

The following figures provided by the Ministry of Defence in 2001 make curious reading. They list these causes of death:

Road traffic accidents 61
Accidental gunshot wounds 37
Suicide 10
Electrocution 10
Drowning 9
Missing 6
Falling under trains 5
Murder by British soldiers 2
Judicial hanging for murder . . . 1
Natural causes including illness .46

No mention is made of the Servicewoman abducted, tortured, raped and murdered, or of the murder of an airman by an airman at RAF Deversoir, and there were four British Servicemen judicially hanged for murder. The Roll of Honour at the end of this book should make interesting reading for the author of the MOD figures listed above.

One night I attended, in darkness, the scene of a road accident where several African soldiers were killed. Fifty years later it was finally confirmed that the incident was an enemy ambush. The official report states that the attack occurred at 3.30 in the afternoon. If this was not the incident that I attended, then there must have been another that was not recorded. A large number of the sixty-one road traffic deaths should rightly be recorded as death by terrorist action.

Elsewhere you will read of the gallant actions of Major Wharton and Flying Officer Snelling. The MoD records them as dying as a result of civil disturbance. AC2 James Rankin's death is described as the result of a suspected ambush. LAC Andrew Kirk died of injuries sustained in a civil disturbance. Even the death of AC2 Thomas Murray, murdered by gunshot by robbers in Ismailia, is slanted away from terrorist action by mention of the robbery. Major Wharton and Flying Officer Snelling

17th September 2002

Dear Mr Findlay,

Thank you for your further letter of 7th September seeking recognition in the form of a medal for all those who served in the Suez Canal Zone during the early 1950s, following the receipt of my letter of 25th June.

I'm sorry to disappoint you, but having read your letter carefully, I'm not sure how I can answer your question without appearing flippant and it is certainly not my intention to appear rude. Those in Command of the Armed Forces during the early 1950s were fully aware of the situation in the Canal Zone because they were there. While much of the routine correspondence from that period has been destroyed many years ago there are documents held in the Public Record Office (PRO) at Kew which make it clear that the Services were well aware of the unpleasant conditions in the Canal Zone at that time. However, the institution of a medal is not automatic, as I know you realise, and the fact that no formal request was ever made for a medal in respect of service at the time is evidence that those senior officers in Command did not feel that a case could be justified. My best advice to you, especially as I understand from your letters that you are writing a book on the subject, is to research the matter carefully from the surviving papers at the PRO. You can do this free of charge simply by visiting the archive. The source documents which were written at the time are the best place to investigate this matter.

However, since I wrote to you there have been developments which I can pass on to you. Sir Richard Wilson, the then Cabinet Secretary and Chairman of the Committee on the Grant of Honours, Decorations and Medals (known as the HD Committee), held a meeting with MPs and selected representatives of the major Canal Zone veterans' organisations earlier in the summer. Following this meeting Dr Moonie responded to a written response to a Parliamentary Question on 23rd July on the subject of a Canal Zone medal. He said that the Government consider it important to respect the principle that where there is a clear, demonstrable decision taken within five years of a campaign that a GSM should not be awarded, that decision should not be reopened. The evidence relating to a consideration of a GSM for the Suez Canal Zone is less clear cut. In view of these exceptional circumstances, the Government are setting up a small sub-committee of the HD Committee under the chairmanship of General Lord Guthrie of Craigiebank to report on the case for an exceptional award of a GSM for the Suez Canal Zone without creating a wider precedent or breaching long-standing principles which underpin the making of such awards.

Under the circumstances it would not therefore be appropriate for the Ministry of Defence to comment further until the sub-committee has published the results of its consideration of this subject.

I hope that this explains the situation.

Yours sincerely

R T Coney

*Here is the unabridged text of two letters I received during my lengthy
correspondence with the Ministry of Defence.*
*Left: A response from R T Coney, Defence Services Secretary (Secretariat)1,
at the Ministry of Defence, St Christopher House, Southwark Street, London.*
*Below: A reply from J J Harding MBE, Info(Exp)Analysis (including HB(A)),
at the Ministry of Defence, Great Scotland Yard, London.*
*I would be interested to know who qualify as the "agreed third parties"
referred to by J J Harding, but obviously authors doing research into
campaigns in which they served don't come up to scratch. And after all,
it was only half a century ago that I was in Suez, and the poor chaps at
the Ministry are still struggling with the First World War.*

13th November 2002

Dear Mr Findlay,

Thank you for your letter to Dr Lewis Moonie dated 13th October which has been
passed to this branch of the Ministry of Defence for reply. I would also like to thank you
for your further letter to my colleague Miss Bandy dated 17th October. Please accept
my apologies for the delay in responding to you.

We of course appreciate the amount of work you have undertaken in producing a list
of both military and civilian deaths in Egypt from 1948 to 1958. However we are not
able to assist with your request for information from personal service records to further
your work.

Departmental practice, reflecting the employer-employee relationship of
confidentiality, means that information from personal Service records is only released
to the next-of-kin or agreed third parties unless the records are in due course
transferred to the public domain through the Public Record Office (PRO) at Kew.

I cannot say at what point records from the 1950s may become available at the PRO,
discussions on this subject are ongoing, but as an indication, the records recently
transferred to the PRO primarily concern the First World War period.

I appreciate that the fact that we are not able to help you will be a disappointment,
but as Miss Bandy mentioned in her letter, the Ministry of Defence's current research
for a definitive tri-service roll of honour will thereby provide recognition of all those
Servicemen and Servicewomen who have lost their lives since 1945.

Yours sincerely,

J J Harding

had their medal ribbons torn off and no doubt their pockets gone through. Should this also be classified as a mere case of robbery?

Only a few deaths, the MoD insist, can be attributed to civil disturbance and action by Egyptian dissidents. A further eight deaths were caused by gunshot wounds where there might have been a dissident involvement. It is high time that the cause of every death was released to the general public. More troops were at risk in Egypt than in many other conflicts because all camps had to be self-reliant for heat, water and power. That Egypt was an unhealthy place is reflected in the number of deaths among children and other Service dependants. The cost in lives of supporting a political decision is frightening.

Postings to Egypt during 1951-54 were used as punishment for Servicemen, according to the late Labour stalwart Barbara Castle in a speech she made in Parliament (Hansard, 11 March 1954).

On the 18 January 1952, a week before the incidents at the Bureau Sanitaire and the police barracks, General Sir Brian Robertson requested that a General Service Medal be awarded to his troops. Dr David Clark MP signed a letter to the effect that New Labour's promise to rectify the wrong in regard to the award of the GSM for service in Egypt was worth 50,000 votes, many of them in marginal constituencies.

The following senior officers supported the claim for the award of a General Service Medal for those who served in Egypt from 1951-54: Field Marshal the Lord Bramall KG, GCB, OBE, MC, JP; Field Marshal Sir John Chappie GCB, CBE, DL; Air Chief Marshal Sir Jock Kennedy GCB, AFC, DL, RAF (Rtd), Lord Lieutenant of Rutland; General Sir Michael Rose KCB, CBE, DSO, QGM; General Sir David Ramsbotham GCB, CBE; Major General Julian Thompson CB, OBE.

As well as the truth about the extent of casualties suffered in Egypt, a number of other secrets are being revealed. During the first Six Day War between Egypt and Israel

A large number of the 61 road traffic deaths should rightly be recorded as death by terrorist action

the RAF refuelled the Egyptian Air Force planes between sorties, thus aiding the Egyptian war effort in accordance with the treaty between the two countries. The sad truth is that not many Egyptian fighter planes survived long enough to require this service.

The unit concerned was No.2 Fuel Transport Company, on attachment to RAF Shallufa and commanded by a Flight Lieutenant Andrews. To drive a heavy goods vehicle, the rank of corporal was required and those few chosen for the refuelling operation went from AC1 through LAC to corporal within a month. Newly promoted corporals Edwards and Waters were instructed to report to RAF Fanara and load up their AEC 6 x 6 2,000-gallon tankers, Reg Nos. 110535 and 115547, with 100-octane fuel and report to a British Army base, part of which was being used by the Egyptian Air Force, with a runway of rolled sand. The corporals' duty was to refuel the old Spitfires and Fiat Machies – similar to our Typhoons and Tempests – being used by the Egyptian Air Force.

The war did not last long, and when the corporals returned to their unit they were instructed to tell no one about their extra-curricular activities, and not to write home about the action. No.2 FTC was swallowed up by 51 MT Company, based at El Hamra, and the corporals were posted to duties elsewhere. One strange tale, said to have occurred in 1952, is reported of the involvement of the

Oxford and Buckinghamshire Light Infantry in a frustrating experience. They were called out to assist a 'dingo' scout car of the Royal Dragoons that had been ambushed near Kantara. When they arrived at the scene they were kept well away from the wrecked car by redcaps, and it was clear that the terrorists had not only killed the crew, but also mutilated their bodies.

The Sudanese tracker studied the sandy terrain and declared that twelve men had been in the ambush party, and that one of them carried a Bren gun. They had set off in the direction of the village that lay ahead but which was concealed by a long low sand dune. The Ox and Bucks regiment, formerly composed mainly of National Servicemen, had recently been reinforced by experienced regular troops. They at once suggested that a pincer movement be instituted to encircle the village, thereby trapping the terrorists within. This obvious military tactic was vetoed by the commissioned officers. The troops were intent on revenge and this may have alarmed those in charge. The Ox and Bucks were therefore ordered to advance as a single body up and over the sand dune. Naturally enough, by the time the village was reached it was completely empty of inhabitants, innocent and guilty alike. It did not take the services of their Sudanese tracker to identify the clear evidence that the entire village had taken to their heels a few moments before the troops arrived. Cooking pots were still hot, and other signs of recent flight obvious.

Elementary military tactics, had they been adopted, would have secured a satisfactory result. The murderers got away and many of the troops who took part thought that it was the result of the policy of appeasement towards the Egyptian Government.

The MoD seems determined to ensure that all those who participated will be long dead before the truth is revealed. By then no one will be interested in a small incident in a far off land, a long time ago.

When research for this book became known, many stories flooded in and, though most were uncorroborated, they made fascinating reading. Mystery surrounds the Royal Navy ammunition dump within the huge Royal Army Ordnance Corps base, 9 B.A.D. Abu Sultan, and whispers of shiny objects that even the klefti wallahs would not touch magnified interest in this building. It seems that old ammunition, gun cotton, booby traps and other unpleasant objects were stored in this huge shed, from which no stock returns were made to Army sources. Mustard gas was mentioned by more than one correspondent.

I am told the staff wore civvies and were escorted to and from an hotel in Ismailia each day. They were, in fact, Navy personnel and an eye-witness reports that when one of them was driven to Post Said where he boarded HMS Bermuda he was piped aboard, a sure sign of senior rank. Rumour had it that the personnel were all of commissioned rank. They certainly failed to fraternise with the other ranks on the camp.

The ordnance in the dump was formerly the property of American, British, Egyptian, Italian, German and even Spanish forces, so its age and origins were shrouded in mystery. Stories of squaddies being threatened with a 252 for simply glancing through the open doors of the compound were commonplace.

A former REME driver, attached to the RAOC, reports that he was ordered to uplift what he describes as shiny shells and take them to a wharf on the Suez Canal for onward movement. Whether they were to be dumped at sea or had some other destination was never explained to him. He was not allowed to leave his truck cab while it was being loaded and unloaded. When the job was finished, he was instructed by a civilian with obvious authority to tell no one where he had been or what he carried. Since he had no idea what it was that he carried, that bit was easy to comply with.

Perhaps someday someone in the know will tell us what was going on.

A WOMAN'S VIEW

When her labour pains started, the ambulance taking Doris Golder to hospital had to be escorted by two lorryloads of armed troops. Here Doris reports on the traumatic life of a soldier's wife in the Canal Zone

At the time of the emergency in the Suez Canal Zone 1951/54 I was a young wife living in privately rented accommodation on the Rue de Chemin-de-fer, Arayshia – not far from the railway bridge. I remember vividly the build up of tension and my anxiety, which started about May 1951. About once every ten days my husband Charles, a warrant officer with the Royal Engineers, had to leave me on my own at night while he attended to camp duties at GHQ Fayid, about twenty-five miles away. I was pregnant at the time, but that did not qualify us for any privileges, such as my husband being excused duty– moreover – none were expected as this was accepted as being part of an Army life.

The active social life that we all used to enjoy was virtually non-existent and we either stayed at home, or shared a few drinks and gossiped with our neighbours resident in the same block. Families living in camp areas in official married quarters were not so badly affected but all movement 'beyond the wire' was restricted.

Convoys carrying personnel from Fayid to Ismailia/Arayshia were frequently stoned or fired at but, fortunately, casualties were few. Other terrorist activities undertaken by the locals included wires strung across roads to decapitate motor cyclists or Land Rover crews, oil/grease spread on roads, usually around blind corners, intended to cause loss of control and crashes, and roadblocks. These took the form of lorries feigning load shedding or engine trouble. Soldiers dismounting to help out would be pounced upon, disarmed, beaten-up, mutilated or killed. It was no secret that happenings of this nature took place on a daily basis throughout the Zone. The Egyptian newspapers were full of news of incidents and Radio Cairo kept us well informed of the acts of their 'freedom fighters'.

In October, several hundred 'students' got off the train from Cairo at the bridge, scrambled down the embankment, and ran amok round the blocks of flats occupied by the service families. The 'authorities' must have known that they were coming and what their intentions were since the train, which should have gone on to Ismailia, stopped at the bridge, well short of the railway station. It was in the process of being turned around when the students, realising their efforts were being thwarted, jumped off.

The rioters broke into property wherever they could, looting and destroying. Our block was set on fire but the Sudanese ghaffir put the fire out when the mob drifted elsewhere. My husband later rewarded this brave man for his timely action by presenting him with a warm coat. Egyptian police followed the rioters at a discreet distance but made no effort to control the lawless conduct. Indeed, they scavenged among the articles that had been thrown out of the doors and windows.

Two points stick in my mind in regard to this incident. The first is that the rabble, although frightening and insulting the British women and children, did not molest them in any way. The second is that although we were only four miles from the Moascar Garrison, no troops were sent to our aid. This event took place on a morning when all the husbands had gone to their places of duty. When they did return, well after the trouble had subsided, every one was armed. Rumour had it that our husbands were deliberately kept in the dark about the incident, and by being held back, undoubtedly prevented bloodshed which would have made a highly charged situation worse.

From then on, every Serviceman carried loaded weapons wherever they went. I remember at this time our fear of answering the door, especially at night, as many stories were circulating regarding the fate of those who had dropped their guard and been attacked. Shopping became very troublesome and could only be done when accompanied by an armed escort, usually one's husband. There were very few shops still trading and they were 'encouraged' to close down by a new batch of 'auxiliary policemen' who appeared. The locals who were brave or greedy enough to remain open had their premises torched by unknown assailants. Our NAAFI was burnt out, but managed to continue trading from a provisions trailer, selling goods brought in from Cyprus.

Early on November 1st, I was admitted to the British Military Hospital, Moascar, to have my son. My labour pains started in the middle of the night and my husband, frightened to death, was forced to wend his way through the pitch black night to the nearest telephone on the other side of the railway bridge. This 300-yard journey was fraught with danger and he later admitted that he imagined possible attack at every corner. The telephone was, fortunately, still operative and in a short time an ambulance, escorted front and rear by two lorryloads of armed troops, arrived.

During my stay in hospital, Charles could have exercised his option of living at his distant base but stayed alone in our flat. It would make visits to hospital easier and would guard our few personal possessions. Later, those items that had been so cherished had to be abandoned.

I was discharged from the BMH in mid-November to a much-deteriorated position. The suburbs were now regularly patrolled by British troops, some in armoured cars. Most families had left for safer places, and all of the RAF families had gone in a well-executed operation. It pains me, as an Army wife to say it, but the RAF seemed much better organised than the Army. My husband would not accept this, and assured me that it was because they had fewer families to deal with.

The odd shot rang out throughout the days and nights, echoing loudly as so many of the building were now empty of residents. Local gangs of bad lads now hid on low balconies or round corners, then jump on the surprised soldiers and steal their weapons. I do not think that they were actual terrorists but simply opportunists taking a chance to acquire something saleable. This made no difference to the offence in the eyes of the Army. Soldiers who lost their arms this way were court martialled.

The tension built up and since there was no possibility of my moving into a proper Army quarter it was decided that I should go home with my new son, Peter. An air passage was requested but I had to wait a few weeks until Peter was old enough to fly. We now had the entire block of flats to ourselves, an eerie experience to put it mildly. Fate, however, brought this matter to a head. Following an uncomfortable week or so, and after a particularly bad night when there was heavy firing all round us, we were ordered to leave. Charles spent the entire night on our balcony, joining in the firing to frighten 'them' off, when the Tannoy of a patrolling armoured car announced that the work convoy had been cancelled and that all families still in the outpost would be evacuated at two hours notice. Only one

Doris Golder and husband Charles, a leading campaigner for recognition of the sacrifices made and hostile conditions endured by the troops in the Canal Zone.

suitcase would be allowed for each person and all other possessions left behind.

We were going to be herded into Lake Timsah Transit Camp, only a few miles down the road, where it would be easier to deal with us and to defend, than this sprawling site. A couple of lads from the Lancashire Fusiliers came to help us on our way and could not do enough to assist. They were so cheerful and confident that it took all the apprehension out of the situation. I will never forget what they did for us. I think that they also helped my husband dispose of his stock of booze, as everyone agreed that it would be a pity to leave it to "come what may". That night we heard from Radio Cairo that this incident was classified as a battle and that they had thrown us out.

A week or so went by at this camp, with my husband running the gauntlet from Ismailia to GHQ Fayid every day, by whatever lift he could scrounge. We were then allocated a tent in the GHQ families' temporary compound at Fayid. These double-skinned EPIPs tents – European personnel, Indian pattern – had sand floors and only basic necessities like beds and bedding, a Tilly lamp, washbasin and stand and a couple of chairs. Home sweet home. It might have been primitive but we felt much safer here than we had felt for some time. The food was adequate as we dined in the sergeant's mess. Charles was only a stone's throw from his job and the airport where he seemed to spend an increasing amount of his time.

There were no complaints... well, not many, and never any made officially. It was accepted that everything possible was being done for us in most difficult circumstances. The whole area was teeming with troops, which must have made heavy demands on all resources. It was intended that we would only be there for a night or two but for some reason my flight was delayed. However, out of the blue, one of my father's friends (I was from a Service family) called round. He immediately offered us accommodation in their quarter in the Fayid Families' Village until the elusive flight came through. Charles readily agreed to this, although it meant us being apart, and he moved to the sergeant's lines. I flew home mid-December and he followed in March 1952 when his extended tour was completed.

During this period I witnessed many instances of quiet courage and it still riles me to think that no claim was ever made to the Egyptian Government for recompense for the items that we lost to looters. We did receive a small amount from British funds for lost furniture but is was nothing compared to the real value.

Historians have largely ignored this period of our history and I feel that it deserves further coverage. On the whole, I enjoyed my 36 years with the colours, first as an officer's daughter and later as the wife of a soldier. The period covered by this report was, without doubt, the most traumatic of my entire Service life.

■ *The Golders were one of more than 600 Service families evacuated from Arayshia. The Royal Dragoons played an important part in escorting the families to safety.*

A few days after Doris was released from hospital, Egyptian police gunned down Major Wharton, RASC and Flying Officer Snelling, RAF only a short distance from her flat. So efficient was the news blackout that the Golders were unaware of the incident.

At the time of this incident, Charles Golder was a WO1 at the tender age of 24. He retired after 22 years service in various parts of the world with the Royal Engineeers to take up a career in teaching, and has been a stalwart of the Canal Zone medal campaign. Charles and Doris are enjoying retirement in Westhoughton, Lancashire.

SIT-REPS

An indication of the level of terrorist activity can be gleaned from official Situation Reports, or Sit-reps, which only rarely were released to serving troops

Here are brief extracts from the Sit-rep for Tel el Kebir for April 1953. Extracts from the report are in bold type. The author's comments are in italics.

There have been twenty successful and five unsuccessful attacks on Service vehicles, most of them armed attacks in daylight. Incidents include the following:

1st April - A Mauritian soldier in the back of a vehicle was shot while driving through Abu Camus. *No report of a death appears against this date so he may or may not have survived.*

6th - Two British soldiers were attacked with axes in the Qassasin area. *A W. Crangle, a sapper of the Royal Engineers posted to Qassasin, died the following day but is not listed as a victim of terrorism.*

12th - A British driver was wounded in the throat while passing through Abu Camus.

16th - A British driver was assaulted and is still unaccounted for. *A Corporal Lamond of the RASC was buried on 17 April. He is not listed as a victim of terrorism, and it is possible that his body was never recovered.*

16th - RAF coach and driver disappeared between Ismailia and Abu Suair. *This coach was driven by LAC Stainton and his body was never recovered.*

19th - East African driver and vehicle missing between the Ismailia Garrison and Hibbert House on the south side of the Sweet Water Canal, Ismailia. *There are no reports of the recovery of this soldier's body. He is therefore not listed as a casualty and his grave, if any, is unmarked.*

22nd - Severe assault on the driver of a jeep at Suez Bridge. The jeep was stolen whilst the Egyptian police on the spot took no action.

25th - Several NAAFI vehicles stolen near Qassasin and the driver of one taken to Cairo. One NAAFI vehicle stolen unroute to Port said, five military vehicles stolen from car park at Port Said. *No report on the fate of the abducted NAAFI staff member has come to light although another Sit-Rep reports the recovery of a NAAFI manager's body.*

27th - British military jeep crewed by a British warrant officer and a sergeant fired on by Egyptian civilians in two taxis on the main Cairo/Ismailia road near Tel el Kebir. British sergeant killed and warrant officer wounded. The two taxis made off towards Cairo. *Sergeant G.F.Fill, Royal Northumberland Fusiliers, was killed in this incident.*

These Moascar Garrison Sit-reps 35 and 36, issued 4 December 1953, give an indication of the level of activity being experienced by all the Services. The personnel involved in an incident had no way of knowing the overall picture and often thought that their area alone was suffering thefts and attacks.

The facts are that between 16 October 1951 and 1 June 1954 there were 1,150 thefts of Army property valued at £160,000. Forty additional cases of theft to the value of £10,000 were being examined, and there were 1,767 thefts of Army tele-communications cable with a replacement value of £66,000. During this period there were eight cases of deliberate sabotage by burning in the Canal Zone, causing damaged estimated at £2million.

21.11. Three Egyptians, one of whom was armed, attempted to hold up WD vehicle in Fanara. Escort fired and Egyptians fled.

21.11. Two Egyptians arrested whilst leaving Tel el Kebir perimeter with WD stores.

22.11. Shots fired into army camp at Moascar. 22.11. Break in at Army Camp Fayid, small quantity of personal property stolen.

22.11. Immediately after a traffic accident, involving a WD vehicle and Egyptian policeman, rifle and ammo was stolen from the vehicle. Thief arrested and rifle and ammo recovered.

22.11. Several shots fired into TEK from different positions.

22.11. Five hundred yards of High tension of overhead cable stolen from Ferry Boyer.

22.11. Patrol discovered four Egyptians removing stores at Port Said. Fire opened and two Egyptians captured.

22.11. Break in at Army Camp Fayid. Small quantity of private property stolen.

22.11. Large quantity of steel piping stolen from Fayid cemetery.

23.11. Egyptian WD employee arrested by Egyptian police and it is believed that he has been taken to Cairo.

23.11. Three Egyptians shot dead by Mauritian guards whilst trying to break into Engineers Stores depot, Fayid.

24/11. WD employee, believed to be Egyptian, arrested by Egyptian police.

24.11. Eight Egyptians seen inside perimeter of RAF Deversoir removing stores. All escaped but three believed wounded.

24.11. Egyptian stole stores from WD vehicle trailer whilst halted at Nefisha level crossing.

24.11. Two Egyptians captured whilst trying to break into club premises Fayid.

25.11. Party of between ten and twenty Egyptians carried out an armed robbery of YMCA Headquarters near Aviary Camp, Ismailia. Five Egyptians entered building and tied up British and Egyptian occupants and stole small quantity of personal property. They then took the keys of two YMCA cars and stole them away. Cars have not been recovered.

25/26.11. Break in at El Kirsh and NAAFI stores stolen.

25/26.11. Break in at RAF Fanara. Three Egyptians captured.

26.11. Two Egyptians seen removing stores near TEK perimeter. Fire opened, Egyptians fled without stores.

26.11. Two Egyptians jumped into vehicle loaded with stores leaving TEK, escorts opened fire, Egyptians fled.

26/11. Two Cypriots both in possession of BFI Cards arrested by Egyptian police in Suez Hotel.

26.11. Four Palestinian employed by RAF arrested by Egyptian police and taken to Ismailia police station.

26/27.11 Break in at RAF Kasfareet but no stores stolen.

27.11. Greek NAAFI Manager of HQ2 Agra canteen missing since 20 November found murdered near Abu Gamus.

27.11. Sten gun stolen from RAF vehicle whilst driver was unloading stores near US Club, Ismailia.

27.11. Break in at family quarters in Fayid area. Small quantity of private property stolen.

27/28.11. 2,000ft of aerial stolen from EHQ receiver station.

29.11. Conservancy vehicle leaving RAF El Firdan was searched and a quantity of stolen MT stores were discovered. On 28th November a contractors vehicle leaving Kasfareet was also searched and stolen stores were discovered.

29.11. Civvy car, property of a British officer, was stolen from French beach Port Tewfik. Fire opened at intruder at RAF Deversoir.

29/30.11. Large-scale theft from NAAFI warehouse El Kirsh.

30.11. Sentries at TEK opened fore on small party of Egyptians seen stealing within the depot. Egyptians fled and stolen property was recovered.

30.11. Egyptian boarded WD vehicle near Qassasin and escort shot him dead.

30.11. Small party of Egyptians stoned a WD vehicle in the El Ballah area. BOR driver opened fire and Egyptians fled, possibly one wounded.

30.11. Two Egyptians apprehended when caught breaking into WD camp at Port Said.

29.11. NAAFI car stolen from outside French Club Port Tewfik at about midnight. Car subsequently found abandoned in Suez area.

1.12. An Egyptian fired three shots through bedroom window of RAF hired quarter in Fanara area. No casualties.

1.12. WD vehicle was boarded by an Egyptian in Suez area, escort opened fore seriously wounding the man.

1.12. Two Egyptians attacked an aircraftsman in Kasfareet village and robbed him. No injuries sustained.

1.12. BOR attacked by Egyptian with knife in Fayid shopping centre. BOR escaped uninjured and Egyptian was arrested.

1.12. Mauritian guard opened fire on three Egyptians attempting to steal from WD stores in Fayid area. Egyptians fled and property was recovered.

30.11. Break in at WD filtration Plant at El Ballah. Small amount of tentage stolen.

3.12. Break in at 10 BOD. First light search revealed one wounded Egyptian and one unhurt. Also attempted break in at 9ESBD where guard opened fire.

2/3.12. Break in at WD camp at Fayid and 60 feet of water piping stolen from Kabrit area. Also break in at RAF Deversoir

4/5.12. Attempted break in at WD camp in Fayid area frustrated by guard who opened fire on thieves. Theft of 1,220 feet of aerial wire from GHQ wireless station.

4.12. Attempted break in by four Egyptians at 8 ESBD. Guards opened fire and one Egyptian was wounded but escaped.

4.12. Four Egyptians arrested whilst attempting to steal piping from cold storage depot, Suez.

3.4.12. Guards opened fire on two occasions at Egyptians seen within perimeter of RAF Deversoir.

EYE IN THE SKY

An Auster spotter plane piloted by Lieutenant Tony Heron played a significant role in the infamous Battle of the Bureau Sanitaire. Phil May of the RAF Regiment, who acted as radio linkman, tells the story

At the time of the battle of the Bureau Sanitaire, I was serving as a Flying Officer with 62 Rifle Squadron RAF Regiment. The Squadron was stationed at RAF El Hamra. Our duties were mainly concerned with the security of vulnerable points, which included a flight detachment providing a permanent guard for the Officer Commanding Middle East Air Force, Air Vice Marshal Sir John Baker, on his house boats located on the edge of Lake Timsah near Ismailia.

In December 1951, I was detached with my flight to command this guard. The flight was based at Air HQ Middle East RAF Ismailia. The airmen were housed in barrack blocks and I lived in the officers' mess, which made a pleasant change after being under canvas in the desert. During this time I became friendly with a young subaltern, Lieutenant A P N Heron, a Royal Artillery pilot. He was also attached to the station with an Auster Air OP spotter aircraft. Because of the friendship an incident occurred which became the highlight of my Middle East tour.

By January 1952 the situation in Ismailia was becoming quite serious, with large numbers of armed Egyptian police auxiliaries and terrorists moving into the town from Cairo. Tony Heron told me that he had been briefed for an operation that was planned for the following day, 25 January 1952, to disarm hostile forces assembling in Ismailia. This was to be carried out by a battalion of the Lancashire Fusiliers, the Parachute Regiment supported by some armoured cars of the Royal Dragoons, and some tanks. He explained that he would be providing an Air OP to cover the operation. As I had flown with him previously he asked me if I would like to accompany him and assist in observing.

The next morning I briefed my 2i/c of the flight, FO Sean McDonnell, that I would be away, and following an early breakfast we took off from RAF Ismailia at first light. We had a type 62 radio set in the Auster, on net with Btn HQ and also Brigade. We commenced circling the town and could see the paras taking up position on an outer ring and the Lancashire Fusiliers were closing in and forming a cordon near the police headquarters, and some appeared to be dug in on the bank near the Sweet Water Canal.

The Egyptian police and auxiliaries were located mostly in the police

■ It was just as well for Tony Heron that FO Phil May had gone along for the ride, because the Auster – which had to fly low and slow to do the job properly – attracted accurate and intense rifle fire at times, and it was a two-man job to provide the vital information to the British troops below.

The part played by heavy tanks in the battle is not mentioned in the wireless log (below), but it is referred to in Phil May's account, and their work was invaluable.

A persistent rumour at the time was that the crew of a Centurion 50-ton tank had drawn by mistake armour-piercing shells instead of fragmen-

HQ building Caracol, and the Bureau Sanitaire (a multi storied, flat-roofed building). As we flew over the area we saw an armoured car from the Royals being fired on from the roof of the BS. It returned fire (tracer) but could not get sufficient elevation for successful results It then moved to a side street. We could clearly see men firing from positions on the roof at our troops, and we continued to circle, reporting movements on the ground.

We noted a considerable increase in the number of armed police on the roof of the BS, who were now dragging up boxes of ammunition. We were asked to report on the numbers on the roof and as we both had difficulty in doing a head count agreed an estimate of between 20 and 30. By this time the enemy were directing some of their fire from the BS at our aircraft. As we were quite low, Lt Heron took evasive action and dived to the east.

We circled the town again and flew back towards the BS buildings and could see what appeared to be 2-inch mortar bombs landing on the building. This had a dramatic and instant effect of clearing the flat roof area till only a few snipers remained there, plus what appeared to be some casualties lying around. We continued circling the town and then flew over Arab Town. I recall returning to the airfield at RAF Ismailia briefly (probably to refuel) and seeing paratroops in the cemetery area NW as we came in to land.

Later, while we continued to fly over the area, we observed support weapons firing into the buildings occupied by the enemy and, later still, the infantry assault covered by a tank giving extremely close support. The paras now seemed to be involved in clearing up on the outskirts of the town, and we returned to RAF Ismailia in time for lunch.

After this action, bombing and shooting incidents continued to occur in the Zone but on a smaller scale. This included the killing of Sister Anthony, a Catholic nun, who was shot in Ismailia whilst caring for children *(Sister Anthony was, in fact, killed five days before this incident.)*

On 26 January, Shepherds Hotel in Cairo was bombed and set on fire by terrorists, and a number of British civilians killed and mutilated by a mob. After this incident the C-in-C British Forces, General Erskine, was reported to have told the Egyptian Prime Minister: "If there is any more of this bloody nonsense the British Army will be in Cairo within the hour."

The Egyptian Prime Minister replied: "But the Egyptian Army will resist you".

Erskine then observed: "In that case, we will take an hour and ten minutes."

If the foregoing is true then General Erskine was a truly brave man, because the British Government at that time was uncertain about declaring a state of emergency, and whether our forces were on active service.

tation ones. The result was that the shells passed right through the buildings.

It must have been a fearsome experience for those inside, but the mistake undoubtedly saved many lives.

Despite requests to cease firing, all twenty of the tank's rounds were fired. Of course, radio headsets can malfunction, and the noise in a tank firing live ammunition is loud and distracting, which may explain why the bombardment continued. But to return the unused rounds would have been to risk the mistake being acknowledged, so...

THE BUREAU BATTLE BLOW BY BLOW

This is the wireless log of the morning of Friday 25 January 1952. The ground control wireless set was positioned on the grass running down to the Sweet Water Canal at the bridge outside Battalion HQ, 1st East Lancashire Regiment. The officer commanding, Lt-Col Jones, was watching the police barracks, called the Caracol. He ordered that the log be kept so that he could know what was going on.

Explanatory notes

Air OP – *Observation post in Royal Artillery Auster piloted by Lt Tony Heron assisted by FO Phil May.*

Bureau Sanitaire – *the secondary police station.*

LF – *The Lancashire Fusiliers.*

Acorn – *Signal code for the intelligence officer.*

Caracol – *The main police station.*

Seagull – *Signal code for the second in command.*

Royals – *The Royal Dragoon Guards.*

Auxiliaries – *Auxiliary Egyptian police, mostly without uniforms and not well disciplined.*

3 Para – *3rd Parachute Regiment.*

Arashiya – *An Arab quarter of Ismailia.*

Sunray – *Signal code for commander.*

FS – *Field Security.*

41 Fd Regt – *41 Field Regiment, Royal Artillery.*

Colonel Malik – *The Egyptian Army liaison officer with the British.*

ELR – *1st East Lancashire Regiment.*

The wireless log

06.37
Police in firing position on roof. (Air Op)

06.40
Commander reports that owing to lack of officers in Caracol he will probably have to use force. (Cmdr Rover)

06.45
No one on roof, police skulking under trees in rear. (Air Op)

06.49
Lot (8) of police on Bureau Sanitaire roof armed with rifles. (Air Op)

06.55
LFs received above message. (1LF)

06.58
(20) Police on north building of Bureau Sanitaire, one on south building. (Air Op)

07.00
SW corner of north building of Bureau Sanitaire defended. Position of oil drums with 10 police on ground. (Air Op)

07.05
Police on roof of Bureau Sanitaire appear to be drawing ammunition. (Air Op)

07.07
3 Riflemen on south end of

Bureau Sanitaire. (Air Op)

07.09
Police taking up positions round Bureau Sanitaire on ground. (Control to 1LF and Cmdr Rover)

07.15
Inform Acorn: very fat officer wearing khaki SD on roof of Bureau Sanitaire. (Air Op)

07.13
Vehicle fired on from roof of Bureau Sanitaire. (?)

07.15
Battle going on in Bureau Sanitaire. (Control to 1LF)

07.18
Northwest side of Bureau Sanitaire: police collected. Only 10 on east side. (Air Op)

07.23
Battle still in progress. (Control to 1LF)

07.26
Malik with Egyptian general. Egyptian general refuses to leave house until firing ceases. Caracol ordered to cease firing and to hang out a white flag. Egyptian general will then go down to Caracol. (1LF)

07.27
Caracol surrounded. Officers keep arriving. Ordered to get wogs out. No success. Cmdr not anxious to open fire. Hopes wogs see sense. Bureau Sanitaire certainly firing. Round of blank fired, all fired back, general shooting. Wants to have 07.26 message verified. Verified by Seagull. Sounds promising. Remaining outside Caracol.

(Cmdr)

07.47
Almost all the police have left the roof of the Bureau Sanitaire. Only 5 or 6 still there plus 1 or 2 bodies. (Air Op)

07.48
Situation status quo: not anxious to blow the place down. Awaiting Major-General. Then if fire still being received from Bureau Sanitaire will try to get Major-General to Bureau Sanitaire. (Cmdr)

07.49
General does not intend to get police out. (Seagull)

07.50
Arms and thugs hidden in Stalio's gardens in rear of cordon. Rue Abbas Makim. (1 ELR)

07.53
Am of opinion must blow place down. Can I wait a few hours to get sense out of General. (Cmdr)

07.54
Tell police that they have acted honourably and to come out. (Cmdr)

07.55
Use fire hoses (Seagull to Bde Cmdr)
Follow up first suggestion in Bureau Sanitaire and Caracol. (Cmdr to Seagull)

08.00
Our people have stopped firing at Bureau Sanitaire. (B Sqdn Royals)

08.13
Malik says he has reached a complete impasse. In that

case tell General his Caracol will be severely damaged. Lives on his head. (Seagull to Cmdr)
Big Sunray says good thing if regular police could come out with arms. NOT auxiliaries. Pass to Malik. (Bde Cmdr to Seagull)

08.24
Malik told General. General will concert officers in Caracol to see if they will accept these terms. Is doubtful if they will. (Seagull to Cmdr)

08.35
Armed wogs running west and east in Arab Town outside cordon area of 1 E Lancs Regt. 1 E Lancs Regt. is engaging them. Only a few of them. That is the sniping that you can hear. (Control to Cmdr)

Sit-Rep from 3 Para: No. of persons in cage: Army 4; 1 Officer and 36 ORs railway police. 26 OR army police. Police cas 1 OR shot dead, north side of railway line. Own cas 1 wounded. Arms and ammo impounded. 60 assorted rifles. 1 x .38 revolver. Small amount of ammo. Law and order maintained in Arashiya. (3 Para to Seagull)

08.51
Still parleying with Caracol. Think things look like happening. (Cmdr or Seagull)

09.35
Seagull to set. What is position about (Egyptian) army? (Sunray)

A Royal Artillery Auster like this was used to provide air observation during the Battle of the Bureau Sanitaire.

1 shot fired from Egyptian camp killed 1 LF. Camp covered. Normal activity among Egyptians. (Seagull)

Make point clear to big Sunray. Warn Douglas to be prepared. Have no success at Caracol. Am opening with 2 pounders. Tanks will return fire with fire Besa. *Heavy machine gun.* (from Cmdr to Seagull)

2 dead, 3 wounded: our casualties. (Seagull)

09.40
Don't endanger lives unnecessarily. (Seagull to 1LF)

09.45
Ask Sunray to call me. (Seagull)

09.55

3 ORs killed. 5 wounded – 40 ORs, 1 officer. (from 1LF)

09.57
2 police officers brought in by sub units. Found hiding in cupboard in hotel in Ismailia. 1 officer believed to hold the rank of colonel. (3 Para)

10.00
Called to ask whether Caracol is to go in. (Seagull)

Caracol has gone in. (Cmdr)

Pause after softening up. Another broadcast now to police. (Seagull to Bde Cmdr).

10.01
Ambulance to French Square. (1LF)

10.07
Further ambulances sent to French Square.So you will be getting one more. (To 1LF)

10.09
Confirm report that Bureau Sanitaire has surrendered. (To 1LF)

We confirm that (1LF)

10.10
Do you require FS team now? (To 1LF)

10.12
Liaison officer to set. Cancelled. *Crossed out in original copy.*

10.14
Liaison officer on set. Will you confirm that Caracol has surrendered? Do you want FS? (Seagull)

No. Caracol has shown no sign of surrendering. Unconfirmed reports that bureau Sanitaire has surrendered. Report about

Caracol quite incorrect. (Sunray)

10.14
What is true position at Bureau Sanitaire? (Sunray to Seagull)

10.15
1LF Sunray to set. (On other set)

10.22
Rumour of surrender in Bureau Sanitaire is incorrect. Ascertain number are now coming out with hands up (acc by armd cmdr). Tonight I want to relieve LFs. If possible I would like another unit to take over. (Sunray)

Cas to LF. 7 wounded and 3 killed. (Seagull)

10.30
LO to set. tell Sunray or LO to call me. (Seagull)

10.32
Agreed that our 2nd Battalion be made available this evening. Had report from Caracol that police want ambulance for wounded. Unwilling to surrender. Ambulances not to be sent until surrender. (Seagull)

10.46
Small parties coming out of Bureau Sanitaire. FS to be sent. (From 1LF)

10.47
1 or 2 police on top of Bureau Sanitaire. (Air Op)

10.50
All police will now be considered POW. None to be evacuated. (Seagull)

Heard rumours that 200

people surrendered in Bureau Sanitaire. (Sunray)

Small parties coming out. (Seagull)

10.50
Party of police being marched towards French Square. (Air Op)

10.50
We are now in French Square. (Cmdr)

10.56
At Caracol by green bus is deep pit which contains 6 police. Pit leads to door underground. (Air Op)

10.57
FS men have been sent. (To 1LF)

11.03
I think Bureau Sanitaire is finished. Large crowds have surrendered (200 or 300) and more coming in. Get transport to move them.

41 Fld Regt are providing transport. (Seagull)

11.06
Will you arrange for transport to move prisoners now. (Sunray to Seagull)

Arrange through gunner rep. (Control to 1LF)

11.15
We have 2 Egyptian Red Crescent officials who want to pass cordon. Can they pass? (3 Para)

11.20
Who are these officials? If doctors, yes. If not let me know who they are. (Control to 3 Para)

11.22

Still one or two people being winkled out of Bureau Sanitaire. (Air Op)

11.25
Are these officials doctors? (Control)

No they are not doctors. They call themselves Red Crescent officials. (3 Para)

11.27
Use initiative. If part of ambulance let them through. Search them. (Control to 3 Para)

11.30
Egyptian POW being taken away. App. No. 400. (1LF to control)

11.34
Is Malik with you? (Sunray)

No. Not for 3 hrs. Probably on bridge. (Seagull)

Want him urgently. (Sunray to Seagull)

11.37
Please confirm whether Egyptian ambulances can collect wounded from Bureau Sanitaire. (Control to 1LF)

11.41
Egyptian ambulances will be let through if OK with Sunray. (1LF to control)

11.43
Egyptian ambulances will come through your cordon after searching. When return check wounded number. (To 1LF and 1ELR)

11.45
Malik is not on bridge. May be in HQ in Moascar. Phone him. (Seagull to control)

11.46
Have you received supplies of tear gas? (Control to 1LF)

11.55
Malik, Egyptian army officer, and a member of Egyptian Red Crescent have gone through barrier into Ismailia looking for ambulances. (1 ELR to control)

12.00
Everyone to look for Colonel Malik. He is to be told to report to Sunray. Urgent.

12.15
Coming out of Caracol surrendering now. (B Sqdn Royals to control)

12.17
21 Elderly people have come out so far, elderly sergeant type. (B Sqdn Royals)

12.20
Ask your Sunray to report this location straight away. (Control to 3 Para)

12.23
Police officer just come out of Caracol to see Brigadier. Being sent in jeep.

12.25
Sunray has left location.

12.25
Contacted Colonel Mallett. (BM Rover) *Should be Malik?*

12.30
Have you sent police captain down to this location as well as Colonel Mallett? (Control to BM) *Should be Malik?*

No. He is still outside Caracol. He is being sent down. (BM)

12.31
Confirm whether 400 Egyptian police have been

removed? (Control to 1LF)

All except about 80 men. (1LF)

12.34
33 thugs and 1 woman surrendered at back of Caracol now. 100 prisoners including police. (B Sqdn Royals)

12.37
What percentage are thugs and what percentage police? (Control to B Sqdn Royals)

12.39
3 ORs killed. 1 officer wounded. 11 ORs wounded. (1LF to control)

12.45
Total figure is 300 now. Taking some sorting out. Percentage follows. All from Caracol. (B Sqdn Royals)

12.46
Sunray at Caracol.

12.51
19B check: 40 police killed. 3 to 4 hundred rifles SMLE. 1000s rds .300. No. of carbines (believed Italian). (B Sqdn Royals)

12.54
19B 400 from Caracol – Djellabahs, greatcoats, uniforms. Impossible to say which are police. (B Sqdn Royals)

13.00
Netting call.

13.15
Proceed to Ferry Point and check reports that there are 6 Egyptian tanks on other side. (To Air Ops)

13.20
No tanks but there are 6

armoured cars directly opposite Ferry Point. (Air Op)

13.23
Like to confirm that LFs reserve Coy are going through Ismailia picking up the odd policeman. Pass general warning - no looting. (Sunray to Seagull)

13.24
Reserve Coy go through Ismailia mopping up police. No looting. (Seagull to 1LF)

13.25
Send three 3-ton vehicles to collect arms and ammo from Bureau Sanitaire. (1LF to Control)

13.26
Police officers from Caracol to be sent to Timsah Leave Camp. See they are well fed. (Sunray to Seagull)

13.33
Sunray requires a packet of cigarettes at Caracol. *Crossed out in original*

13.40
Five 3-tonners will be at Bureau Sanitaire at 14.00 hours. (Control to 1LF)

13.45
May this unit stand down? (Sapper to control)

Yes, except from small recce party. (Control to Sapper)

13.50
36 dead, 60 wounded, 557 rifles captured at Bureau Sanitaire. (B Sqdn Royals to Control)

13.52
DI Sweep of this area begins 14.15. (1LF to Control)

AWARD FOR GALLANTRY

One of the real heroes of the battle of the Bureau Sanitaire was Corporal (Acting Sergeant) Harry Foster of the Lancashire Fusiliers, who won the George Medal for his bravery in the action. For his gallantry the Queen awarded Sgt Foster the George Medal, the second highest honour that can be awarded in peacetime. Here is the citation:

Sergeant Foster was platoon sergeant of 8 Platoon of C Company on the morning of 25 January 1952. At about 09.00 hours his platoon was ordered to enter the courtyard of the Egyptian Police Barracks in the Bureau Sanitaire, Ismailia, and to clear the left wing of the building.

The Egyptian Police were covering the courtyard with heavy rifle fire, and in the first five minutes of the action Sgt Foster received a bullet wound in the right upper arm. He ignored this and carried on. The platoon was held up about halfway across the courtyard and Sgt Foster moved about in the open, putting LMGs into fire positions and encouraging his men. About five minutes later he was again hit, in the leg but ignored this wound and remained at his post.

Under cover of MG fire from the tanks in support, the platoon managed to reach the building and gain lodgement. Resistance was strong, and Sgt Foster led a party throwing grenades. Shortly after this, and about half an hour after receiving his first wound, he was hit again by a rifle bullet in the leg, this time severely. Although in great pain he refused assistance – he was evacuated only on the direct order of his platoon commander.

Throughout the action Sgt Foster had shown complete disregard for his own safety and his gallantry and good leadership were an example to all ranks of his company.

Harry Foster is honoured for his gallantry in the regimental museum of the Royal Regiment of Fusiliers, at Wellington Barracks in Bury. The Royal Regiment of Fusiliers was formed in 1968 from a number of regiments, including the Lancashire Fusiliers, .

A photograph on the wall of the museum shows the late Sgt Foster standing outside Buckingham Palace with his family after receiving his George Medal from the Queen.

The citation at the museum reads: "His complete disregard for his own safety, in going forward whilst wounded, saved the lives of three members of his platoon."

ROLL OF HONOUR

The following names of non-World War dead who lie in Egypt are listed in alphabetical order and include civilians, Service dependants and others who died before and after the period of 1951-54. All casualties are named under the cemetery in which they were buried, with date of interment. Plot, Row and Grave numbers are abbreviated, e.g. P14 RF G7.

In some cases, the Service number available is known to be inaccurate but every care has been taken in the preparation of the list, which has been kindly supplied by the Egypt Award Alliance Memorial Association.

When aircrew or passengers died in flying incidents over the sea, and as a result their bodies were never recovered, their names are unlisted. The men who simply disappeared are listed at the end of this chapter. The Ministry of Defence advise that they have no list of those evacuated as seriously wounded, and who subsequently succumbed to their injuries.

All of them died because they were serving in this theatre. Please study the names, note the ages, and remember the dead.

FAYID WAR CEMETERY

ACHOLA J., Private 18175334 African Pioneer Corps (East Africa), 10 March 1954. P14 RF G7.

ADAMS J.J.W., Airman 4032980 RAF, 9 December 1950, age 20. P18 RB G16. **Died of injuries received in road traffic accident on 8 December 1950.**

AHFAT A.F., Private 18085374 African Pioneer Corps (East Africa), 2048 Mauritius Company, 3 December 1951. P16 RA G2. **Killed in vehicle ambush.**

ALBERT S., Private 18088324 African Pioneer Corps (East Africa), 2212 Mauritius Company, 20 January 1952. P14 RG G3.

ALDER R.E., Aircrew 369762 RAF, 12 January 1953. P34 RA G1. **Killed in crash of Hastings aircraft TG502 near RAF Shallufa while flying from RAF Fayid.**

ALLAGHAPEN K., Private 18081049 African Pioneer Corps (East Africa), 2048 Mauritius Company, 3 December 1951. P16 RF G2. **Killed in vehicle ambush.**

ALLEN B., AC2 4072697 RAF Regiment, 56 Rifle Squadron, 18 January 1952, age 18. P18 RB G26.

ALLEN J.H., Captain 173726 Royal Army Pay Corps, 4 October 1950. P18 RB G4.

ANSELL R., L/Corporal T/19039862 RASC, 27 August 1952, age 23. P18 RD G37. **Killed by terrorist action.**

ANTOINE L.G., Private 18026291 African Pioneer Corps (East Africa), 2048 Mauritius Company, 3 December 1951. P14 RG G1. **Killed in vehicle ambush.**

APOLLON H., Private 18084938 African Pioneer Corps (East Africa), 2048 Mauritius Company, 19 November 1951. P14 RF G6.

APPLETON J.R., Airman 39773 RAF, 29 March 1949. P13 RA G16.

ARCHERS G., Civilian, 1 October 1953. P34 RC G4.

ARLISS S.A., Civilian, 107 MU (RAF), 16 August 1952. P15 RA G11.

ARNOLD E., Gunner 22231123 Royal Artillery, 25 November 1951, age 24. P18 RA G43.

ASHTON B.G., Airman RAF, 2 May 1951. P118 RC G7. **Killed when Valetta VLN156 crashed.**

ASHWORTH A.S., Sergeant 149587 RASC, 4 September 1949, age 35. P13 RD G3.

ATHERTON S., Airman 991742 RAF, 21 January 1954. P34 RD G17.

AYAROO M., Private 18089540 African Pioneer Corps (East Africa), 2048 Mauritius Company, 3 December 1951. P16 RF G6. **Killed in vehicle ambush.**

BAILEY A.C., Sergeant 22548066 Royal Pioneer Corps, 7 September 1955. P35 RA G6.

BAILEY M.F., Lieutenant 322074 6th Airborne REME, 8 November 1951, age 26. P18 RA G6.

BAINTON G., Craftsman 21050433 REME, 3 May 1949. P13 RA G24.

BAKER R.M., Civilian, Service dependant, 5 January 1953, son of W.O Baker 10 BOD (Geneifa). P13 RD G34.

BALA C-O., Private 18180208 African Pioneer Corps (East Africa), 20 April 1954. P14 RG G4.

BALL E.J., Sapper 3910598 Royal Engineers, 7 November 1948. P18 RF G14.

BAMFORD G.A., Private 22475462 Army Catering Corps, 28 April 1952, age 19. P18 RC G31.

BANKS G., Sergeant 554961 16th/5th Lancers RAC, 3 October 1949. P13 RD G19.

BARBER E.K., Airman 1388748 RAF, 6 March 1948. P13 RB G8. **Listed as one of seven airmen said to have been killed in the same road traffic accident.**

BARNARD B.C., Airman 3510306 RAF, 12 January 1953. P34 RA G15. **Killed in crash of Hastings aircraft TG602 near RAF Shallufa while flying from RAF Fayid.**

BARRATT N., Sapper 14176337 Royal Engineers, 169 Railway Workshops, 14 July 1948. P13 RC G25.

BATSTONE H., Airman 3129339 RAF, 4 July 1953. P34 RD G4.

BATTRICK C.J., Driver T/21181233 RASC, 2 May 1951, age 21. P18 RC G17. **Killed when Valetta VNL156 crashed.**

BATTY L.T., Driver 19168593 RASC, 18 March 1949. P13 RA G10.

BEARD J.M., Airman 578638 RAF, 2 May 1951. P18 RC G11. **Killed when Valetta VLN156 crashed.**

BEDSON J., Civilian, Service dependant, 26 May 1951. P18 RC G11.

BEECH D.C., Driver T/22635382 RASC, 93 Company, 2 July 1953, age 19. P34 RE G4. **Killed by terrorist action.**

BEEKO R., Private 18081255 African Pioneer Corps (East Africa), 2046 Mauritius Company, 25 September 1951. P16 RE G1. **Killed by terrorist action.**

BELL J.A., Private, 1st Battalion Cheshire Regiment, 13 October 1952, age 23. P18 RD G10.

BELLWOOD M., Civilian, 19 July 1953. P34 RD G10.

BENNETT E., Civilian, Service dependant, 3 March 1952, daughter of Corporal Bennett. P18 RC G8.

BENNETT R.A., Sergeant 592329 RAF, 109 MU, 23 November 1954, age 22. P35 RD G10. **Killed by terrorist action.**

BERRINGER A.M., Civilian, Service dependant, 11 February 1949, father of Captain A.M.Berringer RAOC. P13 RG G25.

BETT J., L/Bombardier 14473436 Royal Artillery,. HAA Battery, 11 December 1952, age 23. P13 RG G24.

BETTS A.J.T., Sergeant 14459270 RASC, 23 November 1948. P13 RG G3.

BETTS W., Guardsman 2614267 3rd Battalion Grenadier Guards, 24 August 1952, age 39. P18 RD G35. **Known as Busty Betts, because he had been up and down through the ranks throughout his military career. He died as a result of injuries received in a road accident involving a British Services ambulance.**

BHICA H.R., Private 18009324 African Pioneer Corps (East Africa), 30 March 1949. P16 RB G4.

BHOLO R., Private 18081566 African Pioneer Corps (East Africa), 2048 Mauritius Company, 3 December 1951. P16 RE G5. **Killed in vehicle ambush.**

BHULAGOO B., Private 18084540 African Pioneer Corps (East Africa), 18 July 1949. P16 RC G5.

BIBBY T., Private Army Catering Corps, attached 33 Company RAMC, 29 July 1953, age 18. P34 RA G10.

BLACKBURN P., Corporal 22379763 REME, 30 July 1951, age 22. P18 RC G30. **Killed by terrorist action.**

BLACKWELL H.E., Driver T/19154704 RASC, 30 September 1948. P13 RE G15.

BOLTWOD J.A., Civilian, Service dependant, 12 August 1950. P18 RA G32.

BOMHAM J., Private 22165036 1st Battalion The Loyal Regiment (North Lancashire), 9 August 1951, age 21. P18 RA G2. **Killed by terrorist action.**

BONNE J.A.A., Private 13404338 African Pioneer Corps (East Africa), 11 September 1948. P14 RB G6.

BONNER E., Sapper 22798024 Royal Engineers, (Engineer Base Egypt), 21 July 1953, age 19. P34 RD G14. **Accidentally killed on Mortar range.**

BOOKER T.E., Private 22998994 1st Battalion Royal Warwickshire Regiment, 20 July 1955. P35 RE G21.

BOOTUM H., Private 1823228 African Pioneer Corps (East Africa), 2048 Mauritius Company, 6 December 1948. P16 RB G2.

BOYES S., Civilian, 13 August 1952. P18 RD G27.

BRACK C., Private 18024844 African Pioneer Corps (East Africa), Mauritius Company, 6 December 1948. P14 RC G5.

BRADBURY F., Corporal 22211998 Royal Engineers, 11 December 1951, age 40. P18 RB G9.

BRADER R.M., AC1 2392943 RAF, 324 Wing,19 October 1949. P13 RE G2.

BRADLEY Judith, Civilian, 7 July 1950. P18 RA G19.

BRADNOCK E., Flt/Sergeant RAF, 443 Air Training Corps, 11 May 1950. P18 RA G3. **Riding as a passenger in Lincoln SX957 he died as a result of a mid-air collision with Vampire VZ188. Eleven airmen died in this incident.**

BRENNAN B., L/Corporal 19034404 Royal Irish Fusiliers, 12 March 1949. P13 RA G6.

BRENNAND G., Private 22620422 1st Battalion South Lancashire Regiment, 23 May 1953, age 20. P34 RA G6.

BRIEN J., Leading Aircraftsman 190225 RAF, 10 November 1948, age 40. P13 RF G22.

BRIMLEY K.W., Flight Lieutenant 925993 RAF, 216 Squadron, 2 April 1954. P5 RA G13. **Pilot, one of three killed when Valetta VW205 crashed in the Canal Zone.**

BRISTOW S.D., Private 21031830 RAOC, 3 September 1948. P13 RE G1.

BROADBENT H., Airman 562411 RAF, 6 January 1951. P18 RB G27. **Killed by terrorist action.**

BROMLY R.J., Flying Officer 160996 RAF, 107 MU, 1 September 1951. P18 RA G8. **Killed in road accident at Fanara.**

BROSTER T.D., Airman 2358389 RAF, 7 March 1948. P13 RB G6. **Died in BMH of injuries received in road accident on 6 March 1948. Six other airmen said to have been killed in the same road traffic accident.**

BROWN (Mrs), Civilian, 9 December 1948, age 40. P13 RG G9

BROWN A., Bombardier 22536703 Royal Artillery, 26 Field Regiment, 26 August 1954. P35 RC G5. **Killed by terrorist action.**

BROWN Brendan, Civilian, 17 February 1951. P18 RB G33.

BROWN Margaret, Civilian, 17 August 1951, age 6. P18 RA G6.

BROWN W.J., Private 19158020 RAOC, 13 April 1948, age 19. P13 RC G7.

BRUTON P.F.L., Corporal T/21187507 RASC, 2 May 1951, age 21. P18 RC G15. **Killed when Valetta VNL156 crashed.**

BUCKLE R.H.F., Airman 3036500 RAF, 148 Shallufa, 11 May 1950, age 23. P18 RA G1. **Navigator of Lincoln SX957 involved in mid-air collision with Vampire VZ188. Eleven airmen were killed in this incident.**

BUCKLES Carol Anne, Civilian, Service dependant, 14 November 1951, daughter of Sgt Buckles. P18 RA G36.

BULL W.L., Pilot Officer 607063 RAF, 249 Squadron, 8 December 1950. P18 RB 10. **Killed when his Vampire fighter crashed.**

BURKE T., Sergeant 3651046 Military Provost Staff Corps, 51st M.P DB, 4 August 1951, age 45. P18 RC G36. **Killed by terrorist action.**

BURKILL C., Airman 1590192 RAF, 12 January 1953. P34 RA G5. **Killed in crash of Hastings aircraft TG602 near RAF Shallufa while flying from RAF Fayid.**

BUTCHER Ann Muriel, Civilian, 23 July 1950. P18 RA G11.

BUTTERWORTH J., Sister 280270 Queen Alexandria's Imperial Military Nursing Service, 28 September 1948. P13 RE G9.

BRYNAND L., Civilian, Service dependant, 1 February 1950, age one, son of 618300 Sgt L Brynand RAF. P13 RF G7.

CAMPBELL A.M.C., L/Corporal 22324596 Royal Engineers, 9 ESBO Suez, 2 October 1951, age 20. P18 RA G16. **Killed by terrorist action.**

CAMPBELL C.E., Civilian, Service dependant, 28 February 1950, age one, daughter of 44855 Major C.E.Campbell of Royal Tank Regiment. P13 RF G23.

CANSDALE H.E., Signalman 14072667 Royal Corps of Signals, 3rd GHQ Signals Regiment, 5 February 1948, age 20. P13 RA G19.

CAREY R.J., Driver T/21023504 RASC, 4 February 1950. P13 RF G13.

CARLTON V.P., Sapper 22403963 Royal Engineers, 8 ESBD, 26 May 1955. P35 RE G7.

CARTER F.J., Corporal T/21016707 RASC, 9 February 1952, age 31. P18 RB G38. **Murdered by Corporal Tom Houghton, age 23, 74 Company RASC.**

CARVER W.E., Major 18782 British Army, 152 Transit Camp Fayid, 31 January 1948. P13 RA G15.

CASIMIR A., Private 18012732 African Pioneer Corps (East Africa), 2065 Mauritius Company, 23 March 1948. P14 RA G5.

CASTLEDINE Wendy Ann, Civilian, Service dependant, 30 July 1949, daughter of 4972972 Warrant Officer1 Castledine, Brigade GHQ. P13 RB G21.

CAUNTER L.F., Squadron Leader 21009 RAF, 107 MU, 25 October 1949. P13 RE G8.

CHADWICK C.J.D., Leading Aircraftsman 2538396 RAF Fayid, 30 December 1951. P18 RD G30.

CHAPMAN G., Civilian, 5 September 1951. P18 RA G10.

CHARALAMBOS N., Civilian, 5 July 1954. P35 RB G18.

CHELAKIS N., Civilian, 12 November 1951. P14 RF G4.

CHIDDA R., Driver 139050135 African Pioneer Corps (East Africa), 13 (M) Company, 31 March 1949. P16 RC G7.

CHONGA., Private 18115698 African Pioneer Corps (East Africa), 2209 Mauritius Company, 29 September 1953. P14 RE G6.

CIRIC P., Corporal British Army, 21 December 1948. P14 RD G2.

CLARKE E.J., Airman 572231 RAF, 18 March 1949. P13 RA G8.

CLARKE G.T., Pilot Officer 748034 RAF, 107 MU, 11 August 1953. P34 RA G18. **Killed while piloting Harvard KF329.**

CLISSETT D.R., Driver T/22156157 RASC, 20 July 1950. P18 RA G26.

COLEMAN J., Signalman 19092166 Royal Corps of Signals, 4 September 1948. P13 RE G3.

COLETTE D., Private 18086917 African Pioneer Corps (East Africa), Rodriguez Company, 3 July 1953. P14 RD G7.

COLLIER R., L/Corporal 22548900 Royal Corps of Signals, 10 January 1953, age 19. P18 RD G36.

COLLINS, W., Trooper 19148109 16th/5th Lancers, RAC, 26 July 1948. P13 RD G6.

COLWILL H.C., Company Sergeant Major PLY/X819 Royal Marines, 20 July 1948. P13 RD G4.

COMPTON B., Civilian, 13 July 1952. P18 RD G7.

CONNELL J.M., Airman 3502220 RAF, 31 January 1949. P13 RG G23.

CONSTANTINE SERUNJONI S., Private 18174996 Royal Pioneer Corps (East Africa), 2203 Company, 7 August 1954. P14 RG G8. **Killed by terrorist action.**

COPELAND R.G.G., Major 190476 11th Hussars, RAC, 20 December 1952, age 32. P18 RD G26.

COPP S., Corporal 2229041 Army Catering Corps, attached 17 Brigade GHQ, 25 July 1951, age 21. P18 RC G28. **Killed by terrorist action.**

CORBETT R., Airman 4021573 RAF, 20 October 1948. P13 RE G25.

COULSON P.B., Captain 1st Battalion Royal Horse Artillery, 5 July 1950. P18 RA G17. Joint grave with COULSON Suzanne Elizabeth, Civilian, Service dependant, 7 July 1950, age one.

COUTTS P.R., Flying Officer 2533253 RAF, 213 Squadron, 11 March 1954, age 21. P34 RE G14.**Killed when Vampire WL574 he was piloting crashed.**

CRAIG J., Leading Aircraftsman 3131799 RAF, 9 January 1952. P18 RB G28.

CRANGLE W., Sapper 22624079 Royal Engineers, 35 Corps Engineer Regiment, 7 April 1953, age 22. P34 RB G12. **Killed by terrorist action.**

CRIPPS C.A., Sapper 22819325 Royal Engineers, 8 ESBD, 26 May 1955, age 22. P35 RE G9.

CRIPPS R.P., L/Bombardier 242306150 Royal Artillery, GHQ Group MELF, 10 November 1952. P18 RB G23.

CRITCHLEY J., 2nd Lieutenant 3390263 RASC, 10 November 1948. P13 RF G20

CUMMINS A.S., Airman 4022074 RAF, 3 July 1949. P13 RB G11.

CUNNINGHAM I.D.S., Flying Officer 607043 RAF, 219 Squadron, 12 February 1952. P18 RB G44. **Killed in flying incident when piloting Mosquito RF988 at RAF Kabrit.**

CURTIS P., Sergeant 22305704 Royal Artillery, 26 Field Regiment, 14 August 1954, age 22. P35 RB G24. **Killed by terrorist action.**

CURTIS R.T., Gunner 22365352 Royal Artillery, 5 November 1951. P18 RA G29.

DABBS K.J., Airman RAF Deversoir, 19 September 1952. P18 RD G2. **Died of leukaemia not detected during pre-embarkation medical.**

DABROWSKI, Civilian, 148 Squadron, 11 May 1950. P18 RA G9. **Killed when his Vampire VZ188 was involved in a mid-air collision with Lincoln SX957 of 148 Squadron RAF. Eleven airmen lost their lives in this incident.**

■ The high death rate suffered by the African Pioneer Corps can partly be explained by the knowledge that they were present in Egypt during the whole period of operations.

In the main they were recruited in Mauritius, an island country with a population of well under 900,000. The Rodriguez island is 565km from Mauritius and has a population of only some 22,000. The Seychelles (1,600km east of Mombassa, Kenya) has a population of only 60,000 scattered throughout its 85 islands.

It follows that the tragedies must have impacted on nearly every community at some time. Poverty may have been the spur to continued recruitment.

I remember them as a happy and carefree bunch who were extremely rough footballers despite playing against studded boots in their bare feet.

DAINYS P., Civilian, 10 February 1950. P14 RE G7.

DALY J.D., Fusilier 21182922 Royal Irish Fusiliers, 12 September 1949. P13 RD G13.

DARBY Janet, Civilian, Service dependant, 3 February 1950, age one, daughter of J Darby 30 Corps RASC. P13 RF G9.

DART G.W., Airman RAF, 26 July 1954. P35 RB G14.

DAVIES C.J.L., Civilian, 5 July 1950. P18 RA G15.

DAVIES H.G., Sapper 21048285 Royal Engineers, A Branch GHQ, 2 October 1948. P13 RE G21.

DAVIES P., Civilian, 9 March 1951. P18 RB G37.

DAVIES Robert, Civilian, Service dependant, 29 May 1949, son of Corporal R Davies 547527 RAF. P13 RB G7.

DAVIS Jane, Civilian, 14 February 1954. P34 RE G6.

DAVISON A., Private 22400730 RAMC, 15 December 1951. P18 RB G13.

DAYKIN J.R., Driver T/22448305 RASC, 7 September 1952. P18 RD G45.

DE FRANCE R.W., Airman 772656 RAF, 8 December 1950. P18 RB G14. **Killed in road traffic accident.**

DEBBONNAIRE B., Leading Aircraftsman RAF, 107 MU, 29 March 1953. P34 RB G6

DEMAINE P., Signalman 22105469 Royal Corps of Signals, 25 February 1950. P13 RF G21.

DEMOSTHENOUS C., Labourer 6017 4th Cypriot Labour Unit, Labour Corps, 8 May 1953. P34 RB G18.

DIAMAS J., Private 18025252 African Pioneer Corps (East Africa), 25 January 1949. P14 RD G6.

DICKINSON J.R., Sapper 22309718 Royal Engineers, 3 December 1951, age 23. P18 RB G5. **Killed in vehicle ambush.**

DOCHERTY P.L., Corporal 21126008 REME, 30 July 1953. P34 RC G17.

DOHERTY P., Airman 4013835 RAF, 28 April 1948. P13 RC G13.

DONAUGHY M.B., Major 101191 Royal Corps of Signals, 21 March 1949, age 49. P13 RA G12.

DONNELLY W.G., Airman 4027933 RAF, 25 September 1954. P35 RC G13. **Killed by terrorist action.**

DOUGLAS G., Aircraftsman 1st Class 2463964 RAF, 14 April 1951, age 19. P18 RB G41. **Killed by terrorist action.**

DOWNES R., Private 22893289 1st Battalion Cheshire Regiment, 19 April 1954. P35 RA G9.

DOWNEY R., Private 14194096 Army Catering Corps, 5 July 1948. P13 RD G12.

DOYLE P.J., Civilian, 28 August 1950. P18 RA G38.

DUNN B.G., Private 22635497 RAOC, 1st Infantry Division, 2 April 1953. P34 RB G10.

DUNNETT K.W., Gunner 21034447 Royal Artillery, 28 January 1949. P13 RG G19.

DUPORTAIL L.P., L/Corporal 18023466 African Pioneer Corps (East Africa), 2051 Mauritius Company, 23 July 1948. P14 RA G3.

EARL J., Trooper 21001002 Royal Tank Regiment, R.A.C, 24 July 1949. P13 RC G14.

EDWARDS F., Pilot 111 3011939 RAF, 208 Squadron, 14 July 1948. P13 RC G2. **Killed when his Spitfire TP450 suffered a mid-air collision with Spitfire TP292 piloted by F/O Frederick Jelly of 208 Squadron RAF.**

EDWARDS R., Civilian, Service dependant, age one, 17 November 1948, son of 511629 W.O.R Edwards RAF. P13 RF G24.

EDWARDS R.W., Sergeant T/22038428 RASC, 13 February 1954, age 23. P34 RE G4. **Killed by terrorist action.**

EKOKOU A.O., Private 18777316 African Pioneer Corps (East Africa), 2212 Company, 8 May 1954. P14 RG G6.

EJOKO EPILU E., Private 18177902 African Pioneer Corps (East Africa), 2208 Company, 21 October 1954. P35 RD G22. **Killed by terrorist action.**

ELEY Anita, Civilian, 3 December 1953. P34 RC G18.

ELLICOTT Susan, Civilian, Service dependant, 22 August 1948, daughter of Captain Ellicott. P13 RD G22.

ELLIOTT H.S., Staff Sergeant 22542828 RAPC, 4 July 1952. P18 RD G5.

ELLIS A., Private 22417344 RAMC, 2 May 1952, age 20. P18 RC G35.

EYERS J.J., Civilian, Service dependant, 24 August 1953. P34 RB G7.

FAIR F., L/Corporal 22234568 REME, attached 44 Tank Company, 15 September 1954. P35 RC G11. **Killed by terrorist action.**

FAIRLEY H.G.P., Sapper 22506819 Royal Engineers, Engineer Group, age 18. P18 RB G24.

FANNIE E., Private 40641 African Pioneer Corps (East Africa), 2065 Seychelles Company, 28 July 1952. P14 RA G6

FANNON F.H., L/Corporal 22559164 2nd Parachute Regiment, AAC, 9 April 1952. P18 RC G18.

FEATHERSTONE E.S., Driver RASC, 13 January 1950, age 23. P13 RF G1.

FELTOE C.F., Corporal 22655251 2nd Green Howards (Yorkshire Regiment), 24 March 1954, age 20. P34 RE G16.

FENION W.S., Gunner 11 4872914 RAF, 148 Squadron, 11 May 1950. P18 RA G5. **Killed in mid-air collision between Vampire BZ188 and Lincoln SX957.**

FERNANDAISE F., Private 48066 African Pioneer Corps (East Africa), 2065 Seychelles Company, 27 January 1953. P14 RC G2.

FIELD P.H., Captain 338747 Northamptonshire Regiment, 21 May 1954. P35 RA G21.

FIRTH Susan, Civilian, Service dependant, 1 November 1951. P18 RA G22.

FISHER A.E., Signalman 22355871 Royal Corps of Signals, 18 September 1950. P18 RA G42.

FITZHERBERT E.T., Lieutenant 390338 3rd Battalion Grenadier Guards, 9 March 1952, age 23. P18 RC G12. **Presumed drowned when he and a fellow officer failed to return from sailing on the Great Bitter Lake.**

FLANAGAN K.J., Leading Aircraftsman 2543482 RAF, 109 MU, 18 July 1953. P34 RA G4.

FLANAGAN R., Trooper 5th Dragoon Guards Princess Charlotte of Wales's, Shandar, 11 August 1953. P35 RB G1.

FLETCHER R.H., Private 22487932 RAMC, 1 November 1951, age 19. P18 RA G25.

FORD J.B., Senior Technician 534789 RAF, 109 MU, 4 July 1953, age 37. P34 RE G11.

FORD R., L/Corporal 22573602 Royal Corps of Signals, attached 29 Field Regiment Royal Artillery, 3 July 1953. P34 RE G9.

FORSTER F., Lieutenant 397888 Royal Artillery, 1908 Light 651 AOP, 26 February 1954. P34 RE G8.

FOWLER M.R., Driver Royal Corps of Signals, 4 December 1953, age 19. P34 RD G1.

FOXWELL M.R., L/Corporal 22437559 British Army, 3 December 1951. P18 RB G1. **Shot dead in an ambush by Egyptian Police while providing escort to the Assistant Provost Marshal.**

FRASER A.M., Airman 3503178 RAF, 10 March 1949. P13 RA G4.

GAISH E.R., Electrical Mechanic 1st Class SMX864324 Royal Navy, HMS Chevron, 24 May 1953. P34 RC G11.

GAVIGAN H., Private 22730009 Highland Light Infantry (City of Glasgow Regiment), 19 November 1953, age 19. P34 RC G10.

GEORGIADIS S., Civilian, 2 December 1953. P34 RC G16. **This is almost certainly the NAAFI manager abducted and murdered by Egyptian terrorists. His body was recovered on 27 November, having been missing since 20 November 1953.**

GERARD L.C., L/Corporal 18008170 African Pioneer Corps (East Africa), Mauritius Company, 23 July 1952. P14 RA G4.

GIBBON M., Civilian, Service dependant, 3 October 1948, age 27. P13 RE G23.

GIBSON L.P., Wing Commander RAF, 109 MU, 30 December 1954. P35 RD G18. **Killed by terrorist action.**

GODFREY D.F., Airman 750136 RAF, 27 May 1952. P18 RD G1.

GODFREY T., L/Corporal 19060294 Royal Irish Fusiliers, 12 September 1949. P13 RD G11.

GOODHALL A.H., Private 22525378 Cheshire Regiment, 30 December 1953. P34 RD G7.

GOUDENARD L., Civilian, 28 May 1948, age one. P13 RC G21.

GRAHAM D.D.A., Airman 2292960 RAF, 6 March 1948. P13 RB G12. **Listed as one of seven airmen said to have been killed in the same road traffic accident.**

GRANT A., Civilian, Service dependant, 15 August 1948, age 24, wife of Captain Grant 343692 RPC. P13 RD G18.

GRAY D., Driver T/22774712 RASC, 44 Company, 6 October 1953. P34 RC G6.

GRAY T., L/Corporal T/22286820 RASC, 13 July 1950. P18 RA G24.

GRECH J., Civilian, 107 MU RAF, 14 May 1955. P35 RE G5.

GREEN W., Staff Sergeant 14028154 Royal Engineers, B Company (D) DCRE, 5 February 1948, age 24. P13 RA G21.

GREGSON D.L., Lieutenant 441783 3rd Battalion Grenadier Guards, 9 March 1952. P18 RC G14. **Presumed drowned when he and a fellow officer failed to return from sailing on the Great Bitter Lake.**

GRIEVE A.J., 2nd Lieutenant 441783 Royal Tank Regiment, 1st Battalion RAC, 27 August 1955. P35 RA G4.

GRIFFIN P.A., Trooper 22671063 Royal Tank Regiment, 1st Battalion RAC, 4 April 1954. P35 RA G3.

GRIFFITHS L.H., Guardsman 22545149 3rd Battalion Grenadier Guards, 20 September 1953. P34 RB G17. **Electrocuted while ironing his uniform.**

GRIFFITHS R.G., Trooper 22143904 RAC, Royal Tank Regiment, 28 March 1950. P13 RG G4.

GUMBABISSOON., Private 18086673 African Pioneer Corps (East Africa), 2048 Mauritius Company, 3 December 1951. P16 RF G4. **Killed in vehicle ambush.**

GUTTY M., Private 18026099 African Pioneer Corps (East Africa), 2038 Mauritius Company, 7 July 1949. P16 RC G1.

HALL N.G.T., Driver T/22172821 RASC, 2 May 1951. P18 RC G19. **Killed when Valetta VNL156 crashed.**

HAMILTON D., Driver T/22373465 RASC, 3 November 1951. P18 RA G27. **Killed by terrorist action.**

HAMILTON L.F.H., Corporal 713873 RAF, 23 May 1952. P18 RC G45.

HANDSLEY R.C., Civilian, 18 April 1952. P18 RC G25.

HANRAHAN Bridget, Civilian, Service dependant, 11 December 1950. P18 RB G18.

HARRIS D.A., Airman 4000587 RAF, 9 January 1949, age 20. P13 RB G18.

HARRIS G.E., Airman 3501484 RAF, 1 March 1949. P13 RA G2.

HARRIS G.R., Gunner 22313918 Royal Artillery, 71st HAA, 30 July 1951. P18 RC G38. **Killed by terrorist action.**

HARRISON J., Sapper 22474502 Royal Engineers, 3 March 1953, age 20. P34 RB G2.

HARTLEY B., Airman 4011107 RAF, 12 April 1948. P13 RC G3.

HARTRIDGE Norma, Civilian, Service dependant, 30 July 1951, wife of Captain Hartridge RASC. PC R18 G40.

HARVEY Rose, Civilian, Service dependant, 4 February 1950, wife of BSM Harvey Royal Artillery, GHQ Fayid. P13 RF G11.

HARWOOD J.F.W., Private 19188935 RASC, 29 October 1948, age 19. P13 RF G10.

HASKELL K., Private 21031722 REME, 29 September 1948. P13 RE G13.

HASSAN A.K., Private 18009959 African Pioneer Corps (East Africa), Mauritius Company, 17 July 1948. P15 RA G1.

HATHAWAY F.J., Corporal 14731995 Royal Engineers, E & M South, 7 October 1950. P18 RB G6.

HAVELOCK A.S., Sapper 22662385 Royal Engineers, HQ Movement Transport Suez, 19 January 1952. P18 RD G14. **Thought to have been killed when a bomb concealed by terrorists in a fruit barrow was detonated on the YMCA bridge.**

HAYLOR I.C.S., Private 22550925 1st Battalion Cheshire Regiment, 17 May 1952. P18 RC G41

HEALY J., Bombardier 21127388 Royal Artillery, 80 LAA, 21 August 1949, age 26. P13 RC G24

HEAP A.N.H., Pilot 607049 RAF, 22 October 1951, age 22. P18 RA G18. **Killed when his Vampire crashed at RAF Shallufa.**

HEAPHY F.M.J., Private 22397088 2nd Battalion Parachute Regiment, AAC, 10 February 1952, age 19. P18 RB G40.

HEBDEN W., Corporal RASC, 40 Company, 6 February 1952. P18 RB G34. **Killed by terrorist action.**

HEEROO B., African Pioneer Corps (East Africa), Private Mauritius Company, 21 February 1953. P16 RB G1.

HENDRICK R.P., Gunner 22435975 Royal Artillery, 82 Location Battery (Deversoir), 25 December 1951. P18 RB G19. **Killed by terrorist action.**

HESLOP Peter Frank, Civilian, 27 May 1953.

HEWITT J., Fusilier 1st Battalion Lancashire Fusiliers, 3 January 1951, age 19. P18 RB G25. **Killed by terrorist action.**

HEWSON J.I., L/Corporal 79072933 RAOC, 11 August 1948. P13 RD G16.

HIBBERT D., L/Corporal 22754070 Royal Military Police, 1st Div Provost Company, 17 July 1954. P35 RB G22. **Killed while riding a motorcycle when involved in head-on collision with a three-ton truck driven by an East African Pioneer.**

HIGGINBOTTOM, Civilian, Service dependant, 10 May 1949, age 6, son of Rifleman B.F. Higginbottom, 284 Field Sec SUEZ. P13 RB G1.

HIGGINS C., Private 22443664 REME, 27 August 1952. P18 RD G39.

HIGGINS D.W., Private 22988192 RAOC, 10 BOD, 6 September 1954. P35 RC G9. **Killed by terrorist action.**

HIGGINS Gerald Colin, Civilian, Service dependant, 8 August 1949, age one, son of SQMS G Higgins, Barrack Stores Suez. P13 RC G16.

HIGGINS J., Captain 214468 Royal Pioneer Corps, PCLU 904, 3 October 1952. P18 RD G8.

HIGHAM J., Trooper 22444241, 4th Battalion Royal Tank Regiment, RAC, 31 January 1952. P18 RB G32.

HILL F.A., Leading Seaman P/JX292525 Royal Navy, HMS Glasgow, 7 September 1953. P34 RB G13.

HILTON Gail Jennifer, Civilian, Service dependant, 15 August 1951. P18 RA G4.

HINCHLIFFE, L/Corporal 22796125 2nd Battalion Royal Inniskilling Fusiliers, 9 July 1953. P34 RA G2. **Died following negligent discharge of a rifle.**

HINDESS T., Corporal RAF, 109 MU, 25 September 1948. P13 RE G5.

HIRST A.G.H., 2nd Lieutenant 411969, 1st (Royal) Dragoons, 21 July 1951. P18 RC G36. **A week before he died Lieutenant Hirst rescued a swimmer in difficulties in the Gulf waters south of Suez. To carry out this brave act he ran barefoot over broken desert ground that lacerated his feet. Less than a week later he died od a virulent strain of poliomyelitis.**

HOBSON W.H., Lieutenant 24925 KOYLI, 30 January 1952. P18 RB G30.

HODGKINSON R., Private 22007034 RASC, 30 September 1948. P13 RE G17.

HOLLAWAY H., Driver 22559254 Royal Corps of Signals, attached 29 Field Regiment Royal Artillery, 8 July 1953. P34 RE G15.

HOLLINGWORTH O., Private W350775 WRAC, 21 October 1949. P13 RE G4.

HOLLOWAY F.E., Civilian, 16 November 1949. P13 RE G14.

HOLME A.J., Leading Aircraftsman 2395888 RAF, 109 MU, 21 December 1951, age 19. P18 RB G17.

HOMANS K.T., Fusilier 22856682 2nd Battalion Royal Inniskilling Fusiliers, 26 August 1953, age 18. P34 RB G9. **Died following negligent discharge of a rifle.**

HOPGOOD C.J., Major 366565 British Army, 24 April 1950. P13 RG G12.

HOPGOOD R.S.H., Lieutenant 366190 RASC, 26 March 1949. P13 RA G14.

HORTON F.P., Sapper 19174374 Royal Engineers, 12611 PORT OPER SQD, 27 February 1948. P13 RB G4.

HOURY E.H., Civilian, 21 January 1954. P34 RD G15.

HOWARD P.R., Staff Sergeant CH/X894 Royal Marines, 45 Commando, 1 July 1949. P13 RB G9.

HOWS Roger, Civilian, Service dependant, 19 September 1951, age one. P18 RA G12.

HUGGETT P.F.J., Craftsman 22896797 REME, 29 November 1953. P34 RC

G12. **Shot in the chest by fellow soldier Craftsman Brennan while on guard duty. The two soldiers were discussing what they would do if a terrorist climbed over the perimeter wire and Craftsman Brennan stated he would put "one up the spout and pull the trigger". This he did. He was court-martialled for his actions.**

HUGGINS, Civilian, Service dependant, 18 October 1955, son of W.O.Huggins J.T. 847674, HQ LAD REME. P35 RA G14.

HUNT Cecilia, Civilian, Service dependant, 3 July 1949, age 35, wife of Major C.Hunt Royal Artillery, HQ OSD. P13 RB G13.

HUNT R.C., Signaller 22413355 Royal Corps of Signals, 3 GHQ, 11 September 1951, age 19. P18 RA G35.

JACKSON D., Airman 3508849 RAF, 28 September 1951. P18 RA G14. Killed by terrorist action.

JACKSON R., Leading Aircraftsman 2543423 RAF, 107 MU, 11 August 1953. P34 RA G16.

JELLY F.W., Flying Officer RAF, 208 Squadron, 14 July 1949. P13 RC G4.

JEPSON, Civilian, Service dependant, 21 September 1954, son of Sergeant S.M.Jepson 578742 RAF. P35 RC G13.

JESSIMAN I.R., Signalman, Royal Corps of Signals, 2 ECS, 25 April 1950. P13 RG G14.

JOHNSON C.F., Sapper 227951143 Royal Engineers, Engineers Base, 23 July 1953. P34 RD G12.

JOHNSTONE T.J., Stoker Mechanic Royal Navy, HMS Saintes, 3 December 1953. P34 RC.

JONES A.L., Staff Sergeant 14452353 RASC, 6 October 1949. P13 RD G21.

JONES C., Private 22741516 RAMC, 9 August 1953. P34 RA G14.

JONES Peter Raymond, Civilian, 13 October 1950. P18 RB G8.

JONES R.J., Sapper 23039587 Royal Engineers, 47 Survey Squadron, 19 November 1954. P35 RD G8. **Killed by terrorist action.**

JOSEPH M.M., Corporal 13908460 African Pioneer Corps (East Africa), 2049 Company, 13 April 1953. P14 RA G2.

JOUBERT D., L/Corporal 41016 African Pioneer Corps (East Africa), 2065 Seychelles Company, 13 April 1953. P14 RD G1.

KAVANAGH L., Aircraftsman 1st Class 2492656 RAF, 11 March 1952, age 22. P18 RC G10.

KENCH T.A.W., Airman 1922188 RAF, 7 February 1953. P18 RD G42.

KHOORDY P., Private 18085653 African Pioneer Corps (East Africa), 2053 Mauritius Company, 27 November 1949. P14 RE G5. **Killed by terrorist action.**

KHUDU M., Private EC/3069 African Pioneer Corps (East Africa), 2318 Bechuana Company (Suez), HCT, 11 November 1948. P14 RC G3.

KILANGO M., Private 18119977 African Pioneer Corps (East Africa), 2220 Company, 4 February 1953. P14 RC G4.

KILUTU M., Private N/61731 African Pioneer Corps (East Africa), 2208 Company, 9 February 1955. P35 RD G24.

KIMBERLEY I.E., Leading Aircraftswoman 2815071 WRAF, 3 August 1952, age 19. P18 RD G21. **Died of brain tumour.**

KING C.E.J., Civilian, 23 September 1950. P18 RA G46.

KIOKO J., Private EA61677 African Pioneer Corps (East Africa), 2224 Company, 13 April 1953. P14 RC G8.

KIRKWOOD T.M.G., Aircrew 578279 RAF, 12 January 1953. P34 RA G17. **Killed in crash of Hastings aircraft TG602 near RAF Shallufa while flying from Fayid.**

KISUMU O., Corporal 58137 African Pioneer Corps (East Africa), 2202 Company, 13 November 1952. P14 RB G5.

KIZITO Y., Private 18176969 African Pioneer Corps (East Africa), 2219 Company, 13 December 1953. P14 RF G3.

KNIGHT A.T., Airman 55484 RAF, 3 January 1948, age 28. P6 RE G19.

KNIGHT R., Airman 2364135 RAF, 22 October 1948. P13 RF G2.

KUBI B., Private 18188014 African Pioneer Corps (East Africa), 2224 Company, 23 February 1952. P14 RG G5.

KUTWAROO S., Private 18082909 African Pioneer Corps (East Africa), Mauritius Company, 16 January 1953. P16 RA G7.

LABONNE H., Private 18008692 African Pioneer Corps (East Africa), 2046 Mauritius Company, 28 October 1948. P15 RA G3.

LAKE Angel K., Civilian, Service dependant, 20 April 1949, daughter of Warrant Officer11 A.K.Lake HQ8 Infantry Brigade Suez. P13 RA G22.

LALL R.H.C., Major 189010 Royal Sussex Regiment, 15 July 1952. P18 RD G9.

LAMBERT R.W., Guardsman 22683599 Coldstream Guards, 29 September 1953. P34 RC G2.

LAMOND J.P., Corporal T/22546494 RASC, 148 Field Bakery, 17 April 1953. P34 RB G14. **Killed by terrorist action.**

LANGRIDGE D.G., Civilian, Service dependant, 1 March 1952, son of Warrant Officer11 Langridge, RAOC. P18 RC G6.

LARNER J.P., Corporal 22194469 British Army, 4th Company, GHQ Group, 8 April 1951. P18 RB G39. **Killed by terrorist action.**

LAVENDER F., Staff Sergeant 254143 REME, 19 Armed W/shops. 29 July 1954. P35 RB G16.

LAW A.L., Civilian, 14 November 1952. P18 RD G18.

LAYFIELD T.B., 2nd Lieutenant 393960 4th Royal Tank Regiment, RAC, 7 October 1949. P13 RD G23.

LEACH Renie, Civilian, Service dependant, 15 February 1951. P18 RB G31.

LEATON K., Corporal 22068615 Royal Corps of Signals, ECSR, 19 November 1951. P18 RA G41.

LEBABO M., Private AS/40303 African Pioneer Corps (HCT), 2311 Company, 6 April 1948. P14 RA G7.

LEE A., Private 4802507 Royal Lincolnshire Regiment, 15 July 1948. P13 RB G15.

LEE C.J., Airman 2454112 RAF, 25 July 1950. P18 RA G28.

LEE R.E., Private S/22743923 RASC, 12 August 1953. P34 RB G3. **Killed by terrorist action.**

LEECH L.E., L/Corporal T/22656358 RASC, 73 Company, 2 July 1953. P34 RE G5. **Killed by terrorist action.**

LEEVES L.J., L/Corporal PO/X5902 Royal Marine Commando, 24 January 1949. P13 RG G17.

LEOPOLD E., L/Corporal 18025870 African Pioneer Corps (East Africa), 2062 Rodriguez Company, 15 January 1949. P14 RD G4.

LESPOIR J., Private 18026220 African Pioneer Corps (East Africa), 27 October 1948. P14 RB G8.

LEWIS C.A., Airman 147596 RAF, 10 September 1955. P35 RA G8.

LILLIOT A.J., Driver 19161605 RASC, 10 November 1948. P13 RF G18.

LISETTE J.B., Private 18007179 African Pioneer Corps (East Africa), 2062 Mauritius Company, 4 August 1951. P14 RF G2. **Killed by terrorist action.**

LITUYANI, Sergeant 58412 African Pioneer Corps (East Africa), 2218 Company, 11 September 1948. P14 RB G7.

LLOYD J.H., Civilian, 11 November 1954. P35 RD G2.

LLOYD PRICE R.J., Colonel 44947 Royal Artillery, 17 May 1950. P13 RG G16.

LONGDEN D.R., Airman 4031139 RAF, 109 MU (Abyad), 4 July 1954. P35 RB G12.

LOUBSER. P.G., Airman 4016805 RAF, 148 Squadron, 11 May 1950. P18 RA G7. **Killed in mid-air collision between Vampire BZ188 and Lincoln SX957. Eleven airmen were killed in this incident.**

LUDLOW E.H., Civilian, 25 July 1952. P18 RD G17

LUGG K.C., Private 22880022 British Army, 1 Company GHQ Group, 4 April 1954. P35 RA G1.

MACANDREW., L/Corporal 22621558 Royal Corps of Signals, 25 May 1953. P34 RC G13.

MACCANN J., Driver 22917983 RASC, 22 July 1955. P35 RE G13.

MACHIN F.D., Sergeant S/4612766 RASC, 16 July 1948, age 33. P13 RD G2.

MACLACHLAN P., Private 22843290 1st Battalion York and Lancaster Regiment, 9 May 1954. P35 RA G17.

MAHLOLO T., Private AS/41231, 2315 Company, African Pioneer Corps (HCT), 18 July 1948. P14 RB G4.

MAINWARRING D.G., Signalman 14182711 Royal Corps of Signals, 2 Squadron Egypt Company, 17 February 1948. P13 RB G2.

MALCOLMSON Roger Stuart, Civilian, Service dependant, 7 April 1950, age one, son of Captain R.S.Malcolmson RAOC. P13 RG G6.

MANUEL C., Sergeant 13906151 African Pioneer Corps (East Africa), 13 November 1949. P14 RE G3.

MAPSTONE P.G., Airman 915201 RAF, 5 February 1951, age 36. P18 RB G29. **Killed by terrorist action.**

MARIGADOO R., Private 18086587 African Pioneer Corps (East Africa), 2048 Mauritius Company, 3 December 1951. P16 RE G3. **Killed in vehicle ambush.**

MARSHALL C., Craftsman 23202475 REME, 12 December 1954. P35 RD G14. **Killed by terrorist action.**

MARSHALL D.E., Signalman 23202475 Royal Corps of Signals, 3 GHQ. 11 November 1949. P13 RE G12.

MARSTON A.W., Private 14189067 Royal Staffordshire Regiment, 10 December 1948. P13 RG G7.

MARTINGS L., Corporal AS/26680 African Pioneer Corps (HCT), 2313 Company, 29 January 1948. P14 RA G1.

MASON B.G., Civilian, 17 May 1953. P34 RC G5.

MASON H.W., Captain 342499 RASC, 74 Company, 11 February 1952. P18 RB G36. Murdered by Corporal Tom Houghton, age 23, 74 Company RASC.

MATHIESON H.M., Fusilier 19035943 Royal Irish Fusiliers, 12 September 1949. P13 RD G9.

MATHIEU J., Sergeant African Pioneer Corps (East Africa), 2048 Mauritius Company, 3 December 1951. P14 RF G8. **Killed in vehicle ambush.**

MAWSON G., Private 22909617 1st Battalion York and Lancaster Regiment, 13 November 1954. P35 RD G4. **Killed by terrorist action.**

MAY A.R., Airman 4119448 RAF, 12 August 1955. P35 RA G2.

MAYMAND Raymond Terence, Civilian, Service dependant, 22 September 1950. P18 RA G44.

McALLISTER M., Craftsman 22561165 REME, 29 May 1954. P35 RB G4.

McAULEY J.M.F., Civilian, Service dependant, 28 September 1952. P18 RD G6.

McCALLUM J., Flight Lieutenant 124173 RAF, 107 MU, 5 July 1949. P13 RB G23.

McCARTHY I.M., Warrant Officer 1 3960492 South Wales Borderers, 14 October 1955. P35 RA G12.

McEWAN J., Staff Sergeant 7668622 RAPC, 92nd Company (Fayid), 17 January 1948. P6 RE G23.

McHARDY M., Nurse 371640 Queen Alexandria's Imperial Army Nursing Service, 28 August 1948. P13 RD G24.

McINTYRE W., Civilian, 7 July 1953. P34 RD G6.

McKELVIE W., Staff Sergeant 22251551 RAOC, 22 December 1950. P18 RB G20.

McLAREN J.S., Driver 22316232 RASC, 13 July 1951. P18 RC G34. **Killed by terrorist action.**

McLEAN-MOFFATT W., Civilian, GHQ, 8 November 1951. P18 RA G31.

McNALLY P., Civilian, Service dependant, 2 October 1948, age 23. P13 RE G19.

McNEILL L.A., Airman 1130768 RAF, 8 September 1949. P13 RD G8.

McNULTY R.J., Corporal 4006184 RAF, 324 Wing, 28 November 1949. P13 RE G18.

McPHEE E., Airman 4001890 RAF, 4 October 1948. P13 RD G17.

MELLORS W.H.S., Airman 183295 RAF, 11 March 1953. P34 RB G4.

MELTON D.V., Corporal T/14088468 RASC, 668 Company, 9 April 1948. P13 RC G1.

MENZIES, Civilian, Service dependant, 10 November 1954, son of 2263436 Pte H Menzies, HQ Fayid Garrison. P35 RC G23.

MIDDLETON D.J., Fusilier 22202447 1st Battalion Lancashire Fusiliers, 24 September 1950. P18 RB G2.

MIDDLETON R., Corporal 21191163 REME, 18April 1952. P18 RC G27

MILLARD D.P., Civilian, 8 December 1951. P18 RB G7.

MILLET R.B., Airman 3504069 RAF, 14 July 1949. P13 RC G6.

MILNE E.R., Airman 3104508 RAF, 17 July 1948. P13 RD G14.

MILNE G. S., Airman 4013121 RAF, 3 August 1950. P18 RA G30.

MILNE J.S., Craftsman 22454346 REME, attached 35 Corps Engineering Regiment Royal Artillery, 19 October 1952, age 22. P18 RD G12.

MILTON D.J.M., Airman 31222224 RAF, 12 August 1950. P18 RA G34.

MOGIE J.J., Private S/22775804 RASC, 120 Supply Platoon, 14 July 1953. P34 RD G8. **Killed by terrorist action.**

MOLLOY P., Private 21060828 RASC, 28 December 1948. P13 RG G13.

MOONEY J., C.Q.M Sergeant 13119247 Royal Pioneer Corps, 23 December 1949. P13 RE G22.

MOORE T.J., Private 22486285 RASC, 22 October 1951. P18 RA G20.

MOOTOO, Private 2052 African Pioneer Corps (East Africa), Mauritius Company, 14 October 1949. P14 RE G1.

MOOTOOS A., Private 18091246 African Pioneer Corps (East Africa), 2046 Company, 2 October 1953. P14 Re G8.

MORGAN C.J., Trooper 19168148 16th/5th Lancers, RAC, 29 April 1948. P13 RC G11.

MORGAN T.P., Signalman 22763931 Royal Corps of Signals, 1st Infantry Division, 6 October 1954. P35 RC G17. **Killed by terrorist action.**

MORRIS H.A., Corporal RM/8206 Royal Marine Commando, 21 January 1954. P34 RD G13.

MORRIS J.H., Aircraftsman 1st Class 3039443 RAF, 6 March 1948, age 20. P13 RB G14. **Listed as one of seven airmen said to have been killed in the same road traffic accident.**

MORRISON S., Corporal 3502539 RAF, 128 MU, 23 November 1948. P13 RG G1.

MOTHIBEDI K., Private EC/10332 African Pioneer Corps (HTC), 2318 Bechuana Company, 1 January 1948, age 23. P31 RG G7.

MOUSSA S. J., Private 18138308 African Pioneer Corps (East Africa), 30 March 1954. P15 RB G6.

MUNDEN R.C., Major 67135 Gloucester Regiment, 24 February 1950. P13 RF G19.

MUNOHOR B., Private 18023758 African Pioneer Corps (East Africa), 2052 Mauritius Company, 23 October 1948. P16 RA G5.

MURIA K., Private 18119977 African Pioneer Corps (East Africa), 2220 Company, 4 February 1953. P35 RD G34.

MURPHY, Civilian, Service dependant, 24 September 1955, son of Warrant Officer G.F.Murphy RAF Hospital Fayid. P35 RA G10.

MURRAY T., Airman 4060025 RAF, 15 May 1953. P34 RC G3. **Murdered when shot by robbers in Ismailia.**

MUSAPHORE E., Private 18084672 African Pioneer Corps (East Africa), 8 August 1949. P15 RA G5.

MWAMGANGI, Private 18118592 African Pioneer Corps (East Africa), 2208 Company, 14 July 1953. P14 RE G2.

MUNGALI N., Private N/61574 African Pioneer Corps (East Africa), 2205 Company, 8 September 1952. P14 RB G3.

NICHOLLS J.R.N., Corporal T/22204897 RASC, 2 May 1951. P18 RC G13. **Killed when Valetta VNL156 crashed.**

NICHOLLS Patricia Ann, Civilian, Service dependant, 1 August 1955, daughter of C.Nicholls 4012719 RAF. P35 RE G23.

NOCK W.C., Staff Sergeant 7601262 REME, 16 Para Works, 10 May 1952, P18 RC G39.

NORRIS William Philip, Civilian, Service dependant, 24 May 1949, age one, son of Sergeant P.Norris 79916, 4 Royal Tank Regiment. P13 RB G3.

NYOCO, Private 61903 African Pioneer Corps (East Africa), 2203 Company, 17 August 1952. P14 RG G1

O'CONNELL J., Airman 2340930 RAF, 16 December 1948. P13 RG G11.

ODULA K., Corporal 58137 African Pioneer Corps (East Africa), 2202 Company, 13 November 1952. P14 RB G5.

OGG W.J.A., Airman 3132663 RAF, 8 August 1952. P18 RD G23

OKASAM F S/O., Private 18174128 African Pioneer Corps (East Africa), 2224 Company, 13 February 1955. P35 RE G1.

OKECHE, Private 18778302 African Pioneer Corps (East Africa), 19 March 1954. P14 RG G2. **Killed by terrorist action.**

OKELO, Private 59554 African Pioneer Corps (East Africa), 2205 Company, 27 February 1953. P14 RC G6.

OKKER V.C., Airman 2516403 RAF, 12 January 1953. P34 RA G3. **Killed in crash of Hastings aircraft TG602 near RAF Shallufa while flying from RAF Fayid.**

OLLITE M.A., Private 18030681 African Pioneer Corps (East Africa), 28 October 1949. P15 RA G7.

OKOTH O., Private 18174112 African Pioneer Corps (East Africa), 2203 Company, 8 November 1953. P14 RF G1.

O'TOOLE J., Airman 2414612 RAF, 19 September 1952. P18 RD G4.

OWEN N.B., Civilian, Service dependant, 23 February 1952, son of Captain Owen RASC. P18 RC G2.

PADDINGTON J.E., Aircraftsman 1st Class 4050848 RAF, 18 May 1953, age 26. P34 RC G7.

PADGETT D., Captain RASC, 9 BAD, 13 February 1948, age 20. P13 RA G25.

PADHOOM T., Private 18028229 African Pioneer Corps (East Africa), 2062 Rodriguez Company, 15 July 1949. P16 RC G3.

PALMER G., Craftsman 22465476 RASC, 58 CAR COMPANY, 10 February 1952. P18 RB G42. **Killed by terrorist action.**

PANNIFER J.E., Airman 117400 RAF, 26 January 1950. P13 RF G3.

PARMESSUR D., Private 18084844 African Pioneer Corps (East Africa), 2046 Mauritius Company, 13 January 1951. P16 RD G6.

PARSLEY D., Pilot Officer 204468 RAF, 5 July 1949, age 21. P13 RB G25.

PATON, Civilian, Service dependant, 11 April 1954. P35 RA G5.

PAVLIDIS J.P., Civilian, 12 December 1953. P34 RD G3.

PAWSON G.M., Private 19140467 RAOC, 22 August 1948. P13 RD G20.

PAYNTER G., 2nd Lieutenant 433209 1st Battalion Scots Guards, 14 April 1954. P35 RA G7. **Died after a short illness.**

PEDIANI J.H.D., L/Corporal 21032426 Royal Engineers, 4 Company GHQ, 31 January 1949, age 19. P13 RG G21. **Cause of death recorded as "congestive cardiac failure". The condition was not detected during his pre-embarkation medical.**

PETIT S., Corporal 18008563 African Pioneer Corps (East Africa), 2052 Mauritius Company, 4 August 1952. P14 RA G8.

PHILLIPS Kenneth, Civilian, 23 December 1950. P18 RB G22.

PICKERING W., Sapper 21056976 Royal Engineers, 23 December 1950. P18 RB G22.

PIERRE W., Private 13907805 African Pioneer Corps (East Africa), 28 May 1948. P14 RB G2.

PINCOMBE B., Major 77621 Bedfordshire and Hertfordshire Regiment, 20 July 1949. P13 RC G12.

POTTER J.C., Captain 265343 Royal Artillery, 14 April 1948. P13 RC G5.

POTTINGER G.W., Sapper 22998870 Royal Engineers, 19 July 1955. P35 RE G19.

POVAH A.F., Civilian, 12 July 1951. P18 RC G26.

POWELL T.O., Sergeant 2238006 RAF, 216 Squadron, 2 April 1954. P35 RA G15. **Signaller, one of three killed when Valetta crashed in the Canal Zone.**

PRICE Jennifer Mary, Civilian, 29 April 1951. P18 RC G1.

PRICE M.E., L/Corporal 22390421 Royal Berkshire Regiment, 4 May 1952. P18 RC G37. **Shot dead by accident in the armoury at 156 Transit Camp, Port Said.**

PRITYCHARD A.C., Driver 19030606 RASC, 30 Company, 8 December 1949. P13 RE G20

PRYOR C.F., Airman 4017921 RAF, 109 MU, 8 July 1953. P34 RE G17.

QUIBELL J.V., Sapper 22840537 Royal Engineers, 7 March 1954, age 18. P34 RE G12.

QUINN J.F., Sergeant 7264166 British Army, HQ Suez Corps, 21 February 1952. P18 RB G46.

RAMDOO R., Private 18028563 African Pioneer Corps (East Africa), 26 April 1949. P16 RB G6.

RANSLEY F.C., Lieutenant 373496 Royal Fusiliers, attached 2312 BOY HCTC, 18 January 1948, age 23. P6 RE G25.

REDDALL Hazel Gordon, Civilian, Service dependant, 1 December 1954, age 38, wife of Captain H.G.Reddall. P35 RD G12.

REED P., Driver T/22941338 RASC, 4 Company, 4 July 1954. P35 RB G10. **Killed by terrorist action.**

REYNOLDS R.W., Trooper 21001524 16th/5th Lancers, RAC, 4 July 1948. P13 RD G10.

RICE A.G., Corporal 5185435 North Staffordshire Regiment, 8 September 1949. P13 RD G7.

RICHARDS, Civilian, Service dependant, 12 December 1952, daughter of Private K.Richards HQ3 Brigade (Kabrit). P13 RG G24.

RICHARDS C., Aircraftsman 1st Class 4062641 RAF, 109 MU, 30 July 1953. P34 RD G18.

RICHARDSON W.T.L., Driver 22030501 RAOC, 5 BOD, 28 May 1949. P13 RB G5.

ROBERTS A.G., Private 22186066 RAMC, 23 Para Field Ambulance,16 December 1951. P18 RB G15.

ROBERTS D.E., Civilian, Service dependant, 21 May 1954. P35 RA G23.

ROBERTS H., Private 22590734 RASC, 39 Company, 2 July 1953. P34 RE G3. **Killed by terrorist action.**

ROBERTSHAW W.H., Airman 2359440 RAF, 6 March 1948. P13 RB G16. **Listed as one of seven airmen said to have been killed in the same road traffic accident.**

ROBINSON D., Airman 402995 RAF, 12 April 1952. P18 RC G20

ROBSON P.S., Captain 416971 Royal Corps of Signals, 12 September 1953. P34 RB G15.

ROKOTSI M., Private AS/7943 African Pioneer Corps (HCT), 9 December 1948. P14 RC G7.

ROSE S., Major 203159 Royal Engineers, 4 December 1951, age 42. P18 RB G30. **Captured and murdered by terrorists following a vehicle ambush.**

ROSS I.B., Airman 3084291 RAF, 2 May 1951. P18 RC G9. **Killed when Valetta VLN156 crashed.**

ROSS R.H., Airman 204424 RAF, 26 April 1951. P18 RC G29. **Killed by terrorist action.**

ROWE M.J.G., Civilian, 23 May 1951. P18 RC G23.

RUANE Edmund, Civilian, 16 November 1954, age 30. P35 RD G6.

RUDKIN M.F.S., Major 73205 Royal Tank Regiment, RAC, 3 July 1953, age 35. P34 RD G2.

RUTTER H., Sergeant 22707419 Corps of Military Police, 26 SIB, 26 March 1954, age 19. P34 RE G18. **Killed by terrorist action.**

RYDER J.J., Aircrew RAF, 12 January 1953. P34 RA G9. **Killed in crash of Hastings aircraft at TG602 near RAF Shallufa while flying from RAF Fayid.**

SABY M.M., Private 41141 African Pioneer Corps (East Africa), 2040 Seychelles Company, 20 July 1953. P14 RE G4.

SALMON A.M., Trooper 21027340 4th Battalion Royal Tank Regiment, RAC. 24 September 1948. P13 RE G7.

SALT E.J., L/Corporal 14477225 RASC, 28 September 1948. P13 RE G11.

SAMPSON R.O., Airman 79983 RAF, 3 January 1948. P6 RE G21.

SANBY T., L/Corporal 19038674 16th/5th Lancers, RAC, 22 July 1949. P13 RB G19.

SATTERTHWAITE R.C., Gunner 22613588 Royal Artillery, 73 HAA, 23 February 1953. P18 RD G46. **Killed when dispatch riding to Fayid by motorcycle at night. Terrorists had erected a wire ambush across the road. Recorded as a road accident in official returns.**

SAULA M., Private AS/40234 African Pioneer Corps (HCT), 2311 Company, 16 July 1948. P16 RA G1.

SAUNDERS F., Gunner 22274685 Royal Artillery, 6th Field Regiment, 5 August 1951. P18 RC G46. **Killed by terrorist action.**

SAVILL D.S., Airman 2130426 RAF, 12 January 1953. P34 RA G13. **Killed in crash of Hastings aircraft TG602 near RAF Shallufa while flying from RAF Fayid.**

SAYERS R., Pilot 111606512 RAF, 208 Squadron, 7 January 1949. P13 RA G20. **Shot down by Israeli aircraft when flying an unarmed Spitfire TZ228. After the loss of this and three other Spitfires a Tempest NX207 of 213 Squadron, piloted by F/O David Tattersfield, was attacked and he was shot down and killed.**

SCHMITZ Eva, Civilian, 19 July 1949. P14 RD G8.

SCICLUMA C., Civilian, 16 August 1952. P18 RD G31.

SCOTT D.J., Driver 22734267 Royal Corps of Signals, 3 GHQ, 19 May 1954. P35 RA G19.

SCOTT R.S., Signalman 14038912 Royal Corps of Signals, 13 May 1948. P13 RC G17.

SECRETT F.J., Civilian, 29 July 1955. P35 RE G17.

SELWIN J.J., Civilian. 19 July 1949, age 9. P13 RB G17.

SHADWELL J., Aircraftsman 1st Class 40669789 RAF, Ismailia, attached Admin Workshops, 1 August 1953. P34 RA G12.

SHARP H., Corporal 2388145 RAF, 107 MU, 19 December 1954. P35 RD G16. **Killed by terrorist action.**

SHAW G., Gunner 22252522 Royal Artillery, 6th Field Regiment, 5 August 1951. P18 RC G44. **Killed by terrorist action.**

SHERBURN B., Airman 582487 RAF, 216 Squadron, 2 April 1954. P35 RA G11. **Navigator, one of three who died when Valetta VW205 crashed in the Canal Zone.**

SHUTT Linda, Civilian, Service dependant, 4 May 1948, age one, daughter of F/Sgt Shutt RAF. P13 RC G15.

SKINNER S.A., Airman 4013099 RAF, 109 MU, 12 August 1949. P13 RC G18.

SMELT G., Private 22775209 REME, 28 May 1954. P35 RB G6. **Killed by terrorist action.**

SMITH Colin, Civilian, Service dependant, 28 May 1954. P35 RB G2.

SMITH D.A., Airman 3002534 RAF, 8 December 1950. P18 RB G12. **Killed in road traffic accident.**

SMITH G., Private S/22651384 British Army, GHQ Group, 15 December 1952. P18 RD G28.

SMITH G.M., Warrant Officer 11 1868839 Royal Engineers, 22 Field Engineers, 17 August 1954. P35 RC G1. **Killed by terrorist action.**

SMITH J.E., Airman 538490 RAF, 21 April 1951. P18 RB G43. **Killed by terrorist action.**

SMITH M., Civilian, 3 December 1951. P18 RA G45.

SNEDDON W.B., L/Corporal 7403738 RAMC, 24 October 1948, age 33. P13 RF G9.

SNELLING H.R.A., Flying Officer RAF Fayid, 18 November 1951. P18 RA G37. **Shot and killed by Egyptian police during civil disturbances in Ismailia.**

SOLIMAN A.I., Constable 1547 Civil Police, 2 September 1952. P15 RB G2.

SOLLOUM G.I., Civilian, 16657 109 MU (Abyad) RAF, 17 July 1954. P15 RB G8.

SOMDHOO S., Corporal 13906373 African Pioneer Corps (East Africa), 5 October 1952. P16 RD G2.

SOONDRON G., Corporal 18027940 African Pioneer Corps (East Africa), 2052 Mauritius Company, 5 October 1952. P16 RA G6.

SOPER E.A., Private 19022562 RAMC, 2 February 1948. P13 RF G5.

SOUTHWELL S.J., Corporal 22264620 Royal Engineers, 17 Field Squadron, 22 Field Engineers Regiment, 2 July 1953. P34 RE G1.

SPEARING F., Private 22660621 RAOC, 12 October 1953. P35 RC G8.

SPENCE Margaret Edith, Civilian, Service dependant, 11 October 1949, wife of Captain M.Spence 305853 Royal Lincolnshire Regiment. P13 RC G25.

SPENCER K., Private 22902790 RAOC, 10th Battalion, 11 March 1955, age 19. P35 RD G20.

SPIERS K., Bombardier 19089972 Royal Artillery, 29 Field Regiment, 2 February 1953. P18 RD G40.

SPINKS M.S., Flying Officer 2576373 RAF, 502 Squadron, 26 February 1954. P34 RE G10.

SPRAGGON R., Private 22061579 RAOC, 12 August 1949. P13 RC G20.

SPRY F.A., Bandsman 21015042 Royal Berkshire Regiment, 1 August 1952, age 20. P18 RD G19.

STAFFORD J.G., L/Corporal 14187565 3rd Battalion Grenadier Guards, 2 September 1952. P18 RD G43. **Died in hospital following collapse during dental treatment.**

STEER Janet Mary, Civilian, 13 September 1950. P18 RA G14.

STENBECK H.W.N., L/Corporal 22265487 Royal Corps of Signals, 2nd Air Support, 28 April 1952, age 25. P18 RC G33.

STEPHENSON, Civilian, 18 November 1951. P18 RA G39.

STEWART J.P., Airman 4006088 RAF, 6 March 1948. P13 RB G20. **Listed as one of seven airman said to have been killed in the same road traffic accident.**

STEWART W.D., Trooper 22122039 16th/5th Lancers, RAC, 22 July 1950. P13 RF G16.

STORER W.W., Captain 136144 Royal Corps of Signals, GSV 4BR GHQ MELF, 2 April 1948. P13 RB G22.

STROBEL B., Airman 704461 RAF, 7 September 1949. P13 RD G5.

STUART-FERGUSSON N.J., Civilian, Service dependant, 29 November 1948, age one, son of Group Captain N.J.Stuart-Fergusson RAF. P13 RG G5

SUBDAR A., Corporal 18030104 African Pioneer Corps (East Africa), 12 December 1949. P15 RA G9.

SUMMOGUM S., Private 18024604 African Pioneer Corps (East Africa), 2052 Mauritius Company, 3 December 1951. P16 RE G7. **Killed in vehicle ambush.**

SUNBHOO S., Private 18026033 African Pioneer Corps (East Africa), 2050 Mauritius Company, 3 December 1951. P16 RA G3. **Killed in vehicle ambush.**

SUTHERLAND J.A., Trooper 22142345 16th/5th Lancers, RAC, 15 February 1950. P13 RF G17.

SUTHERLAND W.G., Private 23009609 RASC, 30 Company, 8 November 1954. P35 RC G21. **Killed by terrorist action.**

SYKES Robert George, Civilian, Service dependant, 26 August 1949, son of Corporal Alfred Sykes 3006117 RAF, age 24 hours. P13 RD G1.

SYMINGTON J., L/Corporal 22788314 1st Battalion Royal Tank Regiment, RAC, 30

August 1954. P35 RC G7. **Killed by terrorist action.**

TAITE V., Civilian, 13 November 1952, age 52. P18 RD G20.

TALBOT M., L/Sergeant 22214723 3rd Battalion Coldstream Guards, 28 July 1953. P34 RD G16. **Shot by terrorists and died in BMH of wounds to the neck.**

TALBOT T., Sapper 22120223 Royal Engineers, EST Farara, 22 April 1950. P13 RG G10.

TARGETT R.P., Flying Officer 57842 RAF, 128 MU, 11 February 1948. P13 RA G23.

TATHAM J., Airman 619526 RAF, 26 April 1951, age 36. P18 RB G45. **Killed by terrorist action.**

TAYLOR B., Trooper 19190057 16th/5thLancers, RAC, 28 May 1948. P13 RC G23.

TAYLOR G.W., Sapper 225743101 Royal Engineers, 42 Survey Engineer Unit, 2 May 1953. P34 RC G9.

TELFORD Marie Therese, Civilian, Service dependant, 22 April 1955, daughter of Warrant Officer Telford 4689452 10 BOD Geneifa. P35 RE G3.

TATHANA H., Private AS/18736 African Pioneer Corps (HCT), 2310 Company, 1 November 1948. P14 RC G1.

THOMAS D.J., Corporal 22567363 REME, 26 July 1955. P35 RE G15.

THOMAS L.A., Airman 2542564 RAF, 32 Squadron, 23 July 1953. P34 RA G8.

THOMPSON G., Sapper 22795083 Royal Engineers, 22 Field Regiment, 7 February 1954. P3 RE G2.

THOMPSON J., Aircraftsman 2420897 RAF, 62 Squadron, 28 May 1950. P13 RG G20.

THOMPSON J.J., Gunner 22470136 Royal Artillery, 16 July 1952. P18 RD G15.

THOMPSON J.R., Private 22898981 RAOC, 11 January 1954, age 18. P34 RD G9.

THOMPSON R., Signalman 22126322 Royal Corps of Signals, 3 GHQ Signals, 22 May 1950. P13 RG G18.

THOMPSON W.J., Third Engineer Merchant Navy, SS HUMPHREY GALE, 29 August 1952. P18 RD G41.

THOMSON J.G.S., Civilian, 12 January 1952. P18 RD G32.

THOMSON R.H., Private 22636703 Royal Scots, 21 October 1954, age 20. P35 RC G19. **Killed by terrorist action.**

TIMMINS T.W., Sergeant (Acting) 22382362 RAMC, 1 July 1954, age 22. P35 RB G8.

TIMMIS I.J., Signalman 22108632 Royal Corps of Signals, 4th Air Form Signals, 31 October 1949. P13 RE G10.

TIMSON P., Trooper 19165568 4th Battalion Royal Tank Regiment, RAC (Shandur), 4 April 1948. P13 RB G24.

TRIGG A., Signaller 22804492 Royal Corps of Signals, 6 May 1953. P34 RB G16.

TRIMMER G.G., Civilian, 6 March 1951. P18 RB G35.

TRUNDLEY J.G., Signalman 22046110 Royal Corps of Signals, 2 ECS Regiment, 15 September 1949. P13 RD G15.

TRUSCOTT G., Private 14149095 Army Catering Corps, 17 May 1948. P13 RC G19.

TULL J.T., Private RAMC, 15 August 1949. P13 RC G22.

TUPPEN W.D., Civilian, Service dependant, 3 February 1948, age 48. P13 RA G17.

TURNER L.N.R., Corporal 610960 RAF, 107 MU, 13 December 1951. P18 RB G11.

TUTT Lillian, Civilian, Service dependant, 30 April 1951. P18 RC G3.

TYLER C.A., Warrant Officer 11, 2616822 Military Provost Staff Corps, 51 MP DB, 28 February 1952. P18 RC G4. **Killed by terrorist action.**

UNDERWOOD G.L., Marine POX 6234 Royal Marines, HMS Glasgow, 28 August 1953. P34 RB G11.

UPTON J.A., Aircraftsman RAF, 11 July 1954. P35 RB G20. **Killed by terrorist action.**

VAUGHAN E., Private 22472178 Royal Sussex Regiment, 29 November 1952, age 21. P18 RD G22.

WADE A.R., Seaman Merchant Navy, HT 2 Empire Fowey, 11 July 1950. P18 RA G21.

WADE H.R., Airman 4073929 RAF, 12 January 1953. P34 RA G7. **Killed in crash of Hastings aircraft TG602 near RAF Shallufa while flying from RAF Fayid.**

WAITE S., Signalman 22606148 Royal Corps of Signals, attached 29 Field Regiment Royal Artillery, 4 July 1953. P34 RE G7.

WAKOLI A., Private 18176106 African Pioneer Corps (East Africa), 12 February 1954. P14 RF G5.

WALKER D., Airman 4001277 RAF, 6 November 1948. P13 RF G12.

WALKER P.A., Gunner 1157603 1st Battalion Royal Horse Artillery, 15 April 1949. P13 RA G18.

WALLER F.S., Corporal 22206001 16th/5th Lancers, RAC, 20 July 1949. P13 RC G10.

WALSH Janet, Civilian, Service dependant, 12 July 1950, age one, daughter of Major E.J.Walsh Manchester Regiment. P13 RG G22.

WALSH J.C., L/Corporal 22522629 Royal Engineers, 35 Corps Engineers Regiment, 14 November 1952. P18 RD G16.

WALSH L.E., Aircraftsman 1st Class 4010976 RAF, 107 MU, 5 January 1950. P13 RE G24.

WARREN R.H., Sergeant 2582764 Royal Corps of Signals, RAF Signals Regiment, 15 January 1954. P34 RD G11.

WATKINS R., Captain 281650 Royal Artillery, Para Brigade, 17 April 1952, age 33. P18 RC G22.

WATSON, Civilian, Service dependant, 27 November 1949, son of Sergeant N.G.Watson 80 LAA Regiment. P13 RE G16.

WATSON B.F., Civilian, 15 May 1951. P18 RC G21.

WATSON R., Pilot 11, 3040517 RAF, 324 Wing, 10 February 1950, age 24. P13 RF G15. **Killed when his Tempest NX252 suffered engine failure on landing at RAF Deversoir.**

WEARMOUTH J.M., Private 19163159 RAOC, 31 December 1948. P13 RG G15.

WHELAN Michael James, Civilian, Service dependant, 3 March 1950, son of LAC M.J.Whelan 4005479 RAF. P13 RG G2.

WHITBREAD W.L., Captain 37758 Royal Fusiliers, 10 August 1952, age 40. P18 RD G25.

WHITE E.M., Driver T/22729588 RASC, 73 Air Dispatch Company, 14 August 1953, age 19. P34 RB G5.

WHITE J., Seaman Merchant Navy, MV Swanvalley, 1 January 1952. P18 RB G21.

WHITE J.G., Private 22642554 RASC, 19 May 1953. P34 RC G1.

WHITE J.G.C., Private 22999686 RAOC, 23 October 1955. P35 RA G16.

WHITFORD D., Civilian, Service dependant, 15 July 1952, son of L/Corporal W.Whitford 22540010 Royal Signals. P18 RD G13.

WHITTAKER B.N., Airman 564802 RAF, 13 July 1950. P18 RA G23.

WILKINSON G.M., Aircrew 610650 RAF, 12 January 1953. P34 RA G11. **Killed in crash of Hastings aircraft TG602 near RAF Shallufa while flying from RAF Fayid.**

WILLIAMS A., Civilian, 10 BDC, 20 February 1953. P18 RD G44.

WILLIAMS E.A., Private 19037550 Army Air Corps, 18 May 1952. P18 RC G43.

WILLIAMS F.A., Captain 166354 Royal Artillery, 23 October 1948. P13 R G4.

WILSON H., L/Corporal 22233326 Royal Corps of Signals, 3 HQ Signals Regiment, 7 July 1951. P18 RC G32. **Killed by terrorist action.**

WINN R.J., Driver 22721208 RASC, 31 March 1953. P34 RB G8.

WOOD K.A., Trooper 22963168 The Queen's Bays (2nd Dragoon Guards), 20 July 1955. P35 RE G11.

WOODHEAD R., Private 22479964 East Lancashire Regiment, 22 August 1952. P18 RD G33.

WOOLARD R., Airman 2361274 RAF, 6 March 1948. P13 RB G10. **Listed as one of seven airmen said to have been killed in the same road traffic accident.**

WOOTON D.A., Lieutenant 383312 Royal Artillery, 23 July 1952. P18 RD G11.

WRAGG A.C., Craftsman 14150468 REME, 2 Pt Workshops, 23 April 1948. P13 RC G9.

WRIGHT Sylvia Janet, Civilian, Service dependant, 4 March 1954, daughter of Sgt Wright 14409620, 51 MP EDB. P15 RB G4.

YANDELL R.D., Airman F/51254 RAF, 2 May 1951. P18 RC G5. **Killed when Valetta VLN156 crashed.**

YATES R., Major 235184 RAMC, 3 July 1952, age 52. P18 RD G3.

YEATS I.G.M., Civilian, Service dependant, 15 July 1949, age one, father F/Sgt G.M.Yeats 591213 RAF (Abu Sueir). P13 RC G8.

YONGMAN-EATON K., Aircraftsman 4077323 RAF, 2 Works Administration Squadron, 27 January 1953. P18 RD G36.

YOZEFU, Private 18179510 African Pioneer Corps (East Africa), 2221 Company, 27 August 1954. P16 RB G3. **Killed by terrorist action.**

YUILE David, Civilian, Service dependant, 20 April 1950, stillborn son of Corporal M.J.Yuile 4005046 RAF. P13 RG G8.

ZARB E.S., Civilian, 13 August 1952. P18 RD G29.

ZABLO O., Private N/58256 African Pioneer Corps (East Africa), 2202 Company, 25 March 1952. P14 RG G7.

MOASCAR MEMORIAL CEMETERY

ACTON A.H.B., Lieutenant 297163 2nd Parachute Regiment, AAC, formerly East Surrey Regiment, 21 January 1952, age 23. P13 RE G11. **Fatally shot by a combatant, hidden in one of the crypts, during the search of the Moslem cemetery by the outer cordon in the action at the Bureau Sanitaire. His assailant was shot dead by Donald Atkinson, an A-company member of 2nd Battalion Parachute Regiment now resident in Canada.**

ADAIR, Civilian, Service dependant, 11 December 1951, age 3. P13 RD G8.

ADAMS B.O., Private SL 106668 Royal Canadian Army Service Corps (United Nations Emergency Forces), 20 September 1957. P16 RA G20. **Died of deep shock as a result of 2nd and 3rd degree burns sustained in Jeep accident on 14 September 1957.**

AIRLEY P.G., Private 22487830 1st Battalion Lincolnshire Regiment, 12 December 1951. P13 RD G8. **Died instantly when shot in the head by terrorists while driving a 3-ton truck on the Tel el Kebir-Moascar road. His escort, trained driver J.L.Cooper, took the wheel and drove back through the ambush in an attempt to take Private Airley to a BMH by the shortest route. It was recommended that J.L.Cooper be 'mentioned in dispatches' but no award was granted.**

AKLOO R., Sergeant 18082929 African Pioneer Corps (East Africa), 2045 Mauritius Company, 24 December 1954. P12 RA G15. **Killed by terrorist action.**

ALBERT J.N., Sergeant 19006873 African Pioneer Corps, 2058 Mauritius Company, 25 October 1954. P15 RC G6. **Killed by terrorist action.**

ALEXANDER G.E., Civilian, Service dependant, 18 December 1953, daughter of Squadron Leader Alexander 300023 RAF. P15 RA G9.

ALLEN B., Fusilier 22215305 1st Battalion Lancashire Fusiliers, 4 April 1952. P14 RA G17. **Killed by wounds sustained on 25 January at the Police Station Battle.**

ALLINGTON, Civilian, Service dependant, 13 March 1949, age one. P11 RC G17.

AMBLER R.T., Private T/22061896 RASC, 9 February 1950. P11 RE G17.

ANDRES Anne, Civilian, 20 January 1954. P12 RB G20.

ANTHONY, Civilian, 20 January 1952. P13 RE G10. **Sister Anthony was killed by Egyptian terrorists because she taught British children. An SOS was sent to Moascar Garrison but it did not arrive in time to save her. The terrorists pursued her, ignoring other nuns, in a personal attack.**

ARCHER, Civilian, 23 January 1949. P11 RC G13.

ARMOOGUM S.R., Private 18008730 African Pioneer Corps (East Africa), 2049 Mauritius Company, 2 October 1948. P11 RB G15.

ARMSTRONG J., Staff Sergeant 2718659 APTC, 27 November 1953, age 36. P15 RA G5.

ARSTALL A.J., Private 14189866 Army Catering Corps, Attached HQ MOV Port Said, 22 October 1948. P11 RB G19.

ATKIN E., Private S/14126771 RASC, 6 March 1948. P11 RA G1.

ATKINSON K.R., L/Corporal 223211905 REME, Attached 203 Provost Company, Royal Corps of Military Police, 21 July 1951. P13 RB G2. **Killed by terrorist action.**

AWUONDO O., Private 18116013 African Pioneer Corps (East Africa), 2214 Company, 12 November 1952. P14 RC G1.

AXELBERG E.E., Sapper 22827922 Royal Engineers, 18 January 1954. P15 RA G12. **Died on escort duty as a result of gunshot wounds inflicted by Egyptian terrorists, who escaped by car, after a vehicle ambush.**

AZIE A., Corporal 18007120 African Pioneer Corps (East Africa), 2061 Rodriguez Company, 3 August 1954. P15 RB G19. **Killed by terrorist action.**

BABTISTE D., Private 18088439 African Pioneer Corps (East Africa), 2061 Rodriguez Company, 21 September 1953. P14 RE G12.

BAGNAN L.R., Corporal 18023416 African Pioneer Corps (East Africa), 2051 Mauritius Company, 28 September 1949. P11 RE G2.

BAILEY T.G., Private 22885088 RAOC, BUD, 14 November 1953. P15 RA G3.

BAIRD C.C., Private W/303470 WRAC, 8 December 1954. P15 RC G11. **Killed by terrorist action.**

BALCHIN C., Captain 309129 Royal Engineers, 2 May 1948. P11 RA G10.

BARKER D., QMS (WO11) 5767942 REME, 10 August 1955, age 46. P16 RA G5.

BATIE J., Fourth Officer Merchant Navy, SS British Sailor, 2 October 1949. P11 RE G5.

BEACH Cecilia, Civilian, Service dependant, 8 December 1952, age 8, daughter of Sergeant G.Beech 23208752 Royal Artillery. P14 RC G7.

BEATTIE, Civilian, 21 July 1949, age one. P11 RD G10.

BEATTIE, Civilian, Service dependant, 16 September 1950. P12 RD G17.

BEDFORD A., Trooper 22435195 A Squadron Royal Dragoons, RAC, 26 December 1951. P13 RD G13. **Shot and killed instantly by a corporal mis-using his pistol. The**

corporal was charged with the offence and disappeared from the scene.

BEETHAM Valerie Ann, Civilian, Service dependant, 4 November 1951, age 3. P13 RC G11.

BEGUE A., Private 18086866 African Pioneer Corps (East Africa), 2055 Mauritius Company, 28 December 1950. P12 RE G12.

BEGUE S., Warrant Officer 11 18006204 African Pioneer Corps, 2061 Rodriguez Company, 23 September 1953. P14 RE G13.

BENNETT, Civilian, Service dependant, 4 July 1954, age one, twin son of LAC Bennett 401193 RAF. P13 RB G6 (Joint grave).

BERANADO O., Private 18117659 African Pioneer Corps (East Africa), 2214 Company, 1 September 1952. P14 RB G6.

BILLY, Private 3430 Rhodesian African Rifles, 2 October 1952. P14 RB G12.

BIRCH R.A., Gunner 22184783 Royal Artillery, 80 LAA, 6 July 1951, age 19. P13 RB. **Killed by terrorist action.**

BLOOD, Civilian, Service dependant, 10 March 1951, age 2. P13 RA G3.

BOGUE J.F., Corporal 22264995 REME, attached RAF, 28 March 1953. P14 RD G2.

BORG, Ship's Steward Merchant Navy, SS Empire Shelter, 4 September 1954. P15 RC G1. **Killed by terrorist action.**

BOULTON R.W., Craftsman 14469358 REME, attached 5 BOD RAOC, 21 September 1950. P12 RD G18.

BOUTIA N., Corporal 18023507 African Pioneer Corps (East Africa), 2051 Mauritius Company, 2 October 1948. P11 RB G16.

BOWDEN, Civilian, Service dependant, 20 December 1950, wife of Major J.W.Bowden 371883 3 Hussars. P12 RE G10.

BOWEN J., Captain 320337 RASC, 7 August 1948. P11 RB G8.

BOWERS R., Major 177928 Royal Artillery, 6 October 1948. P11 RB G8.

BOYDELL J., Sergeant 3446527 1st Battalion Lancashire Fusiliers, attached 2 Brigade Main, 18 September 1951. P13 RC G3. **Killed by terrorist action.**

BOYTEN Bernard John, Civilian, Service dependant, 6 November 1951, age 3 months, son of WO11 B.R.Boyten RAOC. P13 RC G12.

BRADBURY H.H., Captain 371502 Royal Engineers, Q Movement Battalion, 3 December 1951. P13 RD G5.

BRISCOEL, L/Bombardier 22207394 Royal Artillery, 41 Field Regiment, 10 May 1951, age 37. P13 RA G17. **Killed by terrorist action.**

BROOKES W.S., L/Corporal 22573220 1st Battalion Highland Light Infantry, 14 July 1953, age 21. P14 RD G12.

BROWN, Civilian, 28 September 1955. P16 RA G7.

BROWN F., CQM Sergeant 2665313, 3rd Battalion Coldstream Guards, 3 January 1952, age 34. P13 RD G16.

BROWN H., Private 22459178 1st Battalion Cheshire Regiment, 19 December 1951, age 19. P13 RD G11.

BROWNING D.H., 2nd Lieutenant 414082 Royal Artillery, 17 February 1951, age 19. P12 RE G20. **Killed by terrorist action.**

BUCHWALD P., German civilian, 8 July 1950. P12 RC G19.

BUCKLEY Edith, Civilian, Service dependant, 30 October 1950, wife of L/Cpl E.Buckley T/6459966 RASC. P12 RE G3.

BUCKO, Private 18083969 African Pioneer Corps (East Africa), 2063 Mauritius Company, 11 July 1950. P12 RA G3.

BURKART E.P., Aircraftsman 4041445 RAF, 128 Squadron Abu Sultan, 25 May 1951. P13 RA G20. **Killed by terrorist action.**

BURNHILL W.R., Major 205862, RAMC, 19 March 1954, P15 RB G4. **Shot dead in terrorist ambush. Captain Issac Wilson was wounded in this incident.**

BURT H.T., Lieutenant Colonel 125782, RAOC, 27 October 1950. P12 RE G2.

BUSHIRE, Private 18116479 African Pioneer Corps (East Africa), 2211 Company, 12 August 1952. P14 RB G3.

BUXEY W., Driver T/22469645, RASC, attached HQ Command, 11 February 1952. P14 RA G4. **Killed by terrorist action.**

BYRON H., Sergeant 2323179 Royal Corps of Signals, 1 July 1949. P11 RD G12.

CAKEKEN, Civilian, 21 April 1950. P12 RC G3.

CAMPBELL A.F., Private 22462981 2nd Battalion Parachute Regiment, AAC, 6 January 1953. P14 RC G5.

CANN D.A., Corporal 2548555 Royal Engineers, MELF 10, 15 March 1954. P15 RB G2. **Killed by terrorist action.**

CARTER L., Gunner 22307022 Royal Artillery, 80 LAA, 27 March 1951, age 19. P13 RA G6. **Killed by terrorist action.**

CAUCHI Alan, Civilian, 8 November 1951. P13 RC G13.

CELINE R., Private 13909092 African Pioneer Corps (East Africa), 2049 Mauritius Company, 27 February 1955. P15 RC G19.

CHALLINOR C., Signalman 22062709 Royal Corps of Signals, 15 July 1949, age 19. P11 RD G9.

CHAPMAN F., Private 22608815 RAOC, Radl Bud (E) TEK, 26 April 1952. P14 RA G9.

CHARLOT V., Private 35371 African Pioneer Corps, 2045 Seychelles Company, 4 November 1948. P11 RC G1.

CHARLOT W., Private 18024551 African Pioneer Corps (East Africa), 2055 Mauritius Company, 7 May 1948. P11 RA G19.

CHEESEBOUGH W.J., Private 22596831 1st Battalion Parachute Regiment, AAC, 21 August 1952. P14 RB G5.

CHENGELEE P., Private 18081850 African Pioneer Corps (East Africa), 2049 Mauritius Company, 18 March 1951. P12 RA G10. **Killed by terrorist action.**

CHESTER P., Driver T/22190465 RASC, 24 July 1950. P12 RD G6.

CHRISTER H.G.P., CSM 3rd Battalion Coldstream Guards, 4 January 1952, age 32. P13 RD G17.

CINI C., Civilian, Warden 8430 Garrison Police Corps, TEK, 1 October 1949. P11 RE G4.

CLARKE F.T., Signaller 22540273 Royal Corps of Signals, 3 Infantry Div, 7 May 1953. P14 RD G4.

COLCLOUGH, Civilian, Service dependant, 22 November 1951. P13 RD G1.

COLLINS Nancy, Private Q/1000084 Queen Alexandria's Royal Army Nursing Corps, 10 August 1951. P13 RB G16. **Killed by terrorist action.**

COOPER H.E., L/Corporal 22685987 Corps of Military Police, No.1 Dog Company, 19 August 1953. P14 RE G9. **The Jeep he was driving was pushed off the road by** an Egyptian lorry. A Lt Hodson survived the attack.

COOPER K., Private 22868877 RAOC, 12 POS, 12 November 1953. P15 RA G1.

COPSON F., Sergeant 2670414, 2nd Battalion Coldstream Guards, 12 January 1952. P13 RE G5. **Killed in during civil disturbance.**

CORNELIUS-WHEELER G.S., 2nd Lieutenant P/382816 RAOC, 21 November 1948. P11 RC G6.

COTTE R.J., Private 18483165 African Pioneer Corps (East Africa), 2053 Mauritius Company, 18 April 1951. P13 RA G10. **Killed by terrorist action.**

COULSON R., Private 22715191, 1st Battalion Bedfordshire and Hertfordshire Regiment, 6 October 1953. P14 RE G14.

COX D.B., Sapper 22765450 Royal Engineers, 21 January 1954. P15 RA G14. **Found dead in railway wagon in Nefeisha marshalling yard by Egyptian civil police. Appeared to have been hit on the head and shot at close range, gun shot wounds to abdomen and chest, believed murdered by Egyptian terrorists.**

COX R.R., Airman 4140697 RAF, 22 January 1955. P15 RC G16.

CRAIGS Alexandra, Civilian, Service dependant, 13 February 1955, age 10 hours, daughter of WO11 Craigs RAOC. P15 RC G18.

CRAWFORD Patricia, Civilian, Service dependant, 8 April 1950. P12 RC G3.

CRESSWELL W., Private 22701979 East Surrey Regiment, 28 July 1953. P14 RE G3.

CROMBIE J.T.D., Sergeant 4005142 RAF Regiment, 30 LAA, 30 November 1951. P13 RD G4.

CUMMING G., L/Corporal 22622760 REME, 7 October 1953. P14 RTE G15.

DANCY R.D., Aircraftsman 1st Class 4108777 RAF, 23 May 1954, age 23. P15 RB G12.

DANNATT C.D., Craftsman 21188149 REME, 2 Base Workshops, 28 January 1952. P13 RE G19.

DAVIE A., Private 22574968 1st Battalion Lincolnshire Regiment, 19 January 1952. P13 RE G8. **One of two killed and six wounded when a terrorist bomb set off anti-terrorist tank mines alongside a manned post on the Sweet Water Canal.**

DAVIES W.D., Civilian, Service dependant, 15 May 1950, age one month, son of Staff Sergeant Davies S/6845982 MELF. P12 RC G11.

DAVIES A.F., Corporal 4030137 RAF, No.3 Police Wing HQ MEAF, 1 May 1950. P12 RC G8.

DAVIES D., Sergeant PL/X5022 Royal Marines, 45 CDO, 6 July 1953. P14 RD G19.

DAVIES-PATRICK H., Sapper 22807298 Royal Engineers, 12 July 1953. P14 RD G20.

Killed by terrorist action.

DAVIS E.M., Civilian, 31 August 1953. P14 RE G10.

DAW T., Sapper 22798544 Royal Engineers, 1207 IWT, 25 April 1953, age 19. P14 RC G20.

DECKER, Civilian, Service dependant, 13 February 1953, age 24 hours, son of Major H.A.Decker RAOC. P14 RC G14.

DEMETRIS, Civilian, LOCCAR, 15 July 1952.

DEVENPORT, Civilian, Service dependant, 28 April 1950. Plot 12 RC G7.

DEWHURST, Civilian, 20 May 1950, age one. P12 RC G12.

DRYLAND, Civilian, Service dependant, 19 November 1950. P12 RE G7.

DRYLAND T.G., Warrant Officer 1 2048050, RAOC, 7 November 1949, age 33. P11 RE G10.

DULLAWAY F., Private 22814067, 1st Battalion East Surrey Regiment, 2 February 1954. P15 RA G18.

DUNBAR-KILBURN R.E.F., Captain 393190 Royal Artillery, attached AOPS Squadron RAF, 28 March 1952. P14 RD G1.

DYSON L., Signalman 22936686 Royal Corps of Signals, 11 July 1954. P15 RB G17. **Killed by terrorist action.**

EASTHAM A.E., Fusilier 22278484 1st Battalion Lancashire Fusiliers, C Company, 25 January 1952, age 28, husband of Martha Eastham of Limavady, Co

Derry. P13 RE G14. **Killed in action at the Bureau Sanitaire.**

EASTHAM H., L/Corporal 19038787, 1st Battalion Lancashire Fusiliers, C Company, 25 January 1952, age 22, son of Mrs Ada Hayes of Preston. P13 RE G12. **Killed in action at the Bureau Sanitaire.**

ECKETT C., Private 22167612 RAOC, 24 August 1950. P12 RD G13.

EDGAR R.G., Driver 22230367 Royal Corps of Signals, 3 August 1952. P14 RB G1.

EDWARDS D.W., Sergeant 22281096 Royal Pioneer Corps, 21 November 1951. P13 RC G19. **Killed by terrorist action.**

EDWARDS N., Civilian (NAAFI), 8 February 1953. P14 RC G12.

ELLIOTT G.P., Major 139793 Royal Artillery, attached 1 Div HQ, 9 January 1952, age 54. P13 RE G2. **Killed in convoy ambush.**

EVANS, Civilian, 14 October 1951. P13 RC G9.

EVANS N., Driver T/22506551 RASC, 13 May 1953. P14 RD G6. **Killed by terrorist action.**

EYNON Terrance, Civilian, Service dependant, 19 July 1950. P12 RD G1.

FABEN Angeline, Civilian, Service dependant, 2 October 1951, daughter of Sgt H.K. Faben 6913422 Royal Engineers. P13 RC G7.

FALCONER J.F., Leading

Aircraftsman 2353841 RAF, 6 April 1949. P11 RC G20.

FANCHETTE G., Private 40826 African Pioneer Corps (East Africa), 2057 Seychelles Company, 28 October 1953. P14 RE G18.

FEARN R., L/Corporal 22236264 Royal Engineers, Workshops A ADM, 18 November 1951. P13 RC G17. **Killed by terrorist action. His body was recovered from the Sweet Water Canal with that of Bombardier Reed.**

FELIX J., Private 40475 African Pioneer corps (East Africa), 2057 Seychelles Company, 6 February 1955. P15 RC G17.

FILL G.F., Sergeant 22287616 Royal Northumberland Fusiliers, 27 April 1953, age 21. P14 RD G3. **Killed when fired on while on the main Ismailia/Cairo Road near Tel el Kebir by Egyptians in civilian clothing. The gunmen escaped in two taxis heading toward Cairo.**

FINDLAY M., Marine RM11460 Royal Marines, 45 Commando, 23 January 1954, age 20. P15 RA G17.

FIRTH T.K., Gunner 22275197 Royal Artillery, 41 Field Regiment, 1 September 1951, age 19. P13 RC G1. **Killed by terrorist action.**

FITZGERALD R.F., Seaman Merchant Navy, SS Black Ranger, Port Said, 9 January 1952. P13 RE G4.

FLEMING B., Guardsman 22217254 Welsh Guards, 28 September 1954, age 22.

P15 RC G3. **Killed by terrorist action.**

FLETCHER D., Private 23061716 South Staffordshire Regiment, 5 July 1955. P16 RA G4.

FLINT G.A., Lieutenant Colonel ZD2252 Princess Patricia's Canadian Light Infantry, RCIC (United Nations Emergency), 26 May 1958. P16 RB G13. **Killed as a result of a firing incident in area of Mount Scopus, Israel.**

FLYNN P., Warrant Officer 512813 RAF Ismailia, 11 November 1952. P14 RB G19.

FORD H.C., Craftsman 19099151 REME, 5 BOD TEK, attached RAOC, 12 March 1948. P11 RA G2.

FOY D., Private 22204873 RAOC, 3 Infantry Brigade Main, 21 April 1951, age 29. P13 RA G12. **Killed by terrorist action.**

FRA L.E., Private 18026259 African Pioneer Corps (East Africa), 2053 Mauritius Company, 24 October 1949. P11 RE G7.

FRANCIS F.J., L/Corporal 22563560 REME, 24 May 1954. P15 RB G13.

FREEGARD H.S., Major MC and Bar 66918 Royal Artillery, 8 January 1952, age 35, husband of Margaret Alice Freegard. P13 RE G1.

FRITH Valerie, Civilian, Service dependant, 14 November 1954, age 3 months, daughter of Staff Sergeant J.H.Frith REME. P15 RC G8.

GALLEO M., Civilian, 9 July 1952. P12 RB G18.

GEEKIE D., Signalman 22800829 Royal Corps of Signals, 28 September 1954. P15 RC G5. **Killed by terrorist action.**

GELLING C., Rifleman 21023359 2nd Battalion King's Royal Rifle Corps, 15 May 1948. P11 RA G13.

GIBBS J., L/Bombardier 19133968 Royal Artillery, 11 May 1949. P11 RD G4.

GILKES Roderick, Civilian, Service dependant, 12 July 1950, age one. P12 RC G13.

GILLIGAN C.N., Craftsman 22429878 REME, 3 Base Workshops, 7 January 1952. P13 RD G19.

GOLDBY J.L., Gunner 21039317 Royal Artillery, UA Tank Battery, 31 August 1950, age 22. P12 RB G3. **Hanged by judicial process by the British authorities for the murder of an Egyptian taxi driver during the attempted theft of a motor vehicle in Cairo.**

GOLDING H.J., Warrant Officer (Class 1) 7584454 RAOC, 24 January 1950. P11 RE G16.

GOLDSMITH K., Sergeant 14035569 AAC, 1 Parachute Regiment, 27 November 1953. P15 RA G6.

GOMES C.H., Civilian, 15 November 1953. P15 RA G4.

GOODALL K.C., Gunner. 22792642 Royal Artillery, 33 Airborne Light Regiment, 8 October 1952. P14 RB G14.

GOODWIN J.A.W., 2nd

Lieutenant 422309 Royal Artillery, 41 Field Regiment, 19 January 1953. P14 RC G9.

GOULDING G., L/Corporal 22216479 Irish Guards, 11 April 1955, age 20. P15 RC G20. **Victim of a shooting accident.**

GRANT J., Private 22659301 Highland Light Infantry (City of Glasgow Regiment), 30 October 1953. P14 RE G19.

GRAVES A.G., Corporal 22717296 Royal Engineers, 11 September 1954. P15 RC G2. **Killed by terrorist action.**

GRAY, Civilian, Service dependant, 29 September 1952, age 5 weeks, son of WO11 E.Gray, ACC. P14 RB G11.

GREENAWAY V.H., Rifleman 14478932 2nd Battalion King's Royal Rifle Corps, 2 April 1948, age 19. P11 RA G7.

GREGOIRE M., Private 18008114 African Pioneer Corps (East Africa), 2048 Mauritius Company, 14 August 1948. P11 RB G11.

GRIFFIN R.S., Airman 199292 RAF, 7 November 1952. P14 RE G20.

GRIFFITHS A., L/Corporal 14292464 RAOC, 610 Command VEM GRP, 3 July 1948. P11 RB G3.

GRINGHAM R.P., Sergeant 2448549 RAF, HQ Unit MEAF, 2 July 1953. P14 RD G17.

GRUBB D.J., Staff QM Sergeant (WO11) 22225843 RAOC, HP BTE, 27 October 1953, age 35. P14 RE G16.

GUNSON R., Gunner 22952767 Royal Artillery, 80 LAA Regiment, 13 November 1953. P15 RA G2.

HALLETT A.B., Craftsman 23024632 REME, 5 March 1955. P15 RA G2.

HAMILTON Keith Robert, Civilian, Service dependant, 19 July 1951, age 5 months, son of Sergeant K.Hamilton REME. P13 RB G10.

HAMMETT J., L/Corporal 23540320 Royal Engineers, 21 January 1954. P15 RA G13. **Killed by terrorist action (file retained by the MoD).**

HAMPTON J.A., Lieutenant 379541 Corps of Royal Military Police, 1 Infantry Div Pro, 17 December 1951. P13 RD G10. **Killed by a bomb thrown at an RMP Land Rover by terrorists (possibly Egyptian policemen), near the Caracol. Two vehicles had visited the Egyptian Police Station on duty and when the second was attacked, the leading Land Rover returned to assist the injured crew. For this action, the senior NCO, a Sergeant McAvoy, was awarded the MBE.**

HANNEY Sheila Margaret, Civilian, Service dependant, 31 January 1952, age one. P14 RA G1.

HARALAMBIDES K., Civilian 687, 26 September 1952. P14 RB G10.

HARDING R.E., Private 19047832, 2nd Battalion Royal Berkshire Regiment, 10 April 1948. P11 RA G8.

HARDY Sally Anne, Civilian, Service dependant, 14 February 1951, age one. P12 RE G19.

HARRIOTT I.G.F., Warrant Officer 1 3594604 1st Battalion East Surrey Regiment, 16 August 1953. P14 RE G8.

HARRIS Patricia Ann, Civilian, 2 September 1950. P12 RD G15.

HARRISON D.F.J., Private 22171638 Royal Lincolnshire Regiment, 10 April 1950. P12 RC G4.

HASELTON H., Corporal 22211476 Royal Engineers, HQ Movements Port Said, 7 November 1950. P12 RE G

HAWKE, Civilian, Service dependant, 3 October 1951, age one. P13 RC G8.

HAYCOCK H.A., Sapper 19044222 Royal Engineers, 10 Railway Squadron, 28 April 1952. P14 RA G11.

HEAD B.R., Craftsman 22317546 REME, 2 BLI/S, 8 July 1951, age 19. P15 RB G8. **Killed by terrorist action.**

HEAL, Civilian, Service dependant, 22 July 1949, age one. P11 RD G15.

HEAL, Civilian, Service dependant, 5 May 1954, son of BSM Heal 33 AD Regiment Royal Artillery. P15 RB G11.

HEFFILL, Civilian, Service dependant, 13 January 1949. P11 RC G11.

HEMMINGS Graham Ernest, Civilian, Service dependant, 27 August 1950, age one, son of Sgt G.E.Hemmings RAF 1353447. P12 RD G14.

HEMSHALL Alan, Civilian, Service dependant, 24 November 1950, age one. P12 RE G8.

HETTIGDON, Civilian, 21 March 1949. P11 RC G18.

HENSMANN F.E., Driver 19182685 RASC, 42 Company, 31 August 1950, age 23. P12 RB G1. **Hanged by the British authorities after being found guilty of the murder of an Egyptian taxi driver during the attempted theft of a vehicle in Cairo.**

HILL I.J., Craftsman 19193402 REME, 7 March 1949, age 19. P11 RC G16.

HILL W.A.G., Craftsman REME, attached H Company 5 BOD, 16 July 1948. P11 RB G2.

HOBSON P.L., Private 22859632 RAOC, 26 February 1954, age 19. P15 RB G1.

HODGMAN L.C., Bombardier 222521819 Royal Artillery, 41 Field Regiment, 10 May 1951, age 27. P13 RA G16. **Killed by terrorist action.**

HODT D., Sapper 22624512, 1207 IWT OP SQUADRON R.E, 20 December 1952. P14 RC G4.

HOGARTH., Civilian, Service dependant, 14 August 1951, age one. P10 RB G17.

HOGARTH J., L/Cpl T/22293477 RASC, 84 Company, 21 November 1951, age 28. P13 RC G18. **Killed by terrorist action.**

HOOPER, Civilian, Service dependant, 19 July 1950, age one. P12 RD G4.

HOSENALLY V., Private MAUR 18081800 Royal Pioneer Corps (East Africa), 2049 M Company, 18 March 1951. P12 RA G11.

HOSSEMALLY B., Private MAUR 13907609 Royal Pioneer Corps (East Africa), 2063 M Company, 21 November 1950. P12 RA G6. **Killed by terrorist action.**

HOSSEN M.M.G., Private MAUR 13909149 Royal Pioneer Corps (East Africa), M Company, Port Said, 3 July 1948, age 25. P7 RF G12.

HOUGHTON T., Private S/22235832 RASC, 483 Sup Company, 24 July 1952, age 23. P12 RB G4. **Hanged by judicial process by the British authorities having been found guilty of the murder of Captain H.W.Mason and Corporal F J.Carter.**

HOWELL A., Private 21121337, 2 Royal Berkshire Regiment, 1 April 1948. P11 RA G6.

HOWS, Civilian, Service dependant, 30 September 1949. P11 RE G3.

HOYLE H., Captain 188141 Royal Engineers, 30 July 1953. P14 RD G16.

HUBARD B.H., Private 22838010 RAOC, 15 December 1953. P15 RA G8.

HULME Robert, Civilian, Service dependant, 12 May 1949. P11 RD G3.

HUNTER Jean, Civilian, Service dependant, 17 May 1952, age one. P14 RA G12.

HUTCHINS, Civilian, 7 February 1951, age 1 year 3 months, daughter of Corporal R.W.Hutchins Royal Signals. P12 RE G18.

HUXSTEP A.C., Corporal S/22395466 RASC, HQ, 27 April 1952. P14 RA G10. **Killed by terrorist action.**

ISLE-BUCK, Civilian, Service dependant, 30 December 1951. P13 RD G14.

JACKSON S., Driver T/21068444 RASC, 56 Trans Camp, 27 April 1952, age 19. P11 RC G12.

JAGURNAUTH M., Private 18091655 African Pioneers Corps (East Africa), 2063 Mauritius Company, 13 July 1953. P12 RA G13.

JENKINS F., Private 22793695 2nd Battalion Parachute Regiment, AAC, 12 July 1953. P14 RE G1.

JENNINGS F., Marine PLY/X1997 Royal Marines, 45 Commando, 18 February 1954, age 34. P15 RA G20.

JEWELL W., Staff Sergeant 2547478 Royal Engineers, 6 January 1953. P14 RC G6.

JOHNSON D.J., Private 23047332 Royal Norfolk Regiment, 9 December 1955. P16 RA G12.

JOHNSON T.O., Private 22572345 3rd Battalion Parachute Regiment, AAC, 3 November 1952, age 19. P14 RB G18.

JOHNSTON R.G., Corporal 4026114 RAF, 3 Police Wing (Ismailia), 18 August 1951. P13 RB G19. **Killed by terrorist action.**

JOLICEUR N.O.E., Private 18007196 African Pioneer Corps (East Africa), 2061 Rodriguez Company, 15 November 1954. P15 RC G9. **Killed by terrorist action.**

JUPE J., L/Corporal 22547714 Royal Engineers, Field Engineer Regiment, 10 January 1953. P14 RC G8.

KAY D.H., Driver T/22420954 RASC, 86 Company, 6 August 1951. P13 RB G14. **Killed by terrorist action.**

KAYONGWE G.F., Private 18179163 African Pioneer Corps (East Africa), 2211 Company, 21 January 1954. P15 RA G16.

KELLY R.A., Private T/2249763 RASC, 30 March 1950, age 19, son of Mrs L.Beale of Wallasey. P12 RC G1.

KELSEY C.L., Captain 170709 Intelligence Corps, 18 November 1951. P13 RC G16. **Killed by terrorist action.**

KEOGH T., Guardsman 22779155 Irish Guards, 18 September 1955. P16 RA G6. **Killed in road traffic accident.**

KERR T., Able Seaman C/JX65786 Royal Navy, HMS Dilwara, 28 March 1954, age 28. P15 RB G6.

KIKEMBOI K., L/Corporal 18116211 African Pioneer Corps (East Africa), 2 October 1955. P16 RA G8.

KILNER H.P., Airman 501190 RAF, 5 November 1950. P12 RE G4.

KIMMINS P., Sergeant 1059265 Army Catering Corps, attached 3rd Parachute Battalion, 3 August 1952, age 44. P14 RB G2.

KING, Civilian, Service dependant, 7 December 1950. P12 RE G9.

KIRK A., Corporal 1907378 RAF, 3 Police Wing (Ismailia), 26 January 1952. P13 RE G15. **Died of injuries sustained in civil disturbances in Ismailia.**

KIRKLAND-LAYAN, Civilian, Service dependant, 9 January 1950. P11 RE G15.

KIRKPATRICK Robert, Civilian, Service dependant, 23 October 1949. P11 RE G6.

KNIGHT A.E., Craftsman 22201015 REME, 2 Base Workshops, 7 January 1952. P13 RD G20.

KNIGHT C.R , Corporal 14480607 1st Battalion Royal Sussex Regiment (Kantara), 13 March 1948. P11 RA G3.

KNIGHT G.F., Driver T/22860887 RASC, 28 April 1954. P15 RB G9. **Killed by terrorist action.**

KNIGHT L.J., L/Bombardier 22305660 Royal Artillery, HQ 2 AGRA, 23 September 1952, age 20. P14 RB G8.

LABONTE A., Private 40147 African Pioneer Corps (East Africa), Seychelles Company, 25 March 1953. P14 RC G19.

LACRUCHE L.R., Private 18081657 African Pioneer Corps (East Africa), 2049 Mauritius Company, 18 March 1951. P13 RA G5. **Killed by terrorist action.**

LALLOO M.E., Private 10801971 African Pioneer Corps (East Africa), 2049 Mauritius Company, 11 July 1954. P15 RB G16. **Killed by terrorist action.**

LAMB, Civilian, Service dependant, 27 December 1948. P11 RC G9.

LANAGHAN J.M., Craftsman 22388720 REME, 9 January 1952. P13 RE G3. **Killed in convoy ambush.**

LASSAM J.D., Craftsman 19139518 REME, attached 610 Command VEH Group, 6 July 1948. P11 RB G4.

LAWRENCE Derek, Civilian, Service dependant, 21 July 1950. P12 RC G17.

LAWS E.M., Civilian, 22 May 1956. P16 RB G1.

LAZAROU L., Civilian, 695 Civil Garrison Police Company, TEK, 29 October 1949. P11 RE G8.

LINNETT G., Civilian, 5 August 1953. P14 RE G5.

LISETTE L., Sergeant 18007512 African Pioneer Corps (East Africa), 2058 Mauritius Company, 23 September 1950. P12 RD G19.

LISTER C.D., L/Corporal 22202774 REME, 13 August 1950. P12 RD G11.

LOGAN H.L., Private 19042451 1st Battalion Argyll and Sutherland Highlanders, 23 May 1948. P11 RA G14.

LORD, Civilian, Service dependant, 2 November 1952, age 2. P14 RB G17.

LOVETT G., Leading Aircraftsman 3507885 RAF (Ismailia), 16 December 1952. P14 RC G3.

LOVIARIS J., Civilian, Warden 863 TEK, NB Garrison Police, 11 January 1951. P12 RE G14.

LOWE J., Fusilier 22587881, 1st Battalion Lancashire Fusiliers, 25 January 1952. P13 RE G13. **Killed in action at Bureau Sanitaire.**

LOWE J.E., Civilian, 17 July 1950. P12 Rd G3.

LUNDIE J., Gunner 2992763 Royal Artillery, 80 LAA, 8 July 1950. P12 RC G20.

LYONS P., Corporal 1st Battalion Royal Inniskilling Fusiliers, 17 July 1952. P14 RA G17. **Accidentally shot by a comrade.**

MACLOU P.A., Private 18006697 African Pioneer Corps (East Africa), 2037 Mauritius Company, 25 January 1948, age 19. P3 RE G1.

MAGEE, Civilian, Service dependant, 8 January 1951, age one. P12 RE G13.

MAGEE, Civilian, Service dependant, 22 December 1950. P12 RE G11.

MAGUIRE T., Guardsman 22478457, 1st Battalion Scots Guards, 25 April 1952. P14 RA G8. **Killed while on stag. The fellow guardsman who shot him claimed it was an accident but was convicted of manslaughter.**

MANSFIELD N.A., Captain 181018 Royal Engineers, 12 July 1949. P11 RD G8.

MAREGA L.P., Private 18081532 African Pioneer Corps (East Africa), 2055 Mauritius Company, 8 April 1951. P13 RA G8. **Killed by terrorist action.**

MARIE L.F., Corporal 18008605 African Pioneer Corps (East Africa), 2046 Mauritius Company, 20 July 1948. P11 RB G6.

MARSDEN, Civilian, Service dependant, 6 July 1949. P11 RD G13.

MARSH B.S.J., Private 22337397 Royal Berkshire Regiment, 7 December 1951, age 20. P13 RD G17. **Attacked by a mob of Egyptians in an out-of-bounds area of Ismailia. Dead on arrival at hospital.**

MARSH J.F., Private 22375866 Army Catering Corps, attached Egypt Command Signals, 17 April 1951, age 19. P13 RA G9.

MARSON D.F., 2415063 RAF, 25 August 1949. P11 RD G19.

MARTIN F.M.G., Private Highland Light Infantry (City of Glasgow Regiment), 13 September 1953. P14 RE G11.

MASON J., Private 21047302 RAOC, 5 (BOD), 11 February 1949. P11 RC G15.

MASON N.E., Convoy Signalman SA126206 Royal Canadian Corps of Signals, 56 Canadian (United Nations Emergency Force), 15 May 1958. P16 RB G11. **Accidentally shot by UNEF maintenance area security guard at approx 02.35 hours.**

MASSANDY F.D., Private 13908105 African Pioneer Corps (East Africa), 2060 Mauritius Company, 9 August 1948. P11 RB G9.

MASSIE J.C.S., Sergeant 22995423 ROAC, 14 October 1955. P16 RA G9.

MASTERS W.M., PO/X1118 Royal Marines, 45 Commando, 6 July 1953. P14 RD G18.

MATTAGLO, Private 18115254 African Pioneer Corps (East Africa), 2207 Company, 24 July 1952. P14 RA G20.

MAZZCI J., Civilian, 14 December 1951, age 40. P12 RB G17.

McCAMMOND G., Private 22316162 RAOC, 23 July 1950. P12 RD G7.

McCORMACK J., Private 22225254 RAOC, 7 April 1950, age 41. P12 RC G2.

McCOWATT C., Sergeant 848042 RAOC, 22 November 1948, age 35. P11 RC G5.

McCUTCHEON., Civilian, Service dependant, 29 March 1950. P11 RE G20.

McDAVID G.E., Trooper SG12420 Royal Canadian Armoured Corps, 56 Recce Squadron (UN Emergency Force), 29 November 1957. P16 RB G7. **Died after a mine explosion near Rafah.**

McDONNELL J., Private 22845543 RAOC, 15 October 1955, age 21. P16 RA G10.

McDOUALL J.C.S., Major 133774 Royal Corps of Signals, GHQ, 17 November 1951. P13 RC G14. **His body was found at the front**

entrance to the Egyptian police barracks. He had been shot at close range.

McERLEAME, Civilian, Service dependant, 2 July 1955, age 5. P16 RA G3.

McGOWAN L.C., Sapper 22783979 Royal Engineers, 25 Field Engineer Regiment, 30 July 1954. P15 RB G15.

McINTOSH, Civilian, Service dependant, 5 July 1950. P12 RC G18.

McIVER D., Private 22202338 1st Battalion Queen's Own Cameron Highlanders, 14 January 1952. P13 RE G7. **Shot in an ambush.**

McKAY T.C., Civilian, Service dependant, 25 July 1951, son of Sergeant R.M.McKay Royal Artillery. P13 RB G11.

McKENZIE, Civilian, Service dependant, 6 May 1949. P11 RD G2.

McKENZIE J., L/Corporal 22208211 1st Battalion Lancashire Fusiliers, 27 January 1952. P13 RE G16. **Killed in action at the Bureau Sanitaire.**

McKNIGHT J.S., Private 14463714 ROAC, 14 September 1948, age 22. P11 RB G13.

McLEAN G., Driver 22808494 Royal Corps of Signals, 2 Agra Squadron, 4 March 1953. P14 RC G15.

McLEOD R., Driver T/19032993 RASC, 16 May 1948. P11 RB G1.

McGUIGAN Dorothy, Civilian, Service dependant, 1 July 1950, wife of Sergeant A.G.McGuigan 1371506 RAF. P12 RD G1.

MEDOR G., Private 35475 African Pioneer Company (East Africa), 2045 Seychelles Company, 1 April 1949. P11 RC G19.

MIC ALLEF-BARTILO Mariella, Civilian, Service dependant, 4 May 1949, age 40. P11 RD G1

MILES J.J., Lieutenant P/262537 Royal Artillery, 24 November 1949, age 26, son of J.W.Miles of Swindon. P11 RE G12.

MILES Shirley Florence Alice, Civilian, Service dependant, 26 February 1951, age 3. P13 RA G1.

MILLS R.B., Private 22616018 RAOC, 16 Independent Para Brigade, Group Ordinance Field Park, 12 May 1953, age 20. P14 RD G5.

MILNE T., Able Seaman Merchant Navy, 4 August 1948. P11 RB G7.

MOHAMED A.K., Signalman CEY/10710937 Royal Corps of Signals, No.2 Company RPCD (MELD), 31 January 1948, age 23. P7 RF G10.

MORRISON G.A., Fusilier 21187639 1st Battalion Royal Irish Fusiliers, 5 November 1949. P11 RE G9.

MOSTYN J.E.N., Captain 35253 RASC, 716 Company, 20 April 1948, age 23. P11 RA G9.

MOURGHEN M.P., Private 18090069 African Pioneer Corps (East Africa), 2051 Mauritius Company, 4 September 1952. P12 RA G12.

MURRAY J.R., Corporal 4080703 RAF (Firdan), 5 February 1953. P14 RC G11.

MURRELLS A., Sergeant 3113571 RAF (Abu Suier), 30 April 1952. P14 RC G2.

MUSYOKA-MYANIKA W., Private 18119456 African Pioneer Corps (East Africa), 2216 Company, 11 February 1953. P14 RC G13.

NARRAINEN N.D., L/Corporal 18024349 African Pioneer Corps, 2053 Mauritius Company, 26 February 1950. P12 RA G2.

NEAL G.W.F., Corporal T1445141 RASC, 286 Tahag Melf Company, 1 April 1948. P11 RA G5.

NEALE R.J., Driver T/22373478 RASC, 12 October 1950. P12 RE G1.

NEAT Joan Mary, Civilian, Service dependant, 5 August 1951, age 35, Church St Eastry, near Sandwich, Kent. P13 RB G16.

NICHOLLS M., Civilian, Service dependant, 24 March 1954. P15 RB G5.

NICOLL, Civilian, Service dependant (66761), 12 December1948. P11 RC G8.

NOBLE C.A., Gunner 22504094 Royal Artillery, 33 Airborne Light Regiment, 20 October 1952, age 19. P14 RB G16.

NORTH Enid Mable, Civilian, Service dependant, 24 July 1951, age 39, wife of Lieutenant S.North. P13 RB G4.

NYAGUTI N., Private 18116714 African Pioneer Corps (East Africa), 2216 Company, 7 July 1953. P14 RD G10.

OLDRIDGE J., Guardsman 22214570 1st Battalion Coldstream Guards, 31 December 1951. P13 RD G15. **Killed by accidental discharge of a rifle.**

ONDIEK W., Private 18116421 African Pioneer Corps (East Africa), 2214 Company, 11 November 1952. P14 RB G29.

OPIYO O., L/Corporal 18176791 African Pioneer Corps (East Africa), 2214 Company, 21 January 1955. P15 RC G15.

O'NEILL J., Driver T22450524 RASC, 5 Field Ambulance (El Ballah), 29 May 1952, age 22. P14 RA G13. **Killed by terrorist action.**

O'SULLIVAN Kevin, Civilian, Service dependant, 8 September 1950, son of Sergeant O'Sullivan 2717662 Royal Corps of Signals. P12 RD G16.

OWADALLY A.R., Private 18023047 African Pioneer Corps (East Africa), 2050 Company, 9 February 1948, age 22. P7 RF G11.

OWEMBA S., L/Corporal 18115067 African Pioneer Corps (East Africa), 2207 Company, 4 July 1952. P14 RA G16.

PALMER Frederick, Civilian, Service dependant, 17 July 1950, age one. P12 RC G10.

PARKER I.S.R., L/Corporal 22201411 Royal Engineers, HQ CRE Works (N), 29 October 1953. P14 RE G17.

PARKER Norman Roger, Civilian, Service dependant, 28 February 1950. P11 RE G18.

PARKINSON H.B., Signalman 22971662 Royal Corps of Signals, 23 December 1954. P15 RC G14. **Killed by terrorist action.**

PARTRIDGE H., Gunner 22336320 Royal Artillery, 19 August 1950. P12 RD G12.

PATTOO L.P., Corporal 18009581 African Pioneer Corps (East Africa), 2049 Mauritius Company, 5 January 1949. P11 RC G14.

PAUL R.A.E., CQM Sergeant 18026810 African Pioneer Corps (East Africa), 2053 Mauritius Company, 2 August 1951. P13 RB G12. **Killed by terrorist action.**

PEARCE, Civilian, Service dependant, 24 January 1951, P12 R6 G17.

PEEL Y., Craftsman 21127162 REME, attached HQ BTE, 24 July 1951. P13 RB G3. **Killed by terrorist action.**

PELL R., Private 19189563 RAOC, 27 September 1948, age 19. P11 RB G14.

PENNELL K.E., Corporal SB138623 Royal Canadian Corps of Signals (United Nations Emergency Force), 15 September 1957. P16 RA G19. **Died as a result of a vehicle accident on the Suez -Ismailia road.**

PERRY C.M., Private 22715216 1st Battalion Bedfordshire and Herefordshire Regiment, 20 March 1953. P14 RC G18.

PERRY J.M.E., Signalman 19179103 Royal Corps of Signals, 15 May 1948, age 19. P11 RA G12.

PERSU M., Private 18082641 African Pioneer Corps (East Africa), 2057 Mauritius Company, 4 January 1951. P12 RA G8. **Killed by terrorist action.**

PETERS F.S., 143604 ROAC, 11 May 1948, age 44. P11 RA G11.

PHILLIPS Raymond Anthony, Civilian, Service dependant, 22 May 1949. P11 RD G6.

PICK G.H., Major 214482 RAOC, 9 August 1948, age 42. P11 RB G10.

PIKE G.J., Private 22437587 1st Battalion Parachute Regiment, AAC, 21 August 1952. P14 RB G4.

PLAICHE D., Corporal 1808379 African Pioneer Corps (East Africa), 2061 Rodriguez Company, 3 August 1954. P15 RB G20. **Killed by terrorist action.**

POLAND H.A., Private 22104768 RAOC, 31 July 1949, age 18. P11 RD G16.

POPLE L., Driver 22695653 Royal Corps of Signals, 28 January 1953. P14 RC G10.

POTHANAH H., Private 18137388 African Pioneer Corps (East Africa), 2042 Mauritius Company, 31 December 1954. P12 RA G16. **Killed by terrorist action.**

POUNTNEY, Civilian, 29 August 1951, age one. P13 RB G20.

PRESCOTT Ezarine Ann, Civilian, Service dependant, 5 May 1950. P12 RC G9.

PREVOST J.R., Private 18024980 African Pioneer Corps (East Africa), 2059 Mauritius Company, 22 January 1948, age 26. P3 RD G5.

PRICE F.M., Sergeant 845713 Royal Artillery, 15 November 1948, age 35. P11 RC G3.

PRINGLE-PATTISON A.R.G., Major 71207 1st Battalion Queen's Own Cameron Highlanders, 14 January 1952, age 34, husband of Dorothy Rosemary Pringle-Pattison of Edinburgh. P13 RE G6. **Shot and killed in an ambush.**

PRONGER A., Private 22306780 Royal Berkshire Regiment, 10 December 1951. P13 RD G6. **Attacked by an Egyptian mob in an out-of-bounds area of Ismailia. Dead on arrival at hospital.**

RADCLIFFE D.R., Captain 362719 Royal Engineers, 35 Engineer Regiment, 24 October 1951. P13 RC G10.

RAHONAWTH S., Private 18025282 African Pioneer Corps (East Africa), 2059 Mauritius Company, 21 October 1949. P12 RA G1.

RAINE Anthony Ronald, Civilian, Service dependant, 27 July 1950. P12 RD G9.

RAMDHANY N., Private 18085486 African Pioneer Corps (East Africa), 2045 Mauritius Company, 26 May 1952. P12 RA G17.

RAMPEAR L., Private 18082625 African Pioneer Corps (East Africa), 2047 Mauritius Company, 28 December 1950. P12 RA G7.

RANCE, Civilian, Service dependant, 14 July 1950. P12 RC G14.

RANKIN J., Leading Aircraftsman 3514782 RAF, SD List, 15 March 1954. P15 RB G3. **Died in suspected ambush.**

RAWCLIFFE G., Private 22431490 1st Battalion East Lancashire Regiment, 4 July 1952, age 22. P14 RA G14.

RAYWOOD P., Private 22173772 RAOC, 26 April 1951, age 20. P13 RA G14. **Killed by terrorist action.**

REED B., Bombardier 22238905 Royal Artillery, attached 211 Trans Camp, 24 November 1951. P13 RC G20. **Killed by terrorist attack, his body recovered from Sweet Water Canal with that of L/Cpl Fearn.**

REVELL B.R.J., 2nd Lieutenant RASC, 7 November 1948. P11 RC G2.

REYNOLDS G., Guardsman 22335843 Grenadier Guards, 25 November 1951, age 20. P13 RD G2. **Killed in road traffic accident.**

RICKARDS, Civilian, Service dependant, 337 LAD TCK, 14 October 1948. P11 RB G18.

RIMELL W.C.P., Craftsman 22801548 REME, 5 March 1955. P16 RA G1.

ROBERTS, Civilian, 13 November 1950. P12 RE G6.

ROBERTS J.T., Corporal SF8590 Royal Canadian Army Service Corps (UN Emergency Force), 56 Command Transport Company, 10 July 1957. P16 RB G15. **Absented himself during overnight stop near Port Suez while on convoy duty. Body recovered in the morning. Drowning stated as cause of death.**

ROBERTS J.W., Gunner 14906851 Royal Artillery, 23 January 1948, age 21. P3 RD G6.

ROBERTS W.B., Leading Aircraftsman 4023536 RAF, 20(M) Unit (E), Port Fouad, 6 January 1952. P13 RD G18.

ROBERTS W.O., Driver T/22597763 RASC, 34 Company (GT), 8 August 1953. P14 RE G6. **Killed by terrorist action.**

ROBINSON M., L/Corporal 22728872, 1st Border Regiment, 23 July 1953, age 18. P14 RD G15. **Drowned in Lake Timsah when off duty.**

RODGERS E., Lieutenant 127916 RAPC, 23 May 1948, age 49. P11 RA G15.

ROGERS F., Gunner 22601462 Royal Artillery, 80 LAA, 25 July 1952. P14 RA G18.

ROMAN A., Corporal 5380272 Royal Corps of Signals, 41 Field Regiment (F Troop 1 Div Signals), 18 December 1949. P11 RE G14.

ROPER, Civilian, Service dependant, 28 March 1951, child of Sergeant P.Roper 6203594 RASC. P13 RA G7 (Joint grave).

ROPER S., Civilian, Service dependant, 13 May 1952, age one. P13 RA G7 (Joint grave).

ROPER P.H., L/Corporal S/22390956 RASC, 84 Company, 29 January 1952, age 19. P13 RE G20.

ROSSAN D., Private 18083006 African Pioneer Corps (East Africa), 2047 Mauritius Company, 11 January 1951. P12 RA G9. **Killed by terrorist action.**

SADLER M.A., Driver T/4547765 RASC, 286 Company, TAHAG MELF, 1 April 1948. P11 RA G4.

SALT G., L/Corporal 22828149 Corps of Royal Military Police, 203 Provost Company, 11 August 1953. P14 RE G7. **Almost certainly the RMP killed at night when ambushed by wire while carrying urgent dispatches by motorcycle from Port Said to Fayid.**

SALTER T., Private 22683705 1st Battalion East Surrey Regiment, 16 July 1953, age 19, son of W.Slater of Tolworth, Surrey. P14 RD G14.

SANASEE M.G., Private 18083755 African Pioneer Corps (East Africa), 2049 Mauritius Company, 18 March 1951. P13 RA G4. **Killed by terrorist action.**

SAWYER I.A., Private SK17653 Royal Canadian Army Service Corps, 56

■ The bodies of Driver Edward Hensmann, RASC, and Corporal Tom Houghton, age 23, 74 Coy RASC, are buried in Moascar Cemetery. Both were judicially hanged for murder.

The bodies of Driver Hensmann and Corporal Houghton have been buried in graves arranged at a different angle to every other grave in the cemetery.

Oddly, the accomplices of Edward Hensmann, who were found guilty of the same offence in the same trial, have been buried normally.

Canadian Transport Company (United Nations Emergency Force), 22 April 1958. P16 RB G9. **Killed as a result of a road traffic accident at approx 22.10 hours near Rafah.**

SCARTH, Civilian, Service dependant, 7 October 1950. P12 RD G20.

SELLORS John, Civilian, Service dependant, 16 September 1951, age one. P13 RC G2.

SEVERS D.G.B., Corporal 22385629, 1st Battalion Lincolnshire Regiment, 29 September 1951. P13 RC G6. **Killed by terrorist action.**

SHARP, Civilian, Service dependant, 1 July 1949. P11 RD G7.

SHARP, Civilian, Service dependant, 22 May 1949. P11 RD G5.

SHARPE John Christopher Eric, Civilian, Service dependant, 9 July 1951, age one. P13 RB G7.

SHAW J., Driver 22275133 RAOC, 12 January 1951, age 19. P12 RE G15. **Killed by terrorist action.**

SHEARS Jennifer Irene, Civilian, Service dependant, 1 August 1954, age 3, daughter of Sgt L.Shears 22240898 RPC. P15 RB G18.

SHERMAN L.J., Gunner 22287632 Royal Artillery, 41st Field Regiment, 18 September 1951. P13 RC G4. **Killed by terrorist action.**

SHRIMPTON J.G.L., Aircraftsman 1st Class 4073665 RAF,19 March 1953, age 19. P14 RC G17.

SIMPSON R.J., Civilian, NAAFI, 15 December 1954. P15 RC G13.

SKELTON D.R.W., Private 19148890 REME, 309 L of C Workshops, 27 May 1948. P11 RA G16.

SMART D.A., Craftsman 22870357 REME, 26 December 1953. P15 RA G10. **Killed by terrorist action.**

SMITH, Civilian, Service dependant, 17 July 1950, age one. P12 RC G15.

SMITH, Civilian, Service dependant, 4 July 1951. P13 RB G5.

SMITH A.N., Guardsman 22213548, 3rd Battalion Grenadier Guards, 29 December 1952. P13 RE G18. **While on stag at Tel el Kebir he and his companion followed terrorists across a minefield and both were killed by the explosion of a mine.**

SMITH F., Guardsman 21006032 3rd Battalion Grenadier Guards, 27 January 1952, age 22. P13 RE G17. **While on stag at Tel el Kebir he and his companion followed terrorists across a minefield and both were killed by the explosion of a mine.**

SMITH R.E., Gunner 22208649 Royal Artillery, Anti-tank Battery, 31 August 1950. P12 RB G2. **Hanged by the British authorities for the murder of an Cairo taxi driver during an attempt to steal a motor vehicle.**

SOMERVILLE A., Private 22696015 3rd Battalion Parachute Regiment, AAC, 20 May 1953. P14 RD G7.

SOORAH J.F., Private 18024837 African Pioneer Corps (East Africa), 2057 Mauritius GP Company, 6 September 1949. P11 RE G1.

SOYFOO A.R., Private 18089822 African Pioneer Corps (East Africa), 2038 Mauritius Company, 28 February 1954. P12 RA G14.

SPENCER M.J., Corporal

22033474 Royal Engineers, DCRE, 4 August 1949. P11 RD G17.

SPIERS A.P., Private 19083759 Royal Berkshire Regiment, Transit Camp, 25 October 1948. P11 RB G20.

SPILLANE C., Signalman 22325891 Royal Corps of Signals, Egypt Comm. Signals, 28 November 1951. P13 RD G3.

STAINSBY, Civilian, Service dependant, 17 August 1951. P13 RB G18.

STAMMER, Civilian, Service dependant, 9 May 1950, age one. P12 RC G10.

STAPLES J.S., Private 19056287 RAMC, BMH El Ballah, 7 July 1948. P11 RA G20.

STARK I.L., Sergeant SA118631 Royal Canadian Engineers,(United Nations Emergency Force), 27 September 1957. P16 RB G5. **Killed at approx 16.00 hours as a result of mine explosion near Rafah.**

STARK R., L/Corporal 22169339 Royal Corps of Signals, Egypt Command, 14 May 1951. P13 RA G18. **Killed by terrorist action.**

STOTT D.M., Driver T/23237028 RASC, 22 October 1955. P16 RA G11.

STRACHAN N.B., WO11 S/O 553161 REME, 15 April 1956. P16 RA G16.

STRINGER W.G., Major 657986 Royal Engineers, 13 April 1954. P15 RB G7.

STURMEY R., Corporal 22431035 Royal Corps of

Signals, 28 September 1954. P15 RC G4. **Killed by terrorist action.**

SUMMON, Private 18027810 African Pioneer Corps (East Africa), 2050 Mauritius Company, 24 July 1950. P12 RA G5.

SUNNER, Civilian, Service dependant, 12 December 1949. P11 RE G13.

SWEET D.L., Signalman 22345305 Royal Corps of Signals, 3 L of C Signals, 8 February 1952. P14 RA G3.

TAYLOR, Civilian, Service dependant, 26 December 1955. P16 RA G13.

TAYLOR E.G., Sapper 22812240 Royal Engineers, 50 Field Squadron, 11 July 1953. P14 RD G11.

TAYLOR G., Private 22879366 RAOC, 5 November 1954. P15 RC G7.

TAYLOR J.R., Sapper 22257736 Royal Engineers, 13 March 1952. **Killed by terrorist action.**

0TAYLOR H., Gunner 22013826 Royal Artillery, 9 December 1948. age 18. P11 RC G7.

TEELUCK P., Private 18082067 African Pioneer Corps East Africa), 2038 Mauritius Company, 20 July 1950. P12 RA G4.

TEERHOO A.R., Private 13909281 African Pioneer Corps (East Africa), 2059 Mauritius GP Company, 30 August 1949. P11 RD G20.

THARBY H., Private 22768610, 1st Battalion Bedfordshire and

Hertfordshire Regiment, 7 February 1954. P15 RA G19.

THEOVILLE F., Private 18023746 African Pioneer Corps (East Africa), 2052 Mauritius Company, 4 May 1948. P11 RA G17.

THOMAS, Civilian, 18 November 1948. P11 RC G4.

THOMAS, Civilian, 24 November 1949. P11 RE G11.

THOMPSON G., Captain 274190 RASC, 1 January 1949. P11 RC G10.

THOMPSON D.J., Sapper 2275106 Royal Engineers, 18 January 1951, age 19. P12 RE G16. **Killed by terrorist action.**

THOREAU M., Private 40175 African Pioneer Corps (East Africa), 2040 Seychelles Company, Pioneer Works, 1 February 1952. P14 RA G2.

THORNER B., Driver T/22665741 RASC, 22 May 1953. P14 RD G8.**Killed by terrorist action.**

TILLEY J.D.R.J., CSM (WO11) 5499162 RAOC, 21 January 1954, age 36. P15 RA G15. **Brought in dead to British Military Hospital, Moascar: cause of death – natural causes. MoD state they are unable to give any further information without the written permission of the next of kin.**

TILLMAN J.W., Sapper 22665207 Royal Engineers, 1 January 1954. P15 RA G11.

TIMSON J., Private 21187694 2nd Battalion Royal Lincolnshire Regiment, 27

August 1948, age 18. P11 RB G12.

TOOLSEY A., Private 18027664 African Pioneer Corps (East Africa), 2057 Mauritius Company, 6 July 1948, age 21. P10 RB G8.

TULEY, Civilian, Service dependant, 19 May 1951. P13 RA G19.

TUNNEY H., Private 22479687 1st Battalion Border Regiment, 1 March 1952. P14 RA G5. **While the SIB were investigating the loss of beer being unloading from lighters, they found two small tins of Spam in Private Tunney's unattended small pack. Charged and convicted of theft despite his protestations of innocence, he was awarded a spell in the glasshouse. On release, while being transported to the pick-up point, he saw his Border Regiment truck approaching. In his excitement, he tried to leap from one moving vehicle to the other and was killed.**

TURNER Brian David, Civilian, Service dependant, 27 April 1951, age one. P13 RA G13.

UREN B.J., L/Corporal W/371539 WRAC, 8 December 1954. P15 RC G12. **Killed by terrorist action.**

VALABDA, Civilian, Service dependant, 7 July 1949, age one. P11 RD G14.

VAN STRAUBENZEE C.C., Royal Canadian Armoured Corps, 56 Recce Squadron (United Nations Emergency

Force), 10 May 1957. P16 RA G12. **Died when his Ferret scout car overturned when swerving to avoid a crowd of Egyptians. Rioting Egyptians?**

VARNEY D.H., Leading Aircraftsman 4042912 RAF (Ismailia), 24 July 1952. P14 RA G19.

VAUX J.B., Private 22693709 1st Battalion Parachute Regiment, AAC, 30 May 1954. P15 RB G14. **Killed by terrorist action.**

VEZINA H.R., Sapper SE119102 Royal Canadian Engineers, 1 Middle East Detachment (United Nations Emergency Force), 9 March 1957, age 29. P16 RA G17. **Died of Acute Myocardial Infarction.**

WAGHORN B., Civilian Sub-Inspector 1640 CND Warden Company TEK, 26 September 1962. P14 RB G9.

WALKER E.F.J., Leading Aircraftsman 4014167 RAF (Ismailia), 10 July 1951, age 22. P13 RB G9. **Killed by terrorist action.**

WALL F., Private S/22587839 RASC, 16 July 1953. P14 RD G13.

WALLACE H.K., Guardsman 22215738 1st Battalion Scots Guards, 18 April 1954. P15 RB G8.

WALLER J.S., Private 22876547 RAOC, 18 January 1956, age 20. P16 RA G14.

WALSH D., Sapper 22787939 Royal Engineers, 39 Field Squadron, 29 July 1953. P14 RE G4.

WARBOYS S., Private 22464685 1st Battalion Lincolnshire Regiment, 20 January 1952. P13 RE G9. **One of two who died when another six were wounded as a terrorist bomb set off anti-tank mines alongside a manned post on the Sweet Water Canal on 19 January 1952.**

WATKINS R., Sapper 22774544 Royal Engineers, 25 Field Regiment, 14 October 1952. P14 RA G15.

WATSON B., Signaller 22623442 Royal Corps of Signals, 3 Loc Signals Regiment, 16 March 1953, age 22. P14 RC G16.

WEBSTER S., Gunner 22279035 Royal Artillery, 33 Airborne Light Regiment, 8 October 1953.

WEBSTER V.E., L/Corporal 19180375, 2 Battalion Middlesex Regiment, 5 July 1948. P11 RA G18.

WEEKS L.C., Captain 201160 Royal Corps of Signals, 1 Squadron Egypt Command, 10 August 1951. P13 RB G15. **Killed by terrorist action.**

WELCH, Civilian, Service dependant, 2 May 1951, age 3 months, son of L/Corporal J.D.Welch REME. P13 RA G15.

WELLS M.E., Captain 434034 C/O Intelligence Corps, 4 February 1956. P16 RA G15.

WESTWICK Peter Matthew, Civilian, Service dependant, 19 April 1951, age one. P13 RA G11.

WHARTON R.H., Major 101369 RASC, 18 November 1951. P13 RC G15. **Shot and killed by Egyptian police during disturbances in Ismailia.**

WHEATMAN R.I., Civilian, 3 August 1950. P12 RD G10.

WHEATON T., Staff Sergeant 22207343 Royal Artillery, 30 July 1949. P11 RD G11.

WHITE L.C., Private 22887555 Bedfordshire and Hertfordshire Regiment, 18 November 1954. P15 RC G10. **Killed by terrorist action.**

WILDEY, Civilian, Service dependant, 6 August 1949, age one. P11 RD G18.

WILLIAMS D.D., Private S/22420290 RASC, 482 Supply Platoon, 22 December 1951. P RD G12.

WILSON A.R., L/Corporal 22237452 REME, 2 Base Workshops, 22 September 1951. P13 RTC G5. **Killed by terrorist action.**

WILSON J., Private 22596010 Army Catering Corps, attached 203 Company Royal Military Police, 24 July 1953. P14 RE G2.

WILSON W.B., Sergeant 18115486 African Pioneer Corps (East Africa), 2207 Company, 11 November 1952. P14 RB G20.

WISDEN G.A., Private 22605740 RAOC, Base VEH Depot (E), 31 August 1952. P14 RB G7.

WOOD J., Private 19135763 RAOC, attached REME, 19 July 1948. P11 RB G5.

WOODWARD, Civilian, 24 July 1950, age 26. P12 RD G8.

WRIGHT Jonathon, Civilian, Service dependant, 13 July 1950, age one. P12 RD G2.

WRIGHT P., Signalman 22398884 Royal Corps of Signals, Egypt Command, 3 March 1951. P13 RA G2. **Killed by terrorist action.**

YOUL J.A., Lieutenant 460130 RASC, 30 May 1953. P14 RD G9. **Killed by terrorist action.**

YUILE J., Civilian, Service dependant, 4 December 1953, son of Corporal J.Y.Yuile RAF 4005041. P15 RA G7.

ISMAILIA MEMORIAL CEMETERY

ANTHONY Elizabeth May, Civilian, Service dependant, 11 March 1948, age one, daughter of Capt G.H.Anthony GHQ RE. PM1 RA G26.

BILLINGS Christina Joan, Civilian, Service dependant, 23 January 1948, age 21, daughter of Capt Billings 2nd Battalion North Staffordshire Regiment. PM1 RA G25.

HAZELWOOD Michael, Civilian, 26 August 1948, age one. PM1 RA G10.

HILL Michael George, Civilian, 4 July 1948, age one. PM1 RA G27.

LERWILL Leila Bernice, Civilian, Service dependant, 20 January 1948, age 2, daughter of Lt-Col G Lerwill Middlesex Regiment. PM1 RA G24.

LLOYD-DAVIS Gordon, Civilian, 10 February 1956. PM15 RA G6.

MACLEAN John, Civilian, 6 May 1950, age 53. PM15 RA G3.

OLIVER Cecil Paul, Civilian, 19 May 1955, age 55. PM15 RA G4.

PAICE A.F., Civilian, Service dependant, 9 August 1948. PM1 RA G18.

SCRIVEN Pauline Ruth, Civilian, Service dependant, 16 August 1948, age 5. PM1 RA G9.

STEER Marion, Civilian, Service dependant, 6 July 1948, age one. PM1 RA G20.

VINE John Douglas, Civilian, 30 March 1950, age 2. PM6 RC G12.

NO KNOWN GRAVES

■ *The following personnel were abducted and killed by Egyptians and have no known graves. Six of them were travelling in pairs when taken.*

STAINTON D., LAC. Driver of a Bedford Coach Reg No 27-AC-36. Left camp 18 April 1953 on a duty run and failed to return. The bus was never found.

PYPER R.W., Gunner 22800177 Royal Artillery. Disappeared 11.01.54.

DIXON C.J.W., Driver 22682695 RASC. Disappeared 11.01.54.

MOORE W.J., Sergeant 22306151 Royal Artillery. Disappeared 22.01.54.

ARTHURS J., Lance Bombadier 22522902 Royal Artillery. Disappeared 22.01.54.

FITZGERALD J.M., Signalman 22712001 Royal Signals. Disappeared 15.03.54.

RAYBOULD H., Signalman 22559512 Royal Signals. Disappeared 15.03.54.

SMETHURST M.J., Sergeant 1815877 Royal Air Force. Disappeared 12.02.52.

SHEEHAN A.E., Flight Lieutenant 3507330. Royal Air Force. Disappeared 03.11.56.

AITCHERLEY D., Air Vice Marshal, Royal Air Force. Failed to arrive in Cyprus when flying his personal Meteor from the Canal Zone. Posted missing, presumed dead, around 10.06.1952.

CASUALTIES FROM THE CRASH OF YORK G-ANSY

A York transport aircraft blew up while ferrying military personnel from the Suez area back to the United Kingdom on 18 February 1956, killing all on board. En-route from Cyprus, Avro York G-ANSY refuelled at Malta. Shortly after it became airborne at Malta-Luqa airport, one engine caught fire and the aircraft stalled and crashed. All forty-five passengers and five crew aboard were killed. The crew of the York,

operated by Scottish Airlines, were: Captain Frank COKER, pilot; First Officer R.GORVIN, co-pilot; J.HAY, radio officer; R.BEECHEY, navigation officer; Miss G.UPHAM, air stewardess. There was one Army man aboard, Private A.SMITH of the RAOC.

The RAF and RAF Regiment casualties are listed below alphabetically, giving rank, name, Service number, date of birth and place of birth.

SGT ALBERRY B.F.J., 4292449, O3.09.33, Portland.

LAC BARBOUR A.M., 4014297, 04.04.22, Glasgow

CPL BLY P.J., 2721129, 13.01.36, Scunthorpe

CPL BRACEWELL J., 4111464, 29.08.31, Bradford

LAC BROWN D., 4122086, 29.04.33, Dundee

CPL BURKE C.C., 1909756, 22.12.27, Dublin

LAC BUTCHART S.H., 4081381, 05.08.33, Exeter

LAC CARLTON P.R., 4084971, 27.07.33, Halifax

CPL COLLIER J.D., 4070082, 15.11.32, Rhondda

CPL COX J.R., 1922778, 13.05.33, Hertford

CPL CRAIGIE G.A., 4076740, 08.12.33, Dundee

LAC DRURY-LOWE T., 2718503, 19.05.53, Coulsdon

SAC DUMBILL T.G., 2718862, 24.11.35, Liverpool

CPL EDWARDS J.A., 4091828, 04.02.22, Wellington

CPL FAWCETT J.S.E., 4116734, 14.03.33, Aveley

LAC FITZPATRICK J.L., 4080588, 02.03.34, St Helens

AC1 FLEMING M.J., 4079838, 04.10.34, Wexford

LAC FLEMING W.W., 4079955, 17.12.34, Comber

F/SGT GEORGE H.F., 531122, 22.01.14, London

LAC HAMPSON R., 4092401, 23.03.33, Wrexham

LAC HARRIS E.R., 4092027, 22.01.34, Leominster

SAC HODSON S.A., 3142934, 23.12.35, Market Harborough

LAC HOLLIDA J.M., 4125984, 06.10.35, Worcester

LAC KEATING F.R.J., 4084173, 28.08.33, London

LAC KENYON G., 4099256, 12.03.34, Washington

CPL McKAY J.J., 1923587, 05.03.34, Fort George

LAC MILLAR. D., 4129461, 12.02.33, Dundee

LAC NURSE M.J., 4122093, 23.07.35, Exeter

LAC PARKER D., 4090130, 09.03.35, Leicester

CPL PATERSON A.J., 2718806, 30.11.35, Glasgow

CPL PRATCHETT B.C., 3513692, 21.06.34, Harwich

LAC PYE M., 3513124, 19.05.34, Worcester

CPL ROBERTS T.K., 4125466, 14.02.29, Romford

SGT SPENCE J.W., 4010658, 17.01.27, Loughborough

SGT SPENCER J.A., 643611, 1921, London

CPL STEVEN W., 2558097, 20.12.33, Glasgow

CPL TALBOT W.G., 4104881, 13.12.34, Folkestone

CPL WEARING R.F., 4129185, 07.05.35, Lancaster

LAC WILLIAMS K.E., 4125725, 13.02.35, Liverpool

CPL WILLIAMS R., 4004177, 14.02.29, Staffs

LAC WILSON J.F., 4091342, 17.05.34, Glasgow

SAC WORTLEY G., 4115681, 08.02.35, Consett

AC1 YOUNG R., 4130204, 11.05.35, Aberdeen

SGT ALBERRY B.F.J., 4292449, O3.09.33, Portland.

LAC BARBOUR A.M., 4014297, 04.04.22, Glasgow

CPL BLY P.J., 2721129, 13.01.36, Scunthorpe

CPL BRACEWELL J., 4111464, 29.08.31, Bradford

LAC BROWN D., 4122086, 29.04.33, Dundee

CPL BURKE C.C., 1909756, 22.12.27, Dublin

LAC BUTCHART S.H., 4081381, 05.08.33, Exeter

LAC CARLTON P.R., 4084971, 27.07.33, Halifax

CPL COLLIER J.D., 4070082, 15.11.32, Rhondda

CPL COX J.R., 1922778, 13.05.33, Hertford

CPL CRAIGIE G.A., 4076740, 08.12.33, Dundee

LAC DRURY-LOWE T., 2718503, 19.05.53, Coulsdon

SAC DUMBILL T.G., 2718862, 24.11.35, Liverpool

CPL EDWARDS J.A., 4091828, 04.02.22, Wellington

CPL FAWCETT J.S.E., 4116734, 14.03.33, Aveley

LAC FITZPATRICK J.L., 4080588, 02.03.34, St Helens

AC1 FLEMING M.J., 4079838, 04.10.34, Wexford

LAC FLEMING W.W., 4079955, 17.12.34, Comber

F/SGT GEORGE H.F., 531122, 22.01.14, London

LAC HAMPSON R., 4092401 23.03.33, Wrexham

LAC HARRIS E.R., 4092027, 22.01.34 , Leominster

SAC HODSON S., 3142934, 23.12.35, Mkt H'boro

LAC HOLLIDAY J.M., 4125984, 06.10.35, Worcester

LAC KEATING F.R.J., 4084173, 28.08.33, London

LAC KENYON G., 4099256, 12.03.34, Washington

CPL McKAY J.J., 1923587, 05.03.34, Fort George

LAC MILLAR D., 4129461, 12.02.33, Dundee

LAC NURSE M.J., 4122093, 23.07.35, Exeter

LAC PARKER D., 4090130, 09.03.35, Leicester

CPL PATERSON A.J., 2718806, 30.11.35, Glasgow

CPL PRATCHETT B.C., 3513692, 21.06.34, Harwich

LAC PYE M., 3513124, 19.05.34, Worcester

CPL ROBERTS T.K., 4125466, 14.02.29, Romford

SGT SPENCE J.W., 4010658 17.01.27, Loughborough

SGT SPENCER J.A., 643611 1921, London

CPL STEVEN W., 2558097, 20.12.33, Glasgow

CPL TALBOT W.G., 4104881 13.12.34, Folkestone

CPL WEARING R.F., 4129185, 07.05.35, Lancaster

LAC WILLIAMS K.E., 4125725, 13.02.35, Liverpool

CPL WILLIAMS R., 4004177 14.02.29, Staffs

LAC WILSON J.F., 4091342, 17.05.34, Glasgow

SAC WORTLE. G., 4115681 08.02.35, Consett

AC1 YOUNG R., 4130204, 11.05.35, Aberdeen

■ On 11 May 1950 a Vampire fighter VZ188 piloted by Pilot 2 Stanislaw Dabrowski suffered a mid-air collision with Lincoln SX957 of the 148 Squadron.

The wreckage of the Lincoln may have fallen into the sea because the bodies of only three of the crew of the Lincoln and that of the Vampire pilot are recorded as recovered and buried.

The bodies of the following members of the Lincoln crew are not recorded as buried in the Canal Zone.

This information was supplied by the Ministry of Defence on 31 March 2003.

F/LT PETER VAUGHAN JONES DFC, No.56163, pilot.

F/O ALEXANDER KENNETH MCRIGOR, No.3037093, 2nd pilot.

F/LT LESLIE WILLIAM ARCHER, No.54609, signaller.

ENGINEER 2 DAVID MITCHELL, No.1823806, flight engineer.

GUNNER 1 TERRANCE JOHN CONAGHAN, No.1493487, air gunner.

GUNNER 2 GEORGE SHERWOOD, No.3012853, air gunner.

GUNNER 2 WILLIAM SMITH Fenion, No.1372914, air gunner.

AT LAST...

On 11 June 2003 at 19.30 hours Field Marshal the Lord Bramall confirmed that the Queen had been asked to ratify a decision to award a medal bearing a Canal Zone Clasp for service in Suez, Egypt, between 1951 and 1954. The medal will be the 1918-1962 General Service Medal.

It was explained that Service personnel who completed ninety days' service between 16 October 1951 and 19 October 1954 are eligible for the award, with lesser periods of qualification for those killed, wounded or medivacced.

Medals may be claimed by the individual concerned or, when he or she has died, by the immediate next-of-kin. Applications should be made to the appropriate authority shown below and should, if possible, contain full service particulars, including number, rank, FULL name, date of birth, dates of enlistment and discharge and the name of the regiment or corps where applicable. However, details of service in Egypt are unnecessary as the authorities will examine the individual's records.

Applicants applying on behalf of those who have died will be asked for some proof of relationship. As this will probably involve completing an official form, applicants should await instructions from the Medal Office and should not send any relevant certificates until asked for them.

The addresses for medal applications are listed below.

ROYAL NAVY AND ROYAL MARINES

Naval Pay and Pensions (accounts)
AFPAA (Centurion)
Centurion Building
Grange Road
Gosport
Hampshire PO13 9XA

ARMY (INCLUDING CIVILIAN CLAIMANTS)

Officer in Charge
Army Medal Office
Government Office Building
Worcester Road
Droitwich Spa
Worcester
WA9 8AU

ROYAL AIR FORCE

HQ Personnel Management Centre
Royal Air Force Innsworth
Gloucestershire GL3 1EZ

GLOSSARY OF TERMS

An explanation of terms used in this book and some commonly used by troops. It will be noted that one word could serve as a complete sentence in the interpretation of Arabic by the British. Alternative spellings may apply.

ackers - money; piastres.

aiwa - yes.

alaquifik - I couldn't give a monkey's.

ashenay - why? Very sarcastic; usually answered by ashenkida (why not?).

aqua - fresh water.

bahdin - later.

barrack square - an area of ground, usually square, much loved by drill instructors and RSMs. Much time is spent on it by recruits and others on any form of parade. Usually the surface is of tarmac or concrete but wherever the military are to be found a barrack square will be created even before sleeping accommodation has been established. In such cases it can be created by simply levelling an area of sand. To walk across the square without direct authority is a crime punishable by jankers.

bending drill - defecation in the open. Alternatively, going for a walk with a spade.

billets - accommodation block which can range from a tent in the desert or a Nissen hut to a centrally heated, purpose built, all mod-con building in the UK.

.303 - standard issue Lee Enfield rifle.

bint - young girl.

bokra - tomorrow; put it off until tomorrow; never.

brothel creepers - suede shoes with thick rubber soles.

chai or char - tea; sometimes delivered with doorstep sandwiches at midnight to those on guard duty and served in the NAAFI when no beer was available.

crab fats - Royal Navy term for RAF personnel.

crap hats - RAF and Royal Navy term for Army personnel.

desert chicken - bully beef.

desert rose - a tundish stuck in the sand to use as a urinal.

dhobi wallah - wash bloke; TB spreader.

disasters - plasters.

djellabah - the nightshirt-like apparel worn by working class Egyptians. A cooling garment in summer and a wonderful garment for hiding contraband. At least one British Servicewoman was shot when her nightdress was mistaken for a djellabah as she flitted to a toilet block after dark.

domani - tomorrow; more positive than bokra.

farting around - doing nothing in particular; the RAF on parade.

feloos - money

for the use of - the RAF adjudged that all airmen are simpletons, so on any stores requisition form there was a space to state why such goods were required. Horseshoe nails must be used for that purpose only. That they could be used to join two pieces of wood together is of no consequence. A camp could be falling down for want of a nail, but "them's horse shoe nails" would be the order of the day and their issue forbidden unless a senior officer raised a change-of-use form, when all would be well.

form 252 - in the Army and the Air Force it is the number of the form used to bring a charge against a Serviceman.

gippy tummy - dysentery

gharry - Egyptian horsedrawn carriage.

iggri - hurry up

imshi - go away; sharpish like!

jankers - the invariable end product of the use of a 252. Before normal duty and after duty the miscreant is required to parade at the guardroom, wearing his webbing harness, every hour on the hour. He may also be required to perform menial tasks. Servicemen on jankers are denied the modest delights of the NAAFI

mahleesh - indifferent; could not care less.

mungarea - food.

moya - water (in the desert).

mush - negative; as in **mush quiess**, no good.

NAAFI - Navy, Army and Air Force Institute. In the UK it is a place of rest and relaxation for off-duty Servicemen. When they are on duty, NAAFI vans tour work sites delivering much needed refreshments. In Egypt the NAAFI was short of everything, including staff.

NCO - non-commissioned officer. In the Army a lance corporal is the first step on the road to a field marshal's baton. The equivalent in the Air Force and Navy is a leading aircraftsman and leading seaman respectively. Two stripes are worn by a corporal in the Air Force or Army and crossed anchors denote an equivalent rank in the Navy where, rather confusingly, stripes are awarded for every four years of good conduct, up to a maximum of three. Such stripes are referred to as badges and an ordinary seaman three-badge stoker is held

in high esteem as a man who knows simply everything; in particular, where good pubs are to be found the world over, and how to survive in the Service with the minimum of effort. The highest non-commissioned rank is that of RSM (regimental sergeant major) or SWO (station warrant officer) in the RAF. He is usually a warrant officer, to confuse things further. The only difference between God and a RSM is that God does not think that he is an RSM.

one up the spout - a .303 with a round of ammunition in the breech, ready to be fired. The same term can be applied to a girl who finds herself expecting child.

panther crawl - a method of moving silently across the ground using your elbows and knees or feet. The rifle is held in the hands, slightly raised from the ground, ready for instant action. Practised a lot but rarely used.

Queensberry - the Marquis of Queensberry is credited with making efforts in the prize ring fair and honest. He was the father of Oscar Wilde's boyfriend and was not altogether fair in his dealing with him. His rules are rarely observed when dealing with any enemy.

quick shits - dysentery.

quiess - good; hence, **quiess kateer** – very good.

redcaps - Military Police, identified by a red cap cover.

reveille - the most popular call to duty in the Services as it heralds yet another day of water ski-ing, wining and dining and chatting-up delightful lady Servicewomen.

saida - hello.

schwaiya - a little; **stana schwaiya** - wait a bit.

scruff, the - the Army's affectionate term for the RAF.

snowdrops - RAF Police, identified by a white cap cover.

stag - to be on stag is to be on guard duty. Periods of duty are often referred to as 1st, 2nd or 3rd stag.

Stella - Egyptian-brewed mineral beer. Much loved by permanently thirsty troops.

square-bashing - initial training upon entry to any of the Services, where marching about has a high priority and the barrack square is bashed by the newly issued boots of the recruits.

nikarac/nikabok - foxtrot oscar.

Sweet Water Canal - The Suez canal is salt water so this sewage system, being fed by the fresh water of the Nile, is classified as sweet i.e. unsalted. It is used by the Egyptians living near it for every purpose imaginable and some you would rather not think about.

tala hini - come here.

ticket working - an extremely hazardous method of attempting to gain one's discharge from military service. Only the genuinely mad or bad ever manage to work their ticket.

wadi - watercourse.

WOG - worthy oriental gentlemen, wily oriental geezer or, as the Scots would have it, wee oriental guy. Resides anywhere from Calais eastwards. The term was freely used fifty years ago in those less politically correct times, and it was not a term of abuse but simply a prefix. There were wog taxi drivers, wog shopkeepers, and wog police. It had nothing to do with superiority or inferiority as the following familiar anecdote demonstrates. In the report of an accident between an Egyptian car and a British vehicle the Army driver stated that the car contained two wogs. Instructed to rewrite the report more acceptably, he wrote: "King Farouk was in the back of the car which collided with my lorry. It was driven by another wog."

yimkin - perhaps.

APPENDIX 1

VICTIMS OF BARBARISM

The mutilated bodies of L/Cpl R. Fearn, Royal Engineers, and Bombadier B. Reed, Royal Artillery, who had been missing for six days were yesterday found in the Sweet Water Canal opposite an Egyptian police post in Ismailia. One body was found floating on the surface of the canal yesterday morning, the section of the canal was drained and the body of the other soldier was found at the bottom. He had been badly beaten up; his skull had been smashed in, legs broken and there were bayonet wounds in the body. There are reports that a body of an unidentified officer has also been dumped into the canal, steps are being taken to find out if this is true.

A meeting of the Ikhwan el Muslimeen (Muslim Brotherhood) took place in the native quarter of Ismailia on Wednesday. It has been learnt from reliable sources that the future policy will be to stop all incidents in towns and attacks on service families and concentrate on parties moving over open roads. Mohamed Farghally, the leader of the Canal Zone Branch of the IEM, was present at the meeting. The Egyptians are calling Ismailia the front line town.

All service families have now been evacuated from Ismailia. In four days, 1,200 families have been taken to safer areas. Some will return to England whilst others will go to specially protected areas in the Zone. Ismailia will be put out of bounds to troops not on duty.

11. On the same day, at about 12.10 pm, the Assistant Provost Marshal of the Suez area was returning from a visit to the British Consulate at Port Tewfik. He drove by way of the coast road, which avoids the town of Suez. As he approached the junction of this road with the Suez-Cairo road he heard shooting from the area of the Petrol Point, which is about half a mile down the road from Suez. At the road junction, he saw two lorries and about eighty Egyptian policemen, and he stopped to enquire about the shooting. While he was speaking to an Egyptian police officer on the first lorry, some police dismounted from the second lorry and fired several shots at two British soldiers in the escorting Jeep which had stopped immediately behind his car. One soldier, L/Cpl Foxwell, was mortally wounded and died in hospital at about 14.00 hours. No shots were fired by the British officer or his escort, after the burst of firing which wounded L/Cpl Foxwell, the Egyptian police officer was able, with some difficulty, to prevent further firing.

111. (1) On the afternoon of 3 December, Major Rose, Deputy Commander of the Royal Engineers in the Suez area, was returning by the coast road from a visit on duty to Port Tewfik in an Army car accompanied by one warrant officer and a private soldier, and followed by a 3-ton lorry driven by a British corporal and carrying eight Mauritanian soldiers. As they turned the corner by the eastern end of the refinery area, they ran into an ambush which concentrated heavy fire on both vehicles. Fire came from a building in the refinery and from a grove of palm trees on the other side of the road. Both vehicles were forced

The treatment of troops captured by the Egyptian terrorists was barbaric, as shown by this official report. The evidence of torture and mutilation was typical of that found on many British bodies recovered from the Sweet Water Canal. It was commonplace for the hands and feet of a captured Serviceman to be severed with spades before they were dumped, dead or alive, in the Canal. Boys in their teens suffered horrible deaths at the hands of men and women who were not trained operatives but opportunists who probably took part in a single act. And the women often were the more brutal.

Details were kept from us, but a few astute serving troops acquired, and kept concealed, copies of reports which have now come to light.

Could it be that we RAF types were the "party of troops" sent to the scene of the ambush? We thought that we were first on the scene, which conflicts with the evidence given in the this report.

into the ditch by the fire. The occupants of the car were thrown clear but, although unhurt, were weaponless, and could not defend themselves. The driver of the lorry dismounted with his arms, and lying on the ground, returned the fire of the attackers. The only two men he actually saw firing at him were both policemen.

After a few minutes a civilian car approached from the east and the warrant officer, commandeering it, was able to escape with the corporal to fetch help. They returned with a party of Bren gun carriers, which, on approaching the scene of the ambush, also came under heavy fire from both sides of the road. This party also observed Egyptian policemen amongst the attackers. Under fire they were able to recover the bodies of five Mauritian soldiers from the lorry. The following day, early in the morning, a party of troops was sent again to the scene of the ambush, and, on making a thorough search, found the bodies of the remaining three Mauritian soldiers and of the British soldier who had been in the car. The body of Major Rose was delivered to the British Military hospital by an Egyptian police officer on 4th December.

111. (2) It appears from the post-mortem reports that the eight Mauritian soldiers and the British soldier were killed by gunshot, but there is evidence also that their bodies were mutilated after death by being struck with a blunt instrument and by stabbing. It is clear from the evidence of the post-mortem report on Major Rose, however, that this officer was most brutally murdered, probably near to the scene of the ambush.

1V. At 16.00 hours on 3rd December, the Infantry Company which had cleared the railway yard, in order that the Petrol Point might be evacuated, withdrew along the road to the north-west and began to establish themselves in positions from which they would be able to go at once to the assistance of any other party of troops which might be attacked. This party were fired on from a scrap yard near their new position. The fire was retuned and, after three Egyptian policemen and one civilian had been killed and four civilians wounded, the remainder surrendered with their arms.

V. At about 4.30pm on 3rd December a party of six Bren gun carriers, which was taking relief to the guard of the Filtration Plant, was fired on near the Plant by three Egyptian policemen. Fire was returned and the operation completed under light fire.

V1. (1) At about noon on the 4th December, another party of six Bren gun carriers taking supplies to the Filtration Plant approached the bridge over the Sweet Water Canal. On seeing a large crowd round the bridge, the carriers stopped some distance away. After about 10 minutes the crowd dispersed and the carriers started to move forward again. As they did so, they were fired on from the other side of the canal, and by an Egyptian policeman and a civilian who were taking cover on the bridge. This fire was returned and three of the carriers established themselves on the bridge and remained there, under fire, while the other three continued on their way to the Filtration Plant. On their return, the whole party withdrew. In this action a British officer and two British soldiers were wounded.

(2) It is known to the British authorities that the firing in this incident was started by an Egyptian policeman firing on the carriers. Egyptian police were also observed to be firing from a tall white building near the bridge.

POST MORTEM REPORT

Major Rose, Royal Engineers.

Post mortem commenced at 15.00, 4 December 1951

<u>Brief history:</u> Brought in dead having been ambushed. Said to have gunshot wounds, and was burnt.

<u>EXTERNAL EXAMINATION</u>

Body of European male about 40 years.

Rigor mortis generalised but just passing off from the neck muscles. Death probably 15 – 20 hours previously.

Deep irregular lacerated wounds down to bone over both eyebrows and extending half way up forehead. The left supre-orbital ridge is broken. The wounds showed signs of reaction and were therefore inflicted before death.

There are other small cuts on various parts of the scalp, which are also ante-mortem, viz: 1 inch above right ear, (appears to have been caused by a spiked instrument) and directed up beneath the scalp for about 1 inch.

On the vortex of the head there is a linear wound with irregular edges about 1.5 inches long and skin deep. There is a similar wound over the right parietal omminence and a wound over the left ear half an inch long.

There is a small cut one-inch long on the chin but this is considered to be post mortem.

On the <u>face</u> there are numerous irregular pitted markings and the nose is flattened out and abraised; and the nasal bones are broken and can be felt to crepitate.

There is a deep cut on the left side of the upper lip.

<u>Posterior surface.</u>

On the back of the trunk there are four small wounds, which are associated with considerable bruising. These wounds are as follows:

(1) Right side of vertebral column with direction towards the left aide and through the vertebral column.

(2) Right side in line of posterior axillary line.

(3) Left side below scapula with direction forward obliquely to right.

(4) Left side near left shoulder.

There is also a severe stab wound in the region of the left elbow joint, the entrance wound being just above the joint and the exit wound leaving the skin below it.

In addition, the left side of the front of the chest, the back of the right hand where it crosses the chest, and the right side of the face in the molar region is charred from burning. The right hand is in cadaveric spasm. These burns appear to have been inflicted post-mortem but slices are taken for histological examination. The right little finger is disjointed at the proximal inter-phalenical joint. This appears to be post-mortem, as there seems to be no reaction around it. There is a cut in the anterior fold of the left axilla. This also appears to be post-mortem since there is no reaction.

<u>INTERNAL APPEARANCES</u>

<u>Oesophagus</u> – Filled with stomach contents, (chewed potatoes).

<u>Tracheas and Main Bronchi</u> – Filled with inhaled sand mucus.

<u>Lungs</u> – The posterior surface of both lower lobes are penetrated by the

This is the post-mortem report on Major Rose, whose car was ambushed on the coast road on December 3 and whose body was delivered to the British Military hospital by an Egyptian police officer on December 4.

instrument causing the stab wounds at the back of the chest.

Heart and great vessels – Extirpation of the thoracic viscor reveals the damage to the thoracic walls.

A large hole is visible on the left side between the 9th and 10th ribs near the costo-vertebral junction. A No.4 Mk 1 bayonet can be inserted through one of the wounds in the back. This passes easily through the hole in the vertebral column and appears inside the thoracic cage between the 9th and 10th ribs. Both sides of the thoracic cavity are filled with blood. In addition there is a considerable amount of haematoma extra-pleurally both right and left posteriorly. The tissues in the neighbourhood of the stab wounds are suffused with extra-vasated blood.

Internally the 6th left rib comminuted by a stab wound in the posterior axillary line. The 5th left rib is also fractured 2 inches from the costal-vertebral junction. On the right side the 8th rib is comminuted 3 inches from the costal-vertebral junction and similarly the 9th rib about 1 inch from the costal-vertebral junction.

Abdominal cavity: The intestines are adheron to the internal abdominal walls by old peritoneal adhesions. The upper surface of the right lobe of the liver has numerous petecheal haemorrhages.

The remaining abdominal organs are normal.

Examination of the spinal canal.

Dissection showed fractured 7th, 8th, 9th and 10th vertebral spines and neural arches.

OPINION

(1) The deceased had his head very forcibly pressed into the sand such that face was severely and deeply lacerated and the nose was flattened, fractured and lacerated. The presence of great amounts of sand in the bronchi proves that he inhaled sand as was therefore alive at the time.

(2) There are four bayonet wounds on the back. Two penetrated into the lungs. One was so severe that it penetrated the vertebral canal, passing completely from right to left side. The vertebral bones were fractured. Since two vertebrae above the main thrust were also broken, it suggests that in order to pull out the bayonet (which was buried to the hilt) a foot may have been applied to the vertebral column just above the main wound, breaking the posterior spines in the effort to pull out the instrument.

(3) No gunshot wounds were discovered.

(4) Death was due to:-

    (i) Suffocation

    (ii) Shock following severe facial injuries, multiple penetrating chest wounds and

    (iii) Through and through wound of spinal canal in thoracic region.

Photographs of the body were taken. A photograph was taken with a bayonet in situ.

Central Medical Laboratory.
Signed: R.S.VINE Lt. Col. RAMC
Specialist in Pathology.
4.12.51

APPENDIX 2

AWAITING EXPLANATION

African Pioneer Corps, Mauritian contingent

Privates SANASEE, CHENGELEE and LACRUCHE, 18 March 1951.

Privates SOONDRON and SOMDHOO, 5 October 1951.

Sergeant WILSON and Private ONDIEK died on 11 November 1952, and the deaths of Privates AWUONDO and ODULA followed on the next two days.

Privates MURIA and KILANGO, 4 February 1953.

Corporal JOSEPH, L/Corporal JOUBERT and Private KIOKO, 13 April 1953.

Army

Captain KELSEY, Intelligence, and L/Corporal FEARN, Royal Engineers, 18 November 1951.

Guardsman REYNOLDS, Grenadier Guards, and Gunner ARNOLD, Royal Artillery, 11 November 1951

Major ROSE, Captain BRADBURY, and Sapper DICKENSON, all Royal Engineers, 3 December 1951.

CQMS BROWN and CSM CHRISTER, both Coldstream Guards, 3 & 4 January 1952.

Staff Sergeant JEWELL, Royal Engineers and Private CAMPBELL, 2 Battalion Parachute Regiment, 6 January 1953.

Major FREEGARD, MC, Royal Artillery, died on 8 January, and Major ELLIOTT, Royal Artillery, and Craftsman LANAGHAM, REME, died the following day.

Sapper HAVELOCK, Royal Engineers, and Private DAVIE, Lincolnshire Regiment, 19 January 1952.

L/Corporal McKENZIE, Lancashire Fusiliers, and Guardsman SMITH, Grenadier Guards, 27 January 1952.

Captain MASON and Driver BUXEY, both RASC, 11 February 1952.

Corporal HUXSTEP and Driver JACKSON, both RASC, 27 April 1952.

L/Corporal STENBECK, Signals, Private RAMFORD, ACC, and Sapper HAYCOCK all died on 28 April 1952.

Staff Sergeant ELLIOTT, RAPC, and Private RAWCLIFFE, East Lancashire Regiment, 4 June 1952.

Sergeant KIMMINS, ACC, and Driver EDGAR, Signals, 3 August 1952.

Privates PIKE and CHEESEBOROUGH, both of 1st Parachute Regiment, 21 August 1952.

L/Corporal ANSELL, RASC, and Private HIGGINS, REME, 27 August 1952.

L/Corporals JUPE, Royal Engineers, and COLLIER, Signals, 10 January 1953.

Signallers TRIGG and CLARKE, 6 & 7 May 1953.

L/Corporal BROOKES, Highland Light Infantry, and Private MOGIE, RASC, 14 June 1953.

L/Corporal ROBINSON, Coldstream Guards, and Sapper Johnson, Royal Engineers, 23 June 1953.

Corporal SOUTHWELL, Royal Engineers, and L/Corporal LEECH, Private ROBERTS, Driver BEECH, all RASC, all died on 2 July 1953.

The circumstances surrounding the untimely deaths of hundreds of Service personnel during 1951-1954 have never been made public, and perhaps never will be if the Foreign Office and the Ministry of Defence have their way.
The release of this information would no doubt change the way history views what went on in the Suez Canal Zone during the years 1951-1954. The double and triple deaths listed here should give us all pause for thought.

L/Corporal FORD, Signals, and Signalman WAITE, died on 3 & 4 July 1953. It is clear they were wounded in the same incident.

Sergeant DAVIES and Marine MASTERS, both of 45 Commando, 6 July 1953.

Private JENKINS, Parachute Regiment and Swapper DAVIES-PATRICK, Royal Engineers, 12 July 1953.

Private BIBBY, ACC, and Sapper WALSH, Royal Engineers, 29 July 1953.

L/Corporal SALT, RMP and Trooper FLANAGAN, Royal Dragoons, 11 August 1953. They may have been involved in the Ox and Bucks incident.

Driver GRAY, RASC, and Private COULSON, 1 Battalion Beds and Herts Regiment, 6 October 1953.

Staff Sergeant ARMSTRONG, APTC, and Sergeant GOLDSMITH, Parachute Regiment, 27 November 1953.

WO11 TILLEY, RAOC, L/Corporal HAMMETT and Sapper COX, both Royal Engineers, all died on 21 January 1954.

Sapper THOMPSON, Royal Engineers, and Private THARBY, Beds and Herts Regiment, 7 February 1954.

Trooper GRIFFIN, RTR, and Private LUGG, GHQ Gp, 4 April 1954.

Craftsman McALLISTER and Private SMELT, both REME, died on 28 and 29 May 1954, almost certainly as a result of the same incident.

Corporal STURMEY, Signalman GEEKIE, both Signals, and Guardsman FLEMING, Welsh Guards, all died on 28 September 1954.

Women's Royal Army Corps

L/Corporal UREN and Private BAIRD, died on 8 December 1954.

Royal Air Force

Airmen TATHAM and ROSS, 26 April 1951.

PO CLARKE and AC1 JACKSON, both of 107MU, 11 August 1953.

F/Lt BRIMLEY, Sergeant POWELL and AC1 DANCY, all of 216 Squadron, 2 April 1954.

Civilians

Captain COULSON, 1 Battalion Royal Horse Artillery, who died on 5 July 1950, shares a grave with his one-year-old daughter, who died two days later.

The twin sons of an RAF Serviceman died on 4 July 1954.

Appendix 3

Service medals

Campaign	Fatalities	Medal(s)
Indonesia 1945-46	50	Navy/Army/RAF GSM
Palestine 1945-48	233	Navy/Army/RAF GSM
Malaya 1948-61	350	Navy/Army/RAF GSM, plus Malay GSM for Malay units.
Yangste 1949	46	Naval GSM
Korea 1950-53	865	Korea and UN Service Medal
Egypt 1951-54,	54*	Canal Zone GSM
Kenya 1952-56	12,	Africa GSM
Cyprus 1955-58	79	Naval/Army/RAF GSM
Suez 1956	12	Naval/Army/RAF GSM
Borneo-Malaya 1962-66	16	Naval/Army/RAF GSM plus GSM 1962, Brunei Service Medal & Malaya Service Medal.
Radfan 1964	24	GSM 1962
Aden 1964-67	68	GSM 1962
Dhofar 1970-76	24	GSM 1962, Oman GSM, As Sumood and Peace Medal.
N. Ireland 1969	719	GSM 1962
Falklands 1982	255	South Atlantic Medal
Gulf 1991	47	Gulf Medal
Balkans 1992-99	43	UNPROFOR, NATO former Yugoslavia, NATO Kosovo, UNSSM, WEC Medal, UNTAES, UNMIBH, UNMIK.

This shows the known number of fatalities due to enemy action in post-1945 operations, and the campaign medals authorised. Some of the medals were awarded by Commonwealth or foreign countries, but in each campaign British troops qualified for at least one of them.

Disputed figure

Appendix 4

Regiments and Units serving in the Suez Canal Zone between 1951 and 1954

Regiments

1st Battalion The Berkshire Regiment
1st Battalion The Border Regiment
1st Battalion The Buffs
1st Battalion The Cheshire Regiment
1st Battalion The Coldstream Guards
3rd Battalion The Coldstream Guards
1st Royal Dragoons
1st Battalion The Durham Light Infantry
1st Battalion The Royal Fusiliers
1st Battalion The Green Howards
2nd Battalion The Grenadier Guards
3rd Battalion The Grenadier Guards
1st Battalion The Highland Light Infantry
1st Battalion The Royal Inniskilling Fusiliers
1st Battalion The Irish Guards
1st Battalion The Lancashire Fusiliers
1st Battalion The East Lancashire Regiment
1st Battalion The South Lancashire Regiment
1st Battalion The Royal Lincolnshire Regiment
1st Battalion The Oxford and Buckinghamshire
    Light Infantry
1st Battalion The Parachute Regiment
2nd Battalion The Parachute Regiment
3rd Battalion The Parachute Regiment
The Guards Independent Parachute Company
1st Battalion The Queen's Own Cameron
    Highlanders
1st Battalion The Royal Sussex Regiment
1st Battalion The Scots Guards
1st Battalion The Royal Scots
1st Battalion The Welsh Guards
1st Battalion The Bedfordshire and
    Hertfordshire Regiment
A detachment of 400 Rhodesian African Rifles

Royal Artillery

26 Regiment
71 Heavy Anti Aircraft Regiment
73 Heavy Anti Aircraft Regiment
26th Field Regiment 16th Battery
    Sandhams Company
29th Field Regiment
50th Battery 23rd Field Regiment
33rd Parachute Light Regiment
41st Field Regiment
23rd Field Regiment
6th Field Regiment
4th Royal Tank Regiment
19th Armoured Division
4th/7th Royal Dragoon Guards

Royal Engineers

50th Field Squadron
35th Field Squadron

Royal Signals

3rd GHQ Signals Regiment
9 Wireless Troop
'L' Troop Royal Signals
16th Independent Signals Squadron
3rd Division Signals Regiment

Royal Army Service Corps

4th Company
7th Company
30th Company
33rd Company
34th Company
38th Company
40th Company

42nd Company
58th Company
63rd Company
63rd Company RASC Independent
    Parachute Brigade
84th Company
91st Company
126th Company

Royal Army Ordnance Corps

Base Ammunition Depot RAOC Abu Sultan
Ammunition Sub Depot RAOC Lake Timsah
SCOC (Suez Canal Operations Centre)

Royal Electrical and Mechanical Engineers

Light Aid Detachment REME
Base Workshops
16th Airborne Workshops

Royal Army Medical Corps

23rd Parachute Field Ambulance RAMC

Army Catering Corps

Detachments throughout the Canal Zone

Royal Military Police

Military Provost Staff Corps (MPSC)
512 SMPS Royal Military Police
203 Provost Company Royal Military Police

Royal Army Pay Corps

Base Camp, Fayid

Royal Navy Vessels

HMS Glasgow
HMS Checkers
HMS Cheviot
HMS Magpie
HMW Undine
HMS Gambia
HMS Liverpool
HMS Chevron
HMS Retreiver
HMS Barbastel
HMS Ursa

Royal Marines

45 Commando Group
Amphibious Warfare Squadron 40 Commando
40 Commando RM 3 Commando Brigade

RAF Stations

Base Fayid
Base El Shallufa
Base Abu Seweir
Base El Firdan
Base Deversoir
Base Kasfareet
20 MU (E) Port Fouad
Airfield Construction – Air Ministry
    Works Department
RAF Police

RAF Regiment

26 LAA Squadron
28 LAA Squadron
34 LAA Squadron

Women Who Served

QARANC – Queen Alexandra's Royal Army
Nursing Corps
WRAF – Women's Royal Air Force
WRAC – Womens's Royal Army Corps
RAFNS – Princess Marina's RAF Nursing
    Service

APPENDIX 5

REFLECTIONS IN VERSE

Perhaps it was the long, boring hours on guard duty that spurred some to write poems about their thoughts and experiences in Egypt

Egypt

Oh Hell-born land on Earth,
Diabolical, incarnate.
That man should give thee worth,
So false.

Of barren waste and blasted sand,
Scorched, unyielding.
The composition of this land,
Complete.

To parry stroke and thrust of Sun,
Unmerciful, cruel.
Where sand and heat are one,
United.

What, for the lot of man?
Weak, helpless.
Who tries to live his meagre span,
Tormented.

True beauty found in grass and trees,
Pure, green.
And thou hast none of these,
Imposter.

All in all, what is this place?
Brazen, lifeless.
Of mal-design and sheer disgrace?
Egypt.

W.M.B

Stella

I met her first in Cairo,
I fancied her on sight,
But she gave me just a glassy stare
When my lips met hers that night.

To me she was so beautiful,
Tall, with a golden tan,
And her effervescent sparkle,
Would please most any man.

She was so cool and tempting,
Her dress was paper thin,
And as I madly tore it off
I knew that I would win.

I held her tightly in that bar,
I was hot, my throat was dry.
I took her without a struggle,
There was no protesting cry.

I took her back to share with my friends,
She was passed from man to man.
She was drained of all she had to give,
As only soldiers can.

Now, as I lie upon my bed,
I wish that she were here,
But I've only the empty bottle
That was filled with Stella beer.

Ken Burrows

Egypt's Mona Lisa

The sexual life of the camel
Is better than most people think.
At the height of the mating season
He'll try to get rove up the Sphinx.

But the Sphinx's abdominal passage
Is blocked by the sands of the Nile,
Which accounts for the hump on the camel
And the Sphinx's inscrutable smile.

Anon

APPENDIX 6

A DIARY KEPT IN THE CANAL ZONE 1951–1952

1951

15 October Egyptian Parliament abrogates Anglo/Egyptian Treaty.

16 October British Forces put on alert. Riots in Port Said, Ismailia, Suez. 'A' Squadron Royals sent to Ismailia and Port Said. Married families evacuated from Suez to camp. Billeted in the tents vacated by 'A' Squadron. Lancashire Fusiliers restore order in Ismailia.

17 October Platoon of 3 Brigade HQ capture El Firdan railway bridge – troops of 'A' Squadron stand by. Two Egyptians killed. Egyptians suspend rail system – withdraw dock labour and begin pulling out the 66,000 civilian workers from the Canal Zone During the next month the British replace the labour force by drafting 4,000 Mauritian Pioneer Troops, 3,500 civilians from Cyprus and Malta 5,000 Air Force technicians from the UK. Troops take over all the Egyptian workers duties.

18 October Two troops of 'C' Squadron Royals, consisting of a Coy/Sqdn/Btn, are dispatched to Wilforce to block the Cairo/Suez road from the Egyptian army should they decide to advance on Suez. This force remained in position until March 1952 located at Kilo 99. 'B' Squadron Royals joined Crusader Force to form a screen against threatened Egyptian army attacks in the area of Ribeiqui Station. The Force assembled at night just north of Fayid airport. At first light the artillery registered targets and the RAF dropped leaflets. The Egyptians withdrew their forces, which included tanks. At l3.00 hours the Crusader Force returned to camp, but the squadron maintained patrols on the Erskine line.

17 November In Ismailia two Royal Berkshire men are killed by a mob and one RMP is killed when shots are fired from a Police Station.

18 November Whilst trying to restrain the Egyptian auxiliaries from shooting up civilian quarters, one Army officer, one RAF officer and one RMP are killed by a mob in Ismailia.The bodies of six murdered soldiers are recovered from the Sweet Water Canal.

3 December Action in Suez by East Kents, the Buffs and Royal Sussex against auxiliaries following shooting fatalities. The Buffs had six men wounded in the skirmishing. A Platoon of the Royal Sussex charged an Egyptian position and one of their men was wounded. Four auxiliaries were killed, three wounded and twenty-five captured. On this day a small convoy of Mauritian troops was ambushed and five killed. The mutilated bodies of one officer, one sapper and three more Mauritians were later recovered.

Personal recollections from the journal and signals diaries kept by Sergeant Don Mallinder, 1 Royal Dragoon Guards. Don now lives in New Zealand.

4 December Snipers from the village of Kafr Adfu hindered the re-supply of the troops guarding the water filtration plant. Royal Sussex had one officer and one soldier badly wounded. 1 Parachute Regiment and one troop of 4 RTR used bulldozers to partially destroy the village.

17 December Bomb thrown at RMP jeep killing one officer. Fire directed at other security forces. 'A' squadron Royals troop silences auxiliaries by firing Besa machine guns and 2 pounders. Jeep is recovered Another 'A' Squadron troop rescues an RAF convoy trapped under fire on the Tel El Kebir road. The Royals fitter half-track truck on its way to support this troop comes under fire whilst in transit through Ismailia. The fitter, a George Small, opened fire with a Bren gun and silenced the auxiliaries who were positioned in a Mosque. The Royals 'A' Squadron Leader whilst on a recce around French Square finds a mob attempting to set fire to a British three-ton truck and disperses them by driving his jeep at them

1952

3 January Suez water filtration plant attacked again by snipers from Kafr Adfu village. 1 troop 4 RTR take control of village by firing one shot each of a 20 pounder shell to subdue the auxiliaries. 2 Parachute Regiment clears village near Abu Sueir to keep Moascar Road open.

5/8 January Auxiliaries place snipers along the Moascar/Cairo Road and as a result all movements have to be escorted.

12 January Military train ambushed approaching Tel El Kebir. Cameron Highlanders suffer two men badly wounded as a result of a mine laid across their path. 3 Coldstream guards supported by 4/7 Dragoon Guards remove the auxiliaries. They clear the village of El Hammada, killing 12, wounding 15 and capturing 21. The Guards lose one sergeant killed.

13 January 26 Field Regiment engaged near village of Tel El Kebir. 5 auxiliaries killed. Attack on British troops Egypt HQ at Moascar. 'A' Squadron Royals restored order.

14 January Patrol of Cameron Highlanders lose one officer and one soldier killed and one man wounded in skirmish. 6 auxiliaries killed around Tel el Kebir. Grenadier Guards shoot dead a desperado trying to assassinate the Brigadier with a pistol. 26 Field Regiment bombard Tel El Kebir and El Hammada villages at last light.

15 January 26 Field Regiment again bombard Tel El Kebir and El Hammada to subdue sniper fire.

16 January Grenadier Guards cordon off two villages and the Coldstream Guards attack at dawn, covered by aircraft and a troop of Royals 'B' Squadron. 2 auxiliaries killed, 160 captured including a Major-General. A Royals Trooper Hesketh won a commendation for his actions.

19 January Ismailia – Bomb exploded setting off anti-tank mines alongside a manned post on the Sweet Water Canal. Royal Lincolns lose two men killed and six wounded. A troop of Royals killed 3 auxiliaries. Sister Anthony shot dead in convent by terrorists. Royal Lincolns, supported by 'B' Squadron Royals attack

BYRNE

Kilo 99 on the Cairo-Suez road. Troops were based here to block the road should the Egyptian army decide to advance on Suez.

an area to clear it of auxiliaries. Royals control fire by aiming machine guns at roof tops and buildings.

20 January Houses alongside the Sweet Water Canal are cleared of residents to prevent a recurrence of yesterday's activity.

21 January Parachute Regiment fight their way into Ismailia Moslem cemetery and lose one officer killed in the action. 4 Egyptians killed and a large ammunition dump discovered. Among the ordinance recovered was 6,000 rounds of Bofers shells.

26 January Auxiliaries attack a British arms dump at Shallufa.

25 January The incident at the Bureau Sanitaire and the Caracol (*dealt with elsewhere in this book*).

APPENDIX 7

ADDRESSES OF INTEREST TO THOSE WHO SERVED IN THE SUEZ CANAL ZONE

The Royal British Legion
48 Pall Mall
London
SW1Y 5JY
08457 725725

The Royal British Legion Scotland
New Haig House
Logie Green Road
Edinburgh
EH7 4HR
0131 557 2782

SSAFA (Sailor's Soldier's and Airmen's Family Association) – Forces Help
19 Quenn Elizabeth Street
London
SE1 2LP
020 7403 8783

The Canal Zoners
172 Cromwell Road
Hounslow
Middlesex
TW3 3QS
020 8814 2135

Suez Veterans Association
103 Gay Gardens
Dagenham
Essex
RM10 7TH
020 8262 7839

Egypt Award Memorial Alliance
56 Queen Elizabeth Drive
Chapel Downs
Crediton
Devon
EX17 2EJ
01363 776386

National Army Museum
Royal Hospital Road
Chelsea
London
SW3 4HT
020 7730 0717

INDEX